New Directions in Campaigns and Elections

The ground upon which campaigns and elections are contested has been shifting rapidly in the last decade. Radical and ongoing changes to the way elections are administered and campaigns are financed; new approaches to polling, campaign management and advertising, and voter mobilization; and recent developments in the organization of political parties and interest groups, the operation of the media, and the behavior of voters require close examination. *New Directions in Campaigns and Elections* guides students through the tangle of recent developments in real-world politics, drawing on the insights of innovative scholarship on these topics.

More than any other aspects of American politics, campaigns and elections have been affected—in many cases transformed—by new communication technologies, a recurring theme throughout the volume. This tightly organized collection of original contributions raises important normative questions, grounds students' thinking in cutting-edge empirical research, and balances applied politics with scholarly insights. Like other volumes in the *New Directions in American Politics* series, the focused exploration of the latest developments across a comprehensive range of topics makes this an ideal companion for students eager to understand the rapidly changing political environment of the U.S. electoral process.

Stephen K. Medvic is associate professor of government at Franklin and Marshall College. He is the author of *Political Consultants in U.S. Congressional Elections* and the textbook *Campaigns and Elections: Players and Processes*, as well as co-editor of *Shades of Gray: Perspectives on Campaign Ethics*.

New Directions in American Politics

The Routledge series *New Directions in American Politics* is composed of contributed volumes covering key areas of study in the field of American politics and government. Each title provides a state-of-the-art overview of current trends in its respective subfield, with an eye toward cutting-edge research accessible to advanced undergraduate and beginning graduate students. While the volumes touch on the main topics of relevant study, they are not meant to cover the "nuts and bolts" of the subject. Rather, they engage readers in the most recent scholarship, real-world controversies, and theoretical debates with the aim of getting students excited about the same issues that animate scholars.

New Directions in Campaigns and Elections

Edited by Stephen K. Medvic

 Routledge
Taylor & Francis Group

NEW YORK AND LONDON

First published 2011
by Routledge
270 Madison Avenue, New York, NY 10016

Simultaneously published in the UK
by Routledge
2 Park Square, Milton Park, Abingdon, Oxon OX14 4RN

Routledge is an imprint of the Taylor & Francis Group, an informa business

© 2011 Taylor & Francis

The right of Stephen K. Medvic to be identified as the author
of the editorial material, and of the authors for their individual
chapters, has been asserted by them in accordance with
sections 77 and 78 of the Copyright, Designs and Patents Act
1988.

Typeset in Minion by Wearset Ltd, Boldon, Tyne and Wear
Printed and bound in the United States of America on acid-
free paper by Sheridan Books, Inc.

Library of Congress Cataloging-in-Publication Data
New directions in campaigns and elections/edited by Stephen
K. Medvic.
p. cm. – (New directions in American politics)
1. Political campaigns–United States. 2. Elections–United
States. I. Medvic, Stephen K.
JK2281.N482 2011
324.70973–dc22   2010033282

ISBN13: 978-0-415-87882-1 (hbk)
ISBN13: 978-0-415-87883-8 (pbk)
ISBN13: 978-0-203-85299-6 (ebk)

For Laura,
With love and gratitude

Contents

Figures

Tables

Preface

The Dynamic Nature of Campaigns and Elections

It is common for political scientists to regard campaigns and elections as relatively static events in American politics. Campaigns occur at regular, indeed legally prescribed intervals and much of what candidates do to win votes is tried-and-true. Some variation on "it's time for a change," for instance, is a perennial campaign theme. Furthermore, much of our understanding of how elections work is based on research that is decades old. For example, we have known since the mid-twentieth century that party identification is the most important predictor of how a person will cast his or her vote.

Upon further reflection, however, campaigns and elections may be considered to be among the most dynamic phenomena that political scientists study. This is particularly true in the United States, because few democracies in the world hold as many elections as we do. The result is that there are numerous opportunities for campaigns and elections to change over a short period of time. This may be most obvious with respect to campaigns, where ever-evolving technology enables candidates to appeal for support, organize volunteers, and mobilize voters in ways that were unimaginable just a few years, if not months, ago. But elections, and the patterns we observe in them, also change. From the late 1960s through the 1980s, for example, we witnessed a fairly steep rise in split-ticket voting, only to see that trend reversed in the last few presidential elections.

This book attempts to identify the most significant developments in campaigns and elections in recent years. The chapters are written by well-respected scholars in the field and are based on their identification of important trends in the practical world of campaigns and elections, the latest insights from academic research, or both. The book is not intended to provide comprehensive coverage of each of its topics, though many authors do provide a brief overview of the current literature on their particular subjects. Instead, the chapters describe, as the book's title suggests, "new directions" in each of the 14 aspects of campaigns and elections included in this volume.

The book begins with two chapters that examine the legal foundation of campaigns and elections. The first, by Thad Hall and M. Kathleen Moore, addresses the administration of elections with a particular focus upon the changes that were implemented in the wake of the contentious 2000 presidential election and on suggestions for further reforms to the operation of elections. David Magleby's chapter on campaign finance reviews recent developments in the regulation of campaign money and charts trends in the sources of such money, as well as how it is raised and spent.

The next four chapters (i.e., Chapters 3–6) turn attention to the essential elements of campaigns. Brian Schaffner explores public opinion polling, with an emphasis on cutting-edge innovations in survey research including the adoption of Internet surveys. My own contribution examines the use of information and communication technology and its impact on campaign management and organization. In their chapter on campaign advertising, Bryce Corrigan and Ted Brader investigate recent methodological and theoretical developments in the study of advertising effects. Robert A. Jackson follows with a chapter on voter mobilization in which he reviews current research on the effectiveness of campaigns at getting voters to the polls, assesses the field experiment approach to the study of mobilization, and identifies the latest get-out-the-vote tactics employed by campaign operatives.

Chapters 7 through 10 deal with the major non-candidate actors in campaigns and elections. Jeffrey M. Stonecash examines the resurgence of political party unity, attempts by party leaders to craft unified party images, and the tensions this creates for parties pursuing majorities. Clyde Wilcox revisits basic questions about interest groups—such as what constitutes an interest group and what counts as electoral activity—and calls for further theoretical progress in order to make sense of recent developments in electioneering by such groups. Diana Owen's chapter on the media traces the emergence of the current communications environment and explores fruitful avenues for future research, including a proposed mapping of the election media system. Andrew Dowdle, Pearl K. Ford, and Todd G. Shields tackle a number of challenges facing the traditional model of voting behavior, including the ideological polarization of elites and its effect on voters, changes to voting patterns in the South, the influence of religion, and the distinctive behavior of women and minorities.

Chapters 11 through 13 explore developments in elections. In their chapter on congressional elections, Jamie L. Carson and Carrie P. Eaves grapple with a puzzle—if, as we know they do, incumbents have tremendous advantages in elections, why do at least some of them lose every election cycle? Scott D. McClurg and Philip Habel describe how presidential campaigns both respond to and contribute to the increasing fragmentation of the electorate. And Timothy B. Krebs and Jonathan Winburn examine trends in both state and local elections, and detail the ways in which elections at those levels differ. In the final chapter, Chapter 14, Todd Donovan and Shaun Bowler explain how election reform occurs and consider the effects of three major reforms—term limits, direct democracy, and proportional representation.

The chapters in this book address important empirical, theoretical, and methodological questions. The creation of a variety of new datasets and the easy accessibility of such data allow researchers the opportunity to study aspects of campaigns and elections that heretofore have been unexplored. However, as always, empirical investigation should be based on sound theoretical foundations. The contributors to this volume remind us that even in areas with decades of received scholarly wisdom, new research questions are constantly emerging.

Although these chapters were written independently, a number of themes emerge in the book. One such theme is the causes and consequences of ideological and partisan polarization in American politics. Another is the critical importance of technology in changing the ways candidates communicate with voters, voters interact with candidates and parties, and the media cover campaign and elections. Finally, the importance of electoral competition to democracy is a theme that runs through the entire book. From campaign finance and redistricting rules to targeted persuasion and mobilization efforts and the incumbency advantage, nearly every aspect of American campaigns and elections has some impact on competition between the parties. That competition, in turn, is essential to democracy. Understanding the factors that foster—or inhibit—electoral competition may be the most important contribution the chapters in this volume make.

This book was obviously a collaborative effort and I thank each of the contributors for their diligence and cooperation. I would also like to thank Michael Kerns for his vision for the *New Directions in American Politics* series at Routledge and for allowing me the opportunity to contribute to it with this volume. His sage advice helped shape the book from beginning to end. Mary Altman provided patient assistance throughout the process and I appreciate her help. Finally, I owe tremendous thanks to my loving (and much loved) wife Laura, to whom this book is dedicated. Without her support I could not have completed this project—or much else for that matter.

S.K.M.
Lancaster, PA

Contributors

Shaun Bowler is Professor of Political Science at the University of California, Riverside. He is co-author and co-editor of several books, including *Direct Democracy's Impact on American Political Institutions* (with Amihai Glazer. Palgrave, 2008); *Reforming the Republic: Democratic Institutions for the New America* (with Todd Donovan. Prentice Hall, 2004); *Demanding Choices: Opinion, Voting and Direct Democracy* (with Todd Donovan. University of Michigan Press, 2000); and *Party Discipline and Parliamentary Government* (with David Farrell and Richard Katz. Ohio State University Press, 1999).

Ted Brader is Associate Professor of Political Science at the University of Michigan and research associate professor in the Center for Political Studies at the Institute for Social Research. He is the author of *Campaigning for Hearts and Minds* and currently serves as Associate Principal Investigator for the American National Election Studies and for Time-sharing Experiments for the Social Sciences. His research focuses on the role of emotions in politics, political partisanship, media effects on public opinion, and other topics in political psychology.

Jamie L. Carson is an Associate Professor of Political Science at The University of Georgia. He received his Ph.D. from Michigan State University in 2003 where he was a Fellow in the Political Institutions and Public Choice Program. His primary research interests are in congressional politics and elections, American political development, and separation of powers. He has published in a wide variety of academic journals and is currently working on a book examining late nineteenth- and early twentieth-century congressional elections in the U.S. House of Representatives.

Bryce Corrigan is a Ph.D. candidate in the Department of Political Science at the University of Michigan and a visiting Fellow at Vanderbilt University. His research develops strategies for flexible statistical inference from rolling cross-sections and other incomplete panel data structures, which he applies to investigate the dynamics of citizens' learning and persuasion during political campaigns.

Todd Donovan is Professor of Political Science at Western Washington University. He is co-author and co-editor of several books, including *State and Local Politics: Institutions and Reform* (with Chris Mooney and Dan Smith. Wadsworth, 2011); *Why Iowa? How Caucuses and Sequential Elections Improve the Presidential Nomination Process* (with David Redlawsk and Caroline Tolbert. University of Chicago Press, 2011); *Democracy in the States: Experiments in Election Reform* (with Bruce Cain and Caroline Tolbert. Brookings Institutions Press, 2008); and *Electoral Reform and Minority Representation* (with Shaun Bowler and David Brockington. Ohio State University Press, 2003).

Andrew Dowdle is an Associate Professor of Political Science at the University of Arkansas and Editor of the *American Review of Politics*. His work has appeared in a number of scholarly journals including *American Politics Research, Political Research Quarterly* and *Presidential Studies Quarterly*.

Carrie P. Eaves is a Ph.D. candidate in political science at the University of Georgia. She received an MPA from the University of Georgia in 2006. Her primary research interests are American political institutions and congressional elections. She has a publication forthcoming in *Legislative Studies Quarterly*.

Pearl K. Ford is an Assistant Professor of Political Science and African American Studies at the University of Arkansas. Her scholarship and teaching interests focus on African American politics, electoral behavior, and the intersection of race, class, and political institutions. A native of Savannah Georgia, she holds a Ph.D. in political science from Howard University.

Philip Habel is Assistant Professor of Political Science at Southern Illinois University Carbondale. His research interests include political communication and political behavior. His work has appeared in *Legislative Studies Quarterly, Political Analysis*, and *Social Science Quarterly*.

Thad Hall is an Associate Professor of Political Science at the University of Utah. He has authored or co-authored four books, including *Point, Click, and Vote: The Future of Internet Voting* and *Electronic Elections: The Perils and Promise of Digital Democracy*, and has written numerous articles on election administration and voting technologies.

Robert A. Jackson is Professor of Political Science at Florida State University.

Timothy B. Krebs is an Associate Professor of Political Science at the University of New Mexico. His work on urban politics and policy has appeared in the *American Journal of Political Science, Political Research Quarterly, Social Science Quarterly, American Politics Research, Urban Affairs Review, Journal of Urban Affairs*, and *Public Administration Review*. He is currently studying the role of mayoral partisanship in city fiscal policy and the nature of deracialized speech in mayoral campaigns.

David B. Magleby is currently Distinguished Professor of Political Science, Senior Research Fellow at the Center for the Study of Elections and Democracy, and Dean of the College of Family, Home and Social Science at Brigham Young University. In the area of campaign finance he has edited or co-edited nine books. His research has been funded by the Pew Charitable Trusts, the Carnegie Corporation, the JEHT Foundation, the Joyce Foundation, the National Science Foundation, and the Rockefeller Brothers Fund. He has been a Fulbright Scholar at Oxford University.

Scott D. McClurg (Ph.D., Washington University, 2000) is an Associate Professor of Political Science at Southern Illinois University. He has published work on campaigns and voting behavior in the *American Journal of Political Science, Political Research Quarterly,* and *American Politics Research.* He has made multiple appearances on local St. Louis and Southern Illinois television stations to discuss the presidential elections in 2000, 2004, and 2008.

Stephen K. Medvic is Associate Professor and Chair of the Government Department at Franklin & Marshall College. His research and teaching interests include campaigns and elections, political parties, the media and politics, and public opinion. In addition to numerous academic articles and book chapters, he is the author of *Campaigns and Elections: Players and Processes* (Wadsworth Cengage 2009) and *Political Consultants in U.S. Congressional Elections* (Ohio State University Press 2001). He is also co-editor of *Shades of Gray: Perspectives on Campaign Ethics* (Brookings Institution Press 2002) and associate editor of the *Guide to Political Campaigns in America* (CQ Press 2005).

M. Kathleen Moore is a graduate student in public administration and policy at the University of Utah, where she is studying election administration and methods.

Diana Owen is Associate Professor of Political Science and Director of American Studies at Georgetown University, and teaches in the Communication, Culture, and Technology graduate program. She received her doctorate in political science from the University of Wisconsin-Madison. She is the author, with Richard Davis, of *New Media and American Politics* (Oxford 1998) and *Media Messages in American Presidential Elections* (Greenwood 1991), and editor of *The Internet and Politics: Citizens, Voters, and Activists,* with Sarah Oates and Rachel Gibson (Routledge 2006) and editor of *Making a Difference: The Internet and Elections in Comparative Perspective,* with Richard Davis, Stephen Ward, and David Taras (Lexington 2009).

Brian F. Schaffner is an Associate Professor in the Department of Political Science at the University of Massachusetts, Amherst. His research focuses on public opinion, campaigns and elections, political parties, and legislative politics. He is co-editor of the book *Winning with Words: The Origins & Impact of Political Framing*, and his research has appeared in over a dozen refereed journal articles, including the *American Political Science Review*, the *American Journal of Political Science*, *Public Opinion Quarterly*, *Political Communication*, *Political Research Quarterly*, *Legislative Studies Quarterly*, and *Social Science Quarterly*. Schaffner is also a regular contributor to the award-winning political site Pollster.com.

Todd G. Shields (BA, Miami University, 1990; MA, University of Kentucky, 1991; Ph.D., University of Kentucky, 1994) is a Professor in the Department of Political Science. He is also Director of the Diane D. Blair Center of Southern Politics and Society and Associate Director of the Fulbright Institute of International Relations. His research interests lie broadly in applied statistics and American elections. He has published dozens of journal articles and is the co-author or co-editor of four books, including *The Persuadable Voter: Wedge Issues in Presidential Campaigns*, the winner of the Robert E. Lane award for the best book in political psychology awarded by the American Political Science Association in 2009. He is also the co-author of *Money Matters: The Effects of Campaign Finance Reform on Congressional Elections* and the co-editor of *The Clinton Riddle: Interdisciplinary Perspectives of the 42nd President* and *New Voices in the Old South: How Women and Minorities Influence Southern Politics*. He is currently working on edited volumes examining the scholarly legacies of V.O. Key Jr. and C. Van Woodward, two of the most influential scholars in the fields of southern politics and history. He generally teaches courses in research methods, applied statistics, and survey research.

Jeffrey M. Stonecash is Maxwell Professor in the Maxwell School, Syracuse University. He does research on political parties and changes in their electoral bases. His recent books are *Class and Party in American Politics* (2000), *Diverging Parties* with Mack Mariani and Mark Brewer (2002), *Political Polling* (2003; 2008, 2nd edn), *Parties Matter* (2006), *Governing New York State* (2006), *Split: Class and Cultural Divisions in American Politics* with Mark Brewer (2007), *Reassessing the Incumbency Effect* (Cambridge University Press, 2008), *Dynamics of American Political Parties* with Mark Brewer (Cambridge, 2009), and *Counter-Realignment: Political Change in the Northeast* with Howard Reiter (Cambridge, 2010). He edited *New Directions in American Political Parties* (Routledge, 2010). He is now working on a book about changes in the relationship between presidential and House results since 1900.

Clyde Wilcox is Professor of Government at Georgetown University. He has published widely on campaign finance, interest groups, elections and voting, public opinion, religion and politics, gender politics, and science fiction and politics. He has served as an expert witness on campaign finance cases for the Justice Department and the Federal Election Commission, and consulted on campaign finance issues with the Organization of American States and the National Endowment for Democracy. Over the past few years he has lectured on interest groups and elections in a number of countries across five continents.

Jonathan Winburn is Assistant Professor of Political Science at the University of Mississippi. His research interests include redistricting, representation, and state legislative elections with a recent book published by Lexington Books and journal articles in *Political Research Quarterly* and *State Politics and Policy Quarterly* on these topics.

## Chapter 1

Election Administration

Setting the Rules of the Game

Thad Hall and M. Kathleen Moore

The 2000 election brought to the fore questions about how we administer elections in America. Although there was a large focus immediately after the election on the rules governing vote-counting standards and on the technology used for voting—the "butterfly ballot" and punch card voting problems—it was immediately evident that the people who administer elections are also important. The face of Katherine Harris, the Republican Secretary of State of Florida, became an immediate symbol of the conflicts that exist in the United States with election administration. Harris was both the official at the state level responsible for the implementation of elections in Florida and co-chair of George W. Bush's Florida campaign. This conflict highlighted the fact that, in much of America, we govern our elections through partisan elected officials.

The Florida election debacle also illustrated that elections in the United States are highly delegated affairs. Voters vote in elections that are run not by state officials but by local election officials, and there are more than 10,000 such officials nationally. These officials are also often partisans who have specific political interests in election outcomes. They are often not full-time election officials; elections are but one of a panoply of activities that they administer in their jobs as county clerks, auditors, recorders, probate judges, and many other local government activities. These local election officials, in turn, generally delegate the implementation of Election Day voting activities to voting precincts, which are managed and run by poll workers—low-paid individuals who agree to work twelve or more hours on Election Day to implement the election procedures for 1000 or so voters in their community.

The delegation that is involved in running elections is extensive (Alvarez and Hall 2006). Between the federal government, the state election offices, local election officials, and polling places, elections require extensive coordination across multiple levels of government. This coordination is made more difficult because elections have a restrictive timeline. The implementation of early and absentee voting can lessen the volume of voters visiting the polls on Election Day. Conventional voting remains a single-day event; hiring a sizeable temporary workforce to run the Election Day activities and finding enough appropriate locations to hold the election in precincts in a jurisdiction presents a challenge. Election administration may be viewed in terms of nested principal–agent relationships: principals rely on agents that, in turn, rely on other agents. Statutory requirements, decentralized administrative structures, and elements of partisanship at all levels further complicate the adverse selection and moral hazard problems characteristic of principal–agent arrangements.

In this chapter we focus on this issue of election administration, considering how states delegate responsibility to local election officials and how these officials, in turn, delegate responsibility to poll workers in voting precincts. Finally, we examine the implications of these delegation decisions and how they affect the actual administration of elections in the United States. Our goal in this chapter is to illustrate the complexity of the administrative process and the implications of this complexity for the administrative process.

Federal and State Election Administration

As the National Commission on Federal Election Reform noted in its 2001 report, Congress has extensive powers to regulate elections under the Constitution (Carter and Ford 2002). The Voting Rights Act, laws governing voting by military and overseas civilians, and the passage of the Help America Vote Act of 2002 (HAVA), all illustrate that Congress has such power. However, when Congress enacted HAVA, it did not create a strong role for the federal government in elections, even though it was within its authority to do so. As Karlan and Ortiz (2002) note, there are several clauses within the Constitution, in addition to several constitutional amendments, that provide Congress with power to govern elections. For example, the elections clause (Article I, Section 1) states that "the times, places, and manner of holding elections ... shall be prescribed in each state ... but the Congress may at any time by law make or alter such regulations." As they note, the courts have ruled that Congress has comprehensive authority under this clause to regulate elections, including the ability to regulate the federal elections process and to create procedures that safeguard the right of eligible voters to vote. Congress may also use its spending powers and the commerce clause to regulate elections as well. The Voting Rights Act is an example of the strong federal involvement Congress can have in regulating how state and local governments administer elections.

HAVA created the Election Assistance Commission (EAC), which subsumed the role that the Office of Election Administration in the Federal Election Commission formerly held. The EAC "is intended to be the national clearinghouse of information on voting equipment, a resource to help states comply with new election standards, and a vehicle for compiling information and reviewing procedures" (Liebschutz and Palazzolo 2005: 508). However, HAVA explicitly did not confer power to the EAC to engage in rule-making or to pass requirements for uniformity across states. The EAC is primarily an advisory body that disburses grant funding provided for by Congress. This activity was especially important in the first years of the EAC, when it gave out funding to states for purchasing new voting technologies and for modernizing state voter registration databases.

The EAC has a four-member board that is nominated by the President, and then confirmed by the Senate, and a relatively small staff for carrying out its mandate. Initially, the EAC had a very difficult time getting its operations started owing to slowness on the part of Congress and the President in appointing members, and a slow start in getting staff online who could account for and distribute funding to the states for technology improvements in a timely manner (Montjoy and Chapin 2005). The agency has also been controversial among states, even though it has little power. At one point, the National Association of Secretaries of State urged Congress to dismantle the EAC entirely. As Elmendorf (2006: 428) has noted, the EAC lacks the basic rule-making powers needed to make reform: "The most straight-forward way of giving an independent agency a role in the development of election law is to authorize the body to implement open-textured standards through rule-making." The EAC has no such authorization; it can merely suggest reforms and offer guidance, as allowed by the restrictions in HAVA.

Instead, the locus of election law in the United States is at the state level. As Alvarez and Hall (2005, 559) note, "Part of the reason for this decentralized model of election administration is constitutional because Articles I and II of the U.S. Constitution largely delegate election procedures for federal offices to the states." Even though the federal government expanded its role in election administration with the passage of HAVA, it still leaves much of the business of election administration in the hands of the states. This means that there remain wide variations in election administration in the United States. Election laws are different across states, and administrative rules and structures vary across many dimensions.

HAVA also illustrated another interesting aspect of election governance in the states, which is that states have historically delegated the role of election administration to the local and municipal levels. Although HAVA repeatedly uses the phrase "a state shall" in delineating the requirements for states under the law, states have, in many cases, pushed these requirements to the local level and not managed the implementation of the law centrally (Liebschutz and Palazzolo 2005). For example, HAVA requires states to have a state-wide voter registration database. Some states have created voter registration databases that are centrally administered at the state level but other states have merely linked together the county or municipally run voter registration systems and called the cobbled-together system a state-wide voter registration system.[1] In the first case the state is being pro-active and assuming the role of administrator as stated in HAVA ("the state shall…") but in the second case the state is continuing the practice of allowing local governments to have control over the election process.

The list of differences in state election laws can be quite amazing to an outside observer (Keyssar 2000). Across the various states, voters use different voting technologies. States have different rules on who has to show identification at the polls. Some states allow voters to vote prior to the election in person in early voting but other states do not. Some states have liberal absentee voting rules and others have quite strict requirements. There are states with Election Day voter registration and states that allow voters to register to vote over the Internet. Most amazingly, the standards for what constitutes a valid vote on a ballot vary across states; what would be counted as a vote for a candidate in one state could go uncounted in another state. This discretion in how states run their elections means that the experience of a voter in the election process varies considerably across states.

This degree of variation in election administration may be viewed in a beneficial manner; local administration of elections and all the variation it entails is core to the American view of participatory government.

> [L]ocal administration of elections can also enhance self-rule, particularly to the extent that it gives Americans more ownership of the voting process, more room for experimentation and innovation, and a structural way to minimize the effects of partisanship and error.
>
> (Ewald 2009: 11)

The argument against sustaining this scale of variation is that it can serve to disenfranchise certain groups—that it exacerbates the effects of partisanship and error. Seemingly trivial administrative decisions can undermine voter confidence and discourage voters from voting even if the variety of decisions were all generated in response to a single statute. Variation in implementation can translate into variation in the rights of voters.

There are many questions that have arisen about the governance of elections at the state level because of the way in which election officials are chosen. In 33 states, there is a state-wide election official—typically the Secretary of State—who is elected through a partisan electoral process. Other states appoint a chief election official or an election commission that governs the administration of elections at the state level (Hasen 2005). Election problems in 2000 in Florida and in 2004 in Ohio illustrate the issues associated with accountability and delegation in elections at the state level. State legislatures typically delegate to the state's Secretary of State or Lt. Governor the power to regulate elections at the state level. However, given that these state officials are often elected and are involved in politics themselves, this delegation can become controversial. In 2000, Florida's Secretary of State "Katherine Harris quickly became a symbol for the idea that the very institutions designed to keep elected officials in check also depend on those same officials for oversight" (Nou 2009: 762). In short, the question was whether the fox was guarding the hen-house. The same questions arose in Ohio in 2004. There, Secretary of State Kenneth Blackwell came under scrutiny when election disputes arose and people questioned whether the state made administrative decisions based on partisan politics. Given that there is a normative ideal that elections will be free and fair, this partisan question is an important one.

Local Election Administration

Examining elections becomes more complex at the local level. With the exception of Hawaii where there is more state control, elections are administered at the local level. The locus of local administration varies across states. In some states, elections are run by counties and in other states elections are administered by municipal governments. Still other states use some combination of the two. These jurisdictions vary widely in their size and capacities to serve voters. In a national study of local election jurisdictions, Kimball et al. (2009) identified 10,370 local jurisdictions in the United States. They found that the median jurisdiction served slightly more than 1,000 voters in the 2004 presidential election. This means that half of all local election jurisdictions are small counties or small towns with very few voters. Considered from the perspective of the number of voters served, they found that approximately 64 percent of voters in the 2004 election lived in one of the 418 largest local election jurisdictions (4 percent of all election jurisdictions nationally).

These jurisdictions vary widely in their capacities for service and the demands asked of them. The smallest jurisdictions, on average, have a single polling place run by five poll workers that has about 350 voters on Election Day. By contrast, the largest jurisdictions serve on average almost 67,000 voters and manage over 750 poll workers, who work in approximately 94 voting precincts. These jurisdictions have very different budget and staffing levels. Small jurisdictions spend, for example, less than $250 on poll worker training, compared to $45,000 in larger jurisdictions (more than 50,000 voters). Surveys by Kimball et al. (2009) and Fischer and Coleman (2008) both find that smaller jurisdictions tend to be run by females who do not have a college degree. Individuals in the largest jurisdictions tend to be better educated and to belong to national professional election organizations. Individuals in smaller jurisdictions are also likely to serve in an array of positions as part of their job, being the elections person, as well as clerk, auditor, recorder, and other positions. Together, these factors suggest that there is a higher level of professionalism in larger jurisdictions related to election administration than there are in smaller jurisdictions.

Data also reveal that the majority of local election officials (LEOs) are elected officials, although some are appointed to their positions and possibly share power with an election board (Kimball and Kropf 2006). The fact that most LEOs are elected raises several important questions. The first is whether electing LEOs reflects the public's preferences for how they should be chosen. In a national survey, Alvarez, Hall, and Llewellyn (2008) found that voters conceptually prefer to have their elections run by a board of individuals who are elected in a non-partisan manner. Voters and non-voters alike prefer power to be distributed among an election board instead of consolidated in a single position. The irony, of course, is that most LEOs are chosen in partisan elections and a single individual runs the elections.

Do differences in the partisanship of election officials actually affect the way in which elections are implemented? In several studies, scholars have found that partisanship does affect the implementation of key election policies and procedures. For example, prior to the 2000 election in Florida, the Secretary of State's Office provided local election officials with a list of potential felons. Counties were to determine whether these individuals should, in fact, be purged from the voter rolls. There is evidence (Stuart 2004) that the purging of felons from the voter registration lists was implemented in a partisan manner; Republican election officials implemented the purge quickly and with little research into whether the felon matches were accurate, and Democratic election officials were slow to implement the purge.

There is evidence that partisan election officials also implement some laws differently depending on the way in which implementation will affect partisan outcomes. The clearest example of this is the area of provisional voting, where Kimball, Kropf, and Battles (2006) found that cross-pressured partisan election officials—a Democratic (Republican) official in a strong Republican (Democratic) jurisdiction—were less likely to count provisional ballots than were partisan election officials in districts that had a partisan leaning which mirrored their own. This variation in approach is "a direct result of Congress's decision not to spell out clearly the requirements for provisional voting, but instead to leave implementation details to the states" (Tokaji 2005: 1228).

Partisanship has also been found to affect other aspects of election administration. Burden et al. (2010) found that, in Wisconsin, jurisdictions with an elected election official had higher turnout compared to jurisdictions with an appointed election official. They argue that elected election officials have more of a customer service focus in their work, meaning that they want more "customers" (i.e., voters) to participate in the "service" (i.e., elections). By contrast, appointed election officials tend to focus on issues of efficiency and economy, which means providing a baseline service at the lowest cost possible.

These views about service also play out in their attitudes toward election reform. Several studies (e.g., Burden et al. 2010; Kimball et al. 2010) have found that elected clerks tend to be more supportive of election reforms than are appointed clerks. For example, Burden et al. (2010) found that elected clerks in Wisconsin were more supportive of Election Day voter registration (EDR), more supportive of absentee voting, and less concerned about the administrative burdens of expanding either EDR or absentee voting. Kimball and Baybeck (2010) also find that attitudes toward reform are shaped by the partisanship of the election official, even if that partisanship differs from the underlying partisanship of the district they represent. Therefore, we see that partisanship of election officials affects the way in which people vote, the reforms that are supported, and the experience voters have on Election Day.

Poll Workers: The Street-level Bureaucrats of Elections

The place where election administration is most important and prominent in the voting process is at the actual time of voting, when voters interact with poll workers. Prior to the 2000 elections, little consideration had been given to the role of poll workers in elections and it was not until after the 2004 elections that these workers were studied systematically. The poll worker is the person who makes elections actually run in the approximately 100,000 polling places nationally. The ability of local election officials to monitor these polling places on Election Day, especially in medium-sized and large cities, is made difficult by the number of precincts that may exist in any given jurisdiction. At the extreme end of the scale, Los Angeles County, California has almost 5,000 precincts that it operates on Election Day but even an average large election jurisdiction has almost 100 polling locations open on Election Day. Whether or not these precincts are effectively run can at best be monitored passively; most counties do not have the staffing necessary to have a permanent county election worker in every precinct. Instead, it is the poll workers who implement the elections and their decisions can have a dramatic effect on the experience voters have when voting.

The historical record illustrates numerous examples of how poll workers have affected the election experience for voters, especially when they have played the role of being the front-line workers in efforts to disenfranchise voters. In the 1900s, poll workers were the ones who ensured that only the "correct" voters voted if they had been able to register. Literacy tests, poll taxes, and other barriers to voting were implemented by poll workers when necessary (Keyssar 2000; Kousser 1974). In Alabama, civil rights organizations sued the state in the 1980s because polling places were still run primarily by white poll workers, even in parts of the state where the population comprised primarily African Americans. This staffing pattern was a legacy of the segregation-era practice of whites running polling places in order to enforce Jim Crow-era barriers to voting. As Montjoy and Brudney (1991: 328) note,

> U.S. District Judge Myron Thompson ... issued a preliminary injunction ordering all but two of the 67 counties [in Alabama] to appoint black poll workers in sufficient numbers to reflect the racial makeup of their precincts ... [because] the pattern of appointing poll officials, violated the Voting Rights Act.

Since the 2000 election, many studies and media reports have identified problems associated with the implementation of elections at polling places by poll workers. For example, research by several scholars has identified problems with how poll workers authenticate voters at the polls. In states with a requirement to show photo identification before voting, voters are not always asked to show such identification. Likewise, in states without a photo identification requirement, voters are often asked to show photo identification before voting (e.g., Alvarez et al. 2009; Baretto et al. 2007; Ansolabehere and Persily 2007; Atkeson et al. 2009). There is also evidence that these laws are implemented differently for white and minority voters. For example, Latino men are asked to show identification more often than are whites or females (Atkeson et al. 2009; Baretto et al. 2007). In-depth studies of the implementation of election law in local jurisdictions have found that a small but significant number of poll workers make significant errors in implementing election laws or procedures. For example, a quarter of poll workers in Los Angeles fail to post the "Voter Bill of Rights" document in their polling place (Baretto et al. 2009). In New Mexico, poll workers have failed to set up the voting machines that are designed to facilitate voting among disabled voters and have failed to safeguard the privacy of ballots when voters encounter a problem in voting (Atkeson et al. 2007, 2009).

These problems concerning the implementation of elections in the polling place suggest that poll workers are key players in the electoral process. A study of voter confidence in the electoral process finds strong support for the idea that poll workers play a critical role in shaping voter confidence in the electoral process and in their confidence that ballots are counted accurately at the polls (Hall et al. 2009). When voters were asked "How confident are you that the electoral process produces fair election outcomes?", voters who rated their poll worker's performance as "excellent" were much more likely to rate their confidence as very high compared to individuals who had less than excellent poll worker encounters. Likewise, when voters were asked, "How confident are you that your ballot was counted accurately?", we again see that having a very positive encounter with the poll worker raises voter confidence dramatically. Neither of these findings should be surprising; after all, if voters encounter a problem with their poll worker they may question how well the poll worker conducts other aspects of their job, such as securing ballots and managing the election process fairly (see also Atkeson and Saunders 2007; Claassen et al. 2008).

More recent work has noted that poll worker evaluations are affected by a variety of factors, including the age of the poll workers, the race of the poll workers, if the voter votes during in-person early voting or on Election Day, and if the voter knows the poll worker (Hall and Stewart 2010). Not surprisingly, voters rate poll workers whom they know higher, but this event is something that occurs less than 20 percent of the time in Election Day voting and less than 10 per cent of the time in early voting. In Election Day voting, voters rate poll workers higher if they are able to interact with a poll worker who looks like them; black voters rate black poll workers higher and white voters rate white poll workers higher. Voters also tend to rate the older poll workers—those over the age of 70—lower than they do younger poll workers. Given that voter confidence is affected by the quality of the poll worker experience they have, the selection of poll workers is an important part of election governance and management.

Recent surveys of poll workers in several states provide us with some descriptive data on the people who run elections at the polls. These data show that poll worker attributes can vary widely across election jurisdictions, with some jurisdictions having poll workers with a much higher average age than workers in other jurisdictions. For example, surveys in three counties in Ohio found that poll workers had average ages of between 55 years in Franklin County (Columbus and home of The Ohio State University) and 67 in Cuyahoga County (Magleby et al. 2008). There are also differences in racial attributes that largely mirror the attributes of the locality from which the poll workers are drawn. However, there are some attributes of poll workers that remain true across jurisdictions. Poll workers are usually older white women; between 66 to 80 percent of poll workers are women in most surveys. Very few poll workers are under the age of 30; one study found the median age of poll workers to be 65 years old. Workers typically have greater than high school education. Most poll workers have served for multiple elections; Magleby et al. (2008) found that poll workers in Ohio and Utah had worked between eight and 11 elections on average.

Poll workers are responsible for all aspects of the polling location's Election Day operations: setting up and taking down voting equipment, posting signs, handling ballots, assisting disabled voters, verifying voter registration, applying identification and provisional voting laws, etc. It is the responsibility of election administrators to train poll workers to be able to handle the demands of the precinct. Training must cover a broad range of topics in a short amount of time. Training schedules need to be convenient for workers to encourage participation. Typically, training is conducted in lecture-style sessions with an open section for worker questions. Some states offer training completely online (electiononline.org 2007).

Why does training matter? Training is important because the quality of the training that poll workers receive has ramifications beyond poll worker competence. The characteristics of the job training which poll workers receive have been shown to influence poll worker confidence and satisfaction (Hall et al. 2007). Researchers studied 2006 surveys of poll workers from jurisdictions that utilized identical brand-new voting technology, yet employed differing training techniques to instruct poll workers on how to use the technology. These studies found that "[h]aving good hands-on training increased confidence [among the poll workers] that the ballots would be counted accurately" (Hall et al. 2007). Poll workers from jurisdictions that relied solely on lecture-style training sessions were more likely to report that the training content differed from actual Election Day experiences; the training did not prepare them for the work. In short, training ensures that poll workers implement the election at the polls more accurately than they might otherwise have done and makes them more confident in their work. For the voter, this means that the election experience is likely to be better managed and, in turn, raise the confidence of the voter in the electoral process.

Election Management and Experiences across States

If differences in election management only affected an individual's experience but did not affect the overall election process, it would not be so significant that there are variations in election administration across the United States. However, as we have discussed previously, there are critical distinctions that occur across different election environments. For example, the partisanship of election officials can affect whether a voter's provisional ballot is counted and the level of turnout (with higher turnout occurring in localities with partisan election officials). We also know that poll workers implement laws differently across precincts, including laws governing voter authentication and general activities that make elections run smoothly at the polls. In this section we consider how election management varies across states and how these variations affect voter turnout and voter confidence in the electoral process.

One of the first key aspects of election management that varies across states is the way in which voters are authenticated before they vote. As noted previously, following HAVA, some states developed more stringent ID requirements. Studies from New Mexico and elsewhere showed that state laws can vary greatly in the requirements for voters to show or not to show identification and that these laws can be implemented in highly variant ways (Atkeson et al. 2010). Researchers have found that partisan affiliation and individual poll worker characteristics were not driving the decision to ask for identification. The intent behind these identification requirements was to prevent voter fraud. However, when implemented, a possible side effect of the requirements is discouraging potential voters from participation. If the identification requirement is applied incorrectly to a legitimate voter, he or she could be required to vote provisionally (an option that comes with a decrease in the probability that the vote is properly counted (Pitts 2008)).

But what do differences in state identification laws mean for turnout? In a seminal study, Alvarez, Bailey, and Katz (2007) find that stricter voter identification laws can affect turnout among certain populations of voters. These scholars used data from the United States Census Current Population Survey for four election cycles to examine the changes in individual turnout that occurred with the introduction of new voter identification requirements in the states. The goal of this study was to see how moving from one voter identification requirement to a more strict requirement affected turnout. They focused specifically on key subpopulations to see if there was a disproportionate impact on the turnout rates of certain groups, such as the poor, minorities, and the elderly. The results of their analysis were that stricter identification laws did not result in significantly different levels of turnout between different racial groups or among voters of different age categories. However, stricter identification laws do affect voters who are less well educated—their turnout is lower in states with stricter voter education laws—and among less wealthy voters, who again have lower turnout in strict identification states.

Voter identification laws are an example of how policy choice can affect specific voters in their quest to cast a ballot. Very strict voter identification laws most affect the low-income voter but all voters are subject to the vagaries of how a given set of poll workers will implement the law when the voter arrives at the polls. This problem of implementation again illustrates the principal–agent problem in elections, where the voter is subject to different voting experiences based on the quality of the poll workers whom they encounter and the mode of voting that they choose to utilize to cast their ballot.

Voting Technology and Experiences

Voting technology is another aspect of elections that varies across jurisdictions. Unlike most countries where there is a standard method of voting used nationwide—most commonly voting on a paper ballot for a very small number of races—in the United States voting technologies vary across states and often within states. Multiple voting technologies may be utilized simultaneously in one state on a single Election Day (Saltman 2006). Even in a state with a single Election Day voting technology, voters may use a different technology to vote if they cast their ballot absentee. In addition, some states use electronically counted paper ballots as a primary voting method but also have some form of electronic voting in the precinct as well, to accommodate the needs of voters with disabilities as required under HAVA. Prior to 2000, many jurisdictions were using paper punch card or lever voting systems; now, optical scan ballots and direct recording electronic (DRE) voting machines are more common (see Caltech/MIT Voting Technology Project 2001). HAVA did not dictate the adoption of a particular voting technology. States can pick the voting technology that they want to use—as long as they do not use punch card ballots or lever machines—and some states allow their local election jurisdictions to select the voting technology used.

HAVA's requirements to update voting equipment coupled with the state block grants to fund equipment purchases created a connection between state and local election officials and voting technology developers and vendors. Voting technology presents yet another principal–agent relationship in election administration: "The need for technological innovation coupled with recent outlays in federal funding guarantee that private actors will be entrusted with central electoral functions" (Nou 2009). State and local election officials must delegate important responsibilities to private industry and the vendors hold the upper hand when it comes to having important information about how the voting technology works.

The goal of HAVA was to have states adopt new voting systems that would reduce voter errors and prevent the United States from having a repeat of the 2000 election in Florida. However, although HAVA required states to upgrade voting technology, the legislation was silent on mechanisms to help voters revise errors on their ballots: "HAVA does *not* require that voting systems provide actual notice and opportunity to correct mistakes" (Tokaji 2005: 1215) and the EAC does not have the power to mandate that states adopt voting technologies that meet certain federal standards.

As was mentioned before, in many states the decision of what voting technology should be adopted was left up to local election officials. Survey data show that the decision of what technology will be adopted by a locality can often rest on the attitudes of the election official about various voting systems (Moynihan and Silva 2008). The perceptions of local election officials of HAVA were predicated largely on their knowledge about HAVA, their perception that HAVA could be funded in their jurisdiction without a revenue shortfall, and their attitudes about the role the federal government should play in elections. Attitudes toward the type of technology they supported for voting also depended on their attitudes toward technology generally—people who have faith in technology had more faith in electronic voting. The type of voting technology the voter uses to vote is determined largely by the perceptions and attitudes of their election official, and not necessarily by data regarding which voting technology may work best for their voting population.

Studies have shown that certain voting technologies which contain features that help voters know if they have made a mistake can reduce the overall residual vote rate (Hamner et al. 2010).[2] Researchers used data from the 2000 and 2004 presidential elections to evaluate the impact of upgrades in voting technology on residual votes. Analysis demonstrated that the reduction was greatest with DREs that alert voters if they fail to vote in a race (typically referred to as an under-vote) and deny voters the ability to vote more than once in a race where only one vote is allowed (an over-vote). In addition, the ballot error rate is also substantially reduced with the use of optical scan ballots when this technology is programmed so that the vote tabulator alerts the voter that there is an error with their ballot (either an over-vote or an under-vote). The difference between the two technologies is that the optical scan voting system allows voters to know that a mistake was made and to subsequently correct the mistake, but it is not always obvious where the mistake occurs on the optical scan ballot.

These differences also vary across different brands of voting machines; simply put, all voting machines are not made equal. In an important recent study, researchers at several universities had voters use different voting machines to accomplish specific voting tasks, such as changing their vote, voting for a write-in candidate, and otherwise voting on these different voting technologies (Herrnson et al. 2008). They found marked differences in the experience voters have using different types of DRE voting machines because these machines use different ways of showing a ballot and often provide voters with different ways of actually voting. They also found differences between DREs and paper systems and differences between perceived ease of voting and actual accuracy of what the voters did.

This work extended research that had been conducted previously by the Caltech/MIT Voting Technology Project (2001), Bullock and Hood (2002), and Tomz and Van Houweling (2003) which found differences between voting technologies in the accuracy of capturing votes. Tomz and Van Houweling's work is especially important because they found that white and African American voters interact with the same technologies differently, with African Americans more likely to have ballots with residual votes when they were not given feedback that they had made an error.

Quality of Election Administration

One measure of election administration quality is voter confidence. Voter confidence means the level of confidence a voter has that his or her vote has been accurately counted. This confidence is tied directly to the electorate's view of the legitimacy of the elected government. If election processes do not satisfy voters, the resulting elections will not be viewed as legitimate by the electorate. Alvarez and Hall (2006) advocate reducing the number of principal–agent relationships utilized in election administration. However, several authors (e.g., Alvarez et al. 2008; Atkeson and Saunders 2007) found that confidence was tied to the mode of voting: lower confidence levels were associated with non-Election Day methods. The authors caution that implementing non-traditional voting methods which remove the voters from the polling place (voting without the poll worker–voter interaction) could be detrimental to voter confidence. Other researchers have found that the technological method of voting does not affect voter behavior or perceptions of the integrity of the voting process; other aspects of election administration (poll worker interactions, length of lines at polls) had a significant impact upon voters' confidence in the process (e.g., Hall and Stewart 2010; Stein et al. 2008). We would like to know what administrative features could be employed to mitigate the negative aspects of principal–agency in election administration while enhancing voter confidence. If we can find solutions that satisfy both of these requirements, we can enhance the quality of election administration.

One solution that would square with many of these findings is the utilization of Election Day vote centers (EDVCs) over the traditional residential precinct locations. Under the EDVC model there are fewer polling locations, but they are located in high-traffic areas which usually means that they are closer to public transit options and business centers. Voters from the entire jurisdiction can go to any vote center they choose; they are not required to visit their residential polling location. The EDVC is equipped with a jurisdiction-wide registration database, so that poll workers can look up any voter regardless of precinct. EDVCs ease the staffing burdens for LEOs; since there are fewer polling locations under this model, and fewer poll workers are required to adequately staff the locations. Researchers studied EDVC in Larimer County, Colorado, and found that EDVCs increased the participation of all individuals and particularly of individuals who were unlikely to vote under the traditional precinct-based model (Stein and Vonnahme 2008). The use of EDVC would definitely cut down on the volume of delegation which LEOs must undertake to staff fewer voting locations, and EDVCs would still provide the poll worker–voter interaction that was found to be so important to voter confidence.

Alvarez and Hall (2008) discuss the benefit of adopting standard operating procedures (SOPs) for elections to increase the legitimacy of elections. SOPs help mitigate the principal–agent dilemma by systematically eliminating a portion of the agent's discretion. Election administration operates with scant resources to compensate or directly monitor employees. Most employees have little job-related training or experience. Standardization can provide the guidance that is not present when individuals with little or no institutional knowledge are relied upon to carry out the work of the organization. An SOP that clarifies the procedure to transmit final vote tallies to central offices removes the ability of a precinct worker to devise a potentially insecure transmission method. Regulations that detail the maintenance procedures for voting equipment in between elections guard against the possibility that staff select an inappropriate maintenance provider that could tamper with equipment. If SOPs are explicit, less decision-making is possible for agents and the potential for variation is diminished. SOPs can make variations among jurisdictions apparent. Differences in operations are distinct when there is a uniform framework for activities. Beneficial variation may be identified as a best practice while detrimental variation may be identified as a gap or deficiency in the existing SOP. This information may be incorporated into the development or revision of the overall system of SOPs.

Another way to reduce the number of principal–agent relationships is to centralize as many election functions as possible. This leads to the question: What aspects of election administration lend themselves to centralization? Creek and Karnes (2010) propose that the selection of voting equipment is an easily centralized activity: a few state officials could be charged with the task of learning about and testing several different machines, the combined purchasing power of the state could drive down the unit cost, and state-wide contracts could be employed to provide for maintenance of equipment across all jurisdictions. This centralization could provide relief to LEOs to focus less of their energy on technology-related issues and devote more time to local aspects: registration processes, poll worker development, etc.

The local level of election administration is necessary because there are many features of election administration that are ill-suited to centralization.

Selecting precinct poll locations would be a very difficult task to handle remotely; proper site selection is dependent on local knowledge of neighborhoods, traffic patterns, and building specifications. At times, site visits would be necessary to determine whether accessibility requirements can be satisfied. Poll worker recruitment requires local administration; in a Center for the Study of Elections and Democracy report on poll workers, the most common poll worker recruitment methods employed local mechanisms: by another poll worker, at a precinct caucus meeting, by a party official, etc. (Magleby et al. 2008).

Summary

We have focused on the personnel, structure, and complexity of American election administration. Historically, the federal government has abstained from taking over election administration. Instead, states have been allowed to create election systems as they choose, within the confines of a limited federal role. Even after the 2000 election crisis and the passage of HAVA in 2002, the federal government has allowed the states to retain most of their autonomy in this area.

However, the responsibility to carry out the business of elections is not concentrated at the state level of government. State election officers assume varying degrees of involvement—sometimes actively engaged in the finer details of the election process or merely involved when there is a public, system-wide failure. Local election officials have the greatest tasks of overseeing registration and voting operations. Poll workers are the street-level election officials who ultimately facilitate (or thwart) the voting process. At any level, potential partisanship of individuals involved in elections can influence election policies and vote count outcomes.

Shared responsibility and the need to provide coverage to all jurisdictions necessitates that election operations utilize extensive chains of delegation. The federal government delegates duties to the state-level officials, who delegate to local election officials, who delegate to poll workers. Every delegation brings with it variations in election procedures which means that voters living in different states, or in different precincts or even standing in different lines at the same polling station on Election Day can have fundamentally different voting experiences. Variation occurs in the type of voting technology utilized, the laws that apply in the state, how those laws are interpreted and implemented by poll workers, the capacity of the polling location to serve voters, the quality of the training received by poll workers, and the competency of poll workers.

The quality of election administration may be quantified through voter confidence—the degree to which a voter believes his or her vote has been counted correctly. Research indicates that voters feel more confident when they vote through traditional methods (in person at a polling place) and have positive interactions with poll workers. Since confidence is tied to some delegated aspects of election administration, particularly the poll worker–voter interaction, some options to mitigate the negative potential of delegation (while retaining the positive benefits to voter confidence) in election administration were discussed: Election Day vote centers, adopting standard operating procedures, and centralizing decision-making with regard to voting technology at the state level. However, as long as there is voting in polling places, elections will always need to retain a local component; there are some aspects that can never be centralized at the state level or higher such as selecting polling locations and the training and recruiting of poll workers. This local involvement does not mean that the states and federal governments cannot play a more robust role in the electoral process.

Future Research

Because of the inherently local characteristics of election administration, there will always be a need for studies from a variety of jurisdictions throughout the United States. A local focus is required because the variation in laws, equipment, and people necessitates knowing the characteristics of the local administration to begin to analyze the overall impact of the system on voter confidence, policy implementation, residual vote rates, voting participation, experiences of voters, etc. Changes in laws, voting methods, and technologies will always require examination of how these changes impact upon voter access and confidence.

We know about poll workers who have served through numerous elections; we do not know as much about attritional poll workers. When first-time poll workers do not return, the resources invested in training them and the knowledge they gain from their Election Day work experience leaves with them. When surveys are conducted on recent poll workers, respondents have not necessarily decided whether to continue being a poll worker or not; data might indicate lower attrition rates than are experienced when staffing poll workers for the next election. Studies that track cohorts of poll workers would be useful in identifying the individual characteristics and structural factors that are associated with workers who serve for a single election and then discontinue service.

The costs of election administration and basic return on investment questions have not been fully examined. The Census reports federal, state, and local governmental finances but does not require a separate reporting category for election administration.[3] In addition, since a local election official usually has a variety of responsibilities unconnected to elections, his office's budget does not necessarily make election-related expenses distinct. Local and state comprehensive annual financial reports do not always present election expenses separate from other governmental functions. It would be interesting to see how expenditures affect voter experience and poll worker retention, and how spending relates to the partisanship of election officials.

Notes

1. For a discussion of the issues of state control of voter registration, see the *election-line.org* report. Available at www.pewcenteronthestates.org/report_detail.aspx?id= 35430.
2. A residual vote occurs when a voter fails to have a vote counted for a specific race in an election. The residual vote total is calculated by subtracting the number of votes in a specific race in the election from all ballots cast. The rate is the residual vote total divided by the total number of votes cast in the election.
3. www.census.gov/govs/.

Chapter 2

Campaign Finance
Adapting to a Changing Regulatory Environment

David B. Magleby

The past decade has seen substantial legislative and judicial activity in the regulation of campaign finance. This was at least partly in response to changes in
the ways parties, groups, and individuals raised and spent money in federal
elections. The 1996 election marked an important turning point, with a substantial increase in parties' and groups' spending on elections apart from
money they contributed to candidates. The changing policy and political environments, including federal legislation and court decisions, call for new and
creative research strategies.

Research on campaigns and elections over the past half-century has documented how radio, television, consultants, and new media like the Internet
have changed American electoral democracy (Magleby 2010). When
Woodrow Wilson first used radio to communicate with the nation in 1919,
many Americans saw the new technology as something akin to magic
(Douglas 2004; Loviglio 2005; Campbell 2006). Radio was supplanted by television in the 1950s and 1960s, but remains an important medium for targeted advertising (Magleby forthcoming(b)). By the 1970s, television had
become the major means of communicating with voters in federal elections
and it remains central today. With the advent of cable television, candidates
now assume they need to also advertise on at least some cable stations. As
with radio, some cable stations, such as the Golf Channel or Home and
Garden TV, may reach a particular demographic segment of interest to a
candidate.

One reason money has become even more critical in recent years is that
advertising on television is expensive. Candidates, party committees, and
interest groups, all of whom are bidding for advertising time in a limited
period, have seen costs of advertising rise, sometimes dramatically (Gross and
Miller 2000: 1871–92). It is too soon to know how the Internet will impact
upon campaign communications across the full range of federal elections.
Prior to 2008 the Web was seen as a reinforcing tool more than a persuasion
tool, but some campaigns in 2008, as we will discuss below, found ways to
expand the impact of the Internet. One area in need of further research is how
the Internet will impact upon fundraising and campaigning in the future.

California Assembly Speaker Jesse Unruh famously said, "Money is the mother's milk of politics" (Unruh 1962). The net effect of changes in how money is raised and spent in campaigns since the mid-1990s provides further evidence for the Unruh maxim, at least as applied to campaigns. It is an open question whether campaigns are more expensive because of television, consultants, and new media, or whether, because candidates, party committees, and organized interests have more money to spend, electoral politics has become more expensive. It may be that both are true. However, regardless of what may be causing the growing importance of money in campaigns and elections, the reality is that money matters. This chapter examines recent developments in campaign finance and identifies new directions in research on this topic.

Campaign Finance Regulation

What we know about how campaigns are financed has been greatly enhanced by more effective disclosure requirements enacted into federal law following the Watergate scandal. The Federal Election Campaign Act as amended in 1974 required candidates, political party committees, and individuals and groups seeking to influence the outcome of federal elections to disclose in substantial detail to the Federal Election Commission (FEC) their receipts and expenditures. As Herbert Alexander wrote of 1976, the first election after FECA as amended took effect, the new laws "required fuller disclosure of political funding than ever before" (Alexander 1979: 11).

For two decades, the world of federal election campaign finance was relatively stable and generally observable. That changed in 1996 in two ways. First, political parties, which had pressed for amendments to FECA in the late 1970s to allow parties to raise unlimited amounts of money, including from corporate and union treasury accounts, for party building purposes such as generic advertising and voter registration and mobilization, started using that "soft" money for candidate-specific advertising. The first to make this change was the Clinton/Gore campaign, but the Dole/Kemp campaign quickly followed suit, and party soft money rose dramatically in scale and importance. Party soft money retained FECA's commitment to disclosure but departed from FECA in that it could be raised in unlimited amounts, including from corporations and union treasury funds, and was only limited in expenditure by the requirement of a matching hard money expenditure (Magleby and Squires 2004: 48).

The 1996 election brought a second change in federal election finance as individuals and groups exploited the definition of what constituted an election communication. In *Buckley* v. *Valeo* the Supreme Court defined election advocacy as "express words of advocacy of election or defeat such as 'vote for,' 'elect,' 'support,' 'cast your ballot for,' 'Smith for Congress,' 'vote against,' 'defeat,' 'reject'" (1976). Communications that did not use these "magic words" of election advocacy were presumed by definition to be about issues rather than candidates and were therefore not subject to disclosure requirements or other aspects of FECA. This kind of spending came to be known as "issue advocacy." In 1994 the Christian Coalition was the first to test whether communications that avoided the magic words could also avoid disclosure and spending limits (*FEC v. Christian Coalition* 1999). Then, in 1996, the American Federation of Labor-Congress of Industrial Organizations (AFL-CIO) launched a major effort to unseat Republicans, some elected for the first time in 1994. The organization vowed to spend $35 million (Bradley, Cogan, and Rivers 1997: 12; see also Magleby 2000b: 46). Republican allies soon countered through groups such as TRIAD, a consulting firm, which spent money in competitive districts promoting Republicans and attacking Democrats. These activities were in addition to candidate expenditures and party soft money spending. In competitive contests in 1998, 2000, and 2002 the party soft money and interest group issue advocacy spending sometimes exceeded the spending by the candidates (Magleby 2000c, 2002; Magleby and Monson 2004).

The 1996 election cycle marked another change that at the time was not as important as the surge in soft money and issue advocacy but has come to be very important in the 2004, 2006, and 2008 elections, and promises to remain important in the future. In a case brought by the Colorado Republican Party, the U.S. Supreme Court struck down limitations on political parties' making independent expenditures (*Colorado Republican Committee v. FEC* 1996). In the *Buckley* v. *Valeo* decision the Supreme Court had allowed unlimited independent expenditures by individuals and groups, while permitting disclosure requirements on both the receipt and expenditure of these funds. Under FECA, political party committees were allowed to make limited contributions to candidates and to spend limited amounts of money in coordinated expenditures with candidates. The 1996 ruling allowed parties to make independent expenditures, but only with funds raised under the FECA limits; that is, "hard" money. Party-independent expenditures were a less utilized means of spending money as long as the party committees had the soft money option.

For 15 years, Congress considered again and again reforming the campaign finance system (Dwyre and Farrar-Myers 2001). In 1987 and 1998 there were multiple cloture votes to try to overcome a Senate filibuster against reform. Legislation passed the House in 1998 and 1999 only to die in the Senate, and in 1986 legislation passed the Senate but failed to get the votes needed in the House (Dwyre and Farrar-Myers 2001: 59, 213, 221). In 1992 both Houses passed legislation only to see it vetoed by President George H.W. Bush. Finally, the issue advocacy by some groups in the 2000 presidential primaries and general election, coupled with a visible champion, John McCain, helped prompt Congress to enact the Bipartisan Campaign Reform Act (BCRA) in 2002.

BCRA's most important and enduring element is a ban on party soft money. To help fund election activities in the absence of soft money, BCRA raised individual contribution limits to candidates and party committees, and indexed those limits to inflation. In 2008, the BCRA limit to any candidate was $4600 ($2300 in primary and $2300 in general), and an individual's aggregate contribution limit was $108,200, with no more than $28,500 allowed to go to any one party committee.

The 2002 legislation also included provisions called the "millionaire's amendment," which provided an increase in contribution limits and the possibility of unlimited coordinated expenditures from party committees to individuals running against heavily self-financed candidates (Corrado 2006: 404–1). This amendment was struck down in 2008 by the Supreme Court in *Davis* v. *FEC*.

To provide political parties with assistance in voter registration and getting out the vote, BCRA allows state and local party committees to raise a combination of hard and soft money solely for grassroots voter mobilization activities. These funds, named Levin funds (after Michigan Senator Carl Levin, the author of the amendment allowing such funding), may not be spent on television or radio advertising, nor may they be used in activities that mention a federal candidate's name or that mobilize for an election with a federal candidate on the ballot (Corrado 2006: 363–7).

Addressing the rise in issue ads, BCRA (2002) included language defining electioneering communications as:

> [A]ny broadcast, cable, or satellite communication which refers to a clearly identified candidate for federal office; is made within 60 days before a general, special, or runoff election for the office sought by the candidate; or 30 days before a primary or preference election ... and in the case of a communication which refers to a candidate for an office other than President or Vice President, is targeted to the relevant electorate.

BCRA also restored the longstanding prohibition on unions' and corporations' using general treasury money for such ads.

As with FECA, BCRA was immediately challenged in court and was considered by the Supreme Court on an expedited basis. *McConnell* v. *FEC*, the Court's decision on the constitutionality of BCRA, upheld the soft money ban and left standing the new definition of electioneering communications while declaring unconstitutional a provision requiring parties to decide between the use of limited coordinated or unlimited independent expenditures. The Court also declared unconstitutional a provision forbidding individuals aged 17 and younger making campaign contributions (*McConnell* v. *Federal Election Commission* 2003). Less than four years later, the Supreme Court in *FEC* v. *Wisconsin Right to Life* revisited the BCRA electioneering communications definition. In a five to four decision, Chief Justice John Roberts struck BCRA's language, substituting his own electioneering communication definition:

when an ad is "susceptible of no reasonable interpretation other than as an appeal to vote for or against a specific candidate" (*Federal Election Commission v. Wisconsin Right to Life, Inc.* 2007).

Then in 2010 the Supreme Court returned to campaign finance in *Citizens United v. FEC*, a case involving a documentary movie critical of Senator and presidential candidate Hillary Clinton. In a potentially far-reaching decision, the Court ruled that corporations were free to spend unlimited general treasury funds to advertise for or against a candidate for federal office, even within the time period immediately prior to an election. Simultaneously, the Court overruled the part of *McConnell v. Federal Election Commission* that had upheld BCRA's restrictions on independent corporate expenditures (*Citizens United v. Federal Election Commission* 2010). How *Citizens United* will change the approach taken by corporations in spending money to influence elections remains to be seen. While *Citizens United* was about corporations and not unions, it is likely the case that unions will also be allowed to spend unlimited amounts of treasury funds to influence federal elections. The impact is potentially great, especially given the large amounts of money some corporations have and the substantial spending already done by unions.

Less visibly, the regulatory body charged with this policy area, the Federal Election Commission (FEC), has been frequently challenged in court by both sides for its proposed regulations and has also been hindered by partisan deadlock. For much of the 2008 election cycle the FEC had four of six commissioner slots vacant. With at least four commissioners required for any decisions or actions, this rendered the FEC powerless (Corrado forthcoming). As the FEC continues to change its regulations, candidates will have to adapt and find different ways to utilize the sources of funding available. This in turn means that research on campaign finance will be all the more valuable to policy-makers and the courts as they adjust the rules and processes in this area.

Sources of Money

Money for U.S. federal elections comes from individuals; interest groups including corporations, unions, single-issue groups, and so on; taxpayers; and the candidates themselves. Political parties are a secondary funder of campaigns and elections, but their sources of funding include all of those listed above. A trade union, for example, can make contributions to a candidate, to a political party, and to other interest groups. A core question in researching campaign finance has always been to follow the money from its source to those spending the money to persuade and mobilize voters.

Sources of Money in Presidential Elections

The sources of money for presidential campaigns is different than for U.S. House and U.S. Senate contests, and the sources of funds for incumbents running for Congress are different than for challengers or open-seat candidates. Similarly, the sources of funding for political parties have been somewhat different for Democrats than for Republicans, and have altered with changes in federal law.

Presidential campaigns since BCRA have been largely funded by individuals. Individuals contributed 88 percent of the money raised by Democratic nominee Barack Obama and 54 percent of the money raised by Republican nominee John McCain. Nearly one-quarter (23%) of McCain's funds came from the public grant for the general election (Open Secrets 2009).

Individuals as sources of funding for presidential candidates have increased in importance since BCRA, due in part to the fact that individual contribution limitations were doubled and then indexed to inflation, and to the ban on party soft money, which meant candidates could no longer rely on this unlimited source of funding from their party committees to assist in their campaign efforts.

Even with the soft money ban, parties continue to play a role as a source of funding for presidential candidates. Most party money that is spent on presidential elections is raised from individuals. This has been especially the case for candidates who accept public funding in the general election. Democrat John Kerry in 2004 and Republicans George W. Bush in 2004 and John McCain in 2008 all directed donors to their party committees in the general election campaigns. Ellen Moran, who directed independent expenditures for the Democrats, found that the DNC exceeded its fundraising expectations in 2004 by a factor of "three to four times," in part through Kerry's endorsement. The RNC was also successful in raising hard money in 2004 (Magleby, Monson, and Patterson 2007, 13). The candidates received additional publicity through joint party/candidate committees that ran hybrid ads, communications that mentioned the party and party nominees (Corrado 2006: 1371–38).

However, there are disadvantages to using the joint candidate/party committee funding model. One disadvantage is the candidate losing control of the message. Joint activity cannot be solely about the candidate but must also include a party message. This has the potential to dilute the candidate message and may be particularly damaging in a year when the candidate's party is losing popularity. Joint spending does not allow candidates to distance themselves from the party, as Christian Ferry, McCain's deputy campaign manager, explained following the 2008 campaign:

> In an election where the Republican party brand was damaged, where the incumbent president was a Republican and was incredibly unpopular, where the right track/wrong track number was, prior to September 15, around 30 percent and then after September 15 around 8 percent, being a Republican is not necessarily the way you want to brand yourself if you

want to win the campaign. We had no choice. We had to do things with our entire ticket, we had to do things under the banner of the Republican party. John McCain is a Republican, and so, relying on resources of the RNC made all of our events, a great majority of our mail and phones and most, if not, I'd say, 80 to 90 percent of our field staff were RNC employees working for the benefit of the entire ticket, and that I think was problematic for our chances of success in the fall, ultimately.

(Ferry 2009)

While Ferry's assessment rings true, further research should be done to test the generalizability of the argument. The Obama campaign in particular avoided joint spending to ensure control over their message. As demonstrated above, though the joint spending helped McCain do more advertising than would otherwise have been possible, it also meant that the message had to be adjusted.

Individuals can play a major role in financing presidential candidates by making their own independent expenditures, as George Soros did, spending $4 million in independent expenditures against George W. Bush in 2004 (Patterson 2006: 78). It is not known if money spent in independent expenditures is seen by voters as distinguishable from money spent by other entities in federal elections. The limited data we have suggest that voters do not distinguish the sources of funds; rather they attribute the advertising to one or the other candidate (Magleby 2000a).

While PAC contributions to federal candidates were up substantially in 2008 (32 percent over the 2003–2004 election cycle), PACs again played only a minor role as a source of funds for presidential candidates (Cigler forthcoming). In 2008, for example, 80 percent of PAC contributions to federal candidates went to congressional incumbents (Federal Election Commission 2009b). Further research could productively be done on how PACs raise money and why they spend it as they do.

During much of the FECA period, from 1976 through 1996, public funding was an important source of money to presidential candidates. With only the exceptions of Republicans John Connally (in 1980) and Steve Forbes (in 1996), presidential candidates in both parties accepted public matching funds in the nomination phase of their campaigns, and all party general election candidates during this period accepted the public grant in the general election. With public funding came spending limitations. The source of public funding was a voluntary taxpayer check-off on federal income taxes. Since 2000, taxpayer participation in this source of funding has declined (Campaign Finance Institute 2010), with reasons for this unclear and contested (Pace 1994: 139–52). Candidate participation in the publicly financed system is likely to decline further given the Obama campaign's success in raising money without public funds.

Candidates may provide their campaigns with unlimited amounts of their own money, and some candidates have attempted to use their wealth to advantage. For example, in 2008 Mitt Romney loaned and gave his campaign $44.7 million, nearly 42 percent of his total spending (FEC 2008; see also Open Secrets 2009).[1] Opponents often seek to make spending by self-financed candidates an issue in the campaign, as one of Romney's opponents, former Arkansas governor Mike Huckabee, did in 2008. He criticized Romney's spending of his own money as evidence of a lack of fiscal restraint (Liasson 2008). Yet however loudly opponents of wealthy candidates may complain, it again does not appear that voters penalize candidates who spend lavishly on their own campaigns.

Sources of Money in U.S. House Elections

In competitive contests, House candidates and their political parties have been adept at raising money from outside their district boundaries. Wealthy districts have become the "political ATMs" for other districts (Gimpel, Lee, and Pearson-Merkowitz 2008: 3739–4). More generally, House incumbents rely more than any other type of federal election candidate on PAC contributions. This is due in part to their positions of power in Congress and the constancy of the money chase for House members facing the pressures of an election cycle every two years. Since 1996, 43 percent of money raised by House incumbents came from PACs, compared to 16 percent for House challengers and candidates for open seats (Federal Election Commission 2009a).

The incumbency advantage is even greater for incumbents from the majority party. Democrats, who held the majority in the House for the first twenty years of FECA (1974–1994), enjoyed a substantial fundraising advantage among PACs over Republicans during this period. Writing two decades ago, Candice Nelson and I observed, "There is a clear alliance between Democrats and labor PACs—almost no labor money goes to Republicans." We also noted that corporate PACs gave more to Republicans, but that "by 1988 corporate PAC contributions had become more even" (1990: 808–1).

That balance soon shifted. As Gary Jacobson wrote, the change in party control in the U.S. House in 1994 "transformed the campaign money market" (Jacobson 1997: 152). When Democrats lost majority status, and with it committee control, "business-oriented PACs were free to follow their Republican hearts as well as their pocketbooks in allocating donations" (Goidel, Gross, and Shields 1999: 64). Business PACs continued to be pragmatic by giving to both parties; however, with the GOP in charge they generally favored the Republicans.

House challengers in both parties are often largely invisible to most voters. From 2000 to 2008, for every dollar a House incumbent was able to raise from all sources, a major party House general election challenger raised on average $0.28 (Federal Election Commission 2009a). They are not able to raise enough money to generate publicity and campaign organization sufficient to win the attention of voters. The sources of money for House challengers are mostly individuals. For example, in 2008, House challengers raised on average only 10 percent of their money from PACs (Federal Election Commission 2009a). Some House challengers are largely self-financed, which because there are no limits on what individuals can spend on their own campaigns allows them to neutralize the fundraising advantage enjoyed by incumbents. For example, in 2008, in the Florida Eighth District, Alan Mark Grayson (D) spent $850,000 of his own money (91 percent of his total spend) in a successful bid against four-term incumbent Ric Keller. In the same election, however, James D. Oberweiss (D) of the Illinois Fourteenth District spent a personally financed $3.6 million (77 percent of his total spend), and Mike Erickson (R) in the Oregon Fifth District spent his own $1.6 million (80 percent of his total spend) in failed campaigns (Krigman 2008). Overall, in 2008 challengers' own funds (loans and contributions) constituted on average 22 percent of the money raised by challengers (Federal Election Commission 2009a).

House elections with no incumbent running but with one party dominant in the district resemble incumbent races, with the dominant party candidate often tapping into an individual donor base and raising more PAC money than the opponent in the race. When a competitive district hosts an open-seat contest, both candidates are likely to raise money from individuals in and out of the district and also garner some PAC contributions. These contests also generate substantial interest group and political party spending through independent expenditures, a topic discussed in greater detail later in the chapter.

Political party committees can be a source of modest funding to candidates in House races. In 2008 party committees could contribute $10,000 per election cycle ($5000 in the primary and $5,000 in the general election) to a candidate (Federal Election Commission 2007). If both the party national committee, either the Democratic National Committee (DNC) or the Republican National Committee (RNC), and the party congressional campaign committee contribute the maximum allowable, a candidate can receive $20,000 per election cycle. In addition to contributions to candidates, party committees can spend limited amounts of money in what are called coordinated expenditures with candidates. Coordinated expenditures may be spent on polling, voter registration, voter mobilization, mailings to voters, or television ad and broadcast time (Corrado 2005: 170). In 2008 if a party wanted to "max-out" in contributions and coordinated expenditures with a House candidate they could spend in most races $64,100. For Senate races in populous states the figure could have been as high as $2,304,000 (Federal Election Commission 2007). No House candidate received the full amount in contributions and coordinated expenditures, in part because party committees prefer to spend money on behalf of candidates through independent expenditures. The average contribution to a House incumbent in 2008 for the Republicans was $3223 and the average contribution by the Democrats to a House incumbent was $1193. For challengers the average contribution for the Republicans was $2502 and for the Democrats $2356. Open-seat candidates received on average $9009 from the GOP or $3075 from the Democrats (Federal Election Commission 2009c).

Looking at all sources of funds for U.S. House candidates, it is clear that incumbents in both parties have much more access to PAC money and also outperform challengers among individual donors. The incumbent advantage in sources of funding is not new; it has been a reality for as long as we have had reliable data on sources of funding (Magleby and Nelson 1990: 54). An important area for research is what this enduring difference means for candidate recruitment. Walt Stone, Sandy Maisel, and Cherie Maestas found that potential challengers are aware of incumbents' significant advantage in ability to raise funds (Stone, Maisel, and Maestas 2004: 484). Prospective congressional candidates considering investing more than a year of their time and often substantial personal funds in a candidacy are likely aware that the sources of funding open to them as a challenger are starkly different than those open to their incumbent opponent. This may result in less qualified and less well-connected challengers actually running for office, which in turn only further strengthens the incumbent.

Aside from self-financed challengers, what mechanisms result in challengers' being able to mount visible campaigns? One option might be public financing. The limited experience with public financing in state legislative elections suggests that tax-based incentives for small donors encourage candidates to broaden their base of supporters and to seek contributions among groups they otherwise likely would not (Boatright and Malbin 2005: 813). An enduring question has been: What could be done to foster more competitive House challengers? Money is not the only challenge they face, but it is a substantial one.

Sources of Money in U.S. Senate Elections

U.S. Senate elections are more likely to be seriously contested, and incumbents, challengers, and open-seat candidates are more likely to have access to a network of individual donors. Individual donors contribute 66 percent of all money raised by U.S. Senate candidates, or about 11 percent more than the share individual donors give to U.S. House candidates. Often U.S. Senate challengers have held elective office previously (e.g., state-wide office), and so they bring with them a network of individual donors whom they can tap. Senate elections are also more likely to generate donors and interest outside the state. In fact, small population states such as North or South Dakota, New Hampshire, or Utah can see as much as 90 percent of the individual donors not living in the state of the election.

On average, individual Senate candidates receive more PAC dollars than do individual House candidates, but PAC contributions constitute a smaller percentage of Senate candidates' total receipts because Senate candidates raise so much more money.

The political parties are a modest source of support for Senate candidates. In 2008, party committees could contribute up to $39,900 to a Senate candidate (Federal Election Commission 2007). Some Senate candidates have contributed a substantial amount of their own money to their campaign, as New Jersey's John Corzine did in 2000, in the amount of $60 million (CNN 2004). On average, as a source of funds for Senate candidates, personal funds range between 3 and 4 percent.

How Money is Raised

Candidates, party committees, and PACs raise money in different ways depending on the type of donor being solicited and the amount of money sought. Individual donors remain the most important source of funding. They provide most of the funding for candidates, party committees, and PACs. Despite their importance, relatively few studies exist on donors. The limited attention given to donors is even more glaring in light of the greater importance placed upon individual donors by the BCRA changes (Francia et al. 2003; Brown, Powell, and Wilcox 1995; Graf et al. 2006). Among the questions to be studied in this area are how large and small donors differ along several dimensions—demographics, ideology, motivation, and mode of contribution (e.g., Internet, check, event).

Direct Mail vs. New Media

To date, money has been raised from individuals making small contributions largely through the mail or over the telephone. Not long after FECA took effect the Republican Party invested heavily in direct mail fundraising and the GOP today continues to rely heavily on this method. Although for some candidates and groups the Internet has become a much more common way to raise money from individuals, direct mail fundraising remains very important to both parties and most candidates.

Direct mail for persuasion and mobilization remains an important part of campaigns. Obama was reported to have spent more than $40 million in nonfundraising direct mail alone in 2008 (Gonzalez 2009). The amounts of mail in highly competitive contests can be substantial. For example, in 2008, Colorado voters received 112 unique mail pieces regarding their tightly contested Senate race, and voters in New Mexico's similarly contested First District received 127 unique pieces (Magleby forthcoming(c)).

Over the past decade, the Internet has become a fundraising tool successfully used by some candidates, groups, and party committees. John McCain in 2000 raised $5 million over the Internet, the most successful Internet effort up until that point (Green and Bigelow 2002: 63). Then, in 2004, former Vermont governor Howard Dean raised approximately $20 million through Internet fundraising (Justice 2004). The 2008 campaign saw further advances in the use of the Internet to raise money by Republicans Mitt Romney and Ron Paul, but the Obama campaign's use of the Internet for fundraising in 2008 was much more successful than any prior efforts. Joe Trippi, who managed the Howard Dean campaign in 2004 and worked for the John Edwards campaign in 2008, said of Obama, "He did everything better ... it's like the Dean campaign was the Wright brothers, the Obama campaign was Apollo 11, and we've skipped ... everything in between" (2008). Party committees have also started to see the potential of the Internet as a way to raise money from individuals (Carney 2010).

Interest groups with substantial membership lists can and do use the Internet as a way to raise money for their PAC and other operations. Ideological groups are also using new media to raise money for preferred candidates. ActBlue developed an Internet fundraising tool to enable progressive groups to raise money for Democratic candidates and committees (ActBlue 2010). ActBlue touts its record as having "sent more than $124 million to some 3200 candidates and committees from more than 420,000 donors, with a median contribution of only fifty dollars" (ActBlue 2010). Looking at U.S. House and U.S. Senate elections in 2008, ActBlue helped raise $60 million for Democrats, including $2.4 million for Kay Hagen in the North Carolina U.S. Senate race alone (Magleby forthcoming(b)). A GOP-aligned group, Slatecard, which hopes to counter ActBlue, was founded in 2007. During their first election cycle they raised "more than $650,000 from grassroots supporters for the candidates and committees they support" (Slatecard 2008).

ActBlue and Slatecard have as a primary purpose facilitating individuals making contributions to candidates of the party preferred by the group. Some other ideological interest groups emphasize their issue agenda first but may encourage contributions to candidates as a secondary objective. Groups such as the Association of Trial Lawyers of America (ATLA) provide information to their members on candidates to whom they may consider contributing.

Raising money via the Internet has important advantages. First, the solicitation can be linked to current events, which may motivate giving. During the 2008 presidential campaign, for example, the Obama campaign had not planned on sending an email soliciting funds on the night of the vice-presidential acceptance speech. However, when former New York City mayor Rudy Giuliani and vice-presidential nominee Sarah Palin both criticized Barack Obama's past as a community organizer, the campaign responded with an email which in turn resulted in the largest fundraising day of the campaign (Rospars 2009).[2] In contrast, direct mail pieces have to be written days in advance of their delivery and phone messaging is not nearly as efficient in reaching a mass audience instantaneously. With electronic messaging, as subsequent events occur, the campaign can go back to individual donors asking for additional contributions. One of Obama's repeat small donors, who works as a marketing director for a non-profit organization, said, "They sucked me in. I was getting these daily e-mails and feeling that I was a part of the inner circle. And if anyone is savvy to the tricks of the trade, it's me" (Hutney 2008).

Another advantage of fundraising via the Internet is that the money is available to the campaign instantly, without having to wait for checks to clear. Finally, interacting with donors through the Internet allows the campaign to engage the individual in multiple ways, not just in making financial contributions. This was another of the ways in which the Obama campaign was innovative. The Obama campaign's new media director Joe Rospars (2009) reported:

> The campaign tried to enable folks to take control of the process as much as they were willing at every stage. So if you made phone calls using the myBarackObama sound system or you made a donation or you sent a letter to the editor or joined a grassroots volunteer group at each step you are prompted to not just tell someone but to upload your whole address book and tell everyone you know.

Engaging the Donors

Direct mail and telephone fundraising is largely about the possible transaction of money between the donor and the campaign. What distinguished the Obama campaign was that it genuinely sought to engage voters at several levels, only one of which was a financial contribution. As Obama campaign manager David Plouffe (2009: 77) has written,

> Many of the online contributions were in small amounts, twenty-five and fifty dollars. And almost all of our contributors indicated to us that they also wanted to volunteer. We believed that making a financial contribution would lead people to feel more invested in the campaign and could result in higher degrees of activism.

Allowing individuals to contribute in multiple ways to a campaign not only provided a large group of volunteers, many personal contacts to other voters, and referrals of other possible volunteers and donors, but likely had the effect of increasing subsequent financial contributions. Keeping connected with these individuals required a commitment to databases, data analysis, and to tracking individual participation to make sure it was meaningful (Denton 2009: xii–xiii). While all of this worked well in 2008, whether it can work in other campaigns or even for Obama in the future is an open question. To what extent was the integration of fundraising and other volunteer activity driven by people's desire for change, their opposition to George Bush and the Iraq War, or their fear about the economy? Future research on how campaigns succeed or fail in the integration of fundraising with other forms of engagement will help us better understand if this was a passing phenomenon.

As mentioned above, BCRA provided an incentive for candidates and party committees to focus on individuals able to make more substantial contributions by doubling individual contribution limits and indexing them to inflation. For efficiency and financial impact, candidates put a premium on these individuals who can give max-out contributions. Even Barack Obama, whose campaign did very well among small donors later in the campaign, relied on large donors in the earlier stages. As Obama fundraiser Penny Pritzker told one reporter, "The money did not grow at the grass roots. It wasn't the Internet. We tapped everybody and did every event we could. He'd do seven events in New York, back-to-back-to-back-to-back" (Pritzker 2009: 74). Observer Richard Wolffe calculated that:

Internet donations totaled less than 15 percent of Obama's fund-raising through 2007. Money only started to cascade through the Web after Iowa in early January 2008, and it would take another several months, as the primaries dragged on, for the grass roots to represent half the campaign's fund-raising.

(Ibid.)

To varying degrees the party committees have exploited the BCRA individual donor limits as a means to raise major contributions from individuals. The party committees, who some analysts thought were given a death sentence by BCRA, have instead responded by turning to individual contributions to replace the banned soft money. Table 2.1 reports receipts for individuals to party committees for the period 1996 to 2008. Rather than becoming weak players in federal elections (Milkis 2003), the party committees have substituted independent expenditures for the old soft money expenditures (La Raja 2008: 1971–98). These committees are likely to build on their past successes with large and small donors.

Interest Group Fundraising

Interest groups rely on individuals and other interest groups to provide them with their funds. How the interest group intends to participate in the political and electoral process determines the rules under which the group raises money. If the stated purpose of the groups is to influence the electoral process, more complete disclosure on sources of funds is required. If the primary purpose of the group is more general advocacy or activities like general voter registration efforts, then donors to the group might not be made public.

Political Action Committees, or PACs, are governed by FECA and their sources of funds are limited, as is the case with candidates and party committees.[3] An individual may contribute up to $5000 to any single PAC and up to $37,500 in total to non-federal party entities (PACs) in any given two-year span (Potter 2005: 49). That number is not indexed for inflation. A PAC may

Table 2.1 Individual Contributions to Party Committees, 1996–2008

	1996	1998	2000	2002	2004	2006	2008
DNC	$93,197,921	$48,338,828	$112,157,217	$55,623,021	$356,975,734	$117,948,743	$135,557,004
DSCC	$17,986,267	$18,374,655	$17,506,809	$20,168,297	$57,756,029	$87,232,426	$104,966,958
DCCC	$16,218,464	$13,692,199	$21,844,053	$19,393,788	$50,690,882	$83,158,357	$90,729,507
RNC	$152,801,268	$80,146,222	$193,181,420	$157,825,892	$350,368,907	$213,453,376	$283,936,662
NRSC	$51,539,674	$42,947,511	$33,999,707	$41,533,725	$60,811,444	$65,214,270	$71,035,209
NRCC	$62,937,307	$49,661,821	$67,010,001	$79,175,374	$145,858,047	$112,066,248	$74,929,413
Total D	$171,300,538	$111,482,775	$194,832,261	$139,380,823	$527,993,274	$342,053,829	$403,315,847
Total R	$362,118,765	$240,778,822	$394,787,252	$359,597,911	$654,890,416	$485,689,254	$518,574,608

Source: Federal Election Commission, "Party Financial Activity Summarized for the 2008 Election Cycle: Party Support for Candidates Increases," press release, May 28, 2009 (www.fec.gov/press/press2009/05282009Party/20090528Party.shtml [July 22, 2009]).

Note
The totals include individual contributions to state and local party committees, which are not shown.

also give to other PACs, including leadership PACs, which are PACs formed by members of Congress to raise funds largely to contribute to other members of Congress. The maximum amount that a PAC can give another PAC is $5000.

Leadership PACs have grown in number from 275 in 2004 to 381 in 2008 (Center for Responsive Politics 2009). Candidates can raise the maximum allowable contribution from a PAC for their campaign committee and an additional contribution for their leadership PAC.

PACs vary in how they raise money. PACs associated with corporations and industry groups are allowed to solicit funds directly from members of their organization or trade group, or a similar affiliated group. Other PACs draw funds from individuals who are members of the group. The National Rifle Association, NARAL Pro-Choice America, and the Sierra Club are examples of membership PACs. Some membership PACs reflect individual or professional self-interest, such as the PACs associated with the National Education Association (NEA), the American Medical Association, the National Association of Realtors, or the Service Employees International Union (SEIU). Little is known about how PACs raise their funds and what themes are used in raising that money.

As the country learned in the 2000 presidential primaries with a series of controversial advertisements attacking Senator John McCain, groups could also organize under Section 527 of the Internal Revenue Code and avoid the disclosure requirements of FECA if they avoided using the specific election advocacy words defined in *Buckley* v. *Valeo*. In addition, individuals could make unlimited and undisclosed contributions to these Section 527 organizations. Following the 2000 election cycle, Congress enacted legislation requiring 527s to register with the FEC and file public reports about their donations and donors if they met certain other requirements such as raising $25,000 or more (Storey 2002: 167–87).

Some interest group electioneering, like that done by Republicans for Clean Air in 2000, escaped disclosure because the groups could argue that they were not using magic words like "vote for" or "vote against." BCRA changed that by defining electioneering as mentioning the name or showing the likeness of a candidate to a certain number of people in the area where an election was being held, within a time proximate to the election—but, as mentioned above, the Supreme Court has created a definition of its own. What the Court and Congress are trying to do in defining what is and what is not an electioneering communication is something scholars can assist with. Rather than speculating about what the public perceives to be an election-related message, researchers could provide data on this question through a set of controlled experiments. Such data were gathered on the "magic words" definition. That research found that individual viewers of campaign communication view issue advocacy ads as urging a vote for or against a candidate. Most individuals also saw issue advocacy ads as more about the election or defeat of a candidate than about the candidate's own ads (Magleby 2002). New tests could be constructed using the BCRA definition and Justice Roberts's definition to see the extent to which they conform to voter perceptions.

Interest groups are also organized under other sections of the IRS code. Section 501(c)(3) groups may not make contributions to candidates or political committees and their role in elections is nonpartisan in nature. A contribution to a 501(c)(3) may be deducted as a charitable contribution from the contributor's taxable income. Some may question, however, how nonpartisan voter registration drives can be when they are aimed at demographic groups that largely favor one party over another. Section 501(c)(4) groups are distinct from PACs because their primary purpose is not to influence elections (Corrado et al. 2005: 74–5). However, a 501(c)(4) may spend money supporting or opposing candidates, and these groups, like parties and individuals, may make unlimited independent expenditures.

Many interest groups use two or more of the legal mechanisms described above to raise and spend money. They often have a PAC, a 527 and a 501(c)(4), and/or a 501(c)(3). For example, the Service Employees International Union (SEIU), EMILY's List, and Club for Growth all have a PAC and one or more 501(c) organization.

The 2004 election saw a surge in interest group activity through 527s, with 527s spending $424 million (Cigler 2006: 235). Pro-Democratic groups such as America Coming Together, the Media Fund, and America Votes organized to defeat George W. Bush, while groups like Swift Boat Veterans for Truth ran ads attacking John Kerry, and Progress for America ran ads praising George W. Bush. In 2008 there was less of this kind of activity, a change due in part to both party nominees' going on record as strongly opposed to such expenditures (Magleby forthcoming(a)).

However, 2006 and 2008 saw a new type of interest group activity. A group of investors formed a for-profit corporation aimed at helping progressive groups communicate and electioneer more effectively, based on information about voters (Catalist 2006). Catalist has built a data file on 220 million Americans that includes their names, addresses, whether they voted in past elections, their party registration, and scores of other variables. This data is in turn sold to others with the intent of Catalist's eventually turning a profit. What Catalist did for the Democrats was allow them to compete on an equal footing with the Republicans in micro-targeting individual voters for fundraising, persuasion, and mobilization. How candidates, party committees, and groups use voter files to help register and mobilize voters is an important area for future research.

How Money is Spent

There are promising and important areas needing further research in how money is spent in federal elections. It remains important to monitor the disclosed and limited activity covered by FECA. Candidates, party committees, and interest groups (including individuals acting essentially as an interest group, as George Soros and others have done) continue to be central to the conduct of our electoral democracy.

Individual donors prefer to have their money spent by candidates as much as possible. This is one reason "max-out" individual donors generally give the maximum allowable to candidates rather than give more of their aggregate limit to party committees or PACs.

But spending on elections in ways other than those directed by candidates is substantial and has grown since 1996. How is this spending different than spending by candidates? Do voters see a difference in content or tone? Is this kind of spending less accurate or more negative? We have partial answers to all of these questions but more work is needed.

Studies of spending by candidates find that television advertising and other forms of mass communications are central (Magleby forthcoming(b)). The ground game of voter canvassing, voter registration, and voter mobilization has enjoyed a resurgence of late. The Bush campaign in 2004 made this a high priority and the Obama campaign invested more on the "ground" than Democrats have typically done. As *Newsweek* reported,

> [T]he Obama campaign excelled in its use of the Internet and on the ground with its use of volunteers. They rejected the old practice of gathering volunteers at labor union halls, and so forth, and opted instead for the use of neighborhood teams. They trained volunteers and empowered them to do various tasks from phone calls to door knocks and it proved successful.
>
> (Thomas 2008)

More research on how candidates, political parties, and interest groups pursue "ground" campaigns would help us better understand what works and why.

Independent expenditures by party committees and interest groups have come to play a major role in federal elections. In the aggregate, political party committees spent nearly $225 million independently on congressional contests in 2008 (Magleby forthcoming(d)). An example of a race in which party committee independent expenditures were important in 2008 is the North Carolina U.S. Senate race, where the DSCC used $7.1 million in independent expenditures to help close a gap in funding between Democrat Kaye Hagan and Republican incumbent Elizabeth Dole (Heberlig, Francia, and Greene forthcoming). The DCCC also provided over $200,000 more in independent expenditure funding for Betsy Markey in the Colorado Fourth Congressional District race than the NRCC provided for Marilyn Musgrave. When interest group and party independent expenditures are combined in this contest, Markey's advantage over Musgrave climbs to $2 million (Duffy,

Saunders, and Dunn forthcoming). As in the days of party soft money and interest group issue advocacy, we are now seeing competitive congressional contests where independent expenditures rival or exceed spending by candidates. What does this level of spending do to the content of elections? Do voters understand the difference between a candidate communication and a party or group attack?

While spending by Section 527 and 501(c) organizations did not rise in 2008, it could rise substantially in the future. This is because the particular elements of 2008 that discouraged this activity may be less present in the future and because the Supreme Court in 2010 struck the longstanding prohibition on corporations' using general treasury funds for electioneering in federal elections—prompting a change in regulation that will most likely apply to politically active unions as well. Imagine a large corporation or union deciding it wanted to defeat a particular House or Senate candidate. Out of their profits or general funds they could spend millions of dollars without having to devote time to raising money. We do not know the impact of the Court's departure from decades of limits on this kind of activity, but it could become substantial. As Thomas Mann pointed out, even the threat of a corporation or union having this power could adversely influence lawmaking (forthcoming). Clearly, future research on the financing of federal elections should assess how much corporate and union money enters federal elections and what the impact of that spending is. Also of interest is the question of which corporations or unions choose to spend their general funds on elections and which do not.

Past research has found more non-candidate campaign activity in competitive election environments. For safe seats the patterns of campaign finance have been predictable, with the incumbent or dominant party enjoying substantial financial advantages and the challenger largely invisible. In some past election cycles the number of competitive states in a presidential race or competitive districts or states in congressional elections has been relatively few and as a result voters in the competitive environments have seen extraordinary spending by candidates, party committees, and interest groups. In such environments, what happens to voters when they reach a point of information overload? Will one or both parties seek to expand the playing field of competitive contests?

In these competitive environments politics is very much a team sport, and the candidates are often indistinguishable from their supporting party committees and interest groups. However, because the candidates cannot coordinate with those making the independent expenditures, party committees and interest groups on the same team are not always on the same page. Democrats have recently secured an advantage in this area through the creation of America Votes, an entity that fosters communication among progressive interest groups. By design, America Votes helps environmental and pro-choice groups, unions, and other interests minimize duplication of effort.

Catalist is likely to play a similar strategic role by providing a common database that the groups, party committees, and candidates can all build upon. Given the importance of these relatively few competitive environments in determining which party controls Congress and the White House, an ongoing understanding of the way in which the teams form and function is important.

Conclusion

Given the success at the Supreme Court of those seeking to deregulate our system of campaign finance, an important area of research is what difference contribution limits have made to our electoral democracy. Have they limited the influence of concentrations of wealth on electoral politics? Have they oriented candidates to broaden their base of financial supporters? On what grounds are limits desirable?

We also need to know more about individual donors at all levels, but especially those who make small contributions. What motivates individuals to give? Would tax or other incentives foster greater individual participation in financing our elections? More broadly, given the importance of disclosure as a means for the public to assess the role of money in elections, more needs to be known about how to make disclosure accessible to voters. Given the ease of electronic data transfers, disclosure in the future should be much easier and more timely than in the past.

Our current regulatory policy distinguishes spending by candidates, including money they receive as contributions from party committees and money they spend in coordination with the party, from independent expenditures, spending by 527 organizations, and so on. In practice, this means limiting candidates' ability to work with interest groups and other supporters and, to a great extent, with their own party committees. With litigation likely on this issue in the near future, research is greatly needed. Does this coordination ban make sense, and if so, on what grounds? What data exist to support or refute the ban? The party soft money ban is another predictable area of litigation. As such, research on how party funding works now and would likely work under different rules in the future is critical.

With the judicial and regulatory environment of campaign finance undergoing rapid changes over the past decade, scholars of elections have much work to do. A solid understanding of where campaign funding comes from and how it is used, along with voter perceptions of that use, will—it is hoped—inform policy-makers and the courts as they decide what is and what is not permissible. The topics likely to be decided range from which disclosure may be allowed to whether to reverse the party soft money ban. Research has been important in past decision-making and has that potential in the future as well.

Notes

1. Most of this, $44.6 million, came in the form of loans which Romney later forgave.
2. For a lower estimate of the money raised in that period, see Ben Smith's "Palin Raises $8 Million—for Obama" (2008).
3. A PAC is defined as a multi-candidate committee when it has been registered with the FEC for more than six months, receives contributions from more than fifty-one persons, and contributes to at least five federal candidates.

## Chapter 3

Polling

Innovations in Survey Research

Brian F. Schaffner

Public opinion polls are becoming increasingly prevalent both in the mainstream media as well as academic scholarship focusing on campaigns and elections. At the same time that the demand for survey research is growing, the face of modern polling is being revolutionized by advances in communications technology. On one hand, telephone surveys, the mainstay of the polling industry for the past 50 years, are suffering from very low response rates and the rapid growth of the cell phone-only population. Nearly a quarter of the adult population cannot be reached by pollsters over landlines and fewer than one-third of those who can be reached actually agree to be polled (Curtin, Presser, and Singer 2005). On the other hand, the rapid increase of internet penetration in American homes has made web-based polling a viable and affordable alternative for students of public opinion. Several consortia of scholars have begun institutionalizing new Internet surveys to study campaigns, such as the Cooperative Congressional Election Study (CCES) and the Cooperative Campaign Analysis Project (CCAP). Even the venerable American National Election Study (ANES) has begun to incorporate web-based surveys into its recent studies. Indeed, Internet surveys appear to be democratizing the study of campaigns and elections by making survey research methods available to a wider swathe of political scientists than ever before. Yet, despite the fast-paced adoption of Internet surveys by scholars studying campaigns and elections, significant (and often heated) debate about the validity of this approach persists.

In this chapter, I examine how recent innovations in communications technologies have presented both challenges and opportunities for how survey researchers poll the public and, more specifically, how political scientists study campaigns and elections. I first discuss how phone surveys are being adapted to address these challenges and I then describe the methods being developed to conduct surveys over the Internet. The latter innovation has sparked controversy, which I also detail in this chapter. I follow by discussing some of the innovative work being conducted with Internet surveys before concluding with the claim that despite the methodological hurdles, Internet surveys will become increasingly popular among political scientists over the next decade, largely due to the tremendous promise that these techniques hold for the study of campaigns and elections.

The Changing Landscape of Communications Technologies

Recent innovations in communications technologies have presented pollsters with both opportunities and challenges. As the public adopts these new technologies and abandons others, new ways to contact people and elicit their opinions are emerging while others fade. In particular, a growing number of people have come to rely exclusively on their cell phones, making it difficult to reach them through random digit dialing (Lavrakas et al. 2007). At the same time, the expansion of the Internet has provided a new platform through which pollsters can reach potential respondents. In this section, I document both trends and their implications for survey research.

Growth of the Cell Phone-Only Population

Two decades ago, pollsters could reach nearly the entire American adult population through a single method—random digit dialing. With cell phones still in their infancy, nearly all Americans had a landline telephone at their home, and since caller ID was not widely used, people were also compelled to answer their phones to find out who was calling. The rapid expansion of cellular service in the US has irrevocably changed the landscape of telephone-based survey research. Not only have most Americans taken to using cell phones, but a non-trivial proportion of the American public now relies exclusively on a cell phone. Figure 3.1 presents the percentage of American adults

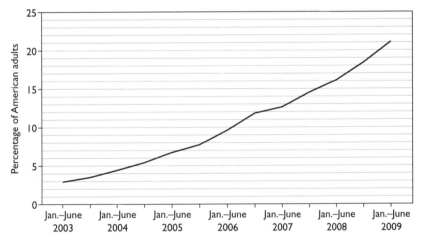

Figure 3.1 The increase in American adults living in a household without a landline telephone.

who report only having a cell phone in their households. As recently as 2003, less than 5 percent of Americans reported that they were cell phone-only; by the end of 2009 that figure exceeded 20 percent. In addition to this substantial proportion of the American public that does not own a landline phone at all, an additional 15 to 20 percent of people who do have landline phones report that they take all or almost all of their phone calls over their cell phones (Blumberg and Luke 2009). When one combines these figures, they amount to a startling 35 to 40 percent of the American public that are now difficult or impossible to reach via landline telephones.

This trend has significant consequences for pollsters. Legally, cell phone exchanges cannot be dialed with the kind of automated technology that pollsters had grown accustomed to using to reduce the costs of conducting surveys over the phone. Having humans manually dial phone numbers requires more time, thereby increasing the cost of a cell phone interview relative to one conducted on a landline. There are other costs as well. The sample of cell phone numbers generally costs more to generate or purchase than a sample of landline numbers and, unlike landlines, a large proportion of cell phone numbers belong to minors. In fact, one study reported that 42 percent of interviews initiated on cell phones had to be terminated because it was determined that the respondent was under the age of 18 (Keeter, Dimock, and Christian 2008). Initiating so many conversations that do not result in valid interviews also costs valuable time and money for survey organizations. Finally, pollsters often offer to reimburse respondents for the cell minutes they use in answering the survey. Altogether, an interview conducted with a respondent on a cell phone costs at least twice as much as a similar interview conducted over a landline (Keeter et al. 2008).

If the cell phone-only population was relatively similar to people who were reachable via landlines, then it would not pose a problem for survey research. However, as Table 3.1 indicates, individuals who only have cell phones differ dramatically from those with landlines when it comes to age, residential mobility, and income. According to the 2008 ANES, nearly 50 percent of Americans under the age of 30 are only reachable via a cell phone; that figure drops to just 4 percent for those over 65. As with many technological innovations, younger Americans have been quicker to adopt and rely on cellular technology compared to their older counterparts. It is also the case that people who have moved more recently are more likely to go without a landline. About half of those Americans who moved in the previous year reported having only a cell phone in 2008, compared to a much smaller share of those who had lived in the same place for more than five years. The act of moving provides people with an opportunity to reassess their telecommunication needs and, when doing so, many appear to decide that they no longer require a landline. Finally, income is also related to whether an individual only has a cell phone. Perhaps because of their limited finances, people with lower incomes are more likely to own only a cell phone or a landline, but they are less likely to have both.

Table 3.1 Age, Residential Mobility, Income, and Telephone Access

Demographic	Cell phone only (%)	Both cell and landline (%)	Landline only (%)
Age			
Under 30	49	46	4
30 to 50	21	68	9
50 to 65	14	71	14
Over 65	4	61	35
Length of residence			
<1 Month	61	33	3
1–6 Months	56	34	9
7–11 Months	46	45	8
1–2 Years	36	54	9
3–4 Years	23	61	15
5+ Years	9	74	17
Income			
<$25,000	24	56	19
$25,000–$50,000	26	64	10
$50,000–$100,000	16	77	7
$100,000>	13	84	3

Source: 2008 American National Election Study.

Because people who can be reached by landlines appear to be systematically different than those without them, pollsters who only call landline telephones must be concerned with coverage bias. Coverage bias may occur when part of the population (e.g., young Americans who only have cell phones) does not exist in the sampling frame (e.g., adults with landline telephones). When the size of the cell phone-only population was smaller, polling organizations were able to adjust for coverage bias by weighting their data according to age and other demographic factors. Thus, even though their polls were reaching fewer young Americans than they had in the past, pollsters could account for this by making the ones they were able to interview count for more. During the 2004 presidential campaign, it appeared that such weighting successfully removed any bias that might have arisen from the exclusion of cell phone-only members of the population (Keeter 2006). However, in 2008, the Pew Center for the People & the Press reported that even after weighting, their landline samples consistently showed less support for Obama than their samples that included cell phone-onlys (Keeter et al. 2008; see also Ansolabehere and Schaffner 2010). This effect likely resulted from the fact that young Americans were much more supportive of Obama, yet they were significantly less likely to be covered in a landline-only survey.

Cell phone-only Americans differ politically in more ways than just their presidential preferences. The fact that cell phone-onlys tend to be younger means that they may also be less likely to vote, since age is positively associated with political participation; that is, older citizens are much more likely to vote (Wolfinger and Rosenstone 1980). Residential mobility is also important in this regard. Previous work has demonstrated that recent movers are also significantly less likely to vote, even when controlling for other characteristics such as age (Squire, Wolfinger, and Glass 1987; Highton 2004). In addition, the fact that cell phone-only Americans are highly mobile may have other consequences related to campaigns. For example, citizens who move around more frequently and do not have landlines may be more challenging targets for campaign mobilization efforts. Citizens are more likely to participate politically when they are asked to do so (Verba, Schlozman, and Brady 1995). Yet, if parties and campaigns find it as costly and difficult to reach those without landlines as pollsters do, then cell phone-only respondents may be less likely to receive these solicitations, and polls that miss these respondents may present scholars with an imperfect picture of the campaign. In fact, Ansolabehere and Schaffner (2009) demonstrate that people with only a cell phone were more than twice as likely as those with landlines to report that neither party contacted them during the 2008 campaign.

Because of these complications, most of the highly-respected polling organizations like Gallup and Pew have turned to conducting dual-mode telephone polls. This process involves calling both landline and cell phone numbers and then combining the interviews to construct a single sample. While this helps to ameliorate the cell phone-only problem, it also increases the cost of conducting a telephone survey. Thus, not all organizations have followed suit. In fact, some organizations have chosen to use a technology that is legally incompatible with conducting interviews via cell phone—Interactive Voice Response (IVR). IVR essentially automates the interview process so that it requires a means of navigation that resembles individuals' experiences when they call customer service numbers. The interviewer for an IVR poll is a pre-programmed voice; respondents answer questions by pressing different numbers on their phone (Blumenthal 2005). Organizations like Rasmussen Reports, Survey USA, and Public Policy Polling use this approach because it is far more affordable than conducting live telephone interviews and results can often be produced in less time. However, even the owner of one of these IVR polling companies has noted that the declining ability to reach young Americans on landline telephones likely means that IVR polling, if not all telephone polling, faces a challenging future (Blumenthal 2009).

Increasing Internet Penetration

While the use of landline telephones has been in steady decline over the past decade, Internet penetration has been continually on the rise. Figure 3.2 shows the dispersion of Internet access across American households during the past decade. By 2009, two-thirds of American households and three out of every four adults had access to the Internet on a daily basis. The most

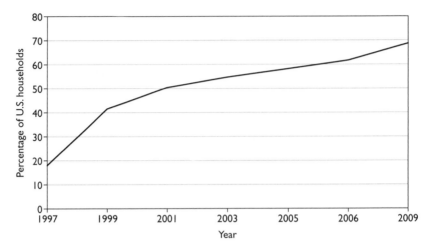

Figure 3.2 American households with access to the Internet.

common Internet activities include sending and reading emails, using search engines to find information, reading the news, checking the weather, and buying products.[1] Americans send private emails and conduct financial transactions over the Internet, so they are unlikely to be concerned about privacy issues when answering survey questions online.

While the increasing use of cellular telephones presents a challenge for survey research, the spread of Internet usage provides an opportunity. Indeed, conducting surveys over an Internet platform has significant potential for reducing the cost of conducting surveys, for making the interview process more dynamic, and finally for potentially yielding higher quality responses. With regard to the first point, personnel costs are dramatically lower for Internet surveys since those polls are self-administered and do not require human interviewers. Data collected online are also efficient because responses may be downloaded directly into a dataset for researchers to start analyzing with little or no effort needed to code responses.

The on-screen interface used to conduct Internet surveys also has a number of advantages. Respondents can engage in a number of tasks that would be difficult or impossible to complete over the phone. Unlike with a telephone survey, Internet respondents may be shown pictures or videos that may relate to the questions they are being asked. It is also easier for respondents to answer questions with a larger number of response options or to place themselves on a scale they can see on the screen compared to one that is described to them over the phone. Even with standard questions, respondents are able to answer computer-based surveys more easily and quickly since it takes less time to read a question and click on the appropriate response item than to listen to someone read those same options and verbalize an answer. For example, in an experiment where respondents were randomly assigned to answer the same questionnaire either online or with an oral interviewer, respondents assigned to the online questionnaire finished in 17.3 minutes compared to 26.6 minutes for those in the oral interview condition (Chang and Krosnick 2010). These findings suggest that an Internet survey could include 35 percent more questions during the same length of time as a telephone or in-person survey. Thus, Internet surveys allow researchers to ask more questions, and a greater variety of questions, compared to telephone polls.

There is also substantial evidence that Internet surveys provide better quality responses (AAPOR 2010). For example, by removing a human interviewer from the process, respondents may become more willing to give honest responses to sensitive questions. One example of such a study was carried about by Link and Mokdad (2005). The researchers randomly assigned respondents to complete an interview either online or by phone. The respondents received identical questions, many of which asked respondents sensitive questions. They found that respondents who answered the survey online rather than over the phone were more likely to report that they engaged in binge drinking and less likely to indicate that they practiced safe sex. These findings suggest that respondents may feel less pressure to provide a response that conforms to social norms when they are not providing those responses to a human interviewer.

One concern raised about online surveys is the possibility that respondents will have an incentive to race through the questionnaire without thinking carefully about the items they are answering or what their responses should be (Krosnick 1999). This behavior—called satisficing—is a challenge for all surveys, but may be particularly problematic for online modules where there is no interviewer present to supervise the interview process. However, recent studies have actually found that satisficing is less likely to occur with computer-based surveys (Chang and Krosnick 2009, 2010). This is likely the case because with an online survey, respondents can proceed at their own pace: they see all of the possible response options in front of them rather than having to listen carefully as the question and response options are read aloud by an interviewer.

Overall, Internet surveys provide a number of potential improvements over the existing model of telephone surveys when it comes to the actual administration of the survey instrument. Removing the interviewer from the process appears to lead to more valid, honest, and efficient responses to survey questions and the visual flexibility of a computer-based survey allows researchers to ask questions in ways that would be impossible over the telephone. Despite these advantages, Internet surveys are still frequently criticized on two main fronts. First, as with surveys conducted over landline telephones, coverage bias is also a concern with Internet polls. While Internet penetration is clearly on the rise, it is still the case that somewhere between a quarter and one-fifth of the population does not have access to the Internet. Furthermore, Internet access is strongly associated with demographic variables such as age, income, and race. Table 3.2 shows the percentage of the public that reported using the Internet based on these factors. Internet use is higher among whites and wealthier Americans than it is for minorities and those with smaller incomes. However, the most significant predictor of Internet usage is age. While nearly all those in the 18–29 age category use the Internet, only about one-third of Americans over the age of 65 do so.

Fortunately, while older Americans are less likely to be online, those who do go on the Internet are much more willing to complete online surveys compared to younger adults, and research has indicated that it is possible to remove non-coverage bias in Internet surveys with statistical modeling (Rivers n.d.; Dever et al. 2008). Furthermore, Internet surveys reach a population that is growing (those who use the Internet regularly) rather than one that is shrinking (those with landlines who are willing to answer calls from unknown numbers). Thus, the coverage bias critique is not particularly problematic for Internet surveys. More challenging criticisms have focused on how online polls select respondents to participate and, accordingly, the extent to which their findings may be generalized as representative of the population of Americans. I describe this debate in greater detail in the following section.

The Debate over Internet Survey Recruitment

While the platform for administering Internet surveys appears to be superior to telephone polls, it is the selection of respondents that ignites more substantial

Table 3.2 Age, Income, Race, and Internet Usage, 2009

Demographic	Internet users (%)
Age	
Under 30	93
30 to 50	81
50 to 65	70
Over 65	38
Race/ethnicity	
Whites	76
Blacks	70
Hispanics	64
Income	
<$30,000	60
$30,000–$50,000	76
$50,000–$75,000	83
$100,000>	94

Source: Pew Research Center's Internet & American Life Project.

debate over the approach. With telephone surveys, the researcher randomly selects telephone numbers to determine which people become part of the sample. The random selection of respondents is important, since it allows the researcher to make certain assumptions about how well the sample is likely to approximate the population of interest. Indeed, it is the random selection of respondents that allows pollsters to calculate margins of error and confidence levels for surveys.

For Internet surveys, random selection becomes a much more challenging hurdle. While nearly all Americans who use the Internet have an email address, it is difficult for pollsters to sample from those addresses. First, unlike with telephone numbers (which are all seven digits with an area code), there is no standard format for email addresses. Thus, pollsters cannot randomly generate email addresses in the same way that they can with telephone numbers. Furthermore, there is no comprehensive listing of email addresses that pollsters can sample from. Even if such a list did exist, further complications would arise from the fact that individuals often have multiple email addresses, some of which they no longer use and others which they may share with family members.

Second, even if pollsters were able to randomly sample email addresses, federal law regulates the type of unsolicited email that may be sent to addresses. Furthermore, spam filters utilized by most email programs may filter out solicitations from pollsters so that many of those emailed would not actually see the message. Concerns about computer viruses also limit the extent to which people are willing to click on links in emails that arrive from unknown sources.

Thus, for pollsters who wish to conduct Internet surveys using a random sample of respondents, a different approach must be taken. This typically involves generating a sample and making initial contact with each respondent either by phone or in person. A pioneer in this technique is Knowledge Networks, a company started in 1999 by political scientists Norman Nie and Douglas Rivers. Knowledge Networks selects its panelists using both address-based and random-digit-dialing sampling strategies. Initial contact is made over the phone and respondents are invited to join the online panel. Where respondents live in a household without Internet access, they are offered a computer and an Internet plan so that they may join the panel. Because this greatly increases the costs of recruitment, respondents do not answer a single survey. Rather, they become a member of a panel that includes approximately 50,000 people who answer an average of two surveys a month on a variety of topics. Panelists eventually rotate off of the panel and are replaced with new recruits.

The approach taken by Knowledge Networks relies on random sampling to recruit members on to the panel and is, therefore, somewhat similar to traditional telephone polls. The main departure is that respondents join a panel and answer a series of surveys over a period of time rather than just responding to a single poll. However, most Internet surveys—referred to as opt-in panels—do not recruit their panelists using random selection. Opt-in Internet surveys are generally conducted by first recruiting individuals to join an Internet panel either by having them click on a web-based advertisement or soliciting their participation through emails sent to lists provided by vendors. This technique is a departure from a probability sampling approach, where the sampling frame is known, as is each person's probability of being selected into the sample.

Opt-in Internet panels have been created by a variety of companies, but I will focus on the approach taken by YouGov/Polimetrix, since its surveys are most commonly used by political scientists.[2] Their selection process begins by recruiting a large number of people to serve on their survey panel through online advertising. The advertisement invites people who are surfing the web to complete a survey about a certain topic, usually related to the website they are currently viewing. After completing a short survey, individuals are then asked if they would like to join the panel and earn rewards (i.e., points that may be redeemed for gift certificates and other items) for every survey they complete. Since YouGov/Polimetrix only recruits people who already have Internet access, the recruitment costs are relatively low and they are able to recruit a panel that is several times larger than what Knowledge Networks maintains. Since not all people are equally likely to respond to recruitment efforts, YouGov/Polimetrix uses targeted advertising to focus particular attention on recruiting groups that are underrepresented on their panel, such as racial and ethnic minorities.

Since YouGov/Polimetrix does not use probability sampling to recruit panelists it relies instead on a technique called sample matching to generate representative samples from its panel. While the technique itself is relatively sophisticated, the basic approach is not particularly difficult to understand. When YouGov/Polimetrix is commissioned to conduct a survey, it begins by taking a random sample from the target population. For example, if a client asks for a survey of 1000 American adults, YouGov/Polimetrix draws a random sample from the Census Bureau's American Community Survey. Of course, YouGov/Polimetrix does not have the ability to contact the people who comprise this sample; rather, it uses this as the target for constructing a sample from its own panel.

The databases from which the target sample is drawn provide basic demographic information for each member of the target population. Thus, once YouGov/Polimetrix draws the target sample, it knows what each member of the random sample should look like on a range of characteristics such as age, race, gender, education, marital status, number of children under 18, family income, employment status, citizenship, state, and metropolitan area. Using all of these variables (and sometimes more), it then selects the closest matching individuals from its Internet panel to essentially replace each person that was randomly selected into the target sample. For example, if one of the individuals selected into the target sample was a 25-year-old married Hispanic woman with a college degree and no children, YouGov/Polimetrix would search for a member of its panel who was also a young, married, college-educated Hispanic woman and she would be asked to take the survey. After matching everyone in the target sample with at least one person from the Internet panel, YouGov/Polimetrix fields the survey to the selected panelists and then weights the responses to ensure that the matched sample is representative of the target sample.

Thus, the most significant distinction between Internet surveys relates to how panelists are recruited to participate. In the Knowledge Networks model, recruitment is based on probability samples, which reduces coverage bias and more closely models traditional survey methods. The YouGov/Polimetrix approach recruits whoever wishes to opt into its Internet panel and then uses the sample matching technique to attempt to create as representative a sample as possible. While the latter approach is more cost-efficient, it is also much more controversial because of how far it strays from traditional sampling methods.

The Controversy

The most robust debate over opt-in Internet surveys involves the question of whether it is possible to use statistical methods to generate samples of respondents that are representative of the target population. The main critique is that since opt-in panels do not use a random (or probability) sampling approach to recruit respondents, one cannot use them to make inferences about the population. Gary Langer, the polling director for ABC News, has frequently made such an argument on his blog:

> Non-probability samples lack the theoretical underpinning on which valid and reliable survey research is based; our policy at ABC News, as at several other national news organizations (including The Associated Press, The New York Times and The Washington Post) is not to report them.
>
> (Langer 2009)[3]

Proponents of opt-in panels typically respond by noting that "all survey respondents 'opt-in'. Would-be respondents (selected via random sampling or not) decide whether to respond or not, or can't be reached at all" (Jackman 2009). The point is that even with contemporary probability-based samples, only about 20 percent of those selected decide to actually participate in the survey. Survey organizations must then weight the data to account for the fact that those who participate have different characteristics than those who choose not to. Dealing with opt-in Internet samples is, then, simply a variation of the same problem that telephone pollsters must deal with when drawing probability samples.

Nevertheless, there is currently a lack of comprehensive and unambiguous data on how opt-in Internet surveys compare to other studies conducted with different sampling strategies and through different modes. Even the studies that have been conducted thus far have been interpreted quite differently by either side in the debate. For example, one study conducted in 2004 compared seven respected opt-in Internet panels to the probability-based Knowledge Networks panel and a probability-based telephone survey.[4] Each survey firm was asked to administer a similar questionnaire to 1000 adults who were representative of the American adult population. The questions used were chosen because they could be validated with government data. For example, respondents were asked questions such as whether they had a passport or a driver's license since these figures could be compared to the actual figures available from the State Department or Federal Highway Administration. The nine surveys were then compared to these population benchmarks to determine how close they came to the actual values they were attempting to estimate.

Despite the strong design of this study, the findings are sufficiently ambiguous to allow both sides in the debate to cite it as evidence supporting their contentions. On the one hand, Rivers conceded that the opt-in Internet panels generated higher error rates than the surveys conducted using probability samples. However, he also noted that the differences were sufficiently small that the opt-in Internet panels might be the better approach in many circumstances. As he wrote in 2009:

> My own interpretation of the 2004 data [...] was that although the opt-in samples were worse than the two probability samples, the differences were small enough—and the cost advantage large enough—to merit further investigation. Even if it were impossible to eliminate the extra 2% of error from opt-in samples, they could still be a better choice for many purposes than an RDD sample that cost several times as much.
>
> (Rivers 2009)

On the other hand, a somewhat revised analysis of the 2004 data yielded findings that indicated larger differences between the opt-in Internet panels and the probability-based surveys. Based on this re-analysis, Yeager et al. conclude: "If a researcher's goal is to document the frequency distribution of a variable in a population accurately, non-probability sample surveys appear to be considerably less suited to that goal than probability sample surveys" (2009: 27).

What the controversy over this report signifies is that there is still much to understand about the value of opt-in Internet surveys relative to traditional probability-based methods. Substantial disagreement remains as well regarding the point at which the additional error in an opt-in Internet survey outweighs the cost-efficiency of the method. If Rivers is correct that the error produced by opt-in Internet surveys constitutes only about a 2 percent increase over probability samples, are the large cost savings from conducting an opt-in Internet poll worth the increased error? Should cost even be a consideration when one is determining which polls are better? And if opt-in Internet surveys are somewhat more error-prone than probability samples, does that mean they should be dismissed as invalid, or just considered slightly less ideal than the alternatives? These are all questions that social scientists and survey researchers are currently struggling to answer.

Furthermore, studies conducted using data collected several years ago are unlikely to shed much light on these questions. After all, Internet usage and penetration has increased significantly during that period and, more importantly, the methods used to recruit panelists and generate representative samples from opt-in panels are undergoing constant innovation. How do opt-in surveys conducted more recently compare to polls using probability samples? From October 12 through November 1, 2008, YouGov/Polimetrix conducted 31,148 interviews with a sample of its opt-in panelists. On November 3 the company released the results of its survey, showing that Barack Obama held 51 percent to 45 percent advantage nationwide over John McCain. The estimate proved to be quite accurate, as Obama won 52.9 percent of the national vote compared to 45.6 percent for McCain. Indeed, the YouGov/Polimetrix estimate came closer to the actual result than the final polls released by well-respected television network polls conducted by NBC, CBS, and Fox; it even produced a closer estimate than the well-regarded Gallup poll. The success of the YouGov/Polimetrix opt-in panel in predicting the final outcome is consistent with previous studies that have documented the "excellent accuracy of online nonprobability sample polls" in predicting election outcomes (AAPOR 2010). Additional analyses have also demonstrated that the YouGov/Polimetrix survey performed as well as or better than surveys based on probability samples when it came to explaining vote choices in 2008 (Rivers and Bailey 2009).

But how accurate are opt-in Internet surveys in measuring other political attitudes that political scientists are often interested in? Figure 3.3 compares the responses from a 2008 YouGov/Polimetrix opt-in survey with similar questions asked during the same period by the ANES and the Pew Center for the People & the Press.[5] As noted above, Pew conducts well-regarded survey research with telephone polls that reach both cell phone and landline numbers. The ANES is often considered to be the gold standard of political surveys, as it uses face-to-face interviews and generally achieves response rates exceeding 50 percent. Thus, both the Pew and ANES surveys offer excellent benchmarks against which to compare the opt-in Internet survey.

Two standard questions political pollsters frequently ask concern approval of the President and approval of Congress. The presidential approval question was available for all three surveys and there was little difference across the three polls. In fact, all three organizations correctly reported disapproval of President Bush at around 70 percent. The YouGov/Polimetrix survey reported

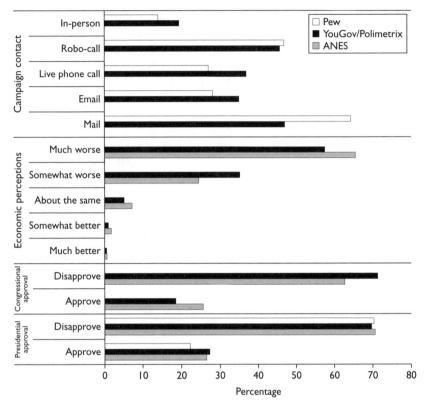

Figure 3.3 Comparison of YouGov/Polimetrix opt-in panel with the ANES and Pew election weekend survey.

an approval rate that was nearly identical to that captured by the ANES, though Pew had a slightly lower approval rate with more respondents reporting that they did not know whether they approved or disapproved of the President. Congressional approval was only available for the YouGov/Polimetrix survey and the ANES. On this question, the ANES found approval of Congress to be about 7 percentage points higher than the opt-in Internet survey.[6] Finally, Figure 3.3 also presents the perceptions of economic conditions reported by respondents to the opt-in survey and the ANES. For the most part, there were few differences across the two surveys. A large majority of respondents to both surveys reported that economic conditions had gotten worse over the past year. However, ANES respondents were about 8 percentage points more likely to say that the economy had gotten "much worse" compared to the Internet panelists.

Since the focus of this chapter is on using surveys to study campaigns, I also included a comparison of whether registered voters reported a variety of different contacts from the parties or candidates during the campaign (the top set of bars in Figure 3.3). On this question, I am only able to compare YouGov/Polimetrix respondents to those who answered the Pew survey. On these measures, opt-in Internet panelists did appear to be somewhat different from people reached by Pew over the telephone. Pew respondents were much more likely to report being contacted by mail, but much less likely to say that they received a live phone call or email from a campaign. The latter difference makes sense since opt-in Internet panelists are more regular users of the Internet and, therefore, would be more likely to communicate by email. It is less clear why Internet panelists would be less likely to receive mail from the campaigns but more likely to receive personal calls.

Overall, Figure 3.3 indicates that on some measures the YouGov/Polimetrix survey produced nearly identical results as the ANES and Pew polls, but on other items such as reported contact during the campaign, the opt-in Internet panel showed somewhat different results. Of course, we do not have a true measure of campaign contact, so we cannot be sure which survey is producing more accurate results. However, it is important to note that different sampling strategies produced respondents that did report somewhat different campaign experiences in 2008.

Using Internet Surveys to Study Campaigns and Elections

While survey researchers are still debating different approaches to conducting Internet surveys, political scientists have been quick to capitalize on this innovation, and the low cost of Internet surveys is revolutionizing the study of campaigns and political behavior. Prior to the advent of online polling, the high costs of telephone and face-to-face surveys made it difficult for most political scientists to field their own surveys. As a result, the field was reliant on the decisions made by a handful of survey organizations, which limited the range of questions that political scientists could address with survey data.

Yet, the introduction of affordable Internet surveys has democratized, to some extent, the study of campaigns and mass political behavior. A wider range of scholars can now afford to write their own survey questions focusing on topics of their choosing. Knowledge Networks was the first organization to offer scholars this access both by providing them with the ability to conduct more affordable surveys, and through a supplementary program (funded by the National Science Foundation) called Time-sharing Experiments for the Social Sciences (TESS). The TESS program has been particularly valuable, as it permits scholars to submit proposals for survey experiments. If the proposal is approved, the scholars' questions are placed on a Knowledge Networks survey free of charge.

Since TESS began in 2003, over 100 projects have been conducted through the program. Many of these studies have expanded what we know about campaigns and elections. For example, a TESS experiment conducted by Vesla Weaver found that evaluations of lighter skinned African American candidates were less race-driven than for those candidates with darker skin (2009). James Fowler and Oleg Smirnov used a TESS experiment to examine whether citizens think that elected officials will govern differently depending on their margin of victory in the previous election (Fowler and Smirnov 2007). And a TESS experiment conducted by Deborah Brooks and John Geer found that "uncivil" attacks during campaigns do not serve to de-mobilize or disengage the public as some political scientists fear (Brooks and Geer 2007).

While TESS has been very successful, the focus exclusively on survey experiments limits what types of projects scholars can pursue through this venue. Thus, in 2006, a large group of scholars organized in teams from more than 30 different universities collaborated to construct the Cooperative Congressional Election Study (CCES). The CCES is conducted with YouGov/Polimetrix's opt-in Internet panel and is a truly cooperative enterprise (Ansolabehere 2007, 2009). Teams of academics can join the CCES by buying a module, which consists of 1000 interviews with respondents before and after the election. Modules may be purchased at a rate of less than $20 per interview and the team purchasing this module gets full control over half of the survey content while the other half is developed jointly by all of the participating teams. This design allows the CCES to achieve several goals simultaneously. First, by coordinating so that half of the questions are asked of all respondents interviewed by all teams, the CCES is able to generate a sufficiently large sample size to allow for scholars to study campaign effects at the state and local level. For example, in 2008, the CCES conducted over 30,000 interviews, including several hundred interviews in most states, and thousands of interviews in more populated states like New York, California, and Texas.

A second goal of the CCES is to provide participants with the ability to have full control over the questions asked of their respondents in the other half of the survey. Each team develops its own questionnaire that is administered to the 1000 respondents designated to that team's module. This provides a large number of political scientists with the opportunity to directly design survey content. Since 2006, over 150 scholars from more than 50 colleges and universities have participated in creating CCES content. Most of the scholars involved in the project had never been previously involved in designing content for public opinion surveys and their participation in the CCES appears to be bringing a fresh approach to the study of campaigns, elections, and public opinion. A search on Google Scholar reveals that the CCES has already generated more than 150 papers and articles since its inception in 2006.

The studies produced by the CCES have already contributed to the field's understanding of many aspects of campaigns, elections, and mass political behavior. With regard to the study of campaigns, for example, Gronke and Toffey capitalized on the large sample size provided by the CCES to determine the effects of contextual and psychological factors on leading citizens to cast early ballots during campaigns (Gronke and Toffey 2008). The large sample size provided by the CCES has also been helpful for a pair of studies demonstrating that ballot initiatives can be influential in mobilizing voters and in affecting citizens' attitudes on the issues that are the subject of the state's ballot initiative (Tolbert, Bowen, and Donovan 2009; Smith and Tolbert 2010). The CCES has also been used to study polarization across a variety of contexts, including investigations into the role of primary voters in causing polarization (Abramowitz 2007) and the extent to which the blogosphere enhances polarization (Lawrence, Sides, and Farrell 2010).

Other scholars have used their CCES modules to ask questions that allow them to examine how citizens perceive candidates' strategies during the campaign. Ridout and Fowler use data from the 2006 CCES to show that advertising has a much greater influence on how citizens perceive the tone of the campaign relative to news coverage (Ridout and Fowler 2009). Schaffner used a question on a module to the 2008 CCES to examine which groups citizens thought Obama and McCain were attempting to target during the 2008 campaign (Schaffner 2010). This paper finds that perceptions of the candidates' strategies differ quite markedly across party lines; partisans generally thought that their party's nominee was focusing on winning over moderate middle-class voters while they saw the opposing candidate as appealing only to his party's base voters.

The research spurred by the CCES has been supplemented by a related project called the Cooperative Campaign Analysis Project (CCAP). The CCAP was initiated in 2008 and followed a similar model as the CCES. Teams of researchers joined together to track the 2008 campaign with a six-wave panel design that was also conducted with YouGov/Polimetrix's opt-in panel. The CCAP focused primarily on tracking the campaign throughout 2008, and it has already contributed to our knowledge of the 2008 election as well as campaigns more generally. For example, Lewis-Beck, Tien, and Nadeau (2010) use CCAP data to demonstrate that racial prejudice likely kept Obama from winning a landslide victory in 2008. Scotto et al. (Forthcoming) used CCAP data to demonstrate the substantial role that economic concerns played in accounting for Obama's victory. A CCAP-based study by Monson, Patterson, and Pope (2009) utilized the panel nature of the data to show that voters who were exposed to the most intense campaign messages were least likely to undergo changes in their partisanship. In addition, Campbell, Monson, and Green used framing experiments placed on the CCAP to examine how information about Obama's and Mitt Romney's religious backgrounds negatively influenced evaluations of those candidates (2009).

One of the most important contributions the CCES and CCAP have to offer for the study of campaigns is the large samples that are not affordable with traditional survey approaches. The CCES conducted interviews with over 30,000 respondents in 2006, 2008, and 2010, while the CCAP followed 20,000 respondents during the 2008 campaign. In the past, political scientists have mostly been limited to relying on studies such as the ANES to study campaigns. Yet, the limited sample size of the ANES makes it difficult to draw conclusions about state-, district-, or market-level campaign effects (Stoker and Bowers 2002). For example, even if one defines the 2008 "battleground states" broadly, the ANES interviewed only 756 respondents in those 11 states. By comparison, the CCES conducted nearly 10,000 interviews in those same states. The differences are even more significant when one wants to examine differences across states. For example, a scholar interested in focusing on campaign effects in Ohio compared to its neighbor state of Indiana would find 1337 Ohioans and 785 Hoosiers in the CCES dataset, but just 85 Ohio respondents and 55 Indiana interviews in the ANES.

Despite the large samples at affordable prices, opt-in Internet panels may not be entirely ideal for studying campaign effects. One particular concern is that the same factors that lead people to be willing to become part of an Internet survey panel may also diminish the extent to which they can be influenced by campaign appeals. A study comparing the 2006 CCES to the 2004 ANES and the National Annenberg Election Study (NAES) found that the opt-in Internet panel generated by Polimetrix was somewhat more ideologically extreme and politically knowledgeable than the face-to-face respondents interviewed by the ANES. The authors noted that such a pattern may make the CCES respondents less susceptible to persuasion effects during the campaign (Hill et al. 2007). However, the authors also note that the CCES sample was fairly close to that produced through RDD technology. Balancing these drawbacks with the greater cost-efficiency of the opt-in Internet model lead the authors to ultimately conclude:

> In a world without resource constraints, the results of our analysis would recommend against use of opt-in Internet samples for studies of political persuasion. In the real world, however, the recommendation is not so clear.... [O]ur partial analysis, based on demographic comparisons with census data, suggests that the bias of RDD sampling methods may be comparable to the bias of a Polimetrix generated (using sample matching) Internet sample. And telephone surveys, though less expensive than face-to-face, are much more expensive than opt-in Internet samples. Thus, our surprising but – we stress – preliminary conclusion is that Internet samples may be preferable to telephone surveys for some kinds of studies.
>
> (Hill et al. 2007: 13)

This begs the question about the types of studies best suited for Internet samples.

In 2010, a task force commissioned by the American Association for Public Opinion Researchers produced a report that provided a number of recommendations regarding how the survey research industry should approach the use of opt-in Internet panels. Their primary recommendation stated that

"Researchers should avoid nonprobability online panels when one of the research objectives is to accurately estimate population values" (AAPOR 2010: 52). The panel did acknowledge that opt-in Internet surveys could be an effective way of conducting some research, particularly where the goal is "understanding how personal characteristics interact with other survey variables such as attitudes, behaviors, and intentions" (53). Indeed, this is the type of research that many political scientists have limited themselves to studying with opt-in Internet surveys. Typically, these studies involve conducting survey experiments with Internet panelists. For example, half of a sample of Internet panelists may be subjected to one party's framing of an issue while the other half is provided with a different framing. Opinions on the issue are then compared depending on which argument the respondents received. The researcher does not attempt to use these data to infer what attitudes are held by the population of American adults; rather, he or she compares opinions in one condition to those in the other condition to determine how influential different frames are. Projects that use opt-in Internet panelists in this way rarely run into objections from the scholarly community.

However, when political scientists attempt to use opt-in Internet panels to draw conclusions about the population of adults or voters, they are likely to face stronger objections. As the AAPOR task force report indicates, such findings currently rest on a less certain methodological footing. Yet, the AAPOR report also acknowledges that "Despite the widespread use of online panels there is still a great deal that is not known with confidence" (54). Furthermore, much of what we know about this technology is already outdated, as the technologies used to produce representative samples from these panels are continually evolving. Take, for example, Hill et al.'s (2007) evaluation of the 2006 CCES. As the authors noted in their conclusion, YouGov/Polimetrix was already adapting their technology at the time they were writing their paper to weight for items such as political interest and partisanship. By successfully weighting for these factors and purposefully recruiting less politically engaged individuals, future YouGov/Polimetrix samples may be less distinctive on these factors and, thus, more appropriate for the study of campaign effects.

The Future of Survey Research in the Study of Campaigns

In this chapter, I have examined how the evolution of polling technology holds the potential to revolutionize the study of campaigns and elections. The advent of opt-in Internet surveys has lowered the barriers to entry for political scientists wanting to conduct survey research and, as a result, a new energy in the study of campaigns, elections, and political behavior appears to have emerged. It is now easier than ever before for political scientists to field surveys that address precisely the questions they are interested in asking. Because Internet surveys are far more cost-effective than other approaches, scholars now have the leverage to collect samples large enough to study campaign effects across different states and localities. With projects such as the CCES and CCAP now in place, the research on American campaigns and elections is poised to take major leaps forward in the coming decade.

Yet, despite the enthusiasm with which many political scientists have embraced these new methods for conducting survey research, it is important for the field to take seriously the concerns raised by critics of these developing approaches. The zeal to collect survey data cheaply and quickly should not overwhelm more fundamental considerations about the quality of those data. Newer and more comprehensive studies are needed to compare contemporary opt-in Internet panels to traditional sampling methods and to gain a better understanding of the best methods for constructing and utilizing an opt-in panel. That said, critics of opt-in Internet panels should take care not to dismiss the method out of hand simply because the process seems so foreign compared to the traditional random-digit-dialing approach. The truth is that increasing coverage bias and declining response rates have rendered the textbook random sample telephone survey a thing of the past for all but the best-funded polling operations.

It is not yet clear whether opt-in Internet panels can generate samples that are at least as accurate as surveys conducted with probability samples. Even if this goal is not achievable, it is almost certainly worth investing in opt-in Internet panels if they can come reasonably close to these benchmarks. After all, as Internet surveys exponentially increase the number of political scientists who have access to the conduct of survey research, the likelihood of potential breakthroughs and innovations in the study of campaigns, elections, and political behavior will likewise grow exponentially.

Notes

1. Based on data collected by the Pew Internet & American Life Project (http://pewinternet.org).
2. YouGov/Polimetrix was also founded by Douglas Rivers following his departure from Knowledge Networks.
3. It is worth noting that other major media organizations, including CBS News and the Economist, have used opt-in Internet surveys extensively over the past several years.
4. Political scientists Jon Krosnick and Douglas Rivers were commissioned to conduct this study and they co-authored a conference paper based on the original results. However, a subsequent study that re-analyzed the data did not include Rivers.
5. The YouGov/Polimetrix poll compared here was conducted for the 2008 Cooperative Congressional Election Study.
6. The discrepancy may be partially explained by the fact that the ANES began interviewing respondents in early September while YouGov/Polimetrix did not commence interviews until early October. The Emergency Economic Stabilization Act (i.e. the bank bailout) passed Congress before YouGov/Polimetrix went into the field, but many of the ANES interviews were conducted before this unpopular legislation was considered by Congress.

## Chapter 4

Campaign Management and Organization

The Use and Impact of Information and Communication Technology

Stephen K. Medvic[1]

One cannot read an article or book on recent developments in campaign technology without being told that the Internet and various information and communication technologies (ICTs) have "transformed" or even "revolutionized" political campaigns (see, e.g., Panagopoulos 2009: 1, 2). The evidence that campaigns are fundamentally different than they were just 15 years ago seems overwhelming. Indeed, it would be foolish to try to claim that campaigns have not changed much in recent years. However, the changes that have taken place in campaigns may also be viewed as simply the latest stage of a process that began with the formation of electoral parties in the early nineteenth century.

Campaigns are primarily about gaining control over chaotic situations. This is true whether the campaign is a military engagement, a corporate marketing effort, or a bid for elective office. An election campaign seeks to control a candidate's (or a party's) message and the voters' decisions (including whether or not to vote and for whom to vote) in situations where much is out of the campaign's control (including the economy, natural disasters, and the actions of other campaign actors such as the opposing candidate and the media). In other words, a campaign is a rational approach to decision-making in a complex environment (Rose 1967).[2] To say campaigns are rational is to say that they seek control by employing technology to process information and deploy human capital, and by developing and implementing strategy based on that information.

This chapter examines the latest developments in campaign management and organization, particularly with respect to the use of ICTs. First, I offer a brief explanation of the history of campaign rationalization beginning in the mid-nineteenth century. Next, I describe the role of ICTs in candidate and non-candidate organizations. Finally, I review the empirical evidence on the extent to which campaigns use ICTs and on the impact of these tools on various campaign goals. Finally, I suggest avenues for future research.

A Brief History of Campaign Bureaucracy and Rationalization[3]

The mid-nineteenth century, according to James Beniger (1986), produced a "crisis of control" in which communication between producers and consumers was extremely inefficient. While production processes were accelerating, feedback from consumers was slow. Solutions to this problem included bureaucratization and rationalization as well as the development of new communications technologies, all of which led to a "Control Revolution" (Beniger 1986). It is no coincidence that modern campaigns developed at precisely the same time.

As political parties began to recognize the crisis of control, they responded by creating campaign bureaucracies in the form of national party committees (e.g., the Democratic National Committee in 1848) and a "group management" model of running presidential campaigns (see Medvic 2005: 162). At the end of the nineteenth century the Control Revolution led to a centralization of campaign management as individual managers such as Mark Hanna began to assume responsibility for presidential campaigns. This centralizing tendency was a form of rationalization, or the attempt to control information by reducing the amount that needs to be processed (Beniger 1986: 15).

In the early twentieth century, campaign rationalization led to the professional campaign manager who was not connected to, and might not even be affiliated with, a party organization (Kelley 1956; Medvic 2005: 162–3). Such managers were hired directly by candidates to handle every aspect of their campaigns. In the 1960s, professional campaign management evolved into the political consulting industry (see Nimmo 1970; Sabato 1981; Johnson 2007). Whereas a manager would handle the day-to-day operation of a single campaign, consultants gave advice to numerous campaigns per election cycle. Initially, this advice was general and strategic in nature. Eventually, consultants became specialists in various aspects of campaign activity, such as polling, media, or fundraising.

There is considerable evidence that hiring professional political consultants helps candidates, especially challengers, run more successful campaigns. This is true both in terms of the amount of money raised and the percentage of vote garnered (Herrnson 1992; Medvic and Lenart 1997; Medvic 2001; Dulio 2004). Consultants bring to campaigns a model of campaigning developed through experience working on dozens, if not hundreds, of campaigns. In addition, and more important for the purpose of this chapter, consultants understand how to use sophisticated technology for communicating with voters.

Technological advances have always found their way into campaigns. Candidates were using the telegraph as early as the 1850s and radio played a role in the campaign of New York Mayor John Hylan in 1921 (Medvic 2009: 99–100). Although radio allowed candidates to communicate with many potential voters simultaneously, its reach was limited. Far less limited was television, which came to dominate campaign media by the 1960s and allowed candidates to communicate with a mass audience. It also radically changed

American politics, including (and perhaps especially) the way campaigns were waged.

In the 1970s, campaign operatives began to rely on computers to process data (Howard 2006: 6–7). As microprocessors evolved in the 1980s, the computer began to be widely used in campaigns. Polls were conducted with the use of computer-assisted telephone interviewing (CATI) systems and desktop computers processed increasingly large amounts of data (Medvic 2009: 103–4). Cable television also emerged in the 1980s, making targeted communications at least theoretically possible. In addition, fax machines were a popular tool in the 1988 presidential campaign (Howard 2006: 7).

The 1990s witnessed the rise of a variety of information and communications technologies (ICTs) including the Internet and cellular telephony. These developments ushered in what Bruce Bimber (2003) refers to as a fourth information revolution. Up until that point, according to Bimber, advances in technology "strengthened the link between resources and command of information" (89). Information was relatively scarce and its collection and management, not to mention the ability to communicate, required bureaucracy.[4]

However, the ubiquity of ICTs has fundamentally altered the situation. Specifically, Bimber argues that the new communication environment—characterized as it is by "information abundance"—encourages the development of "postbureaucratic" organizations (89–109). When information is widely available (and, therefore, cheap), the old bureaucratic structures that were designed to manage scarce information are replaced by organizations that are "less rigidly structured, more malleable, and more responsive to changes in their environments" (102). The division of labor based on expertise, so long a hallmark of bureaucratic organizations, becomes cumbersome and less useful in an environment in which information flows rapidly both inside and outside organizations.

These developments have serious implications for the way campaigns are managed. The following section describes how campaigns are adapting to the new information environment and how they are utilizing ICTs to communicate with supporters and potential voters. I begin by examining competing models of campaign organization as a way of establishing a context within which the use, and eventually the impact, of ICTs may be understood.

Campaign Organizations and the Use of ICTs

Campaign organization is an understudied aspect of American politics. To the extent that there is any research devoted to the subject, it focuses almost exclusively on the organization of political parties (see, e.g., Farrell and Webb 2000). The result is that we have little understanding of how campaign organizations are structured and know only slightly more about how they operate. In addition, we lack a historical benchmark for charting change in campaign organizations over time. Because we do not know how campaigns were organized prior to the fourth information revolution, it is difficult to determine the impact of ICTs upon campaign organizations.

Models of Campaign Organization

There is some theoretical discussion of the structure of campaigns that may be found in the few studies that have examined candidates' campaign organizations. Two models of campaign organization have been posited, though both are based on research that is now 30 or 40 years old. The first of these, which has been referred to as the "comprehensive model," is a hierarchical structure in which "functional specialization, unbroken lines of authority, and complete internal communication" serve to enforce a top-down decision-making arrangement (Lamb and Smith 1968: 21). The comprehensive campaign relies upon a highly bureaucratized organization. Although there is reason to doubt that such a model was ever fully realized (see Levin 1962; Hershey 1974), we should certainly expect to find few comprehensive campaigns in an age of information abundance.

The other model of campaign organization—the "incremental model" (Lamb and Smith 1968: 29)—is, to one degree or another, a more realistic approximation of the way most campaigns operate (or, at least, have operated until very recently). It also appears to share some of the characteristics of the post-bureaucratic organizations which Bimber describes. Like the "professionalized" campaigns which Xandra Kayden (1978) observed in the 1970s, where responsibility and decision-making are diffused (9–10), the incremental campaign disperses authority throughout the organization and accepts input from a variety of sources (Lamb and Smith 1968: 32–3). Although it seeks to capitalize on the diversity of ideas that multiple experts bring to the table, the incremental campaign still assumes that a division of labor exists within the campaign.

It is unlikely that campaign organizations will ever discard a division of labor, but the lines of demarcation between tasks on a campaign are beginning to blur. Indeed, in the post-bureaucratic organization, "the flow of information inside political organizations grows increasingly independent of people's official functions or roles" (Bimber 2003: 102). Thus, individuals are free (and, perhaps, even encouraged) to offer suggestions, and contribute to projects, that may not fall within their bailiwick.

The question facing students of campaigns and campaign management, therefore, is whether the incremental model of campaign organization and decision-making has been refashioned for the fourth information revolution or whether an entirely new model of campaign organization is emerging. Until we have systematic observations of contemporary campaign organizations, it will be impossible to answer that question. In the meantime, we will have to settle for descriptions of what campaigns do and extrapolate about the kind of organization that might support such activities.

Candidate Use of ICTs

Any discussion of the use of new information and communication tools in campaigns must begin with the Internet. Although most observers point to 1996 as the first use of the Internet in campaigns, Richard Davis (1999) notes that the Clinton-Gore campaign used it in 1992 to post documents such as speeches and position papers (86–7). Philip Howard (2006) suggests that e-mail had entered the campaign operative's toolbox by 1992, but notes, "the excitement about new media [in 1992] had less to do with the internet and more to do with direct satellite transmission of [Ross] Perot's thirty-second infomercials into local television markets" (8).

The widespread use of the Internet and the World Wide Web, however, did begin in 1996 (ibid.: 10; Foot and Schneider 2006: 8). By 2000, nearly all major party gubernatorial and U.S. Senate candidates had websites (Owen and Davis 2008: 96).[5] U.S. House candidates lagged behind somewhat in Web presence due to the fact that many House candidates are not serious contenders. By 2002, however, any candidate mounting a respectable campaign for a major office in the United States had a website.

Initially, campaigns used Web pages as "brochureware" (Howard 2006: 12), or simple reproductions of conventional campaign literature. Increasingly, however, candidates have begun to capitalize on the interactivity of the Internet. The emergence of what some have called "Web 2.0" (O'Reilly 2005) allows campaigns to engage potential supporters in a variety of ways, and empowers Web users to collaborate with campaigns and not simply consume their products.

According to Kirsten Foot and Steven Schneider (2006), web campaigning consists of four activities: informing, involving, connecting, and mobilizing (22).[6] These activities are not, of course, mutually exclusive. When a candidate's Web page provides a link to an article announcing an endorsement, the campaign is informing visitors but also connecting them to the media organization or interest group that produced the original article. When potential supporters are asked to "tell a friend" about the campaign by using mechanisms found on a candidate's website, the supporter is invited to get involved as the campaign mobilizes additional support.

Each of the activities identified by Foot and Schneider (2006), to one extent or another, utilizes three web production techniques. The first is co-production, which entails the joint production of Web objects by actors who operate in independent organizations. For instance, a candidate's website may allow contributions to an online message board or comments on a campaign blog. As such, co-production is different than collaboration by individuals within the organization (35–6).

A second web production technique used by campaigns is convergence. Convergence occurs when items that were created offline are placed online (and vice versa). Thus, when television commercials are uploaded to a candidate's website, convergence has taken place. Similarly, door-to-door canvassing organized online or the use of a campaign website's URL in print or broadcast advertising constitutes convergence (36). Finally, linking is the process of connecting two Web pages for the user. This can occur within the framework of the campaign's website (that is, from the homepage to another page on the website) or it can direct the user away from the campaign's site and toward another organization's Web page (38–9).

These web production techniques raise questions about the ability of campaigns to control their messages. We take up those questions below. For now, we turn our attention to the specific ways in which campaigns inform, involve, connect, and mobilize voters. The first of these activities—informing—is perhaps the most obvious use of the Internet and was, as noted above, the only function served by the first campaign websites. Candidate websites provide a considerable amount of information about the sponsoring candidate, including biographical information, news about the campaign, and candidate issue positions.

Indeed, a candidate's issue positions are usually a prominent feature of his or her Web page and the range of issues addressed on the "issues" page is far larger than one would find in the candidate's standard stump speech or even in the campaign ads run over the course of an entire campaign. While candidates are generally believed to follow a strategy of "deliberate priming," emphasizing issues that work to their advantage and ignoring or deflecting those that do not (Medvic 2006), such an approach is not readily apparent on candidate websites. Although candidates occasionally highlight one or two issues on their homepage, it is often difficult to determine which issues a candidate is running on. "Issues" pages will typically prioritize half a dozen or so issues, but there is almost always a link to "other important issues." It is not unusual, however, for a candidate to offer links to his or her positions and statements on a dozen or more issues (see Figure 4.1).

The fact that candidates offer positions on so many more issues on their websites than they discuss in other campaign venues suggests that candidate Web pages are contributing to the ideal democratic dialogue. Indeed, issue statements on candidate websites are often very detailed accounts of what the candidate has done in the past and is pledging to do in the future. But dialogue is a two-way street; candidates have to be addressing one another if dialogue is to occur. Xenos and Foot (2005) have examined the level of dialogue on candidate websites. They note that online dialogue can be direct or indirect. When dialogue is direct, a candidate addresses his or her opponent's issue positions or record explicitly on his or her own website. Indirect dialogue takes place when more than one candidate takes a position on the same issue(s) but does not refer to the opponent's position(s). Xenos and Foot found that only 8 percent of House, Senate, and gubernatorial candidates in 2002 engaged in direct dialogue on their Web pages and that just 32 percent of races exhibited instances of indirect dialogue (178).[7] Recent research, however, has found that many candidates are engaged in negative campaigning on their websites (which, by definition, entails direct dialogue). The

Figure 4.1 A candidate's "issue" page (source: www.himesforcongress.com/site/issues (accessed September 10, 2010)).

amount of negative campaigning online increased dramatically in the three election cycles between 2002 and 2006, to the point where a majority of the Web pages of congressional candidates now include attacks on opponents (Druckman, Kifer, and Parkin 2010).

To the extent that candidates are still unwilling to attack an opponent on their own campaign Web page, they (or the party committees supporting them) have increasingly begun to sponsor auxiliary websites that are devoted to critically examining the opponent's record. In essence, these sites are extended attacks on the opponent. Thus, in 2010, California Senator Barbara Boxer maintained a site entitled "Fiorina Facts," which detailed (critically) the record of her opponent, former Hewlett-Packard CEO Carly Fiorina. For her part, Fiorina sponsored a site called "Failed Senator" (see Figure 4.2), the purpose of which was to document "How Barbara Boxer Has Failed Californians for 30 Years."[8] Thus, while direct dialogue may or may not be occurring on candidates' official websites, there is certainly direct confrontation on these auxiliary sites.

In addition to serving as vehicles for disseminating information, candidate websites are designed to "facilitat[e] interaction between site visitors and the campaign organization" (Foot and Schneider 2006: 70). The importance placed on this "involving" function is illustrated by the fact that visitors to candidate websites routinely encounter a "sign-up" or "donation" page before being directed to the actual homepage. On these pages, potential supporters are asked to provide contact information, and contributions are often solicited.

Once on the candidate's homepage, visitors are bombarded with ways to get involved in the campaign. Options for myriad activities are listed in multiple places. An "Action" menu is typically offered on the navigation bar along the top of the website. Within that menu, visitors can choose to contribute, volunteer, "join the campaign," and "tell a friend." Usually, each of these activities will also have its own hyperlink located in various places on the homepage. Contribution hyperlinks, in particular, may appear multiple times on a single homepage.

Indeed, much has been made of the Internet as a tool for raising campaign funds. Howard Dean's success with online fundraising in the 2004 campaign for the Democratic presidential nomination proved that significant amounts of money could be raised via the Internet. Approximately 40 percent of his over $50 million in contributions were given over the Web (Postelnicu, Martin, and Landreville 2006: 105). Campaigns immediately took notice of Dean's example and began to capitalize on this new way to raise funds. Having emerged as the Democratic presidential nominee in 2004, John Kerry also relied heavily on the Internet to raise money; one-third of his over $234 million was raised online (ibid.).[9] The *Washington Post* reported that in his 2008 bid for the White House, Barack Obama raised $500 million online (Vargas 2008). In other words, Internet fundraising accounted for two-thirds

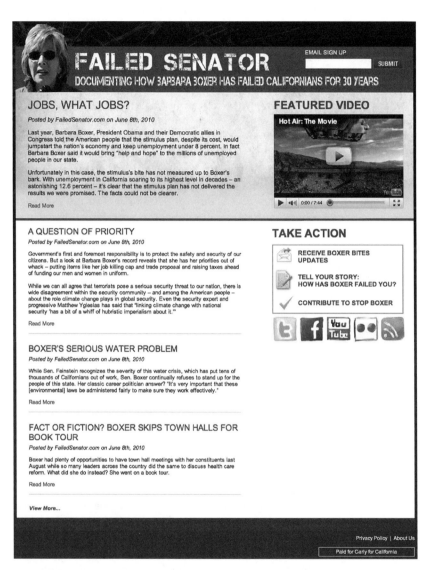

Figure 4.2 A negative auxiliary site (source: www.failedsenator.com (accessed June 11, 2010)).

of Obama's nearly $748 million in total fundraising. Of course, presidential campaigns differ from campaigns at all other levels. Furthermore, the 2008 Obama campaign (and, to a lesser extent, the Dean campaign in 2004) was a unique event. No campaign for U.S. House or Senate, let alone for state legislature or mayor, can command that level of attention and excitement.

Nevertheless, Internet fundraising is now an essential part of all but the most local campaigns for office. Exactly how it has affected the dynamics of campaign fundraising, and whether it has altered campaign organization, is yet to be known. Until reliable data on how campaigns raise money become available, it will be difficult to track the balance of event-based, direct mail, and online contributions to candidates.

Many people hope that the Internet can be used to broaden the pool of potential contributors. The widespread reports indicating that nearly half of all individual contributions to the 2008 Obama campaign were in the amount of $200 or less suggested that online fundraising was fulfilling this hope. However, an analysis by the Campaign Finance Institute found that many such "small" contributions came from repeat givers. When aggregated, only 26 percent of Obama donors gave a *total* of $200 or less to the campaign (Campaign Finance Institute 2008). This number is slightly larger than that of many recent presidential campaigns, though it is roughly identical to the percentage of small donors to President Bush's 2004 campaign.[10]

An analysis of offline and online donors by Panagopoulos and Bergan (2009) also raises doubts about the inclusiveness of Internet fundraising. Online donors are just as likely to be male, white, and married as are offline donors. The former do tend to be significantly younger than offline donors, though the median age of online contributors in the 2004 presidential campaign was 52 (compared to 63.6 for those giving in more traditional ways). Online donors also had higher incomes and were more likely to have at least some graduate education (Panagopoulos and Bergan 2009: 130). The results of a predictive model of online giving suggest that age was negatively related to giving (that is, the younger the person, the more likely he or she is to give online) while self-reported liberalism and online political activism (e.g., visiting candidate or party websites, engaging in online discussions of politics) were positively related (135). Thus, while online donors do differ from traditional donors in some ways, the Internet does not (as yet) appear to have dramatically broadened the pool of contributors.

Of course, soliciting donations is not the only way campaigns ask potential supporters to get involved. As noted earlier, websites provide multiple opportunities to follow the campaign online, volunteer, and share information about (or enthusiasm for) the candidate with one's friends. For example, candidates have recently capitalized on the popularity of the micro-blogging service Twitter by creating accounts that may be followed by supporters of the candidate. Nearly all serious candidates (or their campaigns) "tweet" and their Web pages invite visitors to subscribe to their Twitter feeds.[11] Similarly, candidates encourage visitors to their websites to subscribe to their YouTube channels.

Those seeking to volunteer for a candidate no longer have to show up at the campaign's bricks-and-mortar headquarters. Potential volunteers may sign up online and choose from a variety of activities, including door-to-door canvassing, letter-writing, and hosting house parties. Many candidates also use an online phone bank program that allows volunteers to call targeted voters from home, read a script provided by the campaign, and enter the voters' responses into an online database.

Candidates have also been creative in the ways in which they have encouraged involvement. Hillary Clinton, for example, asked supporters to help her choose her presidential campaign's theme song. Those who "joined" Barack Obama's campaign by providing contact information were often treated as campaign insiders and given information prior to its "official" release through the media. The choice of Joe Biden as the vice-presidential nominee, for example, was first announced via text message to supporters who had given the campaign their cell phone numbers.

In addition to informing and involving, campaigns also connect visitors to other political actors. Connecting is never a primary focus of a candidate's website but there are at least two ways in which the practice can be beneficial to campaigns. The most obvious, and the one most likely to be used by candidates, is to connect visitors to media reports in which the candidate is portrayed positively or the opponent is cast in a negative light. Such reports, because they are from independent sources, lend credibility to the candidate's own claims. The other way in which connecting is useful to candidates is by providing a link to political parties or supportive interest groups. For example, when a local party committee is providing support for a candidate (e.g., a get-out-the-vote effort), the candidate's website can serve as a bridge to the party committee. The danger in linking to outside groups, however, is that the candidate becomes undeniably associated with those groups. If one of them were to engage in questionable activity or make an inappropriate statement, the candidate will have to answer for his or her association with the group. As a result, candidates rarely connect their websites' visitors to the sites of other political actors.

Finally, candidate websites are used to mobilize support for their candidacies. Foot and Schneider (2006) define the practice of online mobilizing as "using the Web to persuade and equip campaign supporters to promote the candidate to others, both online and offline" (131). To some extent, then, mobilizing is a form of involving; indeed, Foot and Schneider write that it "builds on involving, since advocates must first affiliate with the campaign as supporters" (136). Volunteers willing to help "spread the word" will be offered any number of tools for persuading others to support the candidate. Supporters can receive assistance with writing a letter to the editor, printing posters and flyers off the candidate's Web page and distributing them in their communities, and downloading digital campaign logos and images that can be used as wallpaper or screen savers on the supporters' computers.

The most common form of mobilizing is sending an e-mail message directly from the campaign's website. The supporter simply enters the e-mail addresses of his or her friends and family, types a message in the appropriate box (or customizes a default message provided by the campaign), and hits the "send" button. The e-mail the recipient receives can be formatted to look as though it came directly from the sender or it can appear as if the campaign sent it.

Another popular mobilizing practice is using social networking sites such as Facebook and MySpace to build online support that is based somewhere other than the candidate's own Web page. Howard Dean's 2004 presidential campaign relied on the site Meetup.com to spread the word about Dean and to organize volunteers offline (see Silberman 2008). Today, all serious candidates provide hyperlinks to their pages on social networking sites and supporters are encouraged to share their interest in a candidate with their network of friends. The 2008 Obama campaign took social networking a step further and created its own networking site—my.barackobama.com. This site, which "was at the heart of the campaign's new media strategy," allowed users to find other Obama supporters in their areas and to organize events and coordinate other activities such as fundraising (Harfoush 2009: 74). Eventually, over three million accounts were created on my.barackobama.com (ibid.).

Just as candidates link to social networking sites from their own homepages, they also advertise on independent websites in an effort to drive potential supporters to their campaign Web pages. A candidate might, for example, advertise on a neutral site that provides news and information to political junkies. The audience for such sites consists of people who are already interested in politics, are likely to be well informed, and probably have a well-established partisan perspective. Candidates may also target specific groups online. A Republican candidate for the House of Representatives, for example, might advertise on a local conservative blog.

Indeed, campaigns are becoming quite sophisticated in how they target their online advertising. In an attempt to reach young voters, the 2008 Obama campaign reportedly spent nearly $45,000 to place ads within 18 different Xbox 360 online games, including the racing game Burnout Paradise, Guitar Hero, and NHL 09. The ads, which took the form of billboards or signs in various scenes within the games, announced that voting had begun in 10 battleground states that allow early voting (Gorman 2008; Sinclair 2008).[12] The 2008 Senate campaign of Al Franken in Minnesota "nanotargeted" his Internet advertising to appeal to 125 niche groups, using more than 30 million "impressions" (or actual appearances of an ad online). As an example of such targeting, "Minnesotans who were searching for cheap gas or researching fuel-efficient cars saw ads about Franken's plan to lower gas prices" (Koster 2009: 23).

Not all of the ICTs used by campaigns are Web-based. In particular, candidates have begun making great use of short message service (SMS) to deliver text messages to supporters. These messages typically asked supporters to become involved in the campaign in one way or another. They might be asked, for example, to watch a debate or attend a rally. Candidates can also inform supporters of important information via text message. To the extent that supporters provide their zipcodes when they sign up for the service, campaigns can tailor information to particular locations.

Non-Candidate Use of ICTs

Candidates' campaigns are not the only organizations using ICTs. There is now a considerable literature devoted to the study of political parties and new technology (for a review, see Gibson and Ward 2009). As Ward, Gibson, and Nixon (2003) note, parties use websites, in particular, for administrative, campaign, and organizational purposes (12–13). But they also use e-mail, social networking sites, blogs, Twitter, YouTube, and text messaging to keep supporters involved, inform potential voters, disseminate party messages, and organize grass-roots efforts such as volunteer canvassing and get-out-the-vote drives.

Of course, all parties are not the same. Major parties, for instance, have much more of a web presence than do minor parties (Margolis, Resnick, and Levy 2003). Römmele (2003) contends that different types of parties use ICTs for different functions. Parties that seek to maximize votes (or offices), like both the Democratic and Republican Parties, can be expected, according to Römmele, to communicate to voters in a top-down manner with a candidate-centered message. Parties with a concern for intra-party democracy will use ICTs to communicate to members in a bottom-up fashion about the party's platform (12–15). Despite such differences, all parties now rely, more or less, on ICTs to perform their most basic functions. It may be too early to proclaim the advent of "cyber parties" (Margetts 2006), but few doubt that party organization has been affected by new technology. The extent to which this has occurred, and the form such change has taken, are still to be determined by scholars.

Independent efforts on behalf of, or against, candidates are made considerably easier to launch and execute owing to ICTs. Numerous organizations have emerged in recent years to provide an online infrastructure to support or oppose candidates. These organizations have been particularly useful to candidates in the area of fundraising. ActBlue, an online political committee dedicated to raising money for Democratic candidates around the country and at every level of office, is the leading example of such organizations. Since its founding in 2004, ActBlue has raised over $136 million from over 420,000 contributors.[13] A Republican version of ActBlue, called Slatecard, raised over $650,000 in the 2008 election cycle.[14] These organizations make it easy for potential donors to identify a candidate whom they would like to support and get their contributions to that candidate efficiently. When Republican Joe Wilson of South Carolina shouted, "You lie" during President Obama's health care address to Congress in September, 2009, ActBlue helped his opponent,

Rob Miller, raise hundreds of thousands of dollars in a matter of days. At one point, ActBlue reported that they were raising $7 per second for Miller (Scola 2009).

Increasingly, individuals can raise money, or organize volunteers, on their own with the use of new online tools. Blue Swarm, for example, "is a web-based application that allows anyone raising funds on behalf of a candidate to manage their own network of contacts, track pledges received and process donations" (Judd 2010). Similarly, Civio is an online platform for organizing volunteers that can be utilized by campaigns or individuals. Tools like these are typically non-partisan, meaning that the developer makes them available to candidates and supporters of any political party.

There are many other freelance campaign efforts that are made possible by the technology that is available today. Online ads, for example, are relatively easy to produce and can literally be created in one's own home. In 2008, a supporter of Barack Obama produced an ad called "Hillary 1984" (also known as "Vote Different") that parodied a 1984 Apple computer ad.[15] The "mashup" ad placed images of Hillary Clinton on a huge screen that was being watched by hundreds of apparently brainwashed followers. The ad ends with a woman in an Obama tank-top throwing a sledgehammer into the screen, causing Clinton's image to explode as her followers look on in astonishment. The words "On January 14th, the Democratic primary will begin. And you'll see why 2008 won't be like '1984'" appear on the screen as the image fades. The ad immediately went viral and, within days, had been viewed more times than any other presidential campaign ad to that point (Marinucci 2007).

The role of the candidate "tracker" has also been enhanced by technology. Trackers are individuals—sometimes party or campaign staffers, but often volunteers—who follow the opponent and videotape all his or her events, hoping to record a controversial comment or an awkward moment. Because digital technology makes it quite easy to upload the video evidence, a candidate's gaffe is likely to make it on to YouTube within a matter of days, if not hours. During his 2006 re-election bid for the U.S. Senate, former Virginia Senator George Allen twice referred to a tracker of Indian descent from the opposing campaign as "macaca." The statement, which was widely interpreted as a racial slur, was captured on video, which in turn was placed online and quickly went viral. Many observers believe the "macaca video" contributed to Allen's defeat.

During the 2008 campaign, the Democratic Party placed dozens of videos recorded by trackers on their website. The purpose, according to Mike Gehrke of the Democratic National Committee, was to "provide some useful fodder to let a thousand media consultants bloom" (Seelye 2007).[16] In other words, individuals were encouraged to use clips from the trackers' videos to produce their own web ads.

How Widespread is the Use of ICTs in Campaigns?

Many of the examples above are taken from presidential campaigns. In particular, the campaigns of Howard Dean and Barack Obama are believed to have used technology in groundbreaking ways (see, e.g., Teachout and Streeter 2008; Hendricks and Denton 2010). This is not to say that other campaigns have not been technologically innovative. The 2004 Bush re-election campaign, for example, employed very sophisticated—and unprecedented—database management tools for microtargeting and voter mobilization (see Edsall and Grimaldi 2004; Magleby, Monson, and Patterson 2007: 22–3; Hillygus and Shields 2008: 160–1).

Although they provide dramatic examples of how campaigns can put ICTs to effective use, presidential campaigns are not the best models of how campaigns are typically run. Very few campaigns have the resources to build an operation on the level of a presidential campaign. So how widespread is the use of ICTs in non-presidential campaigns? Unfortunately, we can provide only a partial answer to that question. One reason for this is that the adoption of new technology by campaigns is advancing so rapidly that surveys of campaigns conducted only four years ago may now be woefully out of date. Another reason is because the studies that do exist tend to focus on candidate websites and not on ICTs generally. Nevertheless, the results of a few systematic studies do provide a reliable, if limited, picture of the use of technology in non-presidential campaigns.

As noted earlier, by 2002 all serious candidates for major offices had websites and, by 2006, growth in the adoption of websites had reached a plateau according to Gulati and Williams (2009: 69). In the 2006 election cycle, 97 percent of Democratic Senate candidates and 94 percent of Republican Senate candidates had a campaign Web page. On the House side, 88 percent of Democrats and 84 of Republicans had a website (55). The only candidates not to have a presence on the Internet were safe incumbents and challengers who did not mount a serious campaign.

Druckman, Kifer, and Parkin (2009) examined various elements of congressional candidate websites in 2002 and 2004, including whether they utilized multimedia features (video and/or audio files); displayed items on multiple pages; updated information frequently; provided opportunities to personalize the site (e.g., take quizzes, personalize or arrange information, add quantitative or qualitative information); offered links to external sites (e.g., party Web pages or news sites); or provided avenues for two-way communication (e.g., message boards). On average, nearly all (96.8 percent) House and Senate campaigns in their dataset had multiple pages; the vast majority also updated information frequently (80.2 percent) and linked to external sites (72.7 percent). But a minority of sites utilized multimedia (43.7 percent) and very few allowed personalization (25 percent) or two-way communication (9.2 percent) (31).[17]

With respect to which candidates use which elements on their Web pages, Druckman, Kifer, and Parkin (2009) found that "decisions about using Web technology have both practical and political components" (40). Among the results of their analysis is the fact that incumbents were less likely than non-incumbents to have multimedia aspects to their sites and to frequently update information. Thus, some incumbents (more than likely safe ones) feel the need to maintain a Web presence, but do not feel compelled to make it very useful. Incumbents were, however, more likely to provide a link to their parties' websites than were non-incumbents (ibid.: Table 2.3).

Interestingly, Democrats were significantly more likely to allow personalization and two-way communication on their sites than were Republicans (37–40). Similarly, Gulati and Williams (2009) found that Democratic House candidates in 2006 were significantly more likely than Republicans to utilize Web-based tools for engaging and mobilizing supporters (68); Democratic Senate candidates were significantly more likely to use only mobilization tools (67).[18] Just why these partisan differences appear to exist is not entirely clear, but it may be due to the influence of the 2004 Dean campaign. On the other hand, it may reflect structural differences between the parties (e.g., in their bases of support) or even a philosophical difference between the parties' operatives over campaign tactics.[19] However, the most likely explanation is the fact that, between 1995 and 2006, Democrats were the minority party in Congress (notwithstanding a brief period as the majority party in the Senate). Some suggest that the party out of power has more incentive to adopt new campaign technologies in the pursuit of more voters. The extent to which there are, in fact, partisan differences in campaigns' approaches to Internet use is a potentially important area of future research.

Finally, the competitiveness of a race also influenced the elements which candidates used on their websites. The more competitive the race, the more likely a candidate was to utilize multimedia and to update information frequently. On the other hand, close races made a candidate significantly less likely to provide a link to a party Web page and to offer opportunities for two-way communication. Race competitiveness did not significantly influence website personalization, but the direction of the coefficient was negative (Druckman, Kifer, and Parkin 2009, Table 2.3).[20] Thus, candidates in close races provided fresh information in interesting formats, but did not want to alienate independent voters by highlighting their partisan attachments. Perhaps most troubling is the fact that they did not welcome two-way communication (and may not have been anxious to allow users to personalize the website). This implies, as Druckman, Kifer, and Parkin (2009) suggest, a "hesitancy that candidates in tight races have about relinquishing control over their Web site's central message, even if it means that the site will be less engaging" (40).

Data on candidate websites for campaigns below the congressional level are sparse. Herrnson, Stokes-Brown, and Hindman (2007) provide some insight into state legislative candidates' Internet use, but the survey upon which the results are based was conducted in 2001 with candidates who ran for office between 1998 and 2000 (33). Nevertheless, they find that 40 percent of state legislative candidates in their sample had Web pages, 41 percent used e-mail to communicate with voters, and fewer than 20 percent of candidates used e-mail to appeal to undecided voters, used the Internet to recruit volunteers, or solicited campaign contributions online (35). At least with respect to sponsoring a website, the level of state legislative candidates' Internet use was similar to that of U.S. House candidates in 1998 to 2000 (see Gulati and Williams 2009: 54). Thus, we would expect Internet use to have grown among state legislative candidates in the election cycles since 2000. Indeed, Rackaway (2009) found that two-thirds (66.7 percent) of state legislative candidates in Kansas and North Carolina in 2006 had Web pages (a number that, while larger than Herrnson et al.'s earlier figure, still lags behind the level of use by congressional candidates in 2006).

Technology is spreading throughout campaigns at a rapid rate. As a result, the level of use of ICTs by candidates changes, sometimes dramatically, in just an election cycle or two. That makes it very difficult to keep tabs on the trends in ICT use by candidates. Generally speaking, while most serious candidates—even at the state legislative level—now have Web pages, the level of interactivity on those pages appears not to be following the "Obama model" of technology usage. As Gulati and Williams (2009) conclude, Web-based tools "by which citizens coproduce content and interact in two-way communication with the campaign and each other are not being adopted widely or quickly" by candidates below the presidential level (71). Given the lack of a critical mass of supporters in virtually all non-presidential campaigns, the use of ICTs beyond websites by congressional and other non-presidential candidates is likely to also fall far short of the presidential standard.

Future Directions

Clearly, the use of at least some kinds of information and communication technology by candidates and parties is widespread. What is not yet fully understood, however, is the impact that ICTs are having on campaigns. There are two distinct ways in which political scientists might examine that impact.

The first is to determine the ways in which ICTs are transforming campaign organizations. The popularity of Clay Shirky's (2008) *Here Comes Everybody* suggests that there is considerable interest in the possibility of "organizing without organizations" (as Shirky puts it in his subtitle). The idea, very simply, is that ICTs are "eroding the institutional monopoly on large-scale coordination" (Shirky 2008: 143); that is, collective action can now occur without being managed by, or even given direction from, supervisors in a hierarchical structure.

In the campaign world, this view's most vocal champion is Joe Trippi, the campaign manager for Howard Dean's 2004 presidential bid. According to Trippi (2004: 4),

If information is power, then this new technology—which is the first to evenly distribute information—is really distributing power. This power is shifting from institutions that have always been run top down, hording information at the top, telling us how to run our lives, to a new paradigm of power that is democratically distributed and shared by all of us.

Barack Obama seems to share this perspective, at least to a degree. In response to a question from Larry King about the anti-Clinton "1984" viral ad, Obama replied, "one of the things about the Internet is that people generate all kinds of stuff. In some ways, it's the democratization of the campaign process."[21]

Others are skeptical about the ability of the ICTs to democratize campaigns. Philip Howard (2006), for example, believes that new media technology is empowering political elites, not the grass roots (see also Davis 1999; Hindman 2009). According to Howard, "political campaigns in the United States are increasingly manipulative, as managers find new ways to distribute propaganda, mine data, mask political interests, and mislead people unfamiliar with computing technologies" (2006: 3).

In an analysis of early candidate websites, Jennifer Stromer-Galley (2000) found that campaign Web pages allowed media interaction (e.g., audio and video streaming or hyperlinks) but avoided human interaction (i.e., opportunities to communicate with the candidate or a campaign staffer). Stromer-Galley speculates that one of the primary reasons candidates fail to engage in human interaction via their websites is that "they will lose control over the content of their site and over the communication situation in general" (124). A similar concern surely applies to democratized campaign organizations more broadly. The more average citizens are empowered to influence various aspects of campaigns, the more candidates face a new crisis of control. The response of elites to such crises, as Beniger (1986) reminds us, is to use new technology to regain control. Thus, even the supposedly democratized 2008 Obama campaign may be described as "command and control at the top while empowering the bottom to make a difference" (Joe Trippi quoted in Berman 2008).

Much of the debate over how ICTs have transformed campaign organizations will remain unresolved because a demonstration of change requires a comparison to the past. Unfortunately, the fact that campaign organizations have been the subject of very little research over the past 40 years means that such a comparison is impossible. Nevertheless, political scientists can establish a baseline for future claims of organizational change by providing rich descriptions of contemporary campaign organizations—at all levels—and how they utilize ICTs. Howard (2006) describes what he calls "the *hypermedia campaign*" as "an agile political organization defined by its capacity for innovatively adopting digital technologies for express political purposes and its capacity for innovatively adapting its organization structure to conform to new communicative practices" (2; emphasis in original). Political scientists might seek to show exactly how "organization structures" have been adapted and begin charting changes to those structures over time.

The second way in which political scientists might examine the impact of ICTs is to measure the effectiveness of those tools in accomplishing the primary goals of campaigns. Research along this line has begun in earnest, but it is at an early stage of development. Among other things scholars have examined whether or not new technology helps candidates secure more votes (Bimber and Davis 2003; Rackaway 2009; Williams and Gulati 2009), may be used to increase turnout (Bimber and Davis 2003; Dale and Strauss 2009a, 2009b; Nickerson 2009), encourages various forms of activity and engagement with campaigns (Park and Perry 2009), and is an effective tool for fundraising (Panagopoulos and Bergan 2009).

To this point, the scholarship is a mixed bag in terms of the effectiveness of ICTs. They don't appear to help candidates garner votes but they may enable a candidate to raise more money than he or she otherwise would, and they show some promise in stimulating turnout. However, we have much to learn in this area. As ICTs become even more integrated into the everyday lives of citizens, and as candidates begin to rely ever more heavily on such technology to achieve campaign goals, the impact of these tools should become the subject of an increasing number of systematic studies. Until then, we are left to merely speculate about the transformative potential of information and communication technology for campaigns.

Notes

1. I would like to thank David A. Jones of James Madison University for reading a draft of this chapter and providing useful and insightful comments.
2. Of course, given the complexity of the electoral landscape, it is perhaps inevitable that campaigns, as Richard Rose (1967: 195) has concluded, "are only imperfectly and intermittently rational."
3. This section relies heavily on Medvic (2009).
4. It is beyond the scope of this chapter to reconcile Bimber's (2003) view that for most of American political history, information had been "comparatively scarce" (89) with Beniger's (1986) claim that rationalization, which developed during the Industrial Revolution, is an attempt to handle the "rising tide of information" (15) that threatened to overwhelm modern organizations.
5. See Gulati and Williams (2009: 54) for estimates based on all candidates. Major party candidates are more likely to have websites than are minor party candidates. The gap between the two is evident in data provided by Howard (2006: 26-8), who provides estimates for the years 1996 to 2004 for all candidates and for those from major parties.
6. Owen and Davis (2008: 97) suggest that candidates use the Web "to perform two main functions: reinforce supporters and then mobilize them." Davis (1999) offers the following set of campaign website functions: candidate symbolism; information dissemination; opinion gauging; voter reinforcement and get-out-the-vote; and volunteer ID and fundraising (96-109).

7. However, over 80 percent of the races in which both major party candidates had Web pages displayed indirect dialogue (Xenos and Foot 2005: 178).

8. Boxer's cite was found at www.fioriniafacts.com and Fiorina's at www.failedsenator.com. Both were last accessed on June 11, 2010.

9. George W. Bush's Internet haul accounted for just 5 percent of the over $269 million he raised in total (Postelnicu, Martin, and Landreville 2006: 105).

10. Interestingly, 38 percent of Howard Dean's contributors were small donors in 2004, though the comparison is not particularly fair given that Dean dropped out of the race relatively early in the process (see Campaign Finance Institute 2008: Table 2).

11. In reality, campaigns use Twitter more for press relations than for voter communication. Because most political journalists now have Twitter accounts and follow candidates who are on Twitter, campaigns can draw attention to press releases or candidate statements by tweeting them.

12. The ads may be viewed at www.politico.com/static/PPM106_obamascreenshots. html (accessed June 14, 2010).

13. See the organization's running contribution tally on its website at www.actblue. com/ (accessed June 23, 2010). The number of donors is provided on the group's "About" page—www.actblue.com/about (accessed June 23, 2010).

14. See http://slatecard.com/ (accessed June 23, 2010).

15. The ad's creator, Phil de Vellis, had been an employee of Blue State Digital, which provides a variety of online services for candidates. In 2008, Obama and several other Democratic candidates for president retained the company's services. Despite the fact that de Vellis worked for a firm that had been hired by Obama, he claimed to have created the ad at home, using his own personal computer and software. Nevertheless, he resigned from Blue State Digital once his identity became known. See de Vellis' statement at www.huffingtonpost.com/phil-de-vellis-akaparkridge/i-made-the-vote-different_b_43989.html (accessed June 22, 2010). The "Vote Different" ad, which at the time of this writing had been viewed over six million times on YouTube, may be seen at www.youtube.com/watch?v=6h3G-lMZxjo (accessed June 22, 2010).

16. In 2010, the Democrats once again hosted a site—the Accountability Project—on which supporters could upload video they had taken of Republican candidates at campaign events and other public forums. See www.accountabilityproject.com (accessed July 7, 2010).

17. Gulati and Williams (2009) also examined various tools utilized on candidate Web pages, grouping those tools into the categories of "informational content," "involvement and engagement," and "mobilization."

18. Democrats were also more likely than Republicans to have a presence on Facebook in 2006 and they had more support than Republicans in terms of followers on that social networking site (Williams and Gulati 2009: 275–6).

19. It should be noted that some research has found no significant difference between the parties in terms of their candidates' use of technology (see, e.g., Rackaway 2009: 92–3).

20. Gulati and Williams (2009) found that the competitiveness of a race had a negative impact on the amount of informational content which House candidates' provided but made House candidates more likely to utilize mobilization tools on their Web pages (68). The level of competition had no influence on Senate candidates' websites.

21. See the transcript of Obama's interview on *Larry King Live* at http://transcripts. cnn.com/TRANSCRIPTS/0703/19/lkl.01.html (accessed June 29, 2010).

Chapter 5

Campaign Advertising

Reassessing the Impact of Campaign Ads on Political Behavior

Bryce Corrigan and Ted Brader

Political advertising is an oft-derided feature of modern election campaigns. Ads often contain factual distortions, personal attacks, and appeals to anxiety, anger, and prejudice. Many commentators have suggested that these features of ads cause citizens to become frustrated with the political system and the benefits it has to offer, leading them to disengage. That said, campaign ads may play an important role in educating and involving the widest possible audience during elections. Moreover, ads that are actually critical rather than merely self-promotional may turn out to be both the most informative and memorable (Geer 2006). Thus, these features may systematically distort or enhance democratic outcomes, and our understanding of their effects has implications for ongoing political controversies regarding electoral regulations, campaign finance, and broadcast media ownership.

Observers and scholars alike have shown a special interest in the impact of negative (critical), as opposed to positive (self-promotional), advertising. This interest was greatly stimulated by a provocative report, appearing in the mid-1990s, about a multitude of scientific experiments that uncovered large demobilizing effects (reducing turnout by as much as 5 percent) for negative ads in comparison to positive ads (Ansolabehere et al. 1994). Subsequent studies, using a variety of research designs and definitions of what makes an ad "negative" (i.e., "negativity"), claimed to find similar effects, opposite effects, or no effects at all. A recent review of scholarship on the topic (Lau et al. 2007) surmised that the studies collectively signal no clear finding about the relationship between negativity and voter turnout.

Even if this were the end of the story about negativity—and there are reasons to believe it is not—a variety of other factors may shape the impact of campaign ads on their audience. Ads are not merely negative or positive; they also appeal to a variety of emotions, evoke associations to various groups in society, and differ in the extent and nature of their issue content, to name just a few salient attributes. Potential effects also go beyond mobilizing or demobilizing turnout to include influencing what voters learn, and how they form opinions. Finally, though this has received too little attention from scholars to date, people do not respond uniformly to ads, but rather differ in predictable ways based on the psychological—cognitive and emotional—processes set in motion by both their personal characteristics and their situation.

In this chapter, we first review recent scholarship illustrative of promising directions in the study of campaign advertising. With this foundation, we also consider specific proposals for improving the measurement, modeling, and conceptualization of advertising effects that could improve future work. We put some of these recommendations into practice by briefly replicating recent research carried out by ourselves or others.

Recent Developments in the Study of Advertising Effects

We begin by reviewing recent work on the role of negativity, emotional appeals, and audience attributes, in explaining advertising effects. This review is necessarily selective, focusing on just a few factors that may shape advertising effects. We review this work to illustrate what we see as promising directions in research more generally—namely formulation of more nuanced, psychologically motivated hypotheses, development of more detailed data and measures, and use of more robust statistical procedures.[1]

Negativity

After early compelling experimental evidence of a demobilization effect of attack advertising (Ansolabehere and Iyengar 1995), many subsequent studies found either no impact or the opposite effect (e.g., see Finkel and Geer 1998; Freedman and Goldstein 1999; Goldstein and Freedman 2002a). Furthermore, meta-analytic reviews of all available studies found that no confident conclusions may be drawn from the literature as a whole regarding the effects of advertising negativity on turnout (Lau et al. 2007). However, collectively, the studies suggest that attack ads are more memorable than promotional ads, and that exposure to negativity does increase cynicism about government while diminishing feelings of political efficacy (i.e., the sense that one can effectively understand, participate in, and influence political outcomes). These findings imply that, even if negative ads have no clear effect on voter turnout, they may be both effective at communicating facts and have a harmful effect on democratic institutions.

To better understand the evolution of research on the effects of negative advertising as well as its future prospects, it is helpful to consider the ambiguity of the term "negative" itself. Arguments about what negativity *does* tend to be inextricably bound to their theories of what negativity *is*, and definitions of the concept vary. The broadest definition of negativity is tied to the presence of critical statements about an opposing candidate. The presence of criticism in ads may tend to make them more interesting and even more substantive (Jamieson et al. 2000; Geer 2006). Thus, negativity in advertising may have a silver-lining in terms of attracting the attention of voters and equipping them to make better decisions. Other approaches to negativity focus instead on ads that are inappropriate or harsh (e.g., Kahn and Kenney 1999; Fridkin and Kenney 2004), perceived as unfair or deceptive (Jamieson et al. 2000; Freedman and Lawton 2001), or that contain personal attacks (Freedman and Goldstein. 1999). Such ads may be particularly responsible for the deleterious effects associated with negativity, and conversely ads which avoid this while maintaining a critical tone may have a more benign impact (Jamieson et al. 2000).

Meirick (2002) notes that in earlier studies, while scholars discussed definitions of negativity, few actually sought to simultaneously differentiate the effects by distinct types of negativity. An exception is Kahn and Kenney (1999), who investigate the effects of "mudslinging," or inappropriate or harsh attacks, compared to overall levels of criticism in ads. They find that Senate races with more mudslinging exhibited diminished self-reported turnout. In contrast, increased exposure to negative advertising (i.e., ads criticizing the opponent) actually boosted turnout. Taken together, the two findings suggest that two types of negativity—mudslinging and criticism—have divergent consequences, namely demobilizing and mobilizing effects, respectively.[2] Subsequent experimental research also suggests that this distinction matters for the persuasiveness of ads, with mudslinging more likely than criticism to cause a backlash among voters by lowering their opinion of the ad's sponsor (Fridkin and Kenney 2004).

Other recent studies have focused in more detail on the processes that might make negative ads more effective. Meirick (2002) considers the psychological processes triggered by "comparative" or "contrast" ads, which include both attacks on the opponent and promotion of the sponsor, relative to pure attack ads that only derogate the opponent. To learn more about these processes, he exposed subjects to ads from the 2000 congressional elections and asked them to list their thoughts. Pure attack ads led to more counterarguments and more derogation of the source, while comparative ads generated more supportive arguments and bolstering of the source.

Many studies suggest that negative information is more salient and easier to remember than positive information (Lau 1982; Garramone et al. 1990; Geer 2006). Clearly, if citizens tend to learn more from negative ads, this might cast more favorable ethical light on their use. Brooks and Geer (2007) consider the possibility that either criticism or incivility in political ads affects recall of information, but find no clear support for this idea. In an experiment conducted online with a national sample, there were no discernible differences in the recall of information across respondents exposed to positive, negative, or uncivil ads, and only a slight improvement in recall among those exposed to issue-oriented ads. Meanwhile, Koch (2008) finds that people who were exposed to more negative advertising during the 1998 congressional elections in fact made larger errors in describing candidates' policy positions.[3]

Emotional Appeals

During and after the 1980s, journalists and other political observers criticized the Reagan and Bush presidential campaigns for what they perceived as increasing reliance on symbolic imagery that triggers emotions in place of substantive arguments that provoke thoughtful reflection (Jamieson 1992). At the same time, political consultants who are responsible for designing ads seemed increasingly to subscribe to the view that ads should be emotion-based. In fact, research suggests that emotional appeals have dominated logical appeals in presidential television ads since their inception over a half-century ago (Kaid and Johnston 2001).[4]

Despite growing evidence that emotions constitute an independent force shaping citizens' opinions and behavior (Kinder 1994; Marcus et al. 2000), until recently there had been no research testing whether and how political ads influence voters by triggering emotions. One study, for example, examines self-reported emotional responses to real campaign ads shown to subjects under controlled conditions (Tedesco 2002). Emotions were strongly correlated with character assessments of the candidates, and fearful responses in particular were associated with greater political cynicism. Another experiment reveals that emotionally laden images of "cute animals" in print advertisements increased support for environmental organizations, particularly among those who were already more heavily involved in the issue (Huddy and Gunnthorsdottir 2000).

In the most extensive examination to date, Brader (2005, 2006) demonstrates experimentally that ads can influence voters by using imagery and music to elicit stronger emotional reactions. In addition, eliciting enthusiasm and eliciting fear produce quite distinct patterns of effects, patterns that are largely consistent with Affective Intelligence Theory (Marcus et al. 2000). The theory, which draws on neuroscientific studies, posits that emotions arise from distinct systems in the brain designed to adapt behavior to the needs of particular circumstances. One system modulates our commitment to ongoing activities by generating enthusiasm or disappointment in response to success (or failure) in pursuing our goals and desires. Another system serves to interrupt that process with heightened vigilance and (re)thinking when faced with unknown or threatening circumstances. Brader (2005, 2006) indeed finds that enthusiasm appeals in political ads broadly boost political interest and participation, while encouraging voters to stick with their convictions and increasing confidence in their choices. Fear appeals have a more limited ability to boost participation, but loosen the hold of prior convictions, stoke voters' appetite for more topic-relevant information, and render the ad more persuasive.

Personal and Situational Influences

Many studies identify the "typical" or average impact of ads. In other words, they seem to assume that the ad has a uniform impact on all people. However, the psychological processes involved often work in a way that is contingent upon attributes of the individual or the situation. Recently, more studies have sought to understand advertising effects in terms of such individual-level factors and situational contingencies. For example, Kahn and Kenney (2004) predict that the least politically involved citizens ought to be most susceptible to the demobilizing impact of mudslinging. They indeed find that mudslinging campaigns have the strongest demobilizing effects upon those who are less interested in politics, less knowledgeable about politics, or Independents (non-partisan). At the same time, ads that criticize the opponent actually mobilize these same citizens. In light of these results, one might be tempted to believe that critical ads do a better job of reducing information gaps than positive ads, by driving low-knowledge voters to seek out more information than those who are already highly knowledgeable. However, experimental tests suggest that this is not the case (Valentino et al. 2004).

The Elaboration Likelihood Model (ELM) in psychology suggests that per-suasion can be grounded in thoughtful reflection or based on a heuristic process, such as simply paying attention to "source cues" regarding credibility and agreement with one's predispositions (Petty and Cacioppo 1986). Whether an individual relies primarily on superficial cues, or engages in deeper consideration of an argument, is thought to depend upon an indi-vidual's level of personal involvement with the issue. Consistent with these ideas, Yoon and colleagues (2005) find that negative advertising produces heightened cynicism only under conditions fruitful for persuasion—when ads originated from relatively credible candidates, and viewers were relatively highly involved.

There is also evidence to suggest that the impact of emotional appeals is often tied to the political involvement of those exposed. As already noted above, pictures of cute emotionally evocative animals enhanced the persuasive power of environmental print ads predominantly among those already politi-cally active and engaged in environmental issues (Huddy and Gunnthorsdot-tir 2000). Similarly, across a whole range of effects, emotional appeals embedded in the music and imagery of television ads appear to be most effect-ive in changing the behavior of politically knowledgeable or "sophisticated" citizens (Brader 2006). Although these results tend to defy the conventional wisdom that sees emotional appeals as manipulating less informed audiences (Brader 2006), they are consistent with the notion that emotions are "relev-ance detectors" that respond to the personal implications of changes in our situation (Frijda 1986). From this point of view, it makes sense that political ads are better able to stir emotions and change behavior among those who care about and pay the most attention to politics.

The studies discussed thus far largely ignore the temporal dimension of advertising effects. To the extent that cognitive processes set off by exposure are dynamic in character, unfolding and changing over time, we may need to rethink our measurement and understanding of advertising effects. For example, the presence of a source cue may initially undermine the persuasiveness of an ad, if the source is perceived as untrustworthy or as having different values than the viewer. It is possible, though, that such information becomes dissociated from message content over time. Lariscy and colleagues (1999) find that exposing people to attacks on a candidate exhibit this sort of "sleeper effect." Specifically, exposure to a prior defensive counter-argument, or prior information about low source credibility, initially suppressed the impact of negative information. However, the impact of the attack message appeared to increase when new measures were collected in subsequent weeks. Thus, people may recall the disparaging information, but forget crucial details of context that had earlier led them to take the attacks "with a grain of salt." The timing of ads is also relevant if people process information differently at different stages of a political campaign. For example, experiments suggest that ads tend to garner more support by appealing to abstract ideas early on in the campaign and appealing to concrete ideas closer to the election (Kim et al. 2009). We will return to the issue of timing later when discussing new research which suggests that the impact of negativity on turnout may depend upon whether attacks come before or after a person has made up her mind how to vote (Krupnikov 2010).

Some Suggestions for Future Study of Advertising Effects

We believe researchers can further improve our understanding of campaign advertising effects by building on the conceptual and methodological advances observed in recent studies. First, future scholarship would benefit from conceptualizing and measuring exposure in terms of the "dosages" of any given feature of advertising that are administered to the audience. Further, observational studies ought to utilize a cautious baseline for estimating the impact of advertising. To that end, we propose researchers move toward using statistical models that are robust to the kinds of spurious associations that are apt to be problematic in this context, while nonetheless enabling inferences that make as efficient as possible use of limited data. Finally, we hope to see more extensive theorization incorporating explicit psychological premises and attending to the temporal nature of the campaign and electoral decision-making. We discuss each of these proposals in detail, using illustrations from ongoing work.

Measuring the "Dosage" of Advertising Characteristics

How can we best measure political advertising? Ads differ in their propensity to prime group identifications and stereotypes, shape citizens' perceptions of candidate characteristics or policy positions, and evoke emotional responses. Central to our perspective is that, in trying to determine the impact of an actual advertising campaign, these ad qualities are inseparable from aspects of timing and targeting that determine the quantity of voters' exposure. The campaign season begins with proud biographical introductions of the candidates and culminates with urgent "closing arguments" immediately before voters go to the polls. The interim period is, of course, not entirely predictable, but reflects a variety of tactics employed by candidates and their managers unfolding over time, as they try to exploit or limit the damage caused by changing circumstances. Candidates must decide if and when to "go negative" by attacking their opponents, and how to respond if and when the opposition also does so. More broadly, the spatial distribution of candidate, party, and interest group ads reflects not only the electoral geography of salient races but also limited budgets, varying costs across media markets, and attempts to target particular constituency groups. Some ads air only in a single media market, whereas others are dispersed throughout the country. An ad may air only once or many thousands of times.

Not long ago, objective measures that reflected these complexities of quality and quantity of campaign advertising were all but impossible to find. Studies of advertising effects relied on campaign spending or "media-buy" data, self-reported exposure in surveys, expert commentary, and news coverage of campaigns. These may convey important information about campaign messages originating with advertisements, but they also confound citizens' ad exposure with several consequences thereof. Reporters and pundits may focus on a poignant ad that airs a relatively small number of times. Such an ad may be influential in the absence of airings, but in that case it is due to its presence in other media rather than the airing of the ad. Similarly, ads that air thousands of times may escape the notice of media elites, even if they play an important role in the perceptions of ordinary citizens. Respondents' perceptions of the advertising environment in surveys are likely to capture only the most salient features, and confound assessments of the ads themselves with other attitudes they hold toward the candidates and media. In general, people have a difficult time recognizing the bases underlying their judgments, making them unable to isolate campaign advertisements as a factor in producing those judgments. Finally, campaign purchases of media time to air ads are only a crude proxy for who is exposed when and reveal almost nothing about the content of the messages.

Scholars have also undertaken systematic content analyses of ads aired in particular elections, using teams of trained coders to record a large number of attributes for each ad (Kern 1989; Kaid and Johnston 2001; Brader 2006; Geer 2006). Even when such efforts are comprehensive, however, a focus on the ads produced—where each unique ad is a unit of analysis, rather than how many times each ad actually airs—can lead to inaccurate conclusions about such simple facts as who advertised the most and whose campaign featured more attack advertising (Goldstein and Freedman 2002b). However, over the past decade the Wisconsin Advertising Project (WAP) has begun to make available detailed data on the airings of campaign ads. Researchers at the WAP first obtain the data from a commercial media tracking company and then code several basic features of each ad (Goldstein et al. 2002; Goldstein and Strach 2004). Scholars may use these data to study advertising effects by matching the ads aired in a given media market to the behavior of survey respondents from that same location. In an effort to estimate exposure even more precisely, some researchers combine the objective data on precisely when and where various ads aired with estimates of a person's likelihood of exposure to those ads based on their self-reported television viewing habits (Freedman and Goldstein 1999; Freedman et al. 2004; Shah et al. 2007).

The availability of such airings data vastly improves the opportunities for scholars to learn about the content and impact of political ad campaigns. Nonetheless, the question remains as to how best to summarize features of the advertising environment when assessing their effects. For example, one might characterize the overall environment by the percentage of ads possessing some feature of interest. However, in place of such a compositional approach, we advocate estimating the "dosage" of each relevant ad feature received by an individual. The simplest formalization of this idea, the so-called *mixture-amount* model, is used by biologists to quantify the impact of the introduction of a mixture of chemicals (e.g., fertilizers) into the environment when both the composition and total are thought to matter. This model asserts that the effect of a mixture of chemicals in driving some outcome is proportionate to a measure of the total amount introduced multiplied by a measure of the relative preponderance of each particular ingredient. The description of the relationship as proportional means that some ingredients may have a stronger effect than others—for example, some chemicals may be more toxic than others. The total effect of the introduction of a mixture, then, is held to depend upon which chemicals are chosen and their relative impacts, as well as the total amount of the mixture that is introduced.

In the case of political advertising, one can imagine the campaign environment as just such a mixture of varying qualities (e.g., tone, emotionality, group cues, policy arguments) that potentially produce disparate impacts. For example, in our work, we expand upon recent research into advertising tone (negative vs. positive) to consider not only mudslinging and criticism, but also appeals to various discrete emotions. In line with the mixture-amount model, we think of the impact of ad campaigns at any given time as modulated by a person's total exposure to ads with each attribute. Thus, both the qualities and quantities of ads matter.[5]

The mixture-amount concept does not tell us exactly how multiple exposures to ad qualities are linked to citizens' responses. We make the simple assumption that effects of ad attributes "add up" over repeated exposures to form the relevant dosage producing campaign effects. Those who were exposed to an attribute ten times were influenced ten times more than those exposed only once. This means that the total number of airings and the percentage of those airings with each attribute are the relevant measures of amount and mixture.[6] Multiply these together and the dosage of any particular characteristic is the count of ads with that quality (e.g., count of ads criticizing the opponent). If an ad quality is continuous (e.g., a scale measure), we can simply extend the idea of dosage to mean dosage of the ad quality, rather than an absolute count of advertisements. For example, an individual exposed to 1000 airings that are 50 percent issue-oriented and 100 airings that are 100 percent issue-oriented would be scored 1000*50% + 100*100% = 500 + 100 = 600 units of issue-oriented dosage. The same individual could be assigned a measure for personality-oriented dosage, attack advertising, mudslinging, or anything else we believe may be relevant to his or her responses.

Note that, starting from this baseline, researchers may wish to complicate the "simple assumption" about how the impact of ads adds up. There may be strong theoretical reasons to believe effects accumulate in a more non-linear fashion, such as a quality that requires a certain threshold dosage to have any impact, or a quality that has declining marginal impact after a certain dosage level is reached. Scholars to date have done little to incorporate such non-linear conceptualizations into either their theories or their empirical models.

A final subtlety concerns the dynamics of advertising effects. How do the effects of campaign ads "add up" *over time*? This depends not simply on the quantity of advertising but the nature of the effects. Effects may be fleeting, for example, causing a temporary surge in interest, political discussion, or fondness for a candidate that fades after a few hours, days, or weeks. Alternatively, effects may be permanent, such as convincing a person to switch their vote unless or until they encounter new information which reverses that decision. If effects are permanent they should accumulate over the campaign and measurement should focus on the total prior dosage of advertising. However, if effects are fleeting, it becomes much more critical to measure dosage with respect to a particular window of time. Little published work to date addresses the temporal dynamics of adverting effects, and most theories provide scant explicit guidance about the expected persistence of effects in time. In the future, researchers must attend more fully and carefully to the time dimension in constructing both their measures and their theories.

Establishing a Methodological Baseline

What counts as evidence that campaign ads have a specified impact upon citizens' behavior? We would be most comfortable drawing conclusions about advertising effects if we could conduct an idealized experiment during a real political campaign. In this experiment, we might randomly assign some citizens to see an ad (the treatment group) and randomly assign others to see no ad (the control group). We could then compare how the opinions, preferences, or participation of the two groups differed. The average difference between unexposed and exposed individuals would be a good estimate of the typical effect of exposure to that ad for the population involved.[7] To learn about more than the effects of mere exposure, we would want to randomly expose individuals to one of several ads with varying mixtures of ad qualities. If our treatments included a sufficiently broad selection of dosages of various ad qualities, we could then reliably estimate the average causal effect of a unit dose of each quality.

There has been, in fact, a resurgence of such *field experiments*—experimental interventions in the "real world" where the "subjects" are unaware of being studied—in research on politics. However, virtually none have been conducted to study the impact of candidate or party advertising (for a rare exception, see Gerber et al. forthcoming). In practice, it is often not feasible for scholars to conduct such experiments with full ad campaigns, for ethical, logistical, and financial reasons. For sure, where practical obstacles can be overcome, field experiments offer researchers a powerful tool for learning about advertising effects. Even so, questions will remain about how broadly the findings apply where there is a strong likelihood of "selection bias" in overcoming the obstacles (i.e., to what extent are the set of candidates, elections, and advertising attributes for which scholars are allowed to make design decisions and to randomly assign when or where the ads air representative of the larger advertising universe?).

Moreover, sometimes scholars wish to learn about not just the effectiveness of a particular advertising feature, but also the impact of some actual ad campaign or set of ads that was aired in a particular election. For this reason, as well as practicality, scholars must normally settle for a research design that falls well short of the experimental ideal outlined above. One option is to construct advertisements in order to carefully control their attributes and then randomly assign them to individuals in laboratory or survey experiments, sacrificing realism in order to isolate a precise causal relationship. A second option is to collect and merge observational data about advertising exposure, advertising content, and the political behavior of citizens. Variation in advertising over time and space provides analytical leverage for trying to detect corresponding shifts in citizens' responses. This approach offers the hope of making more general inferences about the actual impact of ad campaigns, but makes inferences trickier due to the loss of experimental control and random assignment.

What, more precisely, are the pitfalls of using an observational study to examine advertising effects? Any observed association between behavior and advertising must be interpreted in light of potential confounds—factors other than campaign ads that may explain people's responses and yet be correlated with advertising exposure. Otherwise, we may falsely claim that ads are promoting an effect that is actually caused by one of these other factors. Studies of advertising effects frequently employ a regression model with a set of control variables to "partial out" the effects of potential confounds. Yet, in many cases, it seems likely that some confounding factors remain unaccounted for and thus continue to distort results. For example, television advertising may coincide with other forms of campaign activity in a particular place and time. Campaigns may also target ads with particular qualities at audiences who seem likely to be receptive to the message.[8] These factors can be difficult to measure directly and thus to control statistically (cf. Huber and Arceneaux 2007; Krasno and Green 2008a). We will see an example of this below.

For observational analyses, we therefore suggest considering statistical models that are more conservative than those used for experimental inference (Shadish et al. 2002). Statistical analyses can take advantage of other features of the data (e.g., a temporal dimension, panel structure, grouping factors, or instrumental variables) to reduce the distorting effects of confounds in the absence of randomization (Wooldridge 2007; Imbens and Wooldridge 2009). We next illustrate how to construct such a conservative procedure using the temporal and spatial dimensions of an observational dataset. We compare estimates of advertising effects that use "naive" models, adjusting only for an incomplete set of individual and contextual differences, with more conservative "trend-robust" models that use temporal and spatial characteristics of the data to reduce the potential distortion of confounds.

Substantively, we consider whether tone, mudslinging, and emotionality in televised political ads affect to what extent citizens talk about politics with their families and co-workers. We can think about political discussion as a political activity that, like voter turnout, may be affected by ads. As noted earlier, scholars have proposed that negativity or criticism may pique voters' interest or, alternatively, turn them off from politics. They have also argued that mudslinging demobilizes citizens. High-arousal emotions like enthusiasm, fear, and anger have all been hypothesized to increase political participation (Brader 2006; Marcus et al. 2000; Valentino et al. forthcoming). In the latter studies, pride is often treated as equivalent to enthusiasm and is rarely distinguished in analyses. Although there is good reason to expect similarities between pride and enthusiasm, cognitive appraisal theories of emotion in psychology note some distinctive aspects of pride, one of which is that pride motivates more "expressive" behavior (Lazarus 1991). Ads eliciting pride, therefore, may be particularly likely to increase expressive forms of action such as political discussion. We consider this possibility alongside the previously suggested hypotheses.

The analysis is conducted using data from the 2000 U.S. presidential campaign, which are discussed extensively elsewhere (Brader and Corrigan 2008). What is most important is that the database combines individual-level daily survey data with measures of media market advertising exposure and the qualities of the corresponding ads. The survey data, drawn from the National Annenberg Election Study (NAES), consists of rolling cross-sections, which means that fresh random samples of Americans were contacted and interviewed continuously throughout the general election campaign. Political advertisements were content-coded for tone, mudslinging, and presence of emotional appeals by a team of trained coders. To form measures of the "dosage" of each of these ad qualities to which an individual was potentially exposed, we summed indicators of the qualities over all airings for each media market. Airing dates and locations were identified using the WAP data (Goldstein et al. 2002), covering the largest 75 media markets.

Because our data have a time dimension, we sought to capture in a sensible way the dynamics of any potential advertising effects on political discussion. As the survey measure asks people to report how much they discussed politics during the previous week, we chose to directly model the impact of the past week's exposure to advertising qualities on reported frequency of discussion during that same week. Table 5.1 shows the results. Political discussion is the average level of reported discussion with family and co-workers; it is coded as a scale that runs from 0 to 1. Table 5.1 reports the estimated effects of advertising attributes per 1000 doses.[9] The first column shows the estimated effects on the reported frequency of discussion of two different specifications. In the first we estimate the effects of negativity and mudslinging, relative to positive ads (tone specification), and in the second we estimate those same effects simultaneously with the effects of appealing predominantly to fear, enthusiasm, anger, or pride (tone + emotions specification).

In these "naive" models, we also included a variety of explanatory variables that are believed to be important determinants of participation and turnout in general. These control variables (omitted from Table 5.1)—Media Market Ad Volume, Battleground State, Education, Income, Age, Square of Age, Female, Married, Black, Hispanic, Citizen, Log Residence Length—are intended to help account for the possibility that people who happen to live in the places where more ads are shown are somehow different in their propensity to engage in political discussion, or that battleground states produce increased political discussion through a mechanism other than advertising effects.

If we believe the model is sufficient and rely upon the first column of results in Table 5.1, we would conclude confidently that people exposed to more attack ads and mudslinging during the past week discuss politics more often, but also that these apparent effects are actually driven by the emotional content of ads. The estimates for negativity and mudslinging drop to close to zero when we add the emotional appeal variables. The impact of particular emotional appeals varies considerably. Contrary to what we expect from prior research, enthusiasm appeals appear to modestly depress political discussion by 16 percent (of the scale) for every 1000 ads or "doses" featuring these appeals, holding constant other ad qualities and the total volume of advertising. Fear and anger appeals seem to encourage political discussion at equivalent rates, with 1000 ads sufficient to shift political talk by a quarter of the scale. Finally, consistent with the predictions derived from cognitive appraisal theories, ads appealing to pride dramatically increase political discussion by

Table 5.1 The Effects of Advertising Tone and Emotional Appeals on Political
Discussion during the 2000 Presidential General Election

Key explanatory variables	Estimates by modeling assumption	
	Naïve model	Trend-robust model
Tone Only Specification		
# Negative (attack or contrast)	0.12 (0.04)**	0.05 (0.05)
# Mudslinging	0.23 (0.10)*	0.17 (0.13)
Tone + Emotions Specification		
# Attack/Contrast	0.01 (0.06)	−0.06 (0.87)
# Mudslinging	0.02 (0.12)	0.08 (0.15)
# Fearful	0.24 (0.07)**	0.14 (0.08)+
# Enthusiastic	−0.16 (0.07)*	−0.15 (0.08)+
# Angry	0.26 (0.06)**	0.07 (0.07)
# Prideful	0.66 (0.12)**	0.30 (0.13)*
Sample Size	20,730	20,730

Notes
The table shows marginal effects (and standard errors) for models estimating the
impact of dosages of advertising features appearing in the media market on a respondent's average level of political discussion with family or at work (0–1 scale). Both
advertising dosage and political discussion are measured with reference to the week
preceding the survey interview. Control variables included but not shown: State-level
mean ad volume (trend-robust estimates only), weekly national mean ad volume
(trend-robust estimates only), media market ad volume, battleground state, education, income, age, square of age, female, married, black, hispanic, citizen, log residence length. Both naïve and trend-robust models are maximum likelihood estimators
with random effects for campaign week and state.
Statistical significance thresholds:
+ Marginal at 90% confidence level.
* Significant at 95% confidence level.
**Significant at 99% confidence level.

nearly two-thirds of the scale for exposure to 1000 ads. The effect of pride on
this expressive activity is notably larger than the effect of fear and anger.

Although it appears that we have found some interesting relationships
between recent exposure to emotional advertising appeals and reported rates
of political discussion, we have denoted these models "naive" because we
remain skeptical that the estimates accurately reflect the true magnitudes of
the effects. In particular, we suspect that there are other factors related to both
political discussion and one or more of our explanatory variables—potential
confounds—in no way addressed by the naive models. The models include no
indicators of longstanding interest in politics and the campaign.[10] Furthermore, other campaign factors, such as news coverage, local appearances by
candidates, and other campaign events, or even proximity to Election Day
itself, may drive people to engage in political discussion with their families
and at work. The one contextual factor we included as a control—whether one
lives in a battleground state—may be insufficient to account for these factors.

Note that many potential confounds may be expected to vary in time. So, apparently, do overall levels of advertising and political discussion. Figure 5.1 illustrates the way in which both advertising volume and political discussion (the portion left unexplained by individual-level predictors) are related to time by plotting the aggregate trends in each variable. Note that both variables show clear trends. The trends may completely or partially reflect a real process by which the prior week's advertising drives up levels of political discussion in proportion to the presence of specific ad qualities. If so, our naive analysis would be valid. Alternatively, it may be that the trends in political discussion are responses to news media communications, candidate appearances, major campaign events (e.g., conventions, debates), or the natural buildup of excitement as the election approaches, which all tend to trend upward in intensity along with political advertising. If this is the case, our model is likely to falsely attribute these effects to ads.

These aggregate trends suggest that a more conservative approach to estimating effects is in order, one that takes advantage of the time dimension of the data. In the "trend-robust" models, we include the mean advertising volume at each time point in order to capture trends in potential confounds. Similarly, we include the mean ad volume in each state, purging our estimates of advertising effects of any state-level association between discussion and interest or other confounds related to ad volume. Our estimates of advertising effects from this model are thereby to be interpreted as holding constant overall campaign volume and state-level campaign volume (cf. Bafumi and Gelman 2006).

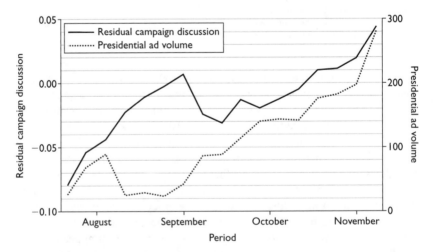

Figure 5.1 The level of political discussion left unexplained by individual characteristics rises as election day draws near, in close correspondence to the rise in campaign advertising (2000 Presidential General Election).

Column 2 of Table 5.1 shows the conservative trend-robust models and invites notably different conclusions than the "naive" models. Now the tone-only specification suggests no effect of negativity or mudslinging. This remains true in the tone+emotions specification and, in addition, the magnitude of several emotional effects has changed and the extent of this change differs across types of appeals. Although we have slightly less confidence in their impact, enthusiasm appeals still appear to depress discussion at roughly the same level. Fear appeals still seem to provoke discussion but our confidence in the estimates is at marginal levels because the estimated impact was cut nearly in half. The estimated effect of anger appeals has dropped so far—by three-quarters—that we are no longer confident they have any impact at all. Finally, estimates for pride appeals are cut by more than half, yet we remain fairly confident in their positive impact on political discussion (this time, increasing political talk by 30 percent of the scale for every 1000 ads).

In summary, because observational studies of advertising effects rest upon strong assumptions, we suggest that future work focus on enabling conservative inferences from these data. We have illustrated one way to do so—by controlling for variation in campaign intensity captured by weekly and state-level mean ad volume. Other strategies are available, though we lack the space to consider them here.[11] Future work should help us to decide which strategies are preferable—which are conservative enough to reduce the risk of finding a spurious advertising effect, but still sufficiently powerful to reveal advertising effects when they are present.

Thinking About Campaigns and Decision-Making in Time

We noted earlier that myriad studies of the impact of negative advertising seem to have produced ambiguous results. Even studies finding mobilizing or demobilizing effects have offered only weak explanations for the psychological processes that might explain such results. New research departs from this pattern. Building on extensive psychological research on pre- and post-decisional processing, Krupnikov (2010) hypothesizes that timing is a critical moderator of the effect of negative advertising on turnout. She predicts that, prior to selecting a candidate, a person ordinarily integrates negative information about a candidate into his or her decision. At this pre-decision stage, the theory makes no firm prediction about the relationship between negativity and the person's likelihood of turning out to vote. However, once a person's mind is made up, the theory predicts that criticizing the person's favored candidate has a demobilizing effect, reducing his or her propensity to vote. The reason is not that people are necessarily "demoralized" to learn that their candidate has unfavorable attributes, but rather stems from the theory of decision processes. Once people make up their minds, the theory holds, they see the unselected choices as unsuitable. If the preferred choice now appears to be similarly unsuitable, then people are unlikely to implement their decision at all—in this case, an individual may decide not to vote.

Krupnikov presents an extensive set of experiments, as well as panel and cross-sectional analyses, providing support for these theoretical propositions. This includes a test of the effects of negative ads using the NAES pre-post election panel survey conducted during the 2000 U.S. presidential election. We replicate that analysis here. The panel was ideal for the purpose because it initially interviewed respondents during the last two weeks of September and re-interviewed them a short time after the November election. Like Krupnikov, we use the WAP data on presidential campaign ad airings to measure likely exposure. Based on her instructions we attempted to construct a model that mimicked as closely as possible the individual-level turnout model of Rosenstone and Hansen (1993), except with the addition of measures of advertising exposure. The key additions to the model for testing Krupnikov's hypothesis are an indicator of decision state at the initial interview, measures of exposure to negative ads both prior and subsequent to that interview (early and late negativity), and an interaction between decision state and late negativity. A methodological control for total state-level ad volume is included, as per the discussion in the previous section.

We find support for Krupnikov's hypothesis even using our conservative measurement strategy. The estimated interaction effect on the log-odds scale was -3.69 and statistically significant ($p < 0.01$). Those who reported making a decision early on were generally more likely to report turning out to vote, but early deciders appear to have been demobilized when exposed to heavy negative advertising subsequent to making up their minds. Figure 5.2 illustrates this demobilization effect. It compares the expected rate of turnout for respondents based on the estimated model, as a function of exposure to advertising negativity and whether they had made up their minds at the first interview. We see that early deciders report almost certainly turning out when they live in markets with low levels of negativity, but those exposed to high levels of negativity are at least 5 to 10 percent less likely to vote.[12]

Distinguishing the effects of ads on turnout by the timing of adverting exposure relative to a person's decision state is just one way to build a psychologically and temporally richer portrait of advertising effects. Future studies would do well to follow this model.

Conclusion

We now have many clues about the role that combative and sometimes ugly political advertisements play in shaping citizens' political behavior. As our review of recent work suggests, however, a monolithic notion of negativity and its effects is no longer viable. Indeed, a variety of qualities that might make ads seem "negative" or "positive," as well as features of the person and situation, are likely to shape the impact of ads in distinct ways. Critical ads

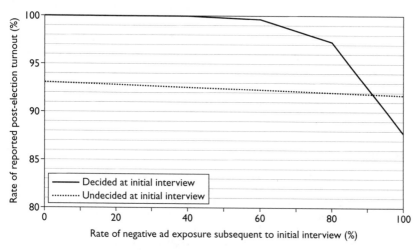

Figure 5.2 The impact of advertising negativity on turnout depends on when voters are exposed relative to making up their minds about the candidates (2000 Presidential General Election).

may often have features that promote citizens' feelings of competence and thus encourage participation (Geer 2006), but under some circumstances a person may no longer enact a decision when that criticism drives them against their preferred alternative (Krupnikov 2010).

The blurring lines between traditional and new media also suggest important directions for future research. People today often read the news and watch ads online using their computers and smart phones. Candidates, parties, and interest groups are increasingly using such technology to circulate ads and other promotional materials, and these information streams may eventually dwarf traditional television advertising. Researchers must be mindful of these developments and adjust their investigations into the effects of "campaign advertising" accordingly.

Although data for studying advertising effects are more readily available than ever before, the complexity of the process poses challenges to our ability to formulate models and draw appropriate inferences. We have discussed the mixture-amount concept as an organizing principle for addressing this complexity. Although we have limited ourselves to the simplest possible operationalization of this concept—a model additively specifying various dosages of ad qualities—we envision that further research may lead to more convincing alternatives depending on the mechanisms proposed by their theories. Similarly, we offered a simple demonstration of a strategy that could be used for drawing circumspect inferences from observational data in the presence of unmeasured potential confounds that are correlated with trends and spatial patterns in advertising and behavioral outcomes of interest.

Perhaps the greatest obstacle for the study of advertising effects is our still fuzzy understanding of how to conceptualize citizens as decision-makers, confronted with a complex and sometimes difficult information environment, and often little willingness or ability to sort fact from fiction. Here too we see promise in recent work (e.g. Martin 2004; Krupnikov 2010) that not only embraces innovative data and methods, but pauses to seek clarity for understanding citizens' responses to political ads in basic psychological premises.

Notes

1. For earlier, less selective overviews, see Goldstein and Ridout (2004), and Iyengar and Simon (2000). To take just one example of a promising line of inquiry we have had to set aside in the present chapter, a number of studies have examined the impact of racial group cues in campaign advertising (Huber and Lapinski 2006, 2008; Mendelberg 1997, 2001, 2008; Valentino et al. 2002).
2. Kahn and Kenney's (1999) measure of mudslinging is based on accusations of campaign managers in post-election interviews, and hence it is hard to know whether it is capturing the same sorts of advertisements consistently across races and over time.
3. Interestingly, Brooks and Geer (2007) report that experimental participants perceived uncivil messages as *less* informative, but they evidently made a greater effort to answer the related recall questions given the pattern of non-response. Koch (2008) finds that people exposed to negative ads believe they were better informed, in comparison to those exposed to positive ads. Thus, in each study, voters tended to misperceive the actual informative impact of the ads.
4. Kaid and Johnston's "videostyle" paradigm asks coders to judge whether an ad makes an emotional appeal without specifying distinct emotions other than fear.
5. For a related discussion focused on measuring advertising exposure and negativity in particular see Stevens (2008, 2009).
6. It is well known that an ad that never airs, or airs only once, can nonetheless reverberate in media circles so that citizens are actually exposed to its content many times during a campaign. In such cases, even the most sophisticated way of measuring exposure to paid advertising may mischaracterize the overall impact of the ads. Moreover, the proliferation of web-interactive journalism, blogging, candidate websites, and video-sharing Internet sites suggests that citizens are exposed increasingly to campaign ads outside of traditional channels and in ways that pose new challenges to measurement. Some recent work does treat media messages and campaign advertisements together (Shah et al. 2007; Yegiyan and Grabe 2007), or considers the media as an intermediary whose coverage and framing of advertising can magnify or diminish advertising effects (Shen 2004; Ridout and Smith 2008; Fowler and Ridout 2009). This seems to us to be an important direction for future research.
7. If the treated individuals vary in their responses to ad exposure, this produces heteroskedasticity (unequal variances) but does not systematically distort our estimates.
8. In addition, the targeted audience may be defined at distinct levels of specificity (e.g., by state, media market, channel, time of day, program viewership).
9. For comparison, consider that media markets which were home to highly competitive races often featured as many as 10,000 to 20,000 or more ads across all races during the 2000 general election (cf. Franz et al. 2008b).

10. We have excluded any explicit measure of political interest, or an implicit measure, partisan strength, because these variables exhibit apparent time dependence and hence may be influenced by advertising.

11. For example, another possibility is the classical difference-in-difference estimator, for which non-parametric versions for continuous treatments have recently been developed (Wooldridge 2007; Imbens and Wooldridge 2009).

12. Although self-reported turnout in the NAES is obviously inflated, Krupnikov (2010) finds comparable results when using measures of validated vote and actual aggregate turnout statistics.

Chapter 6

Voter Mobilization

The Scientific Investigation of Getting the Electorate to the Polls

Robert A. Jackson[1]

> I think we'll be analyzing this election [2008] for years as a seminal, transformative race. The year campaigns leveraged the Internet in ways never imagined. The year we went to warp speed. The year the paradigm got turned upside down and truly became bottom up instead of top down.
>
> Mark McKinnon, Senior Adviser to George W. Bush's
> 2000 and 2004 campaigns[2]

Voter mobilization received heightened attention in the midst of the 2008 presidential campaign. The media and campaign punditry were infatuated with Democratic nominee Barack Obama's efforts to reach out to new voters via new technologies. Mark McKinnon's view, quoted above, reflects a bit of hyperbole, but undoubtedly, future resource-rich campaigns will model many of the innovations of the Obama campaign. Obama won, voter turnout reached levels not seen for decades, and, generally speaking, Obama's mobilization efforts seemed "to work" (see Conway (2009) for an overview). Portending the future by using language suggestive of something akin to a political realignment, Adam Nagourney of the *New York Times* wrote,

> The size and makeup of the electorate could be changed because of efforts by Democrats to register and turn out new black, Hispanic, and younger voters. This shift may have long-lasting ramifications for what the parties do to build enduring coalitions, especially if intensive and technologically-driven voter turnout programs succeed in getting more people to the polls.
>
> (Nagourney 2008: A1)

Being familiar with the field experiments that have become pervasive in the academic literature on voter mobilization, Brian Stelter (2008: A17) suggested that the Obama campaign was effectively running a big "text messaging experiment" (see Dale and Strauss 2009b). Furthermore, the mobilization efforts of 2008 followed on the heels of the frenzied activity of the Bush campaign and of the Kerry campaign, as well as on the part of each candidate's party workers and group supporters, in getting out the Republican base and the Democratic base, respectively, in such battleground states as Ohio in 2004. Describing the situation on the ground heading into Election Day 2004, James Dao wrote,

> So it goes here, throughout Ohio and, indeed, all across nearly a dozen swing states where the election is breathtakingly close. Never in the history of American presidential campaigns will so many people be called, visited, handed literature and cajoled to vote than in the final hours of this race. And the side with the better turnout game is almost certain to win the race.
>
> (Dao 2004: A17)

Clearly, voter mobilization matters to electoral campaigns, and it has also been a subject of longstanding focus in political science. Practitioners' interest has been around as long as candidates have competed in elections, and academics' interest in the topic blazed important trails in the behavioral revolution of the social sciences. Combined with the obvious importance of voter turnout in mass democracies, the readily available (and ever-expanding) supply of data (e.g., the collection of vote returns as dictated by law, the inclusion of turnout questions in most mass opinion surveys on political behavior, and the amenability of mobilization efforts to field experimentation) all but ensures that voter mobilization will continue to be a subject of intense inquiry.

This chapter covers several major domains in this area of research. First, it will review the several decades of "conventional" research on the role of campaigns, elections, and political parties in activating and mobilizing voters. Over the past 15 or so years, this stream has included an especially lively debate regarding the role of negative campaigning as (de-)mobilizer of potential voters. Second, the chapter will review the field experiment approach to studying voter mobilization, which has gained heightened prominence over the past decade. Finally, the chapter will amplify on some of the themes of the opening paragraph. Recent innovations in real-world campaigns, which rely on new electronic technologies, among other things, enable unprecedented micro-targeting and highly focused messaging and mobilization. Not only do many of the findings of the academic literature have direct relevance for real-world campaigns, but the innovations of campaigns in the field should inform the analytical approaches, data collection efforts, and theoretical frameworks of the academic literature.

Do Political Elites Influence Voter Turnout?

The premise that politics generally, and campaign conditions specifically, influence voter turnout has a longstanding history in empirical research on American elections. However, drawing on individual-level survey data, the most well-known turnout investigations, which laid the foundation for our understanding of electoral participation, focused primarily on the characteristics of citizens themselves (e.g., Campbell et al. 1960; Verba and Nie 1972, Wolfinger and Rosenstone 1980; Verba, Scholzman, and Brady 1995). These investigations' answers to the question of why people vote focused primarily on citizen socio-demographics and attitudes. Although providing a great deal of insight, these efforts do not emphasize some factors that are of obvious importance to students of politics—namely differences in the campaign environment. Furthermore, studies that focus on individual-level characteristics are hard-pressed to explain why the level of turnout shifts dramatically from election to election, and why some citizens vote in one election, but sit out another. Thus, in the 1980s, a stream of research reintroduced the importance of politics to the study of turnout, considering citizens and electorates within the context of the campaign environment that surrounds them.

Evaluating the Importance of Campaigns for Voter Turnout

Powerful *prima facie* evidence that campaigns matter is the patterned difference in participation rates between presidential and mid-term elections. As detailed in Campbell's (1960) theory of surge-and-decline, a presidential campaign activates voters. Political elites structure this transient portion of the political environment (Jacobson and Kernell 1983). Strategic elites determine if and when to run for office, how much money to contribute, how much money to spend, and so forth. As candidates, contributors, and political party leaders pursue electoral goals, they influence the election context of potential voters.

The complementary analytical frameworks of information flow and of costs and benefits provide the theoretical underpinning for these mobilization studies. According to Downs (1957), the making of any political decision presupposes a certain minimum of information. At the very least, potential voters must realize that a decision has to be made. To cast a vote, for example, citizens must become aware that a voting opportunity exists and gather, at least, a minimum of information on which to base the vote decision. Since the process of assimilating data consumes scarce resources, as Downs suggests, gathering this information is a costly endeavor. Purposive citizens (i.e., information processors) will attempt to reduce their information costs. When and where possible, they will transfer them.

The campaign environment in which citizens find themselves may attenuate the costs of procuring information and, subsequently, voting. That is, some electoral settings make it much easier to become informed. High-stimulus campaigns that provide easily available information transfer procurement costs, and enhance the likelihood that individuals will become aware of their voting opportunity and act upon it. Since the individual returns from voting are apparently low, the relatively free information provided by candidates and political parties and conveyed, in part, through the media become especially important. Rational citizens are unlikely to do much to inform themselves about whether and how they should vote in a mass election. Furthermore, a campaign that highlights and clarifies the differences between candidates and political parties may give people a reason to vote. In other words, the benefits of voting for one candidate rather than another may become more apparent.

In supplementing individual-level survey data with contextual campaign measures, numerous efforts have examined the importance of campaigns for mobilizing voters at the individual level (e.g., Copeland 1983; Caldeira et al. 1985; Leighley and Nagler 1992; Jackson 1993, 1996a, 2002). Drawing on supplemented American National Election Studies (ANES) cumulative data, Rosenstone and Hansen (1993, see esp. pp. 1778–8) provide the most wide-ranging support, both theoretical and empirical, for political activation in response to competitive electoral contests. The overarching conclusion that emerges from these studies is that a high-stimulus campaign environment, as indicated by greater levels of campaign spending, close contests, and party competitiveness, appears to be important for bringing out voters.

A parallel stream of investigation has assessed the implications of these same campaign indicators for voter turnout at the aggregate or macro level; these aggregate studies attempt to explain variations in the rate or level of turnout across various electoral districts (e.g., state legislative districts, congressional districts, and U.S. states). In the most widely cited of these studies, Patterson and Caldeira (1983: 686; see also Caldeira and Patterson 1982) reach the following conclusion regarding gubernatorial turnout at the state level: "the mobilizing influences of campaign activism and competitiveness have a strong impact on electoral participation." The basic point is clear: "politics matters."

Building on Patterson and Caldeira's approach, Cox and Munger (1989; see also Gilliam 1985; Jackson 1996b) provide a rich treatment that examines congressional district turnout. Their study is important for several reasons. Perhaps most importantly, Cox and Munger revisit the meaning of measures of closeness of outcome in models of turnout (see also Aldrich 1993). Is the apparent effect of such variables the rather direct product of citizens undertaking calculations about the likelihood of their votes making *the* difference on Election Day (i.e., acting in a Downsian, rational actor fashion)? Cox and Munger elucidate clearly an alternative explanation: the influence of closeness may be principally indirect, operating through the behaviors of strategic political elites. That is, candidates, their campaign staffs, political parties, and (potential) financial contributors respond to a close contest by raising and spending more money and putting additional efforts into getting out the vote. In turn, citizens respond to these elite-driven flows of information and stimuli. According to this conception, measures of closeness (including measures based on actual Election Day outcome) operate as surrogates that capture elite activity and effort. However, their final estimates suggest that measures of both closeness and campaign spending exert direct influence on turnout level, providing suggestive evidence for the importance of both elite efforts and calculating citizens (see also Blais 2000: ch. 3).

The Mobilizing Role of Political Parties

In an era of so-called candidate-centered campaigns, it makes sense that a great deal of literature would have focused on such factors as candidate spending levels and the competitiveness of electoral contests. However, lines of research also revisited the role of political parties as agents of mobilization. As V.O. Key (1949: esp. ch. 14) suggested, there is perhaps no substitute for competitive, well-organized parties that offer distinct choices to an electorate. Vibrant party organizations have resources to help get out the vote. Furthermore, a political environment that, election-to-election, presents voters with hard-fought contests between candidates drawn from ideologically distinctive parties conveys to citizens that elections matter. Reciprocally, a history of close contests encourages party elites to activate voters and their party's supporters in particular. Indeed, Burnham describes the mobilization of the mass electorate as "contingent on the existence, competition, and organizational vitality of political parties" (Burnham 1982: 121).

Several efforts focus on the ideological setting of the state party system as an important yet oft-neglected factor in studies of citizen mobilization. These studies view the ideological leanings of state party elites, and of Democratic elites in particular, as fundamental to the participation of voters.[3] Consideration of the impact of elite ideology upon citizen participation rests on the expectation that party activity, as it is undertaken by elites and witnessed by potential voters, may influence the perceived benefits and costs of participation. In short, the values and efforts of political elites give shape and definition to state parties and politics. If, over time, political debate and discussion ignore concerns that are salient to them, citizens should become less likely to participate. Conversely, if they see their interests being represented or receiving attention in political debate and state policy, potential voters should become more likely to participate. The ideological environment sets a tone, and the messages found in elite discourse and conveyed through political activity may serve as a stimulus for participation.

Studies by Hill and Leighley (1996; see also Hill and Leighley 1993) and Brown, Jackson, and Wright (1999) examine the relationship between elite ideology and class-specific mobilization. According to Hill and Leighley (1996), liberal party control (i.e., liberal Democratic elites in control of the state legislature) mobilizes a state's lower income classes, but, surprisingly, only in presidential election years. Brown, Jackson, and Wright (1999) find that liberal party control mobilizes a state's poor in mid-term election years as well. Perhaps the major insight of Brown, Jackson, and Wright's piece is its recognition and incorporation of registration as the critical first hurdle of participation across the United States. They argue that a conception which views citizen decisions to participate as being determined by (short-term) candidate choices, issue positions, and campaign efforts in an election-at-hand tells only part of the story. Although the difficulty of the registration hurdle affects the level of Election Day turnout, citizens must overcome this hurdle several weeks prior in most states. The registration hurdle means that, at least once, citizens must make a decision relevant to participation and overcome obstacles before Election Day and before the campaign has reached its peak. Brown, Jackson, and Wright find that a state's registration level is governed by relatively long-term factors (e.g., party elite liberalism, the difficulty of registration, and state socio-demographic characteristics) and that, reflecting enduring forces in the environment of participation, registration level combines with more proximate campaign and electoral conditions (e.g., the presence of gubernatorial and senatorial races) to structure turnout.[4]

In most other advanced democracies, political parties of the left pitch campaign appeals toward and mobilize the poor and the working class, and these democracies do not observe the marked differences in turnout across those of different socioeconomic status that are associated with the United States (Powell 1986; Jackman 1987; Franklin 2004). Burnham describes the uniqueness of the American setting:

> the institutional mechanisms for social learning among the lower classes—chiefly, of course, the political parties—are so defective that one is left with a kind of apolitical 'state of nature' in which formal schooling is the chief thing that matters.
>
> (Burnham 1982: 168)

Exacerbating the socioeconomic stratification of its electoral participation, the United States is rather unique among democracies in placing the burden of registration upon citizens themselves.

Is the composition of the American voting electorate inherently biased against the poor, the less educated, racial and ethnic minorities, and the young—or can political parties and candidate campaigns effectively target and activate those segments of the electorate whom we have come to expect not to make it to the voting booth in large numbers? Drawing on the evidence from other democracies, it is likely the case that many among the less educated, the poor, young adults, and racial minorities would especially benefit from campaign messages and mobilization efforts targeted at them—giving them a reason or rationale to get to the polls. In fact, Obama's targeting efforts in 2008 reflected a revised logic with a focus on those groups associated with the Left—with the strategy of the Republican Party in the battleground states of 2004 its right-leaning counterpart.

Relying on observational survey data and recall questions, other studies focus on the importance of partisan contacts at the micro level. For example, Rosenstone and Hansen (1993: 171–2) report that being contacted by a political party—either via a phone call or an in-person visit concerning the campaign—increases individual turnout likelihood by almost eight percentage points, other things being equal (see also Kramer 1970; Huckfeldt and Sprague 1992; Wielhouwer and Lockerbie 1994). Although the results of these survey-based efforts are suggestive, several basic problems confront them (see Green and Gerber 2002). First, respondents may inaccurately recall whether they were contacted and whether they voted (problems not unique to the study of canvassing). In particular, those who self-report that they vote appear to exaggerate their level of campaign contact. In addition, political parties and candidate campaigns tend to target likely voters (see Gershtenson 2003). Thus, even if canvassing efforts have absolutely no effect, the survey data would reveal heightened participation among those who are contacted (i.e., endogeneity concerns plague these studies). Instrumental variables provide a possible statistical fix for endogeneity; however, in this case, creating the requisite instrument requires identifying variables that influence the likelihood of being contacted, but *not* the subsequent likelihood of voting—the set of plausible candidates is likely empty. These difficulties associated with using observational survey data to study voter mobilization via canvassing pose a major concern and provide an impetus for resurrecting the field experiment approach, as discussed below.

Negative Campaigning as (De-)Mobilizer?

Whereas this research from the 1980s and early 1990s correctly redirected attention to campaigns and the strategic behavior of candidates as factors that might mobilize voters, most of it conceptualized campaigns and measured the stimuli that they present to the electorate in a rather blunt fashion. The most common approach was to use dummy variables (i.e., 0/1 dichotomous variables) to account simply for whether specific electoral offices were on the ballot (e.g., was it a presidential election year, was a gubernatorial contest present, and so forth), often combined with measures of the level of spending and/or the closeness of election outcomes. In so doing, these studies attempt to capture the general magnitude or volume of the campaign stimuli aimed at an (undifferentiated) electorate. However, such measures are indirect indicators at best. These investigations do not look inside the "black box" of what campaigns are actually doing with their resources and whether they are expending them in ways that are likely to activate voters.

To illustrate: what are some of the limitations in gauging campaign stimuli via candidate expenditures (see Freedman and Goldstein 1999; Goldstein and Freedman 2002a; Goldstein and Ridout 2004)? First, we do not know what proportion of funds was spent on salaries, on polling, on commercials, and so forth. Second, expenditures figures do not take into account the fact that the purchasing power of a dollar varies geographically—one advertising dollar goes further in Nebraska than in New York. Third, there may be marked variation in campaign intensity within a state or an electoral district. For example, residents of Spokane and other parts of eastern Washington likely witness a somewhat different presidential (or U.S. Senate or gubernatorial) campaign than do the residents of Seattle. Expenditures figures do not accommodate this within-state (within-district) variation. Finally, in recent election cycles, spending by candidates' own campaigns is not the only type of spending that takes place in many elections. An exclusive focus on candidate expenditures misses independent and political party expenditures.

Furthermore, these studies largely ignore the tone of campaign messages and implicitly assume away any variation in how different groups of people might respond differentially to campaign messages. One recent vein of turnout research that has considered a nuanced view of campaign information flows and, to a lesser extent, of differential responsiveness across the electorate is research into the relationship between negative campaigning and voter turnout. Given the concerns of academics and campaign reform advocates about both the increasing negativity of political campaigns and declining levels of electoral participation across the last decades of the twentieth century, the possible linkage between the two resonated with a wide audience.

Does attack advertising and so-called "mudslinging" depress turnout, especially among certain types of citizens? Suggesting that negative campaigns demobilize potential voters, the work of Ansolabehere et al. (1994) (see also Ansolabehere and Iyengar 1995) laid the foundation and received a great deal of attention. Furthermore, Ansolabehere and Iyengar (1995) argue that negative campaigns, characterized by so-called "mudslinging," primarily demobilize certain segments of the electorate—most notably Independents (see also Kahn and Kenney 1999; Lau and Pomper 2001, 2004). Despite a great deal of counter-evidence, Ansolabehere et al. (1999) remain steadfast in their claims. They draw much of their evidence from a series of experiments in which participants were exposed to television news broadcasts that contained a variety of campaign ads, including negative ones. Subjects were then asked about their turnout intentions. Ansolabehere et al. (1994) (see also Ansolabehere and Iyengar 1995) also present aggregate models of 1992 U.S. state turnout to support their claims (however, see Brooks 2006). They argue that, controlling for other factors, Senate campaigns which were negative in tone tended to depress turnout that year. Obviously, their results raise important concerns about the long-term health of democratic politics in an era when many campaigns resort to attacks on their opponents.

Several examinations of negativity and voter turnout also assess whether negative campaigns demonstrate greater influence on certain *types* of citizens. As indicated above, Ansolabehere and Iyengar (1995) (see also Lau and Pomper 2001, 2004) suggest that the demobilization effect of negative ads is especially pronounced among Independents—citizens whom they argue are more likely to be open to persuasion by campaign messages. Similarly, Kahn and Kenney (1999) conclude that the demobilizing effect of "mudslinging" is more consequential for Independents, those less interested in politics, and those less knowledgeable about politics. Other efforts, however, do not uncover differential effects across different segments of the electorate (e.g., Finkel and Geer 1998; Freedman and Goldstein 1999; Goldstein and Freedman 2002a), and raise doubts about those presented by Kahn and Kenney (Jackson and Sides 2006).

In contrast, most recent investigations find that, if anything, negative campaigns are associated with heightened voting probabilities and higher levels of turnout—what might be labeled a negativity-mobilization hypothesis (as contrasted with the negativity-demobilization hypothesis) (see Bartels 1996; Finkel and Geer 1998; Freedman and Goldstein 1999; Lau et al. 1999; Wattenberg and Brians 1999; Lau and Pomper 2001; Goldstein and Freedman 2002a; Freedman, Franz, and Goldstein 2004; Hillygus 2005; Geer 2006; Franz et al. 2008a; Jackson and Carsey 2007). These efforts generally conclude that, rather than turning away potential voters, negative campaigns motivate and subsequently activate citizens to go to the polls. Furthermore, several recent efforts suggest that exposure to campaign television advertising produces information gains and increases in political engagement that are especially pronounced among the politically unsophisticated (Freedman, Franz, and Goldstein 2004; Franz et al. 2008a).

Advocates offer a number of compelling arguments supporting the mobilization hypothesis (for an overview, see Finkel and Geer 1998; Geer 2006). First, campaign advertising provides political information to a citizenry notorious for its low store. Beyond simply lowering the costs of acquiring information (Downs 1957), campaigns often highlight and clarify the differences between candidates, thereby giving many people a reason to vote. As Alvarez (1997) suggests, the flow of information in the political environment has implications for voter uncertainty. Advertising facilitates political learning (Freedman et al. 2004), and a truism of American politics is that more knowledgeable citizens are more likely to participate (see also Brians and Wattenberg 1996; Wattenberg and Brians 1999). Second, negative information could be especially pivotal to participation because citizens may weigh it more heavily than positive information when they evaluate candidates. Sigelman and Kugler (2003: 146) speculate that it may take "a loud barrage of brutal attacks to break through the public's wall of inattention, for anything less than that is likely to pass through largely unnoticed." Third, negative campaigns generally, and negative advertisements specifically, may produce stronger emotional and affective responses than do positive ones. According to Finkel and Geer (1998: 577), such reactions could elevate citizens' turnout by "arousing their enthusiasm" for preferred candidates or by increasing the degree to which they care about the outcome of an election.

In addition to normative concerns and theoretical motivations, in no small part, a new and extremely rich data source on campaign television advertisements has facilitated the most recent wave of research on campaign negativity and voter turnout. The Campaign Media Analysis Group (CMAG), a commercial firm that specializes in providing detailed satellite tracking information to campaigns in real time, has provided to Professor Ken Goldstein, now at the University of Wisconsin and current director of the University of Wisconsin Advertising Project (WAP), a wealth of data on television campaign advertising in recent elections in the nation's largest media markets (and, most recently, for the universe of markets). Under Goldstein's direction, these data have been systematically coded, archived, and made available to the research community. Each case in the datasets represents the airing of one ad, and the data contain information about the date and the time of an ad's airing, the television station and program on which it was broadcast, and a coding of its content.

Before these data became available, studies relied on the coding of secondary sources (such as newspaper accounts), experimentally manipulated campaign themes and television advertisements in a laboratory setting, interviewed campaign managers after the election, and/or turned to samples of television advertisements deposited at campaign media archives. Goldstein and Ridout (2004) critique these approaches across-the-board for relying on what are, at best, indirect measures of campaign stimuli; perhaps their major limitation is an inability to capture reliably *campaign* tone and intensity. For example, Finkel and Geer (1998) criticize Ansolabehere et al.'s (1994) analysis of the 1992 Senate campaigns because their measure of campaign negativity (tone) is based on newspaper accounts. Such an approach necessarily conflates variation in actual campaign tone with variation in the press coverage of campaigns. Finkel and Geer argue that "tests of the effects of advertising on 'real world' turnout rate *must be conducted with content analysis of the advertisements themselves*" (Finkel and Geer 1998: 575; emphasis in original). Furthermore, measures based on the proportion of news coverage that is negative also fail to capture how intensely the campaign was fought. Finkel and Geer (1998) employ measures based on a content analysis of the actual ads produced by candidates, as do Kahn and Kenney (1999). Although this strategy accesses more directly the messages candidates send through their advertising, these measures do not account for where or how frequently a particular ad was aired (or for whether it was aired at all).

Many things about the WAP data are noteworthy. For the first time, they provide to researchers reliable and valid information on the universe of ads that were actually aired, as well as the number of times that each ad was aired. The archive includes not only campaign ads paid for by candidates' campaign organizations, but also independent expenditures ads and political party-sponsored ads. In addition, since the data contain the media market in which each spot aired, the researcher can effectively determine the number of ads (and which specific ones) aired in the viewing location of (most) respondents in a national survey. As Franz et al. (2008a) outline, if a survey contains information on respondents' ZIP codes, counties of residence, or area codes, the researcher can locate them within their media market. Thus, the researcher can merge these detailed market-level ad data, including which ads aired on which TV shows and how many times, with the survey data. If the survey also provides information on the television viewing habits of respondents, the variables are in place to create the state-of-the-art advertising exposure measure that Franz et al. recommend.

To provide some flavor of the conclusions based on recent analyses that rely on these detailed advertising data, Freedman, Franz, and Goldstein (2004: 723) indicate that "exposure to campaign advertising can produce citizens who are more interested in a given election, have more to say about the candidates, are more familiar with who is running, and are ultimately more likely to vote." Franz et al. (2008a: 23) refer to TV ads as the "informational multivitamins" of American democracy: "attractively (and expertly) packaged, simple to comprehend, easy to digest."

Two recent studies, however, qualify the newly emergent wisdom regarding the significant mobilizing role of television advertising, as based on the observational findings. Each exploits a natural experiment and reaches the conclusion that television advertising does not mobilize (or, more specifically, did not mobilize in the 2000 presidential election). Huber and Arceneaux (2007) indicate that the apparent mobilizing effect of (presidential) campaign advertising may be a product of advertising exposure being correlated with unmeasured, on-the-ground GOTV efforts. In other words, previous studies may have incorrectly attributed the mobilizing influence of other campaign activities to television advertising. They take advantage of the fact that many individuals in the 2000 presidential election lived in a non-battleground state, yet resided in a media market that crossed over into a battleground state. Thus, these individuals were exposed to heightened television advertising but not to other GOTV efforts. Confining their analysis to respondents in non-battleground states, Huber and Arceneaux (2007: 963) report that they "do not find evidence that advertising increases interest in the campaign or plans to vote." Krasno and Green (2008a) take advantage of the fact that residents of a given state may live in different media markets and thus likely be exposed to different levels of television advertising in a presidential election. Taking into account not only the level, but also the tone of advertising in aggregate models that incorporate state-level fixed effects—where the unit of analysis is the media market by state—they again uncover no evidence of a mobilizing effect for presidential advertising in the 2000 election.[5]

The Field Experiment Approach

Gosnell's (1927; see also Gosnell 1926) pioneering work on voter mobilization in the 1920s introduced many political scientists to the field experiment as a way of conducting social science research. Dividing citizens in each of 12 selected districts in Chicago into those who would be contacted and those who would not, Gosnell engaged in a non-partisan mail canvass to inform those targeted about registration and to encourage them to vote. His guiding assumption: if a larger proportion of the stimulated citizens registered and voted, then the stimuli had an effect. Furthermore, he explored the conditional nature of voter mobilization. For example, he determined that the GOTV notices had a lesser effect among the highly educated and where the local party organization was strong, and the greatest effect among new residents of the city. Green and Gerber (2002) refer to Gosnell's study, technically speaking, as a *controlled field experiment*—distinct from a *randomized* field experiment because Gosnell did not assign subjects to treatment and control conditions on a purely random basis.

Decades later, Gosnell (1948) continued to advocate for the field experiment as a way to study voter mobilization. He wrote:

[T]he experimental method might be employed to investigate the effect of the following upon the size of the poll: house-to-house canvass to get out the vote, a radio campaign to interest people in the election; local discussion groups; an intensive educational campaign in the schools on the rights and duties of citizenship, and other methods to inform and motivate the voter.

(Gosnell 1948: 101)

Building on Gosnell's work, Eldersveld's (1956) field experiments in Ann Arbor in 1953 and 1954 were the first to build pure *randomization* into a voter mobilization design. Randomly assigning subjects into treatment and control groups is central to any experimental design—doing so ensures that there is no expectation of differences, either observable or unobservable, between groups before the treatment, thus enabling the researcher to draw an unbiased inference about causal effect (see De Rooij, Green, and Gerber 2009). Eldersveld randomly assigned (potential) voters to receive telephone calls, mail, and/or personal contact prior to Election Day, assessing the effects of the appeals both separately and in combination. His central finding: the personalized approach is the most effective.

Gosnell and Eldersveld laid a foundation for the recent wave of field experiments on voter mobilization and, no doubt, would look approvingly upon their new-found prominence. Donald Green has been the principal figure advocating for, and facilitating, this wave. A basic design protocol underlies these studies (see Green and Gerber 2008). All incorporate a randomized experimental design in which lists of registered (potential) voters are divided into a treatment group that receives the intervention in question and a control group that does not. Following the election in focus, researchers then examine the public records to determine who voted and who did not. The key statistic is whether those who received the GOTV treatment voted at a higher rate than those assigned to the control group (who did not receive the treatment). Among the GOTV treatments that have been administered in these studies are the following: door-to-door canvassing, leaflets, mail, telephone calls, e-mail, campaign events, and communication through the mass media. Overall, these studies find that how a message is conveyed matters greatly in terms of effectiveness—with personal approaches (e.g., door-to-door canvassing and calls from volunteer phone banks) being much more effective than impersonal approaches (e.g., robotic telephone calls and e-mails) (see Gerber and Green 2000a, 2000b; Nickerson 2007; Green and Gerber 2008). Summarizing this literature, Green and Gerber (2008: 10) indicate that the "gold standard mobilization tactic" is door-to-door canvassing by friends and neighbors.

Among the most interesting and innovative of the field experiments to appear in recent years are those that highlight the social dimension of mobilization. In a study of more than 180,000 households in Michigan, Gerber et al. (2008) report that social pressure transmitted via mailings is extremely effective at mobilizing voters. In the most provocative treatment, Gerber et al. mailed to potential voters a list of the voting record of every registered citizen in their household and of several neighbors, along with notification of the fact that an update would be sent after the election. Turnout increased by more than eight percentage points among those who received this treatment—an effect magnitude rivaling those found in studies that assess the influence of an in-person canvass. In addition, Nickerson (2008) finds that when one member of a two-person household receives an in-person GOTV message, approximately 60 percent of her increased voting likelihood (of nine percentage points or so) is passed on to the member who was not contacted. These results suggest that the turnout decision is socially contagious, perhaps due to social pressure and/or the sharing of voting costs. Thus, the social environment, social norms, and social pressure appear to play major roles in the decision to vote (see also Putnam 2000).

Both the "field" aspect and the "experimental" aspect of the field experiment contribute to its research appeal. The major advantage of the experimental approach is the leverage it provides regarding causal inference. Random assignment of a treatment guarantees an unbiased assessment of the average treatment effect. A complex, multivariate analysis that attempts to encompass the process under investigation via an extensive specification—hopefully as informed by a theoretical model—becomes unnecessary. However, as Green and Gerber (2002) suggest, theory remains relevant (e.g., it may guide the researcher in terms of thinking about the conditions under which a treatment is likely to have a greater (and smaller) effect). Obviously, in the field, not all subjects designated for a (potential) mobilizing treatment will receive it; some may delete a phone message, may not watch or listen to a campaign ad, may not answer the door, and so on. However, Green and

Gerber (2002) highlight that these failures to treat are not as problematic as they may first appear. The experimental data remain informative because the intent to treat is correlated with receipt of the actual treatment but uncorrelated with other determinants of registration and voter turnout. Thus, intent to treat provides an ideal instrumental variable for regression analysis. In fact, Green and Gerber (2002: 811) suggest that another interpretation of, or justification for, random assignment via a field experiment is of a "procedure for generating the instrumental variables necessary for the unbiased estimation of causal parameters."

That these field experiments are being conducted in "real-world" naturalistic settings also has an appeal. Their external validity tends not to be in doubt. The treatments reflect activities that strategic campaign actors either do or could take part in, and they are being administered in the context of actual campaigns to actual potential voters. To provide a contrast frame, the inferential leaps are not as great as those from experiments being conducted in "sterile" behavioral labs on convenience samples of undergraduates.

The resurrection of the field experiment has facilitated marked scientific advance in the study of voter mobilization, and the study of voter mobilization has proven to be the most viable candidate for field experiment research in the study of voting and elections. Treatments that operate on vote choice are likely to be much more controversial and potentially more dubious ethically than are those that operate on voter turnout, especially when the anticipated effect of the latter is mobilization. Although its detractors may suggest that the field experiment is not a design panacea for all areas of study regarding voting and elections, this does not detract from the leverage this approach has provided to the investigation of voter mobilization.

Where Might We Go From Here?

The focus of much of the academic literature on voter turnout is largely removed from the concerns of candidates and their campaigns. Whereas most academic works attempt to explain variation in rates of participation or to provide summary insight into what types of individuals get to the polls and why, strategic political elites are primarily concerned with targeting and mobilizing those citizens who are likely to support *their* candidate. Clearly, from the perspective of campaigns, effective GOTV is built around targeting and focus rather than mass appeals (see Malchow 1998, 2000; Rigamer 1998; Faucheux 1999; Lindauer 1999; Allen 2000). In the world of applied politics, mobilization for the sake of mobilization is an ill-advised strategy. According to Shea, "the campaign should steer clear of un-targeted activities.... Remember GOTV efforts are not about getting voters to the polls, but getting the 'right' voters to the polls" (Shea 1998: 48; see also Shea 1996). From a strategic perspective, the "problem" with generalized appeals is that they inevitably get some of one's opponents' supporters to the polls. Goldstein and Holleque

(2010) provide a critique of Gerber and Green's (2000b) first major contemporary field experiment along similar lines:

> By using random assignment, Gerber and Green ignore the strategic nature of mobilization and distance themselves from the actual phenomenon under investigation. As the 2008 election vividly illustrates, candidates care not at all about high turnout, they care about differential turnout—high turnout among their partisans.... A more accurate estimate could be obtained if an experiment first identified which citizens were most likely to be mobilized, and then used random assignment among those people.
>
> (Goldstein and Holleque 2010: 586)

Via telemarketing efforts, modern campaigns identify their likely supporters (a subset of the electorate) and, subsequently, focus on mobilizing them.[6] Furthermore, the statistical techniques of social science research are migrating into the world of applied politics. Cutting-edge GOTV efforts collect sociodemographic and voting history data to predict citizens' turnout probabilities via regression equations. According to the proponent practitioners, "knowing the probability that a voter will go to the polls is a huge advantage" (Malchow 1998: 46; see also Malchow 2000). Who is the best target for GOTV? The likely supporter who has a 50/50 chance of voting (Malchow 1998: 46). In terms of efficient use of campaign resources, ill-advised targets are those who are almost certain to vote, those who almost certainly will not vote, and, of course, anyone who likely will not vote for your candidate.

In terms of statistical techniques, campaign consultants are drawing upon political science for some insights. However, academic students of turnout could gain some valuable insights from the world of applied campaigning. My directive is not that research on turnout must become more practical or applied in nature. Rather, a greater understanding and recognition of how real-world campaigns operate should facilitate nuanced and richer *theorizing* about voter mobilization. Whereas a great deal of the foundational research on participation focused on explanatory factors that are fixed in any given election (e.g., education, income, age, registration laws), candidates and consultants operate at the margins and take the baseline largely as given. They think quite seriously and in sophisticated ways about the flows of campaign information in this election cycle and what they will mean for the composition of the electorate on Election Day. From this perspective, students of turnout should pay closer attention to such things as the nature of campaign themes and messages and who campaigns target. Voter mobilization is likely a conditional process that depends on both campaign messages and the responsiveness or receptivity of the target audience(s).

As discussed above, the stream of research on negative campaigning and turnout has moved in the direction of providing a nuanced view of flows of campaign information and, to a lesser extent, of the electorate—scholars on both sides have thought quite seriously about the content of campaigns, at least along the dimension of negativity–positivity. Looking at campaigns in a differentiated fashion, this research recognizes a fundamental point about their turnout implications: what campaigns do is probably as important as how much they do. In addition, several of these efforts assess whether negative campaigns demonstrate greater influence on certain *types* of voters (e.g., on Independents or on the politically unsophisticated).

Thinking about the *sources* of campaign information raises additional questions. For example, are there differences in the ways in which incumbent, challenger, and open-seat campaigns activate? How do the mobilization efforts of Republicans differ from those of Democrats? In terms of the nature of mobilization, do on-years differ from off-years? Several studies indicate that a presidential contest provides an overriding stimulus that gets to the polls most of those (peripheral) voters who can be activated (e.g., Jackson 1997; M. Smith 2001). As a follow-up consideration, lower level contests may have greater potential to activate voters in mid-term election years, and research into the mobilizing influence of lower level contests may be well advised to examine these off-years.

Again, a lesson that academics should draw from the practitioners is that strategic campaigns target and attempt to get out *their* voters. Are they effective at doing so? Although a few articles examine the differential turnout influence of campaigns across segments of the electorate, existing research does not provide us with much insight into the answer to this question. Do the content of campaign messages and the emphases of campaigns structure the electorate that shows up at the polls on Election Day (Sides and Karch 2008)? The theories of priming, framing, and issue ownership are among the promising candidates in terms of guiding this style of inquiry. Each of these approaches prompts students of campaigns to think seriously about both the content of campaign appeals and their target audience(s).

Richer theory and data will inform the next generation of voter mobilization studies. In addition to trying to gauge the level of the stream of campaign information, investigators are beginning to wade into the stream and assess its content—and, via field experiments, to even manipulate the flow. Furthermore, researchers should think more carefully about the differential responsiveness of various segments of the electorate. Again, what is the content of the messages that a campaign is presenting to an electorate? Who are the target audiences for these appeals? What types of voters are likely to be more and less responsive? Generally speaking, is it possible for campaigns to shape the composition of the voting electorate in predictable ways? Campaign operatives behave as if the answer to this last question is an unequivocal "yes," but existing data and theories of mobilization do not provide us with sufficient insight.

Notes

1. I would like to thank Suzanne Kirayoglu for research assistance.
2. As quoted in Nagourney (2008).
3. Their rationale is that Democratic elites are especially important to the mobilization of segments of the electorate, such as the poor, who are otherwise unlikely to participate.
4. Arceneaux and Nickerson (2009) outline the importance of taking into account the clustered nature of the data when pooling observations into a "group" based on their location within an electoral district or state. Ignoring the clustered nature of the data (i.e., the fact that the pooled observations are not likely statistically independent) tends to overstate the precision of the estimates for group-level effects. They illustrate this point in relation to the aggregate analysis of Brown, Jackson, and Wright (1999). Furthermore, the impact of statistical clustering should be assessed in any multi-level model that considers survey respondents in electoral context. To date, most of the research on voter mobilization has failed to do so.
5. Franz et al. (2008b) provide a critique of some of the modeling and measurement choices of Krasno and Green (2008a), with a follow-up response from Krasno and Green (2008b).
6. Hillygus and Shields (2008: ch. 6) provide an informative discussion of (micro) targeting in contemporary campaigns. They highlight campaigns' use of wedge issues to prime potentially persuadable, cross-pressured citizens who identify with the other party.

## Chapter 7

Political Parties

The Tensions Between Unified Party Images and Localism

Jeffrey M. Stonecash

Political parties are continually faced with the problem of whether to create a national and relatively uniform policy image for campaigns or allow decentralized campaigns with congressional candidates creating a local image adapted to their race. A clear party image means that the party stakes out a position that contains little ambiguity as to where it stands on policy issues and what its concerns are (Brewer 2009). In 2010, for example, health care reform passed as a Democratic Party proposal and Republicans stood firmly against it. Voters would have little trouble telling which party was on what side of the issue. Democrats were defining themselves as concerned with those who were without insurance and with imposing more rules on insurance companies, and Republicans were defining themselves as against government intrusion and worried about the cost of new programs and deficits.

To the extent that Democrats consistently support programs to provide benefits to various groups and Republicans oppose programs and the taxes to pay for them, the cumulative effect is to reinforce party images. Democrats become seen as liberal, or willing to use government to try to expand opportunity and to help those seen as less fortunate. Republicans become known as conservative, or more concerned with stressing individual responsibility and restraining government and taxes. If representatives of one party vote together and against the other party, and the media regularly report these divisions, this clarifies party positions. Each party acquires a fairly well-defined national policy image. These images will attract and mobilize some voters and alienate others.

The issue of whether to seek to create a clear party image has become more salient in recent years. In the 1960s and 1970s each party had considerable diversity and even the prospect of trying to negotiate a national policy image created conflict within each party (Polsby 2005). The Democrats had numerous conservative Southerners and liberal Northerners. The Republicans had western anti-government conservatives and moderate Northeasterners who were much more comfortable with activist government. Since then considerable realignment has occurred (Brewer and Stonecash 2009). The South has become steadily more Republican (Black and Black 1987, 2002), removing many conservatives from the Democratic Party. The Northeast has become much more Democratic (Ware 2006; Reiter and Stonecash 2011), removing many moderates from the Republican Party. In addition to this realignment, it also appears that geographical sorting is occurring. More and more Republicans live in areas dominated by Republicans and more and more Democrats live in areas dominated by Democrats (Bishop 2008). The result of all these changes is that each party within Congress now has much less internal diversity (Rohde 1991; Polsby 2005).

With less internal diversity, the conditions seem ripe for parties to focus more on clarity and unity of image. More and more members of Congress are seen as winning by larger margins and as "safe" (Jacobson 2009: 303–5). With competition declining, members of each party have more freedom to focus on the concerns of their party. The electoral bases of the parties have become more defined and loyal. Attentive voters are increasingly divided along ideological lines (Abramowitz 2010) and loyal, with higher percentages of those who identify with a party voting for the candidates of that party (Bartels 2000). Given these changes, some argue that it now seems to make more sense for party members to focus on mobilizing their existing constituents than appealing to moderates. Indeed, the genius of a strategist like Karl Rove was presumably his ability to find and mobilize core supporters (Brownstein 2007: 288–9).

As internal diversity has declined, the efforts within parties to push for unity of policy stances and unified support for different policies has increased (Sinclair 2006). In the 1994 House elections Newt Gingrich pushed for and got strong endorsement of a Contract with America that presented ten policy commitments. When President George W. Bush pushed tax cuts and the Patriot Act in the early 2000s the party sought to have complete unity in supporting his agenda. When President Barack Obama proposed a stimulus package and health care reform in 2009 he sought bipartisan support but was ultimately willing to push for just Democratic votes and the image that these were Democratic Party initiatives. The conditions for unity of action and clarity of image are now greater than 30–40 years ago.

The issues addressed in this chapter are how we arrived at the current situation, just how much localism has declined as a relevant factor in party considerations, and to what extent it makes sense for either party to focus on presenting a uniform policy image to voters. While the current portrait of parties is that they are polarized and increasingly presenting a unified stance and image to voters, the question is how accurate that description is of the situation the political parties face.

The first matter addressed is how realignment has changed internal unity over time. These changes provide the basis for greater party unity. The concern is the extent to which presidential and congressional electoral results now overlap. Next, the extent of competition in presidential and congressional elections will be examined to assess how much pressures to be sensitive to swing districts and states have declined. Finally, the implications of these changes for creating unified party images for campaigns will be discussed.

Realignment and Changing Party Unity

In the 1960s and 1970s it would have seemed strange to discuss the merits of a unified party image that would encompass the presidential and congressional wings of either party. The Democratic congressional party was a collection of conservative southerners, northern urban liberals, and some moderates from elsewhere. While congressional parties derived substantial proportions of their members from the South, the party's string of presidential candidates of Kennedy, Johnson, Humphrey, and McGovern conveyed a much more liberal image. The Republicans were a coalition of moderate members from the Northeast and anti-government conservatives from the Midwest and West (Rae 1989). The overall party identity was further muddled by the presidential candidates of Goldwater, Nixon, and then Ford. The more dominant force in Congress was the Conservative Coalition, comprised of conservative southern Democrats and northern Republicans (Patterson 1967). The diversity within each party meant that there was considerable overlap between the parties, with some Democrats more conservative than Republicans and some Republicans more liberal than Democrats.

This diversity within each party soon began to decline. Republicans were pursuing more conservative electorates in the South and gradually achieving success in that region (Aistrup 1996). The South went from being overwhelmingly Democratic to being primarily Republican (Black and Black 1987, 2002). Democrats were seeking more votes in urban areas in the North and they were gradually achieving success. The Northeast went from being heavily Republican to being dominated by Democrats (Reiter and Stonecash 2011). The odd situation of the more liberal Northeast being Republican and the more conservative South being Democratic disappeared. The realignment process was lengthy but it has proceeded steadily and changed the composition of the parties (Stonecash 2006; Brewer and Stonecash 2009).

The changes had three significant consequences for the parties. They brought the electoral bases of the presidential and congressional wings together; reduced the number of moderates within each congressional party; and created greater unity within Congress. Each of these consequences deserves some brief review.

One of the conditions that will make the presidential and congressional wings of parties think about presenting a unified image is sharing the same electoral base. For congressional members to agree to work together and present the same image as their presidential candidates they must be inclined to believe that they have a common base. That base may not be sufficient to gain a majority—a matter to be discussed later—but there needs to be considerable overlap in electoral bases. Members will find this easier if they are representing the same interests and voters. Figure 7.1 indicates the association between presidential candidate votes and the corresponding votes for House (within districts) and Senate (within states) candidates. That is, for House races this involves correlating results for presidents and House candidates within House districts. For Senate races it is the correlation for states with a Senate race in that year with presidential results in those states.

In the early 1900s the results within the relevant jurisdictions for the presidential contest paralleled those for the House and the Senate. When the presidential candidate received strong or weak support in a jurisdiction, the congressional candidates had essentially the same levels of support. The realignment that began in 1948 when President Truman was willing to advocate for civil rights disrupted this association. In the 1960s and 1970s, as the presidential candidates pursued electoral bases different from their existing congressional parties, the separation of results from the two wings of the party became almost complete (Brewer and Stonecash 2009). Then the congressional parties began to shift their success to follow that of presidents, and the correlation between presidential and congressional results began to increase. The presidential–House relationship is very close to being back to the levels of the early 1900s, while the relationship for the Senate still lags. Nevertheless, the trend is toward greater overlap of electoral bases.

As this transition in party bases occurred, it increased the number of moderates within each party. As the Democratic Party moved North (Ware 2006) and became less sympathetic to the South; it became more liberal and alienated southern members who became the moderates within the party. As the

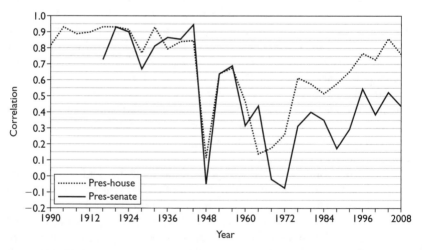

Figure 7.1 Correlation of Democratic presidential results, with results in Senate (by state) and House (by district), 1900–2008.

Republican Party pursued the South and moved away from the Northeast (Reiter and Stonecash 2011) those within the North became moderates uneasy with the direction of the party. Over time the political center and composition of each party changed (Polsby 2005). Those who resisted the ideological movement of the party became moderates and were eventually replaced by party members more compatible with the direction of the party or by the other party (Bond, Fleisher, and Stonecash 2009).

Figure 7.2 provides an indication of changes within the House Republican Party. Keith Poole has created scores that identify the extent to which members of Congress have liberal to conservative voting records within each year.[1] The figure indicates the percentage of the House Republican Party that was liberal, moderate, or conservative in each year. Essentially the same pattern occurred for Democrats in the House and for both parties within the Senate. First, the number of moderates increased and were gradually replaced by conservatives. The party was shedding its moderates and becoming less diverse.

The result has been an increase in the extent of party unity within the House and the Senate. Figure 7.3 provides an indication of this for the Senate. The party unity scores measure the percentage of bills on which a majority of members of one party vote against a majority of the other party. As diversity increased in the 1960s and 1970s the extent of party voting declined. As diversity then declined, the extent of party unity voting increased and is now at levels higher than in the early 1900s. The result, as shown in Figure 7.4, is that the differences in the average voting score between the parties within the House and Senate have steadily increased.

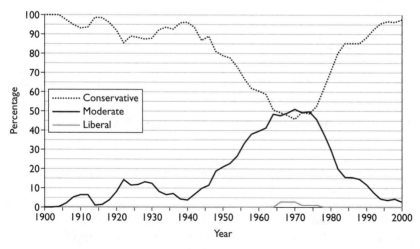

Figure 7.2 Presence of liberals, moderates, and conservatives in the House Republican Party, 1900–2000.

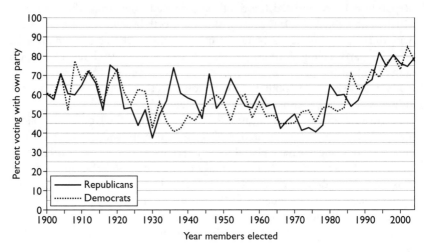

Figure 7.3 Average party unity score by party, Senate, 1900–2006.

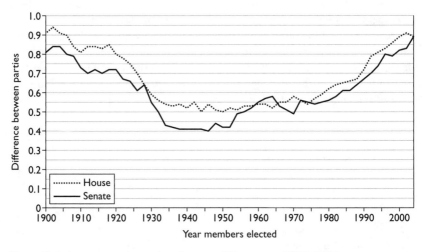

Figure 7.4 Average congressional party differences, 1900–2006.

In summary, the trends of the past several decades have significantly increased the conditions that would make it more likely that parties would seek to create and campaign on a unified image. There is considerable overlap of presidential and congressional results. Each party has fewer moderates to contend with. The extent of party unity in voting is much greater, and the voting records of the parties are now further apart than they have been for some time.

Table 7.1 Number of Republican House Seats by George Bush's Vote Percentages, 2000–2006

Bush %	2000	2004	2006
<40	7	0	1
40–44	15	2	0
45–49	30	15	7
50–54	54	40	31
55–59	56	61	54
60+	60	115	110
Total	222	233	203

Enduring Diversity and the Role of Independents

While there is no doubt that the trends are moving in a direction that makes creating a unified party image more likely, this does not mean that the parties have actually arrived at the point where it makes sense for them to do so. Diversity still exists in party bases. It is also not the case that either party has a majority within the electorate that it can focus on and mobilize. Both of these matters deserve some explanation.

The first matter of importance for parties is how much diversity each contains and how important retaining the diversity of each party is to maintain a majority. From 2000 to 2008 the majority in the House fluctuated, with Republicans holding power from 2000 to 2006 and the Democrats taking a majority in 2006 and holding it in 2008. Table 7.1 indicates how the situation of the House Republican Party varied over time. In 2000 George Bush won a closely contested presidential election. The table indicates the success of House Republicans by Bush's percentage of the vote within districts. (For 2000, his results for 2000 are used and for 2004 and 2006, his 2004 results are used.) In 2000 Bush lost 230 districts. Despite that, House Republicans won in 52 of those districts. Within the majority party in the House, 23.4 percent (52/222) of their seats came from House districts which their president lost. In 2004 Bush improved his situation and only lost 180 districts. His gains appeared to reduce the party's reliance on districts where Bush lost. In 2004 only 17 of their 233 seats came from districts which Bush lost. Despite this gain, the majority within the House was still dependent on members from districts which Bush lost. If they lost the 17 they would have had 216 seats and been in the minority.

By 2006 the general image of President Bush and the Republican Party was declining and it affected their electoral fortunes (Brewer and Stonecash 2009: 1661–83). The party won a total of only eight seats in House districts where Bush lost in 2004. They also won fewer seats where Bush had gotten 50–54 percent of the vote. The combination of outcomes cost them the majority.

Table 7.2 Democratic House Seats by Republican Presidential Success in 2008

Republican presidential results			Democratic House seats		
McCain (%) in 2008	#	% of districts	% won	#	% from
<40	141	32	97.8	138	53.7
40–4	50	12	86.0	43	16.7
45–9	57	13	50.9	29	11.3
50–4	68	16	36.8	25	9.7
55–9	50	11	22.0	11	4.3
60+	69	16	15.9	11	4.3
Total	435			257	

During this time the Republican Party in Congress was largely following the leadership of George Bush and allowing for the creation of a fairly unified image of the party (Jacobson 2007a). The consequence was that the electorate largely reacted negatively to the party as an entity and many Republican members lost. The same situation occurred in 2008. Party members in Congress had agreed to function with high unity of action and image. They paid a significant price for that decision.

Is this a situation confined to only Republicans? The answer is no. Table 7.2 presents the situation for House Democrats following the 2008 elections. The districts in this case are organized by how well Republican John McCain did in 2008. The point is to assess Democratic reliance on seats which their presidential candidate lost. During 2008 there was considerable diversity of presidential voting across the 435 districts. There were 141 districts where McCain received less than 40 percent of the vote and 69 where he received more than 60 percent. The distribution of presidential voting percentages is shown in the third column of Table 7.2. The important matter for the Democrats was how much their majority contained diversity. The party had 257 seats, with 218 required for a majority. They won 25 seats in districts where McCain, even while it was a bad year for his party, won 50–54 percent of the vote. They won 11 where McCain won 55–59 percent—and 11 where he won 60 percent or more. Of their 257-seat majority, 18.3 percent was from districts which their presidential candidate lost. Without those 47 seats the party would have 210 seats and be back in the minority.

The Senate has the same situation, as is shown in Table 7.3. The table indicates Democratic success within states by how well Barack Obama did in the state in 2008. States are first grouped by how well Obama did and then the percentages of seats held are indicated to the right. Following the 2008 election, Democrats had 59 seats and then 60 when Al Franken was eventually declared the winner in Minnesota. It appeared that the party had a solid base for acting as a unified entity. Just as with the House, however, there were

Table 7.3 Democratic Senators by Obama's Vote Percentages, 2008

Distribution of Obama's percentages in state			Democratic Senators		
	2008		% held	D #	% 08
D Pres %	#	%	2008	2008	From
<40	7	14.0	21.4	3	5.0
40–44	8	16.0	25.0	4	6.7
45–49	7	14.0	57.1	8	13.3
50–54	9	18.0	61.1	11	18.3
55–59	9	18.0	77.8	14	23.3
60+	10	20.0	100.0	20	33.3
Total	50			60	

serious risks for party members with creating a unified image before voters. Barack Obama lost 20 states. The difficulty for the Democratic Party was that 15 of their 60 Senators (25 percent) came from states which their president lost. To the extent that the images of the president and the congressional party were tied together, and to the extent that these images declined in popularity, as they did in 2009 and 2010, a unified image would hurt those party members who were in states that were more sympathetic to Republicans.

The problem for each party is simple and it is an enduring one. To the extent that their party gains a majority, that majority is dependent on winning seats in jurisdictions won by the other party. Split outcomes (different winners for presidential and congressional contests) have declined from their peaks in the 1970s and 1980s, but they have not gone away. If presidential election results reflect basic partisan dispositions across states and districts, parties continue to win some portion of their seats in jurisdictions not naturally predisposed to their party. Creating and presenting a unified image may well cost the party members in those jurisdictions less supportive of the party. Members in those seats will resist going along with the image of a unified party for the sake of their own survival. They will also argue to party leaders that trying to create a party image to present to voters may well cost the party the majority.

The Lack of a Majority

The situation which each party faces is that neither has a firm majority within the electorate (Shafer 2003) or across states and House districts. Each party, at least currently, faces the situation where they must reach out to an electorate that is not firmly attached to their view of the world. This lack of a majority is evident in two ways: party identification and the stability of outcomes in House elections.

Since 1952 voters have been asked in the American National Election Study whether they see themselves as a Republican, a Democrat, or something else. These initial reactions are important to the parties because they indicate the base level of support they have.[2] Figure 7.5 shows the percentage of all voters choosing one of the above responses. Democrats, largely owing to attachments within the South, had a near majority until the mid-1960s. Since then they have suffered a steady erosion of their situation, while the independent category has increased.

For roughly the past 30 years neither party has had a majority. Democrats have fluctuated at around 40 percent and the Republican's percentage has varied between the mid- and high 30s. The crucial matter for each party is that they have to reach beyond their relatively certain base if they are going to create a majority. We may have numerous analyses which argue that polarization dominates the process (Brownstein 2007), but it is still the case that there is a swing vote which must be attracted to have a majority. As the results from 2000 to 2008 indicate, the majority can swing from one party to another when a party gains or loses that swing vote.

The lack of a majority is also evident in House elections during the past decade. For a party to have some security in its situation it needs to be able to count on holding a majority of House districts. Table 7.4 indicates the distribution of partisan success for Democrats in the four elections from 2002 to 2008. The boundaries of districts have been unchanged over this time, so this involves comparing the same set of districts over time. The overall success rate of Democrats is shown in the first row, under the figures representing the number of Democratic successes. Of the 435 seats Republicans have won the same seats in all four elections in 44.2 percent of the districts, averaging 67.6

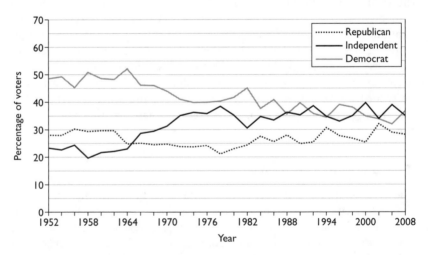

Figure 7.5 Percentage of voters identifying as Democrat or Republican, including leaners, NES Data, 1952–2008.

Table 7.4 Partisan Seat Changes 2002–2008 (Out of Four Elections)

Republican Pres average[a]	% of districts	Number of times seat won by Democrat				
		0	1	2	3	4
		44.2	9.0	2	1.6	44.7
<45	34.6	0	1.3	0	7	96.7
45–9	9.0	28.2	20.5	0	3.6	48.7
50–4	15.7	54.4	17.7	0	2.9	25.0
55+	40.8	80.8	9.6	6	1.7	7.3

Note
a In this case it is possible to obtain the Republican presidential percentage in 2000 for the 2002 district configuration. This is taken from CQ Press' *Congressional Districts in the 2000s: A Portrait of America*. They took the results from 2000 and re-tabulated them for the new districts. The results for 2004 and 2008 are then averaged with the re-tabulated results to give 3 presidential results for same district.

percent of the vote in those districts. Democrats won all four elections in the same seats in 44.7 percent of all seats, averaging 75.0 percent of the vote. Each party has about the same percentage of the 435 seats it can count on but neither party has a certain base that will give it a majority.

The ability of each party to win seats is dependent upon how well their presidential candidate does. To assess this, districts are grouped by the average presidential vote in a district (averaging 2000, 2004, and 2008). That grouping is shown along the left. When a Republican presidential candidate wins 55 percent or more within a district, Republican House candidates win 80.8 percent of the seats in that category four out of four times. However, Republican candidates averaged 55 percent or more of the vote in only 40.8 percent of all House districts, well short of a majority. When a Democratic presidential candidate does well (the Republican gets less than 45 percent of the vote), Democratic House candidates win 96.7 percent of those seats four out of four times. However, this average presidential performance prevailed in only 34.6 percent of all House districts, also well short of a majority. In those cases where the presidential candidates are closer to 50 percent of the vote, party prospects for House candidates are less certain.

Each party may be able to find evidence indicating that their base is larger than these data suggest. Democrats may look at the responses to party identification and conclude that leaners should really be added in as party identifiers. If that is done then, in 2008, 52.3 percent of respondents chose the Democratic Party. The difficulty for the party is that a negative reaction among voters to a policy initiative or economic events could significantly reduce the percentage leaning to the party.

Republicans could look at the distribution of House outcomes from 2002 to 2008 and see that for 9.0 percent of all seats Republicans won the seats three out of four times. They may easily conclude that with George Bush gone and Iraq fading from memory they will be able to regain those seats, add them to the 44.2 percent they won in four out of four elections and return to the majority. The difficulty is that the party's opposition to various bills in 2009 and 2010 may present the party as very conservative and limit party members' ability to regain the seats lost in 2006 or 2008.

For both parties the primary difficulty they may face is that creating a clear liberal or conservative policy image may not help them among those voters or within those districts that are not firmly attached to either party. Again, while there is considerable discussion of polarization and how each party can act to mobilize its base, neither party has a clear base that constitutes a majority.

The Dangers of Pursuing New Voters

The lack of a majority for each party means that they must expand their appeal. How expansion is handled has been a dilemma for parties. Some party members argue that to attract voters the party must create a clear identity about some specific issues and use those issues to try to pull voters to their side. These issues are known as "wedge" issues, or issue positions that are attractive to those in the other party (Hillygus and Shields 2008). To the extent that a party can articulate a clear position on a wedge issue it should be able to attract voters and expand its base. We have numerous examples of such efforts. During the 1960s both President Kennedy and President Johnson concluded that they needed to expand their electoral base in Northern cities and their best possibility to achieve this was among urban blacks (Milkis 2006). This reasoning, plus other factors, resulted in Democratic support for civil rights legislation. Republican candidates wanted to attract southern conservatives and opposed these federal efforts (Aistrup 1996). Republicans in the 1980s and after sought to appeal to religious conservatives by articulating concern about abortion and respect for traditional values in America (Layman 2001; Hetherington and Weiler 2009). These efforts and the dynamics they create are a perpetual part of the flux of American politics (Mellow 2008; Karol 2009).

While the effect of these strategies on attracting voters has received considerable attention, it is also important to note that such moves risk driving some voters in the opposite direction. Democrats lost many conservative whites owing to their positions on civil rights (Edsall and Edsall 1991). Republicans have lost many voters who are pro-choice (Liscio, Stonecash, and Brewer 2011), and they have lost many voters in the Northeast who did not like the social conservative stance of the party (Reiter and Stonecash 2011). As parties pursue clear policy stances that send a signal to attract some voters, they also send a signal to voters who are uneasy about the position. Efforts at expansion can also create losses.

Conclusions and the Future

There are at least two possible patterns that may occur in the near future. One involves the continuation of the situation in which neither party has a majority. The other involves the possibility of one party establishing a thematic image that appeals to those not identifying with either party, thereby bringing them into that party. This could create a near-term majority for one party for a while.

If the former prevails, each party will have to be careful about the image it presents to voters. If one party seeks to create a unified and clear policy image it is unlikely to help elect members of Congress in districts or states where there is not a partisan majority of voters. While the parties in Congress may be more polarized and less amenable to compromising, they continually face the need to win enough elections in swing districts to control the majority. As of now, this means accepting members who must run in jurisdictions not clearly amenable to the policy concerns of the center of each party. There are still districts and states that can go either way and do switch from time to time. Without a sustained majority each party must resist imposing unity on members and must continue the age-old practice of letting some members deviate from the party image. Unless they do, they will elect members when the tide swings their way, but lose those very same members when the electoral tide swings away from them.

The alternative is for the parties to carefully analyze those individuals not currently committed to a party and to seek some commonality with existing party concerns that will broaden identification with the party and result in a majority. The parties are certainly doing that now, but finding that commonality is not easy. There is enormous uncertainty about what appeals might attract independents. Democrats may think that enacting an expansion of access to health care will bring them more voters but it is difficult for voters to sort out the specifics of the legislation to form an assessment. Republicans believe that opposing greater debt and higher taxes will appeal to individuals who believe that government is doing too much. If that stance leads to cuts in desired programs such as Medicare then it may not attract voters. Events such as economic decline or growth can undermine the efficacy of a particular strategy.

While there is considerable uncertainty about the likely effects of adopting clear party images and unified policy stances, each party has an enormous incentive to conduct polls and sort through the results, looking for voter concerns and trying to frame issues in a way that will appeal to those who are unattached. They have no choice but to try to gauge what broad themes might work, all the while living with uncertainty.

Ultimately, a party is unlikely to choose just one of these strategies. They will seek candidates who can win in local jurisdictions while continuing to search for some broad theme that could attract enough voters for a majority.

Notes

1. The term *moderate* refers to a member whose ideological voting record falls between the bases of each political party. In this case a moderate is defined as any member of the House with a voting record between –.2 and 2 on the DW-NOMINATE scale. The data are taken from Keith Poole's web page (www.voteview.com/).
2. Following their initial response, voters are asked a follow-up question. Those who choose a party are asked if they are a strong or weak identifier with that party. Those who say they are independent are asked if they lean toward either party. Those who lean could be assigned here to either party because the evidence indicates that those who lean toward a certain party tend to vote for candidates from that party (Keith et al. 1992). For this analysis, in which the focus is upon certain party identifiers, the initial responses are used.

## Chapter 8

Interest Groups
Back to Basic Questions

Clyde Wilcox

In the summer of 2010, interest groups were already very active in congressional election campaigns. Groups such as MoveOn.Org and Club for Growth had recruited candidates to run against incumbents in party primaries and caucuses, and local networks of Tea Party organizations had organized voters to help some Republican candidates defeat party favorites. Interest groups such as GOPAC and EMILY's List were helping to train candidates and their supporters in skills needed for campaigning in the coming general election. Many interest groups such as the Human Rights Campaign and the National Rifle Association had contributed money to candidates through their political action committees (PACs) and/or encouraged their members to contribute. With the party nominees fixed in many states, groups were already running advertisements on TV, radio, and the Internet, and mailing persuasion pamphlets to potential voters. Other groups were working to develop voter mobilization lists, in some cases canvassing door to door, in other cases matching lists of registered voters with additional information provided by groups or vendors.

With control of both the House and Senate potentially in play, many groups were planning expensive and extensive campaign efforts. Dave Levinthal of the non-partisan Center for Responsive Politics predicted that the 2010 interest group efforts would not only break past records, but that "this could very well obliterate [the record] when all is said and done"(Miller 2010). The Chamber of Commerce was expected to spend some $75 million, and the AFL-CIO had plans to spend up to $100 million. EMILY's List, a pro-choice group that supports Democratic women candidates, expected to spend $43 million.

But most American interest groups were not planning all-out efforts in the 2010 campaigns. Many groups planned to contribute a small amount to a few select candidates, as they have done in past elections, and many organizations have never been involved in electoral politics. Some groups do not participate in elections because US tax law forbids electoral engagement, but other groups try to accomplish their policy goals through other means.

We have been studying the role of interest groups in American elections for decades, and every year there are scores of new studies (Overacker and

West 1932; Sorauf 1988; Rozell, Wilcox, and Madland 2006; Magleby and Patterson 2007; Wilcox and Iida 2010). The studies have used a variety of methods, including formal models (Bailey 2004), statistical analyses of contributions (Ansolabehere, Figueiredo, and James M. Snyder 2003; Hojnacki and Kimball 2001), case studies of organizations (Biersack, Herrnson, and Wilcox 1999), qualitative studies of decision-making (Malbin et al. 2002), and qualitative studies of group activity in particular elections (Magleby and Tanner 2004).

Yet there remains fundamental disagreement about the most basic questions—why groups become involved in elections, how they choose their strategies, what impact their activity has upon campaigns, and what impact their activity has on policy-making. Perhaps most importantly, there is a lack of consensus on how to theoretically understand the way in which interest groups are active, and the implications of the activity for electoral politics.

There are many reasons for this continued disagreement. However, despite an accumulation of hundreds of studies, the most important comparisons remain problematic. It is difficult to compare organizations that choose to be involved in elections to those which do not, or to compare the strategies and tactics of organizations in a systematic way. Ideally we need to compare groups that are active with those that are not, compare the tactics of all groups within an election cycle, and/or compare the decisions by the same groups across election cycles.

Some of these difficulties are rooted in the availability of data. We lack a comprehensive list of all interest groups that would allow us to compare those which are active in elections to those that are not. This is especially true when we consider organizations which are formed solely to influence elections—EMILY's List did not decide to work in elections; it was formed by activists who wanted to influence elections. To fully understand which groups form to influence elections, we would need to compare them to a list of potential groups that did not organize.

Comparing strategies and tactics of organizations within an election cycle is difficult because some group activity is transparent and other activity is not. We can trace with accuracy the contributions by the MoveOn.Org PAC, but it is far harder to measure the flurry of e-mails they send to their members encouraging them to give to candidates, and how much money is raised for the candidates in this way. It is difficult to get clear measures of spending by some types of groups, and so it is hard to see how much organizations spend on recruiting and training candidates, on mobilizing volunteers, and even on some kinds of advertising.

Even when we know the extent of this activity, it is often difficult to find a metric with which to compare. What is the relative value of an endorsement by the NRA, a campaign contribution by a corporate PAC, an hour of phone bank work by a labor union, a handful of volunteers working door to door for a pro-life group, or a well-designed television ad during prime time? It is often impossible to compare how much money or effort an organization spent on these activities, or what their market value might be. When two similar organizations engage in different types of activity, often all we can say effectively is that one mounted a get-out-the-vote (GOTV) campaign and the other aired television advertisements.

Comparing the activity of groups over time is complicated owing to changes in the regulations of group activity, and changes in technology. Congressional lawmaking, regulatory interpretation, and Supreme Court decisions have changed the way in which groups can raise and spend money for various activities. A corporation that wanted to influence elections had different options in 1980, 1994, and 2010. A given corporation might have given money through its PAC in 1980, and encouraged its executives and families to give to candidates. In 1994 the same company might have continued these activities but also have made large "soft money" contributions to political parties. In 2010 these soft money contributions were banned, but the company or its executives could give to the Chamber of Commerce's electoral efforts, and to newly formed organizations by party activists such as American Crossroads, and it might also have communicated with shareholders and employees through its web page and other electronic communication. These very different tactics may reflect changing legal opportunities, not changing strategies.

But an even more fundamental problem is that the concepts "interest group" and "electoral activity" are blurred and contested. To develop theories of interest group behavior in elections, we need to know what organizations and activities to compare. Some organizations active in elections are clearly interest groups, but others are more ambiguous. Some activities by groups clearly constitute electoral activity, but other activity is more difficult to classify.

In this chapter, I will begin with a discussion of questions surrounding the definition of interest groups and of electoral activity, and discuss limitations in existing data. I will then evaluate the promise of different theoretical perspectives on interest groups in elections and suggest new paths for research.

Back to Basics: What is an Interest Group?

The question of how to define an interest group has broad implications for political science, sociology, and economics, and scholars have used somewhat different definitions (Baumgartner and Leech 1998). Each election brings a batch of new and often temporary organizations to American elections, which complicate efforts to define an interest group. There are problems in defining interest groups in the study of lobbying and other activity, but there are two reasons why defining an interest group is especially difficult during campaigns.

First, some actors wish to disguise their identities in electioneering. They may create organizations with attractive names that do their electioneering, for a variety of reasons. For example, corporations may wish to run independent television ads against a candidate, but fear that voters who support the other candidate may boycott the company's products, or that voters would discount their claims as self-interested. During the 2000 campaign, an organization called "Citizens for Better Medicare" (CBM) ran ads attacking Democratic candidates on health care. In 2002 similar ads were run by a different organization, called "American Seniors Association" (ASA). The names of these organizations might suggest to voters that they are citizens groups representing retirees, but both were in fact organized and principally funded by drug companies (Magleby 2004). Advertisements urging voters to support a candidate that are openly funded by drug companies might at best be ineffective and more likely counterproductive, but ads sponsored by organizations of retirees evoke more positive reactions.

We can conceive of CBM and ASA as short-lived interest groups that raised money to influence elections, and therefore put them in the same category as other organizations, but many scholars have treated these organizations primarily as a front for drug company electoral activity. If we take the latter view we should think of CBM not as an organization, but as a tactic of a community of interest groups. Forming and funding the organization is simply part of that strategy.

In other cases, individuals may entirely or primarily fund organizations. In 2000, a group called "Republicans for Clean Air" ran ads in the Republican presidential primaries that helped George Bush in his race against John McCain. The ads were designed to appear to be the product of a group of environmentally conscious Republicans, but in fact they were funded by two wealthy Dallas businessmen who supported George Bush. The "organization" appears to have never had a permanent mailing address, or any of the other characteristics we normally think of as a "group." Many similar organizations pop up during specific campaigns—in 2004 Let Freedom Ring distributed videos extolling George Bush's faith to churches in Ohio and Pennsylvania, but was primarily funded by a single source, with one staffer and a volunteer intern. After the election, the group was disbanded. Should we think of these two organizations as interest groups, or as conduits for the financial resources of individuals?

If we see these organizations as simply conduits for individuals, there are further theoretical complications. Should we think of this activity as linked to these donors' companies, or as partisan or ideological activity? A journalist for the *Wall Street Journal* traced some $20.5 million in campaign contributions over a four-year period to the company Ameriquest and its executives, their spouses, and business associates (Simpson 2007), through individual and PAC contributions, fundraising, and contributions to various other organizations engaged in electoral work. The assumption is that an executive of Ameriquest who gave to a candidate was acting on behalf of the company. Yet when George Soros contributed tens of millions of dollars to 527 committees working to defeat George Bush in 2004, this was not generally seen as an extension of his business interests.

Moreover, if individuals fund a new or even a temporary organization, is that different theoretically than funding a new campaign by an existing organization? Other organizations, including Club for Growth, Planned Parenthood, and NAACP, have launched advertising campaigns entirely funded by single individuals, and the content of these campaigns was doubtlessly negotiated with the donors. In what way is it different to create a new organization, or to simply create a new campaign that is channeled through existing organizations?

Partisan activists may wish to create organizations to carry on electioneering without the party label, so as to appear to represent broader coalitions of citizens. In 2004 Democratic activists together with the heads of some liberal interest groups created a series of 527 committees that were designed to help the Kerry campaign (Weissman and Hassan 2006). Are these organizations best thought of as party surrogates, or as interest groups (Skinner 2005; Boatright 2007)? Similarly, in 2010 former Bush advisor Karl Rove helped create an organization called American Crossroads, in part because he perceived that the Republican Party committees were not effective.

A second reason why defining interest groups is especially difficult during campaigns is that tax law and campaign finance regulations give organizations incentives to create a variety of affiliated and in some cases unaffiliated organizational structures, which are generally referred to by the number of the section of the tax code that describes them. These organizations will be discussed in more detail later in this chapter, but for now the important point is that they can accept different types of contributions, and then pay for different types of activity. Some organizations may have formed a separate segregated fund (PAC) for contributing money to federal candidates, several state-level PACs for contributing to state candidates, a 527 committee that can accept large contributions from wealthy supporters and mount advertising campaigns that can help candidates and parties, a 501(c)3 organization that can help create lists of voters or prepare non-partisan voter mobilization materials, and a 501(c)4 organization that can do some electoral work (Weissman 2009).

Karl Rove and his associates organized American Crossroads as a 527 committee, which can engage in unlimited electoral activity but must eventually disclose the source of its funds. In July they announced the formation of an affiliated 501(c)4 organization that could engage in some electoral activity but would not be required to disclose the identity of donors. The advertisements run by these two affiliated committees may be similar or even identical, but they are organized differently under tax law, as discussed below.

In most cases scholars have conceived of the various organizations that are sponsored by an organization as affiliated with that sponsor, and thus treated their combined electoral activity as reflecting that of the sponsor, even when the new organization has a distinct decision-making structure. Thus the Sierra Club's efforts through its PAC, 527 committee, and 501 (c) 4 are all activities by the Sierra Club in an election. Yet many 527 committees and other organizations are not officially affiliated, but there may be great overlap in funding and personnel. Citizens for Better Medicare was not formally affiliated with the Pharmaceutical Researchers and Manufacturers of America, and Americans Coming Together (ACT) was not officially affiliated with the AFL-CIO. The AFL-CIO and other unions that joined to form ACT have their own 527 committees, so perhaps we should see the decision to form ACT as an effort to more effectively coordinate efforts—reducing collective action costs of a coalition. Alternatively, this decision may have been influenced by large donors like Soros who funded a great deal of the Democratic 527 effort in 2004.

The best qualitative research finesses these definitional issues in a variety of ways. Some work has carefully described the formation and funding of these organizations, and their decision-making, without theorizing about how to classify them (Weissman and Ryan 2006; Weissman 2009). Other work has reported the activity of sets of interest groups, implicitly treating some of these organizations not as independent entities, but rather as strategic decisions by communities of interest groups (Magleby forthcoming(b)).

These definitional issues are especially vexing for quantitative studies of group behavior. These studies frequently try to model the amount of activity undertaken by various types of interest groups, and their allocation decisions. The most common form of this research is to model the decision to form a PAC (among corporations), and PAC allocation strategies (Andres 1985; Masters and Keim 1985; Grenzke 1989; Wilcox 1989; Stratmann 2005).

Of course, not all PACs are interest groups. In the 2010 election, HUCKPAC and SarahPAC were the respective presidential campaign vehicles of Mike Huckabee and Sarah Palin. The PACs sponsored by party leaders and candidates are interesting in their own right (Wilcox and Genest 1991; Corrado 1992), but most (though not all) scholars do not consider them to be independent interest groups and therefore exclude them from these studies.

But more importantly, the decision to form a PAC is only one of the strategic options open to interest groups. Some interest groups do not form PACs, and instead conduct their electoral activity under other organizational forms. The Christian Coalition distributed tens of millions of voter guides while organized as a 501 (c) 4 committee,[1] and some corporations coordinate giving by executives without forming a PAC.[2]

Among organizations that do form PACs, in some cases this constitutes their entire electoral activity, and in other cases it is but a small fraction. For those groups that engage in additional electoral activity, PAC contributions may reflect their overall allocation strategy, but in many cases this will not be true. PAC contributions are made under spending constraints so that large PACs give to many candidates, but issue advocacy campaigns and other electoral activity can be concentrated on a handful of races, or even a single contest. A company PAC may contribute primarily to incumbents in the 2010 elections, but if the company also contributes to the Chamber of Commerce's electioneering efforts then the bulk of that money may go to support GOP challengers and open seat candidates. The distribution of PAC contributions in this case would be a misleading indicator of overall allocations.

Back to Basics II: What is Electoral Activity?

Defining what activites of interest groups are in some sense "electoral" is also difficult, for reasons similar to the problems with defining interest groups. Tax law and campaign finance regulations provide interest groups with incentives to disguise the electoral intentions of some of their activities. These regulations primarily affect the ability of groups to use various resources, including treasury funds and large contributions from patrons, and the requirements that they disclose the source or the money and how it is spent. Frequently the same ad can be financed more easily and disclosed less fully if it falls outside the definition of election activity. Because campaign finance law and tax law have been created and administered separately, let us look at them in sequence.

The Federal Election Campaign Act (FECA) sought initially to regulate contributions and spending by groups and by individuals who were their members. Congress put no limits on communications between an organization and its members, although this activity was required to be disclosed to the Federal Election Commission. The coordination of volunteers and small contributions were both exempt from disclosure, because the democratic values of these activities outweighed any potential danger of corruption.

The Supreme Court overturned spending limits for organizations and individuals, thus allowing organizations to engage in unlimited spending for advertising for or against federal candidates, so long as this activity was not coordinated with the candidate or party. But these "independent expenditure" campaigns must be funded PACs, which raised money from group members in contributions of $5000 or less. The use of membership dues or corporate profits was limited to paying for the costs of running the PAC, and large contributions by patrons could not be contributed to candidates or used to finance independent expenditures.

Political parties and candidates were eager to find ways to channel interest group treasury funds and large contributions from group members and patrons back into campaigns. They argued that some types of activity were not directly focused on federal elections, and thus were outside of the FECA regulations. By the mid-1980s presidential candidates and congressional party leaders were directly soliciting contributions to party "soft money" accounts. These funds were to be used for non-federal (i.e., state and local) elections, and party-building activity including generic party advertising and voter mobilization. But from the start these contributions were channeled into federal elections, and often solicited specifically with the promise that the funds would help specific candidates (Jackson 1988). By the mid-1990s, both parties were using these funds to openly advertise on behalf of specific candidates (see Chapter 2, this volume).

By labeling much of this spending "party building" instead of "influencing elections," parties were able to accept large contributions from corporate and union treasuries, and large personal contributions from corporate officials and other wealthy group members. At first the sources of these soft money accounts were not disclosed; later they were disclosed but not subject to limits. These soft money contributions were banned by the Bipartisan Campaign Reform Act (BCRA) in 2002.

Regulations have also distinguished between advertisements designed to elect a candidate, and advertisements designed to promote an issue. Interest group election advertisements are subject to far more regulations than advertisements that promote policy issues. These "issue advocacy" advertisements may be financed by corporate or interest group treasuries or by very large contributions by interest group members, and are often done in a way that avoids disclosure of the sources of money or even the amount that the organization has spent. In the late 1990s and early 2000s these ads were primarily funded through 527 committees—tax-exempt political committees that did not engage in electioneering and therefore were considered to be outside the FECA regulatory framework.[3] This makes it attractive for an interest group to air advertisements that avoid the technical definitions of an electioneering advertisement, even if these ads are in fact intended to influence potential voters. In 1996, the AFL-CIO spent a reported $35 million in issue advocacy that was clearly designed to influence elections, including many ads that morphed the image of the Republican candidate into that of unpopular party leader Newt Gingrich (Jacobson 1999). In 2004, a group named "Swift Boat Veterans and POWs for Truth" aired a series of advertisements claiming that John Kerry had lied about his war record. In each case, there is little doubt that these ads were intended as electoral instruments, and studies have shown that voters perceived them to be candidate or party advertisements (Magleby 2000a).

The legal criteria for distinguishing issue advocacy from electioneering are narrow and have changed over time. In the 1990s, only ads that contained certain "magic words" such as "vote for" or "defeat" were considered electioneering, so that ads that attacked a candidate but concluded with exhortations to "tell [candidate X] how you feel and be sure to vote in November" were defined as issue advertising. In 2002 Congress defined electioneering advertisements based on when the ad was aired, whether it featured an image or name of the candidate, and how it was targeted. The Supreme Court has recently substituted a more ambiguous standard that electioneering ads are those that are "susceptible to no reasonable interpretation other than as an appeal to vote for or vote against a specific candidate." (*Federal Election Commission* v. *Wisconsin Right to Life, Inc.* 2007). This means that advertisements whose purpose is ambiguous can avoid campaign finance regulations. Interest group activists readily admit that many of the "issue ads" they air are intended to influence elections. But interest groups do mount real issue advocacy campaigns to change public attitudes on issues, including a spate of dueling ads about the possibility of "Clean Coal" aired by groups in 2009. There has not emerged a scholarly consensus on how to distinguish electoral from issue advocacy, with most qualitative work simply making judgment calls and quantitative work frequently ignoring the activity altogether.

Tax law also helps create ambiguous categories in defining electoral activity by groups. Some kinds of voter contacting and mobilization can be financed by 501(c) committees that are tax-exempt charities, to which individuals and groups can make large contributions that are tax deductible, without having their contributions disclosed to the public. Some of these 501(c) committees are sponsored by interest groups that also have PACs and possibly 527 committees, but some are separate entities and some are established ad hoc for particular campaigns. These groups have become increasingly active in national and state elections (Weissman 2009).

Groups organized as 501(c)3 committees are barred from electoral involvement, but they can register voters and encourage voting so long as they do not endorse candidates in the process. Although the IRS guidelines are restrictive, it is legal for an organization to conduct these campaigns in neighborhoods where it is likely that newly registered voters will support one or the other party. Churches can conduct voter registration drives without violating their tax-exempt status, and other 501(c)3 committees can conduct these drives in inner cities, rural areas, or in churches in a community. In the 1980s, Charles Keating, a financier seeking intervention from U.S. Senators, gave more than $800,000 to tax-exempt voter registration groups in an effort to win the favor of Democratic Senator Alan Cranston—a rather clear signal that these organizations were helping the Cranston campaign (Thompson 1993).

Groups organized as 501(c)4 committees are allowed to engage in electoral activity, so long as this does not constitute the principal purpose of the organization. The legal criteria for determining the principle purpose of the organization are somewhat vaguely defined, and applied on a case-by-case basis. Contributions to (c)4 committees are not tax exempt, but the organizations do not pay taxes on income, and they do not disclose the identities of their donors. Although 501(c)4 committees are allowed to engage in electioneering, the "principal purpose" restriction gives them an incentive to describe some of their activities in other ways.

Because courts decide these definitions on a case-by-case basis, the same activity may be labeled as electioneering in one context but not in another. For example, the Christian Coalition in the 1990s claimed to distribute tens of millions of voter guides in conservative churches on the Sunday before elections. Public statements by the group's leaders made it clear that these guides were intended to influence elections, and the organization received contributions from Republican Party committees (Wilcox and Robinson 2010). When the Federal Election Commission charged that the group was engaged in electioneering, a Federal District Court ruled that with narrow exceptions the Coalition's activity did not fall within the definition of electioneering. But in 2003 the Christian Coalition decided not to appeal an IRS decision that the principal purpose of the organization was to influence elections.

What Do Groups Do, and How Do We Know?

With narrowly drawn and sometimes conflicting legal criteria for what constitutes electoral activity, and with a growing proportion of activity undertaken in ways that elude disclosure requirements, many qualitative scholars and top journalists have done heroic work documenting the activities of interest groups in elections. Frequently they are forced to rely on the claims which groups make about their activity, and groups may have incentives to under- or overstate their electioneering. Other scholars have sought to create their own databases to document interest group activity, but what we know about this activity is often incomplete, and revealed in different ways. Below is a partial list of activities by groups, and how we know about them.

- Candidate recruitment. Many interest groups encourage their members or those who support their agenda to run for office, and some have more formal programs to identify potential candidates (Rozell, Wilcox, and Madland 2006). We know about this activity through case studies, especially of women's organizations, and case studies of candidacy decisions (Fowler and McClure 1989). We also have data from surveys of candidates, which in many cases do not distinguish between recruitment by interest groups and by party leaders, friends, and family members. For example, Lawless and Fox demonstrate the importance of recruitment for women's decisions to run for higher office, but their category of "non-elected political activist" includes both party and interest group activists (Lawless and Fox 2005).
- Candidate training. Some organizations offer training to candidates, campaign managers, and/or fundraisers. This can range from formal schools with sessions on canvassing and shaking hands, to distributing documents on how to best discuss issues such as abortion. Some organizations offer this training for a fee, which may be paid by the candidate or activist or by another group. This activity is documented in case studies, but there has been no effort to measure its frequency and extent.
- Contributions to candidates. We know about PAC contributions through carefully maintained and generally high-quality data from the Federal

Election Commission. Group contributions to other organizations that may help a candidate can sometimes be traced, but in many cases we know only what diligent scholars and reporters discover. Interest group contributions to unaffiliated 527 committees are partially transparent through IRS records, but contributions to 501(c)3 committees registering voters or 501(c)4 committees that distribute voter guides are not. Contributions to 501(c)6 committees run by business associations such as the Chamber of Commerce are not transparent.

- Contributions by group members and patrons. In theory we can trace contributions of employees of corporations, although in practice these records are far from complete and it is difficult to know if the contribution is linked to the company. Reporters have frequently written of substantial contributions and fundraising by corporate executives, and the Center for Responsive Politics attempts to trace corporate donors through various tributaries of campaign finance, but contributions to some committees are not disclosed. It is almost impossible to trace contributions from other types of group members—when a member of MoveOn.Org gives because of an e-mailed solicitation by the organization, or a member of Sierra Club responds to an endorsement in a magazine. Occasionally we can see the evidence of coordinated giving—in one election the Association of Trial Lawyers (ATLA) asked their members to contribute $212 to particular candidates, an amount that was large enough to be disclosed and unusual enough to stand out against the flood of other contributions.
- Television and radio advertisements. Because the reporting of these advertisements is not required for all groups, the best data come from the Wisconsin Advertising Project (WAP) (Freedman, Franz, and Goldstein 2004; Franz et al. 2008a), which codes television advertisements in major media markets. The unit of analysis is a single airing of a single advertisement, including the name of the sponsor, targeting information, and other key variables. The project distinguishes between issue ads and campaign ads. Radio advertisements are not included.
- Direct mail. Many organizations mail multiple pieces of information to their members, and to others who they believe may be receptive. Generally these mailings highlight the key issues of the organization, but in some cases the mailings focus on different issues, and are targeted at non-members. Direct mail packets can contain information designed to spur members to volunteer. Some studies have asked a random sample of potential voters to collect all direct mail for analysis, but we do not have systematic nationwide studies (Campbell and Monson 2007; Monson and Oliphant 2007).
- Internet advertising. Many organizations are actively involved in Internet campaigning, and devote significant numbers of web pages to information about candidates. In 2008 and again in 2010, many organizations

created video advertisements that were only shown on the Internet. In 2008, MoveOn.Org sponsored a contest to encourage students to create their own advertisements. Some were broadcast on television, but many were displayed on the organization's web page. Others were displayed on the Facebook pages of their creators. There is no systematic collection of data on Internet advertising.

- Volunteers. A number of organizations train volunteers to work phone banks, to canvas door to door, to register voters, and drive them to the polls. Some of these volunteers are paid, and in some cases this represents an attempt by the organization to disguise its activities. In other cases, however, the best volunteers are simply provided with training and a modest stipend to work outside of their home area. The AFL-CIO bussed hundreds of union members into critical states in the 2008 campaign. This activity is not systematically documented, but case studies of state and local elections have reported various estimates.

Why Basic Questions Matter

Questions about what counts as an interest group and what counts as election activity are critical to the key questions discussed at the start of this chapter and which continue to vex scholars. Moreover, without better measures of interest group activities, it will be difficult to answer these key questions.

Consider, for example, the question of why groups become involved in elections. Scholars have generally posited that electoral activity is connected with an organization's policy goals, so that elections either help groups change policies by establishing lobbying connections, or they help interest groups change politicians in order to advance their goals (Eismeier and Pollock 1986; Evans 1988; Ansolabehere, Snyder, and Tripathi 2002). Indeed, some interest groups contribute substantial sums to candidates who have no opponents, and many PACs have lobbyists as the key decision-makers. Yet some scholars have argued that the contributions made by interest groups are far too small to influence policy-makers, and that they should be conceived instead as simply consumption, or perhaps as fruit baskets and other social niceties (Ansolabehere, Figueiredo, and Snyder 2003; Milyo 2002). Yet our understanding of why groups become active in politics is likely to be flawed if we focus only on those organizations that form PACs, and measure only their PAC contributions. Although the research on PAC formation among corporations has yielded some important conclusions (Andres 1985; Masters and Keim 1985), some companies are involved in elections without substantial, or even any, PAC activity.

Questions about why interest groups adopt and change strategies have been central to the literature (Malbin et al. 2002; Francia 2006; Franz 2008), but to answer this question we must decide if the formation of organizations such as CBM or ACT constitutes strategic choices. It is also essential to trace all activities of interest groups, including not only, for example, a company's PAC contributions but any coordinated giving among its executives and any contributions to the Chamber of Commerce's efforts.[4]

Studies of the impact of interest group activity on elections must include all activity by these organizations. To estimate the effects of get-out-the-vote campaigns we must know their extent, and although voter recall of these contacts is useful, it may not be fully reliable. To estimate the effects of interest group ads we need to know about Internet advertising and mailings. This is important even to the study of candidate spending and campaigns. For example, the question of whether spending leads to greater voter information has typically focused on candidate spending, but in some cases this constitutes the majority of spending in a district or state, and in other cases is dwarfed by interest group efforts (Coleman and Manna 2000).

Finally, among the many challenges facing scholars who seek to study the impact of interest groups upon policy-making is that of measuring all activity and attributing it correctly to its sponsor. One recent study has done a remarkable job of combining lobbying and campaign efforts into comprehensive studies of policy-making (Baumgartner et al. 2009). The consistency of findings in this work is impressive, and it is likely that these findings would remain unchanged with better measures of campaign activity by interest groups. However, in order to fully know how interest group activities influence policy-making we would need to have complete measures of the efforts that these groups make in elections. Although scholars find this activity difficult to trace, it seems likely that lobbyists are eager to claim credit to policymakers.

Rethinking Interest Groups In Elections

It is becoming increasingly difficult to trace the activities of interest groups in elections, and there is increasing fluidity of resources and activities across cooperating organizations. Better disclosure laws are essential not only for scholars, but for the ability of citizens to hold their lawmakers accountable. While we wait for such laws, it is useful to reconsider the way we conceive of interest groups and elections.

Most extant research has conceived of interest groups as interested organizations. These organizations are posited to have policy goals, and their ability to pursue these goals is constrained by their resources, the political environment, law and regulations, and other factors. Organizational characteristics and decision-making rules affect strategic and tactical choices. For example, corporate PACs with lobbyists as key decision-makers give more money to incumbents, and unions and trade associations with federated structures frequently allow state or local bodies some say in allocation decisions (Wright 1985). Organizations may change their leaders or their decision-making structures, and thereafter reach different decisions (Bedlington 1999; Malbin et al. 2002). Of course, changes in leadership and decision-making processes may also be consequences of changes in strategies. These studies have greatly expanded our understanding of the decisions made by individual organizations.

However, as interest group activity in elections becomes increasingly opaque, it may be useful for scholars to focus less on individual organizations and more on group networks. Studies of networks and alliances of interest groups in lobbying are well established, but we need to develop better theories about interest group networks in elections. These theories allow us to treat strategic and tactical decisions by different organizations as connected and mutually contingent.

- Interest groups as communities of interest. Within communities of interest, groups often coordinate strategies, including some tactical specialization. The broad electoral activities of the Sierra Club leave the much smaller League of Conservation Voters free to focus independent expenditures against the "Dirty Dozen." By thinking of groups as networks of interest, it is possible to view activities by CBM and ASA as simply part of the pharmaceutical corporate network, without deciding if they constitute separate organizations or merely strategic choices.

  Scholars have looked at the ecology of group specialization in lobbying and more broadly, but there has been less work on how organizations specialize within campaigns (Gray and Lowery 1996; Bosso 2005). Although there is a substantial literature on the behavior of communities of groups in elections, there has been to date little work that has treated group tactical decisions as partially contingent upon the decisions of other organizations (Evans 1988; Magleby and Tanner 2004; Francia 2006).

- Interest groups as larger political networks. Interest groups can cooperate outside of their community of interest. Groups that work together may be thought of as part of larger political networks that cooperate and share information, in which groups learn from one another. These networks may be formal coalitions, such as the Arlington Group (a coalition of pro-life, pro-family organizations that has monthly meetings), but there are informal networks as well. In the 2000 campaign, the Sierra Club was one of several organizations that helped the NAACP launch an electoral arm that aired TV ads against George Bush (Malbin et al. 2002). In 2004, leaders of the Sierra Club, EMILY's List, and various unions helped to form 527 committees such as Americans Coming Together and The Media Fund to help coordinate their efforts (Weissman and Hassan 2006). In 2008 in a number of states, groups coordinated efforts on behalf of candidates across communities of interest (Magleby forthcoming(b)). If we think of interest groups as political networks, we can study the way in which various groups across issue areas coordinate strategies, where the decisions of one organization may affect those of other groups. This is a very real part of the Washington interest group community, and advances in networking theory and methodology may also allow for better quantitative studies. This is especially useful for studying coalitions within a party that seek to influence nominations.

- Interest groups as partisan networks. In the 1980s, many interest groups worked hard to maintain a bipartisan stance. However, although the Sierra Club and the NRA continue to support candidates of both parties, they increasingly confine their support in one party to safe incumbents, where their activity cannot affect the partisan balance in Congress. Scholars have come to describe interest groups as members of party networks (Schwartz 1990). Both quantitative and qualitative studies have revealed two distinct partisan networks that cooperate with party leaders and seek to maximize the number of legislators from one party (Herrnson 2009; Koger, Masket, and Noel 2009; Magleby forthcoming(b)). Party activists were key players in the formation of ACT and the Media Fund mentioned above, as well as the formation of American Crossroads in 2010. Treating interest groups as members of party networks invites us to trace the interactions with party leaders and interest groups, and to take seriously the strategic stake that groups have in which party controls the majority in Congress (Biersack, Herrnson, and Wilcox 1999). But groups that work together within a party network may work in opposition during party primaries and caucuses, so it may also be useful to think of nodes within a party network, or perhaps as factional networks.
- Interest groups as donor networks. Although it is especially difficult to trace donors with current disclosure laws, it may be profitable to view interest group activity in this way. In the late 2000s, some liberal interest groups proposed electoral projects to donors, and in some cases donors proposed organizational structures to implement them. Indeed, some donors insisted that groups to which they contributed show evidence of a cooperative plan. Donor networks may finance the same activity through different interest groups over time, or even through parties. In 1992 the Christian Coalition mobilized voters for George H.W. Bush, but in 2004 the Bush–Cheney committee and various Republican Party committees engaged in the same activity, frequently using the same messages. This activity was financed by the same types of donors—in many cases the same individuals.

New theorizing about interest groups in elections does not eliminate our need for better data. Indeed, quantitative studies of interest group networks require special measures of group interaction that may be difficult to obtain outside of limited circumstances (Koger, Masket, and Noel 2009; Masket et al. 2009). Although there has been some innovative network analysis using contributions and communications costs, these studies also suffer from the lack of full disclosure of campaign activity (Robbins and Tsvetovat 2008). Because existing quantitative data on connections between interest groups in campaigns are relatively limited, it may be more profitable now to blend quantitative and qualitative studies.

Notes

1. The Christian Coalition lost its tax-exempt status because the IRS concluded that its principal purpose was electoral activity.
2. Corporations that give to candidates without a PAC may not be seeking to avoid disclosure; corporate executives are solicited by candidates and may decide collectively to sponsor a fundraising table at a fundraising event.
3. Section 527 of the US tax code also includes PACs and a variety of other political committees, but in common usage the label has referred to a spate of newly formed committees that engaged primarily in issue advocacy. Congress in 1997 required the disclosure of contributions to and spending by 527 committees to the IRS, but this disclosure is both untimely and incomplete. The Federal Election Commission fined some 527 committees for engaging in electioneering without disclosing the activity to the Commission. Recent court rulings have allowed 527 committees to engage in direct electioneering ads.
4. Some studies have suggested that substantial portions of contributions in state legislative elections are bundled by groups (e.g., Marshall 1999).

Chapter 9

Media

The Complex Interplay of Old and New Forms

Diana Owen

The 2008 presidential election marked a turning point in the evolution of campaign media. It has been characterized as the first twenty-first-century campaign—an intensive campaign managed on multiple fronts that made extensive use of digital technologies alongside traditional strategies (Brownstein 2008). The election media environment now comprises a complex amalgamation of traditional and new media, and the interplay among them. Mainstream media, including television news, newspapers, and news magazines, maintain an important place in elections, while new media, especially online and digital communication platforms, have become more influential. Modern forms of campaign reporting, such as a citizen journalism and blogs, have emerged that complement and compete with the work of professional news organizations.

These developments in the campaign context reflect larger trends in the political media system which is in the midst of a fundamental restructuring that exhibits elements of both consolidation and fragmentation. Media institutions have become increasingly consolidated within a small number of large corporations. Message content is highly redundant across channels, even as the outlets for disseminating information have proliferated. At the same time, the media system has become highly fragmented. The number of available media options offering specialized content directed at specific audiences has multiplied. Micro-targeting, where political messages are tailored for particular segments of the media market, has become standard practice, including during campaigns (Howard 2006; Hillygus and Shields 2008).

These shifts in the media environment are altering the ways in which candidates contest for office, journalists cover elections, political parties and organized groups manage their campaign presence, and voters engage in the political process. To be successful, candidates must run sophisticated campaigns that embrace both established and novel media strategies. Professional journalists have been forced to coexist with amateur content creators. Journalists continue to cover campaigns using time-worn approaches, especially poll-heavy horserace journalism. They have also adopted the personalized, opinionated style of citizen journalism, and practice their craft in both traditional and new media venues. Voters, once relegated to the sidelines by traditional media, have become more active consumers, producers, and disseminators of campaign messages. With fewer professional journalists on the campaign trail (Steinberg 2008), citizen journalists have filled the gaps in on-site coverage of election events.

The developments in election media have influenced the balance of power in campaigns, as the tools available for managing messages have proliferated. Journalists and candidates historically have engaged in a tug-of-war to gain the upper hand in setting the election agenda. Candidates have been able to use new media to communicate to voting blocs at little or no cost, lessening their dependence on traditional "free" media. However, the same social networking and video-sharing sites that provide candidates exposure for little or no cost may be used by citizens to spread their own messages and images outside the control of campaign staffs (Gueorguieva 2008).

This chapter begins with an overview of recent developments in campaign media to provide a context for the subsequent discussion of new avenues for research. These sections will be guided by the basic questions: What are the major trends in campaign media over the last half century? What are the characteristics of the twenty-first-century media campaign? And, what implications do these trends have for the ways in which journalists cover elections, candidates run campaigns, and voters engage in electoral process? The chapter will then consider new directions for election media scholarship, especially the need to reconsider traditional research questions, revise theoretical assumptions, and engage novel methodologies. The opportunities for scholars to carve out new research paths are vast; thus, the discussion here will propose two agendas for research—mapping the election media system and exploring the fragmentation of media-related campaign participation. The chapter concludes with some informed speculation about the future of campaign media, as novel applications are adapted to the election context and new formats gain a stronger foothold.

The Evolution of Campaign Communication

The media system undergoes periodic transformations in response to technological, economic, social, and political developments that can directly influence elections. Advances in print technology, lower paper production and distribution costs, and increased education and higher literacy rates gave rise to the penny press in the 1830s which made news readily available to the mass public. Newspapers contributed to a growth in associational life, including vigorous mass-based political parties that organized behind particular candidates in elections (Schudson 1998). Candidates were evaluated on their ability to deliver oratorical masterpieces that were printed verbatim in the press (Jamieson 1988). Broadcast technology and the availability of radio changed the way in which people experienced politics, as they could now listen to events, like the national nominating conventions, unfold in real time. News magazines referred to 1924 as "the radio year," and predicted that candidates would do much of their campaigning over the airwaves. Radio changed the tone and content of campaign discourse, as candidates adopted a more personal, straightforward style, shortened their speeches, and tailored their messages to reach a broad audience (Clark 1962).

Television gave rise to the modern mass-media campaign, fundamentally altering the dynamics of elections. By 1980, campaigns had become candidate-centric, especially at the presidential level. Post-Watergate reforms of the presidential nominating process diminished the role of party elites and opened up the process to greater participation by the mass electorate. Contenders used television to take their messages directly to the public, circumventing political party control. Campaigns employed media management strategies to generate coverage and staged pseudo events that produced dramatic visuals that conformed to the character of the medium. Televised ads that emulated commercials for consumer products sold candidates using short, simple, direct messages. Broadcast debates, where voters could compare candidates' performances on the same stage, eventually became a staple of campaigns. Candidates abbreviated their speech-making even further, as seconds-long sound bites were more conducive to television coverage than detailed addresses (Patterson 1980; Owen 1991; Hart 1999).

Recent developments in campaign communication coincide with transformations that have been underway for about a quarter of a century. The twenty-first-century media system departs fundamentally from that of earlier eras, and is marked by contradictions: consolidation and fragmentation, broadcasting and narrowcasting, stability and innovation. Traditional mass media affiliated with large conglomerates, such as television nightly news, newspapers, and news magazines, continue to form the backbone of the media system, despite being faced with financial and structural challenges. However, the number and variety of platforms accommodating political content have expanded exponentially. New political media, ranging from old mediums that have assumed new political roles to cutting-edge technologies that facilitate genuine innovations in political communication, have become an integral part of the electoral process.

The broadcast model of communication, which is predicated upon mass media widely disseminating messages of general societal interest, is associated with traditional media, especially television and radio. Historically, this model was predicated upon delivery systems that involve public ownership of scarce resources, especially the radio and television spectrum. These media were subject to regulation and oversight, which included the requirement that programming fulfill a public service imperative (McQuail 2000). The broadcast model is still very much in evidence, as corporate media organizations continue to thrive. Collectively, new media have precipitated movement away from the broadcast model of communication to a narrowcasting model. Many forms of new media disseminate specialized messages aimed at particular individuals or groups. From a business perspective, the term was initially associated with media that were made available to customers by subscription. Narrowcasting has become more broadly construed, and refers to media whose content is selectively directed toward specialized audiences (Mendelsohn and Nadeau 1996). Some election media exhibit characteristics of both broadcasting and narrowcasting models, especially hybrid forms. News websites, for example, make generalized information available to visitors while at the same time limiting specific content to subscribers.

The Era of New Media

The new media era may be viewed in terms of three overlapping phases of development. During the first period, which began in the late 1980s and early 1990s, well-established entertainment media formats supported by old-style communications technologies became more prominent in the political realm. These new media lacked a public service imperative, and their development was motivated heavily by profits. The second phase, initiated in the mid-1990s, was marked by the arrival of novel political platforms made possible by technological innovations, especially computer networks such as the Internet and World Wide Web, and e-mail. These new media were distinguished by their ability to subvert the top-down structure of traditional communication, and the interactivity between users that they made possible. The third phase in the evolution of political media witnessed an expansion of the ways in which technological tools are used for communication. These applications, labeled Web 2.0 when technologists first drew attention to them in 2004, are marked by higher levels of interactive information sharing, engagement, networking, collaboration, and community building than in the past. While audience members could comment on stories written by journalists in the Web 1.0 era, communities of users can now use wikis and social networking sites to collaboratively generate their own content. This phase of media evolution is closely associated with the twenty-first-century media campaign, as the 2008 presidential election stimulated and made visible these innovations in political communication.

Old Media, New Politics

Talk radio is perhaps most emblematic of the first generation of new media. A moribund medium by the 1970s, call-in talk radio was revitalized as a political forum as the First Gulf War and a spate of high-profile legal cases, including the 1991 sexual assault trial of William Kennedy Smith and the 1995 O.J. Simpson murder trial, stimulated public discussion (Davis and Owen 1999). As Baby Boomers' preferences moved from music to talk and their interests shifted from local to national concerns, the medium developed a steady following. Developments in satellite technology made it easy and cost-effective to broadcast talk programs nationally. The new talk radio was nascent in the 1988 presidential contest; four years later it had become a vigorous political force. Talk show hosts, such as popular conservative Rush Limbaugh, continue to use their platform to influence like-minded voters (Barker 2002; Jamieson 2008). Candidates on both sides of the aisle employ talk radio to recruit supporters and energize their base (Owen 1997).

Entertainment media, such as television talk shows and news magazine programs, print tabloids, and music television (MTV), also incorporated more political content into their offerings. Cable television and the proliferation of channels made numerous news and entertainment options available during election campaigns at both local and national levels. These new political media, with their infotainment focus, were able to reach voters who typically did not pay attention to hard news. Some candidates, such as Republican presidential contender George H.W. Bush in 1992, were reluctant to court new media outlets, worrying that they undermined the dignity of the office. Others, such as Bush's opponent Bill Clinton, embraced new media as a mechanism for subverting traditional media gatekeeping that limited candidates' ability to speak for themselves and control their campaign messaging strategies (Patterson 1993, 2002). Clinton donning shades and playing "Heartbreak Hotel" on the sax on the *Arsenio Hall Show* has become a symbol of this early aspect of new media. Trailing in the polls, Clinton used the appearance to appeal to young people and minority voters. During that same election, Ross Perot went on *Larry King Live* and told voters he would run for president if they would organize on his behalf, igniting his Reform Party candidacy. Candidates' talk show appearances have become a campaign staple. David Letterman quipped, "The road to the White House runs through me," as candidates made over 110 appearances on late-night television during the 2008 presidential election (Center for Media and Public Affairs 2008: 1).

The Net Campaign Takes Shape

The Internet has been present in presidential elections since 1992, and is the hallmark of the second phase of new media development. The Clinton campaign established a rudimentary website that functioned primarily as brochure-ware, providing textual information that resembled the candidate's promotional literature, including biographical material and position papers. The site received few visits from voters or journalists. The Bush campaign did not have a web presence (Davis 1999; Bimber and Davis 2003). Clinton's organization also made limited use of the Internet and e-mail to facilitate discussion among elite supporters (Foot and Schneider 2006). The Internet's role in campaigns has grown incrementally since that time, as existing platforms have become more sophisticated and new applications have been developed.

By the 2000 election, all of the major candidates and many minor contenders had websites that primarily featured transcripts of speeches and issue statements (Owen and Davis 2008; Foot and Schneider 2006). Platforms that allowed voters to express their views and debate the merits of candidates, issues, and the campaign, including blogs and discussion boards, had become commonplace by the 2004 election (Lawson-Borders and Kirk 2005). Citizens took on roles similar to reporters by providing information and commentary. Still, the vast majority of campaign news stories, especially those that reached sizable audiences, was produced and distributed by mainstream media organizations (Owen and Davis 2008).

Prior to 2008, only a small proportion of the electorate accessed online campaign media. News sites received limited traffic (Scheufele and Nisbet 2002; Bimber and Davis 2003; Foot and Schneider 2006), and few people took advantage of blogging and online discussion functions during campaigns (Owen and Davis 2008). The percentage of voters who relied on the Internet to learn about the election was 9 percent in 2000 and 13 percent in 2004 (Pew Research Center 2008b). Evidence that exposure to online campaign communication translated into increased interest, knowledge, engagement, or likelihood of voting was mixed. Bimber (2003) found scant support for the contention that online news exposure contributed to political participation, civic engagement, or information seeking (Bimber 2003; Weaver and Drew 2001). Voters tended to access election websites in order to reinforce their political predispositions rather than to learn anything new (Mutz and Martin 2001; Park and Perry 2008). However, Internet news users can exhibit increased levels of political efficacy and participation (Johnson and Kaye 2003; Lupia and Philpot 2005), as well as a greater tendency to vote (Tolbert and McNeal 2003).

The Twenty-First Century Media Campaign

The 2008 presidential contest ushered in a new era in campaigning that coincides with the third phase of the new media's evolution. The communication environment encompassed an elaborate assortment of traditional mass media and new media, and showcased a range of innovations. The campaign marked another step in the development of an election media system where traditional and new sources coexist, complement, compete, and conflict with one another. Election media both drove and were influenced by dramatic advancements in candidates' campaign strategies, which have become more decentralized and specialized (Vaccari 2008). Candidates were able to bypass media gatekeepers and get their message out to voters directly via an assortment of alternative digital platforms, including their own highly sophisticated web presences. They also benefitted from and were targeted by messages generated by organizations and voters independent of candidate committees and political parties. The opportunities for people to follow the campaign and become informed were nearly boundless. The mechanisms for citizen interaction and direct campaign involvement via media were unprecedented.

Traditional Election Media Endure

It is premature to declare the "end of mass media" that some scholars have predicted (Bennett 2005; Miller 2008). Mainstream press coverage remains a fixture of campaigns, especially as the majority of original reporting still emanates from professional journalists. The audience for traditional media continues to outnumber that for new media, as the majority of people rely on mainstream news at least some of the time. Television news remains the public's main source of election information, although the percentage of loyal viewers has dropped as users move to online sources. Sixty-eight percent of voters named television as their primary source in 2008 compared to 76 percent in 2004 (Pew Research Center 2008b). More people still read print newspapers than their online counterparts, although the number of print subscribers has plummeted. In 2010, print papers were read by nearly 100 million adults per day compared to the 74 million unique visitors drawn to newspaper websites per month (Vanacore 2010). A growing audience segment relies on a combination of old and online media (Pew Research Center 2008a).

It is important to recognize developments that influence campaign coverage by the mainstream press that have consequences for new media as well. The 2008 presidential election brought the challenges facing the traditional news industry into full view. Presidential campaigns have become protracted affairs that effectively begin years before the first candidates officially declare their intentions to run. Media coverage is an essential element of the meta-campaign where candidates test their viability, raise funds, recruit key supporters, and attempt to generate awareness among voters. Maintaining interest in an election that may be years in the making is a difficult and resource-intensive task that can tax professional news operations. Financial cutbacks, the result of dropping advertising revenues and declining audiences (Plambeck 2010), coupled with the increased costs associated with newsgathering have caused media organizations to downsize their reporting staffs and limit the number of professional journalists on the campaign trail. Print news reporters who witness events first hand traditionally have been the source of original, in-depth stories that are frequently repurposed by other outlets and can set the agenda for the campaign (Roberts 2008). In 2008, only about two dozen print news organizations assigned journalists to travel "on the bus" with the candidates, reducing the amount of fresh eye-witness copy that was produced by professionals. The perspectives of journalists working for a small number of major publications, including the *New York Times*, the *Wall Street Journal*, the *Washington Post*, the *Los Angeles Times*, the *Chicago Tribune*, and *Newsweek*, were over-represented (Steinberg 2008; Owen 2009).

Established media organizations have been forced to adapt to the shifting communication environment to remain competitive. Traditional media have incorporated elements of both the broadcasting and narrowcasting models into their product, resulting in the development of hybrid media forms. The online counterparts of print newspapers and television news programs have incorporated new media innovations, including blogs and discussion boards, video sharing, and social networking features, into their election reporting. Professional media platforms have included the work of amateurs through eyewitness reporting, commentary, and photo and video postings. Amateur accounts of campaign events, in some instances, became primary source material for professional journalists, who did much of their reporting from the newsroom rather than on the campaign trail.

The Net Campaign Arrives

For years, scholars, political operatives, and journalists have harkened the advent of a new era in political campaigns, prematurely labeling recent presidential elections as "The Internet Election," "Campaign 2.0," and "The Digital Election" (Vaccari 2008). There is substantial evidence to suggest that the "net campaign" had finally arrived in 2008. As Gulati observes, "Not only did the Internet become fully institutionalized as a media platform, but also the range of online applications expanded" (2009: 187). The amount of campaign content populating the Internet increased exponentially in volume and diversity, and the audience grew significantly in size, dedication, and activation.

Perhaps the most significant development of the campaign online in 2008 was the increase in the amount and diversity of user-created content online. Non-professionals made use of the easily accessible tools afforded by the Internet and other digital technologies to generate news and information for public dissemination. Campaign blogs proliferated, running the gamut from rudimentary personal journals to professional quality platforms that resemble online newspapers, such as *Talking Points Memo* and *Huffington Post*. *Scoop08* was an online paper compiled entirely by junior high, high school, and college students with the assistance of an impressive editorial board of experienced journalists. This paper was so successful during the campaign that it was reincarnated after the election as *Scoop44*, a youth-run platform covering the Obama administration. Voters also made path-breaking use of video sharing sites, posting on-the-spot video reports and vlogs, creating original video ads and content streams, and generating sophisticated mash-ups mixing old and new content. These efforts were recognized and appropriated by candidates, campaign organizations, political parties, and journalists, which especially enhanced young voters' role in the electoral process (Owen 2008).

Another indication that 2008 was a landmark campaign for media is the size of the new media audience. While in past campaigns new media served as a supplement to traditional sources, especially television news and newspapers (Owen and Davis 2007), 36 percent of the public regularly depended on online news in 2008 (Pew Research Center 2008a). A majority of voters—nearly 60 percent—consulted the Internet at some point during the campaign, especially to find out information about candidates, issues, and the electoral process. Young people were especially inclined to use digital election media. Twenty-five percent of 18- to 24-year-olds stated that they got their news primarily online versus 7 percent of those over age 45. An expanding cohort of older voters used online sources for election information. In fact, citizens over age 60 were more inclined to read campaign blogs regularly than were younger people (Harris Interactive 2008). The Internet's ability to convey fast-breaking news throughout the campaign contributed to its popularity (Pew Research Center 2008; Gulati 2009; Owen 2009).

There is reason to temper somewhat the enthusiasm about 2008 as a game-changing election. While there were many new opportunities for individuals to take advantage of the Internet's participatory functions, many users treated the online information environment primarily as an extension of traditional media. Voters were far less inclined to engage the interactive features of online communication, even when they were literally right at their fingertips. The public's use of the interactive features of the Internet, including e-mail, text messaging, and social networking sites, in 2008 far exceeded that of previous elections. Still, the number of people who regularly engaged in these forms of interactive communication was relatively small. Only 7 percent of the public communicated with others daily about the campaign through e-mail, text messaging, or social networking sites, with an additional 14 percent doing so once a week. Only 5 percent of the population posted to a blog, discussion board/listserv, Facebook or MySpace page, or any other online platform (Pew Research Center 2008b). Furthermore, the excitement over the novel digital applications that emerged during the nominating campaign waned significantly during the general election, where the old-style, television-dominated mass-media campaign predominated (Owen 2009). Still, the landmark developments of the 2008 presidential contest have carried over to the 2010 midterm elections, and they are likely to take hold more fervently in the 2012 presidential contest.

New Directions in Election Media Research

Research on election campaigns in the current era has largely continued to address long-standing, central questions. Who is producing campaign media messages, for what audiences, and for what purpose? What is the nature of election media content? Who are the audiences for particular kinds of campaign media? How do election media affect voters? Studies have enhanced our knowledge of the role of journalists, candidates, and campaign operatives in producing and distributing campaign messages. There is a cottage industry of

scholarship dealing with campaign communication content, especially cata-
loging the type of information that is disseminated via particular platforms
and how messages are framed by the media. Researchers have examined election media audiences to determine their communication preferences, their
reasons for attending to media, and the effects of campaign messages on their
knowledge, attitudes, and behavior. Political communication scholars guided
by these basic questions have made enormous contributions to our understanding of election media and their effects.

The distinct qualities of the twenty-first century election media environment have compelled researchers to consider standard questions in light of
current developments and to initiate new lines of inquiries. Given the growing
volatility in election media across campaigns, it makes sense to identify the
developments that are lasting and the trends that are transitional. Some questions that might guide research include: What kinds of media are operative
during a given election cycle, and why? What are the functions of particular
media in campaigns, and have these functions been modified over time? The
nature and behavior of election media audiences has changed fundamentally.
The media landscape is populated by communities of users of all sizes and
configurations, rather than by individual audience members, begging the
question: How have the audiences for specific election media formed, stabi-
lized, or changed, and how are they using campaign communication? How
have communities formed around election media? What kinds of campaign
activities do election media promote? The media system is reshaping the relationship between existing institutions as media professionals no longer maintain control over message production and distribution. This development
leads to the question: How is media influence determined and measured in
modern-day election campaigns?

There is a need to revisit established theoretical frameworks and methodologies, and to consider them in light of new election media realities. Karpf's
observation about the blogosphere rings true for election media scholars
today: "One of the chief problems the initial generation of Internet researchers faced was that, as the blogosphere expanded, it was adopted in new and
unexpected manners that didn't fit within the boundaries of our research
program" (Karpf 2009: 68). Theoretical frameworks should consider the
unique characteristics of new media, with their inherent multi-path interactivity, flexibility, unpredictability, and opportunities for more active engagement. Theories should also be developed to generate greater understanding of
the challenge to entrenched media hierarchies and their consequences.

Theories of media uses and gratifications provide an illustration of how
existing theoretical frameworks might be updated. Uses and gratifications
approaches aim to explain the ways in which audience members are motivated to use media to meet particular needs. They assume that the ability of
particular platforms to satisfy people's expectations can lead "to differential
patterns of media exposure, attention, or other related behaviors" (Blumler

and McQuail 1969). Common motivations for media use developed during the mass media era include: (1) information seeking and surveillance/media monitoring, (2) developing and reinforcing a sense of personal identity, integration, social interaction, (3) maintaining personal relationships, and (4) entertainment, diversion, escapism, and relaxation (McQuail, Blumler, and Brown 1972).

Uses and gratifications models have been updated since their inception in the 1940s to reflect advances in communication theory and method as well as changes in the media system (see Ruggeiro 2000). While earlier models assumed a passive audience, scholars, in keeping with changes in media and society, have reconceptualized audience activity as a variable concept that ranges from accidental and passive exposure to user-directed selective exposure to particular media (Levy and Windahl 1984). Digital media, including the Internet, encompass a "new dominion of human activity," and so represent a "new dominion for uses and gratifications researchers" (Ruggeiro 2000). The novel functions of new media are associated with new uses and accompanying gratifications that are more active and goal-directed. The standard inventory of media uses and gratifications has been modified to reflect the interdependent functions and activities associated with new media. These media uses include: (1) consuming, defined as watching, reading, or viewing media, but never using media actively; (2) participating, which involves interactions between users or between users and content, such as sharing election-related e-mails, but not actual content production; and (3) producing, which includes the creation of personal content, such as the production of election-related images, text, video, and ads (Shao 2008).

Uses and gratifications theory can be a useful tool for explaining how and why audiences choose between the plethora of campaign news media. Well-established media uses—surveillance, or maintaining a general awareness of the campaign, and information-seeking about candidates and issues—remain the most prevalent uses of online resources by voters (Davis 1999; Bimber and Davis 2003; Foot and Schneider 2006). Voters still used new media primarily for surveillance and information-seeking in 2008, but they had many options for a more engaged election media experience. The ability not only to comment about, but contribute to, news and information across digital formats transformed what in an earlier era was a passive enterprise to active engagement. The entertainment function of campaign media evolved beyond mere exposure to and enjoyment of election-related comedy. Individuals could readily access a wealth of campaign-related comedy and satire, share amusing material with others, and develop their own content for pleasure. The comedic material available online was some of the most frequently accessed content. Satiric videos, like *Saturday Night Live*'s Tina Fey doing her impression of Republican vice-presidential candidate Sarah Palin, were widely circulated in their original format and as part of user-produced mash-ups.

In addition, orthodox methodologies should be reconsidered in light of the novel characteristics of digital media. Standard content analysis, survey research, and focus groups should be updated for the new media age or used in conjunction with cutting-edge methods. Some of the very same tools that are employed by users of digital media may be used by scholars to collect and analyze data. Electronic sources, such as blogs, discussion forums, and e-mail boxes, can function as archives of material that can be automatically searched, retrieved, extracted, and examined using tools, such as WebCAT and ranks.nl. Audience analysis can also benefit from fresh methodological approaches. People do not consume news online in the same linear fashion that they read the morning newspaper. Instead, they explore news offerings by following a series of links to particular content. Hindman (2009) employed Web crawler techniques to uncover evidence of online communities based around particular topics, and tracked the paths users take to get to the sites that they visit. He discovered that search engines drive users to a shortlist of news sites that receive the majority of news traffic.

Mapping the Election Media System

In the past, it was possible to differentiate types of election media based on their distinct characteristics and functions, and to study them accordingly. Media platforms, for the most part, were uniquely associated with a limited number of communications technologies and delivery systems—print, film, broadcast radio and television, and more recently, cable television, and satellite radio and television. Particular media could be characterized by the source of their messages, the form and substance of their content, and the traits of their audiences which remained fairly stable over time. The functions served by specific platforms, such as providing information, advertising, and entertaining, as well as the litany of potential effects, were fairly well demarcated.

Communications researchers today are exploring territory that is largely uncharted and constantly changing. The distinctions between media based on form and function that long delineated the direction of media research are no longer relevant. The lines between what constitutes election news have been blurred, as professional journalists have been joined by a range of information producers and distributors. The election media environment is shifting at an extraordinary pace due largely to the flexibility and adaptability of digital technologies. Platform innovation, content creation, and message dissemination are no longer the exclusive domain of media and campaign industry professionals. Some forms of campaign media change appreciably from election to election. As we have seen, candidate websites have undergone significant modifications in every election since 1992, evolving from basic brochure-ware to dynamic, multifunctional platforms that provide news and information to voters and journalists. Some communications media that are prominent in one campaign can practically disappear by the next.

A comprehensive and dynamic map of the election media system would benefit researchers in a variety of ways. First, it would track organizational shifts in the campaign media environment, including the rapid deployment of new media, the hybridization and morphing of election media, the evolution of communication formats, and the departure of platforms that can quickly become outmoded. It would also catalog the diverse and expanding functions of twenty-first century election media. Functions associated with passive audiences, such as serving as sources of information and entertainment, have been augmented by functions that stimulate active engagement, such as the creation of user-generated text and videos. In addition, a map of election media would facilitate studies of the increasingly complex interactions between platforms and communicators. Studies might explore the extent to which a symbiotic relationship exists between professional journalists and bloggers, and the degree to which content from party and candidate websites is reprocessed in other media venues.

Mapping a media system that is in constant flux requires new methodological approaches that can track dynamic developments that are consistent with the current media reality. Traditional print manuscripts can only partially convey the elaborate and fluid evolution of election media. A static medium is not entirely appropriate for conveying knowledge about interactive communication forms such as text messaging and social networking. Digital tools, such as online timeline creators, can visually chart the development of particular media as they emerge, evolve, mature, morph, or disappear. They may be used to record the development of hybrid media, indicating when, where, and how new media applications have been incorporated into established media platforms. They can provide concrete illustrations, as opposed to mere written descriptions. They can also allow users to experience interactive media directly, and offer more compelling examples of the phenomena under study. Dippity. com, xtimeline.com, timetoast.com, and timeglider.com are examples of open-source digital platforms that might be employed to map election media. They allow users to create multimedia timelines that integrate text, photos, videos, audio recordings, and events that can be easily shared.

In addition to displaying the evolution of the media system, digital maps/ timelines can become data sources in and of themselves. Digital utilities can be programmed to search vast online archives and organize the accumulated information into databases. The analysis and presentation of data are not limited to established techniques, but can also employ novel approaches, such as interactive, multimedia graphics (see Nisbet 2010; Secor 2010). Dippity. com, for example, has a built-in map interface that allows trends to be displayed hierarchically, by key values, or by definition offering researchers countless possibilities. Particular platforms, such as YouTube, Twitter, or Politico, can be isolated for study. Video-sharing as a concept can be researched across media. Trends in news media websites can be explored during a particular timeframe.

Election Media Diversification and Fragmentation

It is clear that the trademark of the twenty-first century election media system is the escalating number of platforms performing an expanding range of functions that are readily available to voters. The diversification of election media heightens the possibility for campaign audience fragmentation. Voters can specifically tailor their media consumption to conform to their personal tastes, interests, and needs. Users can customize their election media experience based on the content to which they are exposed, the platform through which it is disseminated, and the activities that particular media will enable (Chaffee and Metzger 2001; Tewksbury 2005). At the same time, the overabundance of choice may be a source of frustration to some voters, who must navigate a complex maze of competing platforms and messages. While some voters seek guidance through communities that have formed within the digital culture (Jenkins 2006), others employ mechanisms to simplify their search. They engage in selective exposure, deliberatively choosing to attend to information that reflects their pre-existing beliefs and avoiding content that is antithetical to their views. Some scholars contend that such behavior results in the creation of "echo chambers," where amenable messages are amplified and irrefutable (Jamieson and Cappella 2008). Others have expressed concern that fragmentation of media exposure will lead to social atomization and partisan polarization, especially as citizens will no longer unite around shared mediated political experiences, such as election campaign events (Katz 1996; Prior 2007; Stroud 2007).

Fragmentation of Media Exposure in 2008

Media fragmentation was apparent during the 2008 presidential election, as audience segments were drawn to particular platforms. Young voters, in particular, used digital media that provided novel and accessible outlets for disseminating new information and repurposing old content. Not only did young people access campaign information online, via cell phones, and on their PDAs to the exclusion of traditional sources, they also produced content that gained widespread attention from candidates and the mainstream press.

Comparing the use patterns of specific online media across age groups provides an illustration of the extent to which campaign media orientations can be fragmented. To make this comparison, data from the Pew Internet and American Life Project, November 2008 Post-Election Tracking Survey were analyzed. Table 9.1 depicts the percentage of adults who regularly used specific online campaign media during the 2008 presidential election by age category (18–24, 25–9, 30–45, and 46+). The types of media range from Internet portal news sites, like Google and Yahoo news, the news sites of television, newspaper, and radio organizations, issue-oriented websites, government websites, international news sites, satire sites, alternative media sites, news and campaign blogs and commentary sites, candidate websites, video posting and sharing sites, social networking sites, and discussion forums. The analysis depicts voters' exposure to a wide range of sources during the 2008 election, although the data do not begin to take into account the full spectrum of available media. The data provide evidence of both the consolidation and fragmentation of exposure to election media. Age differences in the regular use of all types of campaign media were apparent and statistically significant. Generally speaking, young people were more inclined to use online election media than other, older cohorts. People over age 46 were the least likely to use any of the online sources. However, patterns of use differed notably across platforms. Websites associated with established media organizations had higher traffic overall than more novel formats. The more novel and innovative platforms, such as satire sites, fact-checking sites, video-sharing sites, social networking sites, and discussion forums, attracted fewer visitors. The percentage of people accessing network television, major newspaper, local news, international news, issue-orientated websites, and blogs was similar for the first three age categories encompassing people aged 18 to 45. The youngest cohort—18- to 24-year-olds—made substantially more use of video-sharing and social networking sites than did other age groups.

Fragmentation of Campaign Activation

The issue of media diversification is commonly addressed in terms of fragmentation of media exposure and its consequences for public opinion and democratic discourse. Constraining the analysis of fragmentation to issues surrounding exposure was most appropriate in an era when mass media dominated, and audience activation via media was limited. Another potential outcome of the diversification of media is the fragmentation of electoral engagement. In the mass media era, journalists and news personalities typically felt that their responsibility was to inform, and not necessarily to engage the public actively in politics. Today, however, campaign media are increasingly providing pathways to both well-established and innovative forms of political participation. As citizens' media experiences become more individualized over time, it is likely that their campaign activation will become more fragmented as well.

Scholars have focused on examining the link between campaign communication and well-established forms of political participation, including volunteering, contributing, contacting, discussing the election with others, expressing opinions, attending campaign events, and voting, and rightly so. Even in an era of burgeoning new media formats, these types of campaign engagement are most prevalent and meaningful (Hindman 2009). Digital media often have enhanced opportunities for voters to take part in these kinds of activities as well as creating occasions for innovative forms of involvement. The most visible of the raft of new applications in 2008, especially those

Table 9.1 Percentage of People Regularly Using Online Election Media in 2008 by Age

Source	18–24 (%)	25–29 (%)	30–45 (%)	46+ (%)	χ^2 sign
Portal news like Google and Yahoo	49	51	39	19	0.00
Network TV (CNN, ABC, MSNBC)	54	55	48	23	0.00
Major newspapers (USA Today, NYT)	29	27	25	13	0.00
Local news	32	38	35	18	0.00
Issue-oriented websites	32	38	35	18	0.00
State or Local government	21	22	17	10	0.00
Alternative (alternet.org, Newsmax)	17	18	17	11	0.00
International news (BBC, Al Jazeera)	8	6	8	4	0.00
Radio news organization (NPR)	21	26	17	8	0.00
Satire (the Onion, Colbert)	25	15	15	5	0.00
Fact checking (Factcheck.org)	11	15	15	8	0.00
News-related or political blogs	25	20	20	9	0.00
Read campaign or political commentary on group site, or blog	37	35	28	16	0.00
Obama Website	45	30	31	23	0.00
McCain Website	28	28	34	15	0.00
Campaign photos, video	21	16	17	8	0.00
Independent audio, video	16	18	19	11	0.00
Networking Site	31	14	8	1	0.00
Discussion forum	14	12	7	3	0.00

Source: Pew Internet and American Life Project, November 2008 Post-Election Tracking Survey. Data analyzed by the author.

related to video-sharing and social networking, were well publicized and subject to scholarly scrutiny. These new forms of involvement included posting amateur campaign YouTube videos and promoting campaign events on Facebook.

Yet other unique forms of campaign engagement have attracted little attention from researchers because few people as yet are taking part in them. For example, voters were micro-targeting colleagues with similar interests by creating and posting specialized campaign content in non-political spaces, such as sports, entertainment, and cooking websites. Individuals created their own campaign websites independent of official candidate organizations that were used to engage people in novel offline activities. One online platform recruited volunteers who were bussed to events, urged to create their own text video presentations about the campaign, and encouraged to disseminate them through their personal platforms. These forms of high-end campaign activation involve dedication and commitment, as well as organizational and technical skills. While such efforts are to date isolated, the cumulative effects potentially can be significant, and may become more relevant in future campaigns.

Scholars might dig more deeply into the digital realm to uncover non-obvious forms of media-related campaign activation. They might catalog activities based on criteria including the level and type of election activity and the specific media platform associated with each form of engagement. Media-related election activities can range from passive forms, such as monitoring campaign media, to interactive forms, like responding to a blog post or forwarding a campaign e-mail, and active forms, including initiating an independent online fundraising effort on behalf of a candidate. A profile of the users engaged in the activity can be developed based on their demographic profile, their political orientations, and their media use habits. The extent of the activation—whether it involves many or just a few people—may also be gauged.

Conclusion

It is risky to make sweeping claims about sea changes in election media in the aftermath of a campaign. Yet there are substantive indicators that the trends witnessed in the 2008 election are not fleeting, but instead herald the arrival of the twenty-first century media election. Not only did voters use the Internet and digital media more often in 2008 than in the past for information seeking, communicating, and participating; their basic orientations to media shifted. Online news media became the main source of information for many, and an integral component of their election media regimen for others. Voters became aware of the electoral applications of social networking and video-sharing platforms. While the political user base for these applications was relatively small, it is bound to expand in subsequent elections.

What happened with election media in 2008 is indicative of the shape of things to come. The review of the evolution of the modern election media system indicates that the growth and diversity of campaign media and innovation has been exponential since 1992. As the foregoing discussion indicates, it is becoming increasingly difficult to differentiate traditional journalism as practiced by professionals from novel platforms that allow amateurs to create and distribute campaign information. *Huffington Post*, for example, is a community blogging platform with over 3000 contributors that physically resembles an online newspaper. The headlines and news agenda are frequently similar to those of daily newspapers, but the story contents differ vastly, with the blog featuring soft news integrated with commentary while online newspapers reflect established journalistic practices.

Election campaigns serve as incubators where innovative media applications are developed and applied. Following the 2008 presidential election, the Obama administration sought to incorporate new media innovations that were effective in connecting the campaign to voters in the election to link up with constituents. As an expanding array of actors with seemingly boundless creativity engages with increasingly sophisticated technologies, the complexity and uncertainty surrounding election media will certainly deepen. The realm of possible online and digital applications suitable to the electoral context has only begun to be exploited.

It is essential that communication research keep pace with the revolutionary developments associated with the twenty-first century election media environment. The application and development of theories, methodologies, and modes of analysis must be forward-thinking. The future of election media research requires that scholars step outside the box of academic conformity, and develop innovative research strategies, utilize new investigative tools, and present their findings in multimedia formats that can best represent the phenomena under investigation.

## Chapter 10

Voting Behavior

Traditional Paradigms and Contemporary Challenges

Andrew Dowdle, Pearl K. Ford, and Todd G. Shields

Comprehending how and why voters behave the way they do is an important aspect in understanding the outcomes of political campaigns and evaluating the health of a democracy. While decades of political science research have shed considerable light on this subject, there is still a great deal of controversy about the relative weight of specific influences and how widely applicable these findings are. In fact, as we argue in this chapter, the growing numbers of voters who do not always follow the standard patterns of presidential voting, such as African Americans, women, Latinos, and other minority groups, present a substantial challenge to existing models of presidential voting behavior and represent the new directions that scholars of voting must focus on in order to understand voting in the twenty-first century.

One of the oldest and most widely accepted paradigms of voter behavior is the "Michigan model," which holds that most voters form an attachment to a political party relatively early on in life, largely the result of familial influence. In the minds of most voters, this sense of affiliation, or "partisan identification," has a greater influence on their vote decision than other factors such as ideology or a candidate's stances on particular issues. While there have been a number of challenges to this model during the past half-century, most political scientists have agreed that the dominant influence in the decision-making process of the typical voter is party identification.

However, the past decade has also produced a number of challengers to the Michigan model that will be reviewed in this chapter. Despite the model's emphasis on partisan identification as opposed to ideology, a number of social and demographic factors such as race, religion, geographic region and gender all play an important role in shaping partisan affiliation and vote choice as well. These variables had an important impact in the elections of the past decade, especially in the 2008 presidential contest. In fact, it is very difficult to fully explain the outcome of the 2008 presidential election without also considering how these emerging groups make decisions and the ways in which they may differ from our popular paradigms.

Seminal Breakthroughs in Voter Research: Are the Voters Fools?

The academic study of voter behavior began around the 1920s. These initial studies were limited in geographic scope and methodologically unsophisticated by today's standards. These early works did, however, call into question the idealized version of the typical citizen as interested, informed, and active in civic life that had been assumed by many scholars.[1] For example, when Charles Merriam and Harold Gosnell (1924) found that a large percentage of Chicago citizens were indifferent and knew very little about their local elections, many political scientists were concerned that the general public might be incapable of making informed and rational decisions about political issues and candidates. Prominent political scientists such as Harold Lasswell actually questioned whether public discussions of controversial issues would lead to outbreaks of violence. Instead of open discourse, irrational voters needed to be guided by more sophisticated and rational political elites as well as academics trained in the social sciences (Lasswell 1930; Ricci 1984).

Although voter interest and electoral turnout increased during the 1930s and 1940s, academic studies of voters during the post-World War II period were overwhelmingly pessimistic.[2] For example, the work by Philip Converse (1964) represents a typical criticism of the inadequacies of the average citizen.[3] According to Converse, the typical American did not possess a well-developed or consistent ideology that drove their political decision-making. Instead, an individual's identification with a particular political party heavily influenced their political decisions. This sense of affiliation, commonly known as party identification, was formed early on in life and nurtured by primary social groups such as the family. Since friends and co-workers are typically from similar backgrounds, they tend to reinforce these beliefs instead of challenging them.[4] The pre-eminence of parental socialization and party identification was solidified by the work of the so-called "Michigan School." Using survey results from the 1948, 1952, and 1956 elections, Angus Campbell, Converse, Warren Miller, and Donald Stokes argued in their seminal work *The American Voter* that because parental socialization occurs early on in life, it has a particularly strong influence. Once party identification forms, this strong psychological attachment remains stable and is unlikely to change during the course of an individual's life (Campbell et al. 1960). Further, because most voters lack a well-developed belief system or ideology (Converse 1964), party identification often served as a lens through which citizens viewed the world, served as the catalyst for which otherwise uninterested citizens were drawn into politics, and served as the mental heuristic for political decisions.

Challenges to the Michigan School

The Michigan School's findings about the importance of partisan identification in individual political decisions formed a powerful paradigm that still influences how many political scientists view voting behavior. *The American Voter*, with its emphasis on sophisticated survey research and sophisticated quantitative analysis, was released at a time when political science was embracing the behavioral revolution and many political scientists were eager to adopt the methodological approaches used by the traditional scientific disciplines. This seminal book was upheld as a paragon of exemplary scholarship.[5]

Eventually, however, criticism of their work began to appear. These doubts included questions about the importance of party identification in countries beyond the United States, the effect that partisan attachment may have on new cohorts of voters, and the possibility that other factors not fully considered in existing research were also primary influences on political decision-making and vote choice. While many critical scholars acknowledged the contributions of the Michigan School, they also questioned the universal applicability of its paradigm.

Criticism mirrored debates about whether the Michigan School's findings were the product of a unique political atmosphere that existed in the post-war United States. Critics contended that individuals living in eras with important polarizing issues, such as the 1850s and 1860s, were much more cognizant of contemporary political controversies (Pomper 1979; Foner 1998). These scholars argued that as the relatively consensual politics of the 1950s were replaced by the more conflictual politics of the 1960s and 1970s—with controversies and struggles ranging from Watergate and the Civil Rights Revolution to the Vietnam War—this led to a more informed and issue-driven public. These new voters were also less positive about parties and more likely to classify themselves as independents (Nie, Verba, and Petrocik 1976).[6]

The apparent decline in the influence of partisanship in the voting calculus of many citizens led to a re-examination of the importance of various factors in the vote choice of American citizens. One of the findings was that while voters sometimes lacked specifics regarding policy issues or candidate assessments, most citizens were able to "reward or punish" incumbents based on whether or not their standard of living was improving or declining. The scholarly consensus today is that voters pay close attention to the economic performance of the party in power, especially when an incumbent president is running for re-election (Fiorina 1981; Nadeau and Lewis-Beck 2001). Even those who argue that other factors besides the economy are important to contemporary voting decisions admit that economic performance often tends to outweigh other factors (Alvarez and Nagler 1998).

Campaigns in an Economic World

Since candidates must win votes to gain office, scholars began to ask how office-seekers dealt with this new environment in which voters relied less on partisan affiliation—and political parties themselves appeared to be losing their ability to mobilize voters on Election Day. Other chapters in this book deal with these various aspects of campaigning in more detail, but generally speaking political campaigns became more candidate-centered as individual office-seekers relied less on political parties to gather resources, provide issue information, or mobilize voters (Wattenberg 1991). In turn, voters responded more to candidate traits and characteristics and less to partisan cues. This phenomenon was especially evident in presidential elections where higher levels of interest and greater access to information concerning the personalities and backgrounds of individual candidates allowed voters to form assessments that might cause them to deviate from their already weakened partisan inclinations.[7] Of course, no one denied the continued importance of party identification, but the original model of voter decision-making was being revised based on changes among voters who were identifying less with the two major political parties and changes among the political candidates who were campaigning more on their own personal strengths rather than on the reputation of their political party.

Revisiting and Reframing the Michigan Model: Issues, Ideology, and Party Identification

As the turbulence of the last third of the twentieth century subsided, a debate began about whether patterns of voter behavior had permanently altered during that period or had begun to revert back to the archetype of the 1950s. Nowhere is that question clearer than in the debate about whether the levels and strengths of partisan affiliation have begun to rebound to the levels of 50 years ago. Although the influence of partisan affiliation on voting declined during the 1960s and early 1970s, it began to rebound during the late 1970s and 1980s—at least in terms of the importance of voting for presidential and congressional elections (Bartels 2000).

There is still a lack of scholarly consensus about the prevalence of issue-related voting. Nowhere was the debate more heated than over the question of whether a number of state ballot measures banning gay and lesbian marriage increased support for Republican candidates (Hillygus and Shields 2005). Some have suggested that the 2004 presidential election represented a fundamental change in how campaigns are executed and this, in turn, has had a great influence on how some people make presidential voting choices. According to Hillygus and Shields (2008) technology has improved so dramatically that candidates are able to target their campaign messages to specific groups of voters in ways that highlight controversial, or 'wedge,' issues. These wedge issues are designed to convince individuals who disagree with their political party on a particular issue (e.g., gay marriage or abortion) to support the opposing party's candidate because of the importance of that particular wedge issue. Of course, the most committed 'die-hard' partisans are unlikely to abandon their party for any reason, but strategic candidates may be able to target pockets of potentially persuadable voters in areas that help them forge Electoral College victories. Ultimately, however, the proportion of the electorate that is potentially persuadable is hotly debated and is related to whether or not contemporary voters are becoming increasingly ideological and, therefore, increasingly partisan in their political outlooks.

Polarized Electorate or Polarized Elites?

One of the most important changes to understanding the contemporary electorate has been the increasing ideological positions of elected officials. Substantial evidence demonstrates that members of Congress have become not only more consistently ideological in their voting patterns but also more extreme in their ideological positions—liberals have become increasingly liberal and conservatives have become increasingly conservative (McCarty, Poole, and Rosenthal 2006).[8] In fact, many of the contemporary congressional office-holders have reached an extreme level of ideological polarization. At no time since Reconstruction have our congressmen and women been further apart on the liberal to conservative dimension, and the number of moderate congressional leaders has declined to just 10 percent.[9]

The political changes leading to polarized and ideologically extreme elected officials has several important implications for how voters make decisions and how the contemporary political context might influence voting behavior. First, the political rhetoric that comes out of both the Democratic and Republican parties is increasingly extreme and emphasizes ideological positions. Ideological rhetoric and positioning is crucially important because it is the information that voters use to make decisions. Rather than viewing political elites as reasoned negotiators forging compromised and pragmatic legislation, electoral officials are viewed as ideological soldiers hardening into uncompromising camps (Levdensuky 2009). Some citizens may react negatively to such ideological posturing while others may become increasingly ideological themselves. To the extent that these patterns continue, contemporary candidates are likely to provide voters with ideologically extreme choices and voters themselves are likely to use different criteria in their voting decisions. At the very least, it suggests that ideological considerations may be increasingly important in the contemporary voting calculus.

Some students of public opinion have indeed argued that voters have followed the lead of elected officials and have become increasingly polarized. Following the 2000 presidential election the ubiquitous red state versus blue state electoral maps visually displayed the apparent dichotomous divide among the American public. Political scientists also echoed the argument that the public was following political elites toward increased ideological polarization. For example, Abramowitz and Saunders (2008) argue that not only has the American public become increasingly ideological, but more citizens have become extreme in their ideological orientations. Further, they argue that regional differences, as well as religious and "red–blue" state cleavages are substantial across the contemporary electorate.[10]

Clearly, if the public has become increasingly ideological, the voting process identified by early research in the 1950s is desperately in need of updating. No longer can we say that the public is "ideologically innocent," nor can we lament the lack of ideological or issue voting across the American electorate. If ideological voting is in fact occurring more frequently, a possible result would be that voters may hold elected officials to greater ideological standards when evaluating their performances, or deciding to elect them in the first place. A further change may be that controversial issues— so-called "wedge" issues—that highlight the ideological gulf between candidates and parties may become increasingly important to candidate evaluations. Controversial subjects such as abortion, gay marriage, and stem cell research are obvious examples of issues that divide the public into opposing camps. To the extent that these controversial wedge issues become the touchstone of increasing numbers of ideologically polarized voters, other concerns and policy areas may decline in importance. Regardless, to the extent that the public is moving into separate ideological camps, such a change would mandate, at minimum, a substantial revision of not only our understanding of how citizens decide whom they will support during an election campaign, but also how elected officials are held responsible for what they do once in office.

These changes open up new directions in voting behavior research. Rather than assuming voter decision-making occurs in a vacuum and is invariant to place and time, we should expect to see changes across elections, across candidates, and across citizens. Some voters will take into consideration campaign messages and, to the extent that these are based on ideological considerations, we should expect to see increased ideological voting among these voters.

As shown in Figure 10.1, contemporary voting behavior has become increasingly related to individual ideology. The figure shows the partial correlation between ideology, party identification, and voting for the Democratic Party presidential candidate since 1952.

While the correlation between party identification and voting for the Democratic Party candidate remains consistently higher than the correlation between ideology and voting for the Democratic Party candidate, the importance of both appear to be on the rise. Following the Nixon campaign in 1972 where the correlation between party identification and party voting fell to just about 0.50, the correlation between party identification and party voting

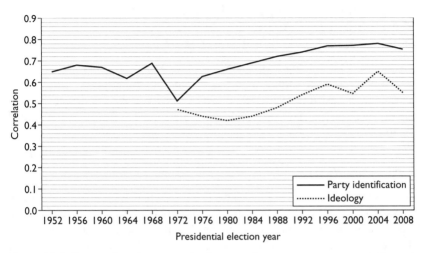

Figure 10.1 Party identification, ideology, and party voting in presidential elections.

increased to approximately 0.76 in the 2008 presidential election. Similarly, the correlation between ideology and party voting increased from a low of 0.423 in the 1980 election to a high of 0.65 in the 2004 presidential election, and 0.55 in 2008. What seems to be occurring is that during the time when political elites became increasingly ideological in their positions, voters responded by making increasingly ideological decisions. As the 2008 CNN presidential exit polls demonstrate, there were clear relationships between ideological perspectives and party voting.

The vast majority of conservatives voted for McCain and the overwhelming majority of liberals voted for Obama. Clearly, voters sorted themselves appropriately along ideological lines in the 2008 presidential election. To the extent that some voters use ideology as the most important aspect of their voting calculus, scholars of voting behavior must revise the 1950s paradigm of ideologically innocent voters and candidates who are evaluated on little more than party identification.

Table 10.1 2008 Presidential Election Voting by Ideology: CNN Exit Poll

	Obama (%)	*McCain (%)*	*Other (%)*
Liberal (22%)	89	10	1
Moderate (44%)	60	39	1
Conservative (34%)	20	78	2

Source: www.cnn.com/ELECTION/2008/results/polls/#val=USP00p1.

Additional Challenges to Understanding Contemporary Voting Behavior: Distinctive Behavior in a Changing Electorate?

In addition to the changes associated with increasingly ideological elites, there are several other dynamics in the contemporary American electorate that challenge the existing orthodoxy of presidential voting. The first is the dramatic changes that have occurred across the southern region of the United States.

Distinctive Voting in Dixie?

Since World War II, the 11 states of the Old Confederacy have continued to capture substantial scholarly attention not only because of their tendency to vote as a block, providing a fortunate presidential candidate with a substantial Electoral College bounty, but because the South has undergone dramatic political changes. The South has moved from a rural agriculture-based economy to the thriving metropolises of Miami, Atlanta, Dallas, and Charlotte. From a more sociological perspective, the South continues to be an increasingly diverse region where immigrants have found jobs and retirees have found milder winters. There has also been an influx of new southerners who are the middle-class African American descendants of those who left the South in the 1920s.

Once a stronghold of the Democratic Party, the Civil Rights Movement in the 1960s and the Republican response in the late 1960s were the catalysts for dramatic partisan shifts during the 1970s, which resulted in the contemporary South becoming a Republican stronghold (Hayes and McKee 2008). Despite the success of the Republican Party in the contemporary South, the influence of the Democratic Party has not disappeared, nor does it appear that the South will experience the same type of one party politics as it once did. According to Black and Black (2002: 3), "[I]f the old solid Democratic South has vanished, a comparably solid Republican South has not developed.... Nor is one likely to emerge." Some have argued, however, that the GOP will continue to grow in strength across the South and there are strong reasons to suspect that such growth will continue (Hayes and McKee 2008). The overwhelming support for the Democratic Party among African Americans creates a clear limit on the gains that the GOP can ultimately obtain. Further, the extent to which Latinos will support the GOP is the clear determinant regarding the long-term domination of the Republican Party in the South.

As shown in Figure 10.2, while the percentage of white southern voters casting ballots for Democratic presidential candidates fell during the early 1980s, there was a slight increase with the candidacies of Bill Clinton in the 1992 and 1996 elections. The percentages, however, fell again in both 2000 and 2004. Obama's candidacy is important owing to the increase in the

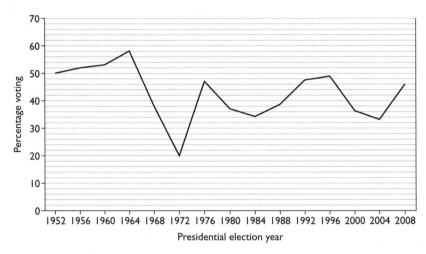

Figure 10.2 White southern Democratic vote for president.

percentages of Democratic votes in the South without the benefit of a moderate southern candidate at the top of the ticket. Obama's ability to bring new minority voters to the polls is extremely encouraging; however, we caution scholars before concluding that the South is ripe for Democratic candidates. Obama's candidacy came at a time when the sitting Republican president, George W. Bush, was incredibly unpopular, even among his own party members. Further, the economy was continuing to fall, and while unemployment continued to rise, the deaths in Iraq and Afghanistan continued to grow.

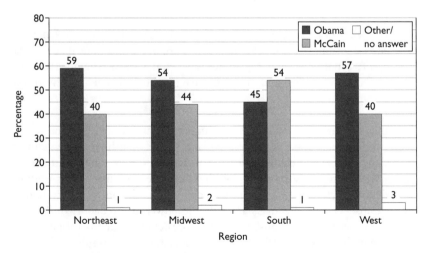

Figure 10.3 2008 presidential vote by region.

While Obama may have taken three southern states, the South was the only region where a majority of exit poll respondents supported McCain over Obama. Clearly the South remains a strong region of support for the GOP—even with an unpopular president, a recession, and an unpopular war.

The contemporary South is a region ripe for change—industry, immigration, education, an aging population, etc.—but are there reasons to believe that the South will continue to be a Republican stronghold for some time? One reason that the South remains such a strongly Republican region is the large concentration and numbers of evangelical Christians within the region. Of course, the South continues to be unique in its homogeneity—particularly in regard to the number and degree of born-again evangelicals.

Religion and Southern Evangelicals: Morality Trumps Economics?

To the extent that political parties and candidates are able to use churches and the homogeneity of the South as an avenue for micro-targeting and mobilizing supporters, the South will continue to be a stronghold for the GOP, at least until the numbers of white evangelicals decline and/or the numbers of non-evangelicals grow. Glaeser and Ward (2006: 133–4) argue that culture and religious divisions have become factors around which American political parties have organized: "The relationship between religion and Republicanism is extremely strong.... Individuals who go to church once a month vote Republican 66 percent of the time; individuals who go to church once per week vote Republican 75 percent of the time." Religious divisions and beliefs allow for political parties to send targeted messages centered on these divides. As Glaeser and Ward (2006: 142) contend,

> We believe that religion has played such an important role in American party divisions because religious groups provide institutions that political parties can use to send targeted messages, and because religious issues are emotionally charged and quite effective in getting people into the voting booth.

Other scholars agree about the growing importance of religion as a crucial factor for contemporary voters, particularly the relationship between church attendance and partisanship (Fiorina et al. 2002). Further, they find that even in the face of controls for party identification, ideological self-classification, presidential performance evaluations, economic evaluations, and candidate evaluations, "Over and above standard (and powerful) predictors of the vote ... in the past three elections (but not before) church attendance has had a highly significant (statistically speaking) association with presidential voting" (Fiorina et al. 2002: 69).

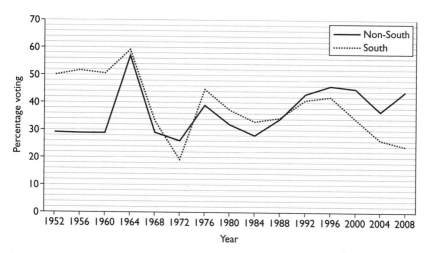

Figure 10.4 Percentage of Protestants voting for Democratic presidential candidate.

What does the increasing importance of religious orientations mean for scholars of voting behavior? At a minimum, it means that while party identification and ideology will continue to be important predictors of voting behavior, religious beliefs (and most likely issues that touch so dramatically upon moral questions) will continue to grow in importance for many voters. While speculative, it seems plausible to assume that in some cases moral issues may have a greater influence on voters because candidates are able to communicate these types of messages through well-networked groups of like-minded believers through churches and associated groups. Further, moral issues are probably more important and ultimately more of a central concern for religious voters than are other issues—even economic issues. In fact, according to Glaeser and Ward (2006: 142),

> [M]any people take their religious views far more seriously than views on other topics, and this may also help us to understand why religion is so often an important part of politics. It may be far easier to motivate voters by appealing to core religious values than to topics like tax policy, and this may be the key reason why religion is so appealing to politicians.

The Politics of Gender

Since the mid-1990s a great deal of research has investigated the so-called "gender gap" in presidential voting. According to most of this research, male voters have become increasingly moved by a conservative position on questions of domestic and foreign policy. Simultaneously, albeit to a lesser extent, women have moved increasingly toward liberal social policies. The result is that women have been more likely to support Democratic presidential candidates while men have been voting increasingly for Republican presidential candidates. In fact, Chaney, Alvarez, and Nagler (1998) find that not only do women and men evaluate the economic conditions of the country differently, with women generally having a more negative evaluation than men, but men are more likely to cast a ballot based on their own personal economic situation while women are more likely to weigh the national economic conditions more heavily in their voting decisions. They also find that much of the gender gap in voting behavior can be explained by the issue preferences that women embrace, particularly their more liberal positions on questions of government responsibility for providing jobs, child care and medical care. Finally, they also report evidence that women are more likely to have an "anti-incumbent" attitude than men and are therefore more likely to punish an incumbent president for downturns in the national economy.

In the 2008 presidential election, we see continued evidence of the different decisions that men and women make in choosing a president. As shown in Figure 10.5, according to the 2009 CNN exit polls, males were split about evenly for both Obama and McCain. Among women, however, 56 percent voted for Obama while only 43 percent supported McCain.

To the extent that the gender gap in presidential voting continues, or even extends to other levels of political office, what does this mean in terms of contemporary voting behavior research? First, the substantial shift of

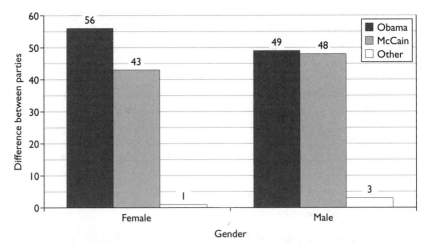

Figure 10.5 Gender composition of the 2008 presidential election (source: www.cnn.com/ELECTION/2008/results/polls/#val=USP00p1).

women choosing the Democratic Party candidate since the early 1980s, and the counter pattern of men choosing the Republican candidate cannot be accounted for by traditional theories of voting behavior that place so much emphasis on the childhood socialization of party identification. If the voting calculus of women and men has changed over the past several years, it is important to understand when and how this change occurred and if the change was unevenly spread across groups of men and women. In this sense, we know that viewing males and females as monolithic groups of voters is an oversimplification of reality, yet we have not fully disentangled the various subgroups of women voters. There are differences among and between groups of female voters and we do not fully understand those differences or when they are relevant. The manner in which candidates attempt to appeal to these distinct groups is also a question without many answers.

As a simple example, if we disaggregate the figure above across race as well as gender, we see that while the gender gap is still evident among white women, the gap among this group is substantially smaller than the enormous gender gaps among African Americans, Latinos, and respondents who indicated that their race was "other" (Figure 10.6).

These clear differences across gender and race point to the next challenge faced by scholars of voting behaviour; namely the lack of scholarship devoted to disentangling how historically marginalized groups make decisions and cast ballots.

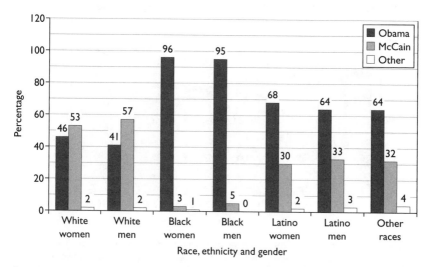

Figure 10.6 Race, ethnicity, and gender in the 2008 presidential electorate (source: www.cnn.com/ELECTION/2008/results/polls/#val=USP 00p1).

Diverse Electorate: Individualism or Linked Fate?

As stated earlier, the American electorate is drastically different demographically, ideologically, economically, and politically than when the "Michigan model" was first posited. As the country has become more diverse, the voting behavior literature has failed to advance in methods and theories to understand the dynamics of political participation for an increasingly diverse electorate. Due to the complexities of the social, historical, and political context in which minorities, particularly African Americans, find themselves, the seminal works in American political behavior are often incomplete explanations for minority voting behavior.

The 2008 presidential election will go on record as the most racially and ethnically diverse in the history of our country. The Pew Research Center reported that nearly one in four votes were cast by non-whites (Pew Research Center 2009a). Of the 131 million persons who voted, blacks made up 12.1 percent, Hispanics 7.4 percent, and Asians 2.5 percent, while whites made up 76.3 percent. Levels of participation significantly increased for eligible black voters. The turnout rate increased from 60.3 percent in 2004 to 65.3 percent in 2008. For Hispanics, the turnout rate rose from 47.2 percent in 2004 to 49.9 percent in 2008. Among Asian voters the rate increased from 44 percent in 2004 to 47.0 percent in 2008, while turnout among white eligible voters fell from 67.2 percent to 66.1 percent (Pew Research Center 2009a). Such changes in the demographic composition of the American electorate indicate that our

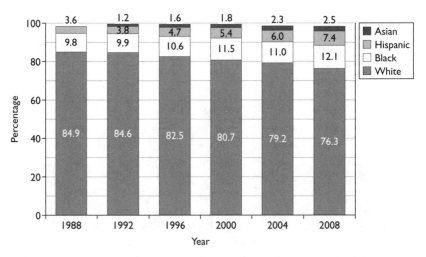

Figure 10.7 Race and ethnic composition of the vote from 1998–2008 (source: Pew Research Center (http://pewresearch.org/ pubs/1209/racial-ethnic-voters-presidential-election).

Note
Whites, African Americans, and Asians include only non-Hispanic populations.

existing models of vote choice, based largely on the voting behavior of Caucasians, is inadequate for understanding the electoral behavior of the contemporary American electorate.

Group identification is seen as a common link between group membership and collective political behavior. This identification involves the merging of individual identity in a group while recognizing interdependence within the group. Dawson (1994) refers to this interdependence as "linked fate," when combined with the desire to address the group's social position through collective action, or group consciousness. While the importance of group consciousness and the concept of "linked fate" has been found to be important in many historically marginalized groups, these forces have been consistently found to be a primary ingredient in the decision-making of African Americans. Individual group member awareness of shared interests or a common fate is what seems to matter in order for the potential for cohesive political action to be realized.

Understanding African American voting behavior, in particular, presents an incredible opportunity for expanding our understanding of voting behavior. Because of overt disenfranchisement from the political system, the African American community developed networks of organizations that provided political socialization and community outreach. The extent to which similar groups and institutions formed and continue to influence the voting behavior of other marginalized groups remains an open question, but most certainly the classical work in political science is unable to adequately explain these processes. For example, is contemporary African American support for the Democratic Party based on group consciousness and "linked fate" as Dawson contends, or do some African Americans support the Democratic Party because of their positions on issues that are important to them, such as fair housing, civil rights, etc.? To the extent that African American support is based on more than childhood socialization into an allegiance with the Democratic Party, the classical models of American political voting behavior fall short as an explanation for this important and growing segment of the American electorate.

Black voting behavior, especially as it relates to the support of black candidates, has been believed to be a function of group identity. Research has found that blacks use what happens to the group as a proxy for individual self-interest (Gurin, Hatchett, and Jackson 1989; Tate 1993; Dawson 1994). The higher one's level of group consciousness, the more likely he or she is to vote for a black candidate or to support policies designed to ameliorate racial inequality. It was predicted that group consciousness would diminish as blacks became more integrated into society and achieved greater economic mobility (Wilson 1978); however, black group consciousness remains high (Dawson 1994, 2001). Thus it is likely that blacks will overwhelmingly support black candidates and elected officials.

African American support for African American politicians is evident in recent poll support of President Barack Obama during his first year in office.

African American support for President Obama during his first year has remained extremely high in comparison to other groups. The Pew Research Center has consistently reported that there is a significant racial divide in the approval ratings for President Obama. In April 2009, 53 percent of white respondents gave Obama a favorable job review, while 33 percent disapproved. In the same poll, an overwhelming percentage of blacks (95%) supported Obama with only 2 percent disapproving. In August 2009 the percentage of whites who approved of Obama's performance declined to 42 percent, with 46 percent disapproving. African American support in August remained consistently strong with a 92 percent approval rating and 4 percent disapproving (Pew Research Center 2009b). This trend remained consistent, with 39 percent of whites approving of Obama and 48 percent disapproving in comparison to 88 percent of blacks approving in December (Pew Research Center 2010).

Latino Voting Behavior

During the 1960s a common argument was that ethnic identity would not persist into the third and fourth generation of immigrants. Raymond Wolfinger (1965) and others did not foresee that new waves of immigrants from Latin America and Asia would create new ethnic groups and strong levels of group identity. For Wolfinger, immigration ended in the early 1900s with the last wave of European immigrants. This significant dynamic of the American demographic picture has transformed the American cultural and political landscape. The uniqueness of immigration from Latin America since the 1960s requires a new understanding of participation and mobilization of American voters.

In today's political environment, group identification is not limited to African Americans. As political parties lose strength there will be continued emphasis upon targeted voter appeals that are likely to emphasize social and ethnic group connections. The targeting of potential Latino voters is likely to reinforce the group identity shared along current political and social realities. Latino immigration has continued at a steady pace which grows the population while solidifying the Latino experience as an immigrant experience. As a result of this wave of immigration, discrimination against Latinos persists and anti-immigration discussions continue. The perception of discrimination along with real discrimination against Latinos will contribute to the group turning inward for support that reinforces its racial/ethnic or group identity (Sanchez 2006).

As the Latino population grows it will continue to gain attention particularly during national elections. Latinos represent the largest ethnic minority group in the United States, surpassing African Americans in 2003. The Latino electorate has grown considerably to an estimated 10 million registrants in 2008. In light of the large increase in Latino population, scholars have argued that Latino voters could become critical swing voters if certain conditions were met (Guerra 1992). Similar conditions have reinforced African American group identity. For example, Latino voters are likely to experience group consciousness in areas where Latinos have significant populations, where there are strategic voter mobilization efforts, there is active engagement of Latino politicians and community leadership, and where there are viable Latino candidates and issues that are relevant for Latino voters. In fact, the historic presence of Governor Bill Richardson (D-NM) in the 2008 Democratic primaries satisfies one of these conditions and was most certainly a key reason for increased Latino participation early in the Democratic primaries. Latino voters were also considered critical to Senator Hillary Clinton's efforts to maintain viability late in the Democratic nomination process. The increased mobilization efforts by the Clinton campaign and Richardson's presence heightened the engagement of Latino voters and the likelihood for participation in the general election.

Overall, two million more Latino voters participated in the 2008 election. The steady increase in Latino participation defies early literature which suggested that Latino electoral participation would be limited as well as the political commentary that Latinos would not vote for an African American candidate (Shaw, de la Garza, and Lee 2000; Verba, Schlozman, and Brady 1995). On the contrary, Obama was quite popular among Latino voters during his time in the Illinois state legislature as well as in the U.S. Senate, winning a majority of Latino voters in the 2008 Illinois Democratic primary (Barreto et al. 2008). Similarly, Tom Bradley in the 1982 California governor's race won an estimated 80 percent of Latino voters. African American mayoral candidates in urban areas have also been successful in securing between 70 and 80 percent of the Latino vote.[11] African American Laura Richardson received over 70 percent of the Latino vote in a special election for the Thirty-seventh House District seat in California although during the primary she received less than 20 percent of the Latino vote (Barreto et al. 2008).

Asian Americans

Current research on Asian American voting is still evolving. Since 2000 there have been growing attempts to understand Asian American decision-making. This significant work found that in 2000 the strongest predictor for support of Democrat Al Gore among Asians was party identification, but research also revealed that geography and national origin played a role in vote choice for Asians in 2000 (Lien, Conway, and Wong 2004). In addition, other factors, such as socioeconomic status, having a sense of linked fate with other Asian Americans, and experience with racial discrimination was not associated strongly with vote choice among Asian Americans. This may be due to the fact that unlike other ethnic groups Asians tend to be the most residentially integrated minority in the U.S. and, like white Americans, enjoy high levels of economic and educational achievement.

Asian voting in 2008, generally, and during the Democratic presidential primaries, specifically, was often discussed in terms of race and ethnicity. Because race in the United States has generally been framed in terms of the relationship between African Americans and whites there is limited understanding of the dynamics of group and race in the Asian population. During the Democratic primaries, Clinton received significant support from Asian voters prompting commentators to ask about Asians' racial loyalties. With which group would Asian Americans find common ground? Trends would suggest that Asian Americans might link their political fortunes with similarly economically and socially situated white Americans and perhaps white candidates. However, Asians have much in common with African Americans such as comprising a phenotypically distinct population subject to discrimination and stereotypes. There is very little research concerning the support of candidates of different racial backgrounds. Much of the research concerning Asian vote choice and race is based on the paradigm of blacks, whites, and now Latinos. Nevertheless, Asian Americans supported Obama in the general election (Ramakrishnan et al. 2009). This fact may force research to move away from previous analysis which argued that Asian Americans might be opposed to supporting African American candidates. Due to the unique housing patterns and socioeconomic status of Asians in comparison to Latinos and blacks, it is possible that party identification and issue preferences play a strong role in Asian American vote choice.

Arab Americans

The research on Arab American political participation is more limited than the study of Asian Americans. The study of Arab Americans and Muslims has only recently attracted scholarly attention.[12] Religiosity in partisan identification has been thoroughly researched over the years as most scholars find that higher levels of individual religiosity and religious commitment and church attendance are associated with stronger Republican Party identification or conservative ideology (Olson and Green 2006; Wilcox and Larson 2006). Religiosity has also been used to explain the significance of African American religious institutions as vehicles for political socialization for persons who sought inclusion in the political process (Tate 1994; Calhoun-Brown 1996). The Church in the black community was significant in the development of the African American Democratic voting block.

How does religiosity influence political behavior when the group is excluded from American society? Unlike African Americans who were excluded due to legalized segregation, Arab Americans do not practice Christianity and have not been fully integrated into American society due to negative perceptions of their faith and culture. Current research has focused largely on American perceptions of Islam and citizens of Middle Eastern descent. There has been very little research investigating the extent to which religiosity operates similarly among non-Christian religious groups, the complicated connections between religion and party identification among non-Christian groups, or if issue positions and religious beliefs play a stronger or weaker role in the decision-making processes of non-Christian groups. As America becomes more culturally, ethnically, and religiously diverse it will be important for research to attempt to understand how non-Christians form partisan identities, how candidates and parties attempt to reach and persuade them, and ultimately how these individuals make electoral decisions.

Conclusion

The 2008 presidential election highlighted both the strengths and limitations of the traditional approaches of voting behavior that political scientists have utilized during the past five decades. In many ways, the 2008 presidential campaign promised to be a unique campaign. The election was the first since 1928 where no sitting president or vice-president ran at any point during the campaign. While foreign policy issues looked to be important during the early stages, they faded as an economic crisis emerged during the final weeks of the contest. As in almost every partisan election, however, party identification continued to be the most important predictor of vote choice. In many ways, voters continued to see the campaign and the candidates through partisan lenses.

However, a number of forces emerged to challenge a mono-causal explanation. The role of ideology in vote choice appears to be more important than ever before in determining how individuals cast ballots. Furthermore, race, region, religion, and gender continue to be powerful forces in influencing vote choice. As the demographic face of the United States continues to change, it will continue to be crucially important for scholars to understand when decision-making across these groups is similar and when it is different. As these groups continue to become larger segments of the voting population, the more important they will become in deciding the leaders of the country and the more important it will be for social scientists to understand how these groups make political decisions.

Notes

1. See Munro (1928) for both a contemporary discussion of Progressive assumptions about the political competence of "all able-bodied citizens" and a criticism of these notions.
2. There were scholars who questioned whether these shortcomings among the citizenry existed or were injurious to democracy. Anthony Downs (1957) argued that while voters were economical with the time and effort they would expend on politics, they would, however, vote for the candidate whom they perceived best matched their preferences on important issues. V.O. Key Jr. (1966) went even further, arguing that "voters are not fools," and that citizens were able to utilize retrospective evaluations in making choices that reflected their preferences and values.

3. Importantly, Converse recently argued that much of his criticism of the average citizen has been exaggerated beyond what he envisioned (Converse 2006).
4. Even those secondary groups oriented toward political action such as labor unions and civic organizations play relatively small roles in political socialization compared to these primary influences (Berelson et al. 1954).
5. See Pomper (1979) for a more detailed analysis of the book's influence on the study of political science.
6. Some later studies argued that this surge in self-identified "independents" consisted mostly of individuals who still leaned toward one of the two major parties. These "leaners" actually thought, acted, and voted in a manner similar to weak partisans (Keith et al. 1992). However, the rise in independents occurred at the same time as a rise in split-ticket voting (Niemi and Weisberg 2001) and the frequency of divided government, though other explanations exist as well (Jacobson 1990b; Burden and Kimball 1998). The drop in partisan affiliation during this period was steeper among Democrats and overall rates of Republican partisanship changed little. However, both parties had fewer strong partisans than during the Eisenhower era.
7. Some scholars criticized the public for forming irrational attachments and evaluations based on idiosyncratic factors such as the physical attractiveness of a candidate. Other scholars argued that voters were trying to identify traits such as honesty, consistency, and competence and to project how these traits would influence their future job performance (Miller, Wattenberg, and Malanchuk 1986).
8. For visual displays of the increasingly polarized Congress, see http://voteview.ucsd. edu/ and for further discussions of McCarty, Poole, and Rosenthal (2006) see http://polarizedamerica.com/.
9. According to McCarty, Pool, and Rosenthal (2006), the bulk of congressional voting during the country's history may be accounted for by two dimensions, or basic questions of political power. The first dimension is the simple struggle over the appropriate role of the government in domestic policy and the economy. Further, they argue that most of the struggle along this dimension may be placed across a standard "liberal" to "moderate" to "conservative" scale, ranging from the most government involvement to the least. The second dimension initially accounted for regional differences in the United States congressional voting as well as the differences in voting patterns during and following the Civil Rights Movement. They argue that now, however, this second dimension has all but disappeared and is now almost completely absent. They contend that race-related issues, such as affirmative action, welfare, Medicaid, etc., are now questions of redistribution. In other words, voting on race-related issues is now accounted for by the first dimension regarding the proper role of government in domestic and economic policy.
10. In regard to religious cleavages Abramowitz and Saunders (2008: 550) contend that "Among white voters, religiosity had a stronger influence on candidate choice than any other social characteristic."
11. See, for example, David Dinkins, New York, 1990; Wellington Webb, Denver, 1984; Ron Kirk, Dallas, 1996; and Harold Washington, Chicago, 1984.
12. Correspondence with *Religion and Politics* editor Ted Jelen on July 8, 2010.

## Chapter 11

Congressional Elections
Why Some Incumbent Candidates Lose

Jamie L. Carson and Carrie P. Eaves

In 2008, Joe Knollenberg, the Republican representative from the 9th district of Michigan, lost his bid for a ninth term in the U.S. House. In the previous election Knollenberg had barely defeated his opponent in the general election, winning just 52 percent of the vote. As a result, the Democratic Congressional Campaign Committee targeted him as a vulnerable incumbent in 2008. The Democrats nominated a well-qualified candidate, Gary Peters, who had served in the Michigan State Senate until he was forced to retire because of state term limits and subsequently went on to serve as the State Lottery Commissioner. Congressman Knollenberg outraised his opponent by more than $1.6 million, yet he still lost his re-election bid. Similarly, Joe Porter, a Republican Congressman from the Nevada 3rd district, was defeated on Election Day. Porter had served in Congress for six years, yet in 2006 he barely won re-election by a margin of 48 to 47 percent. As a result, he was also targeted by Democrats and faced stiff competition from the minority leader of the State Senate Dina Titus. Despite a fairly substantial fundraising advantage, Porter was defeated in 2008.

Incumbents in the U.S. House of Representatives regularly win re-election at a rate well over 90 percent (Jacobson 2009). As a result, pundits and political scientists often bemoan the lack of significant competition in congressional elections. Yet, in the two cases described above (as well as in 17 other House races in 2008), the incumbent failed to win re-election, despite numerous "advantages" associated with the office. More generally, a handful of House and Senate incumbents invariably lose their seats in Congress across individual election cycles. Examining specific trends in these House and Senate elections in which incumbents are defeated could provide vital insight into the declining rates of electoral competition as well as when the rare competitive election might actually emerge.

In this chapter, we assess the current state of research on congressional elections, most notably by highlighting the declining rates of electoral competition in House and Senate races over time. In light of the exponential growth in the amount of scholarship on congressional elections during the past few decades, it would be impossible to thoroughly examine all facets of this research in a single essay. Instead, we focus on a central puzzle in congressional elections research: why some incumbents lose each election cycle despite the inherent advantages accruing to incumbents. We begin our discussion by addressing one element beyond the direct control of individual candidates—the electoral context. Next, we point to three areas of research that offer clues about why electoral competition is declining as well as when the rare competitive election might occur: the actions of incumbents, the role of challengers, and the impact of money in elections. Finally, we conclude our discussion with specific suggestions about new directions for congressional elections research.

Overview of Congressional Elections Research

Since the early 1970s, scholars have devoted a significant amount of attention to the topic of congressional elections research (and House elections in particular). To a certain extent, this emphasis grew out of Mayhew's (1974a) classic observation that we can think of members of Congress as "single-minded seekers of re-election." Building on this valuable insight, students of congressional politics have spent countless hours investigating a wide variety of important and unanswered questions. For instance, why are incumbents re-elected at extraordinarily high rates in House (and, to a lesser extent, Senate) elections? Why do some qualified candidates decide to challenge incumbents while many others choose not to? To what extent are the staggering costs of congressional campaigns a contributing factor to incumbency success rates? These and many other similar questions have motivated some of the more interesting examples of cutting-edge research on congressional elections during the past few decades.

Although much has been learned from this research on congressional elections, there are still a number of unanswered questions that, in our view, have received insufficient attention to date. Take, for instance, Figure 11.1, which has often served as the foundation for many of the inquiries pertaining to congressional elections research. Based on the evidence in the figure, a number of discernible patterns are clear. First, during the past 60 years, a growing proportion of incumbents who have sought re-election in both chambers have been re-elected. Second, the incumbency re-election rate in the Senate has been much more variable compared to the House. Third, there is noticeable volatility in the re-election rates of congressional incumbents, with more noticeable declines in midterm election years. Despite these recognizable trends in House and Senate elections, there is still uncertainty about what explicitly is contributing to each.

Another way to think about the lack of electoral competition depicted in Figure 11.1 is to examine the total number of marginal races in these elections. In Figure 11.2, for instance, we plot the total number of U.S. House races from 1948 to 2008 where the incumbent received between 50 and 55

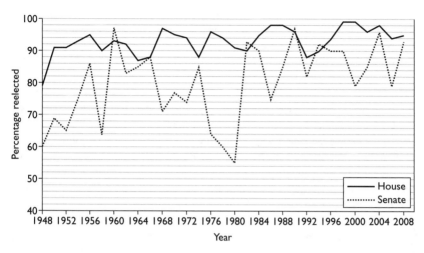

Figure 11.1 Success rates of incumbents seeking re-election, 1948–2008.

percent of the two-party vote (the traditional definition of marginality). Although there are some noticeable spikes in the number of marginal races in election years such as 1956, 1964, 1974, and 1994, overall the pattern shows a fairly visible decline in marginal races over time. In other words, an increasing number of incumbents appear to be winning by larger margins against their opponents in the past few decades. Mayhew (1974b) first noticed this pattern in discussing the "vanishing marginals" in his classic article and the trend appears to have continued in recent decades, with only a modest

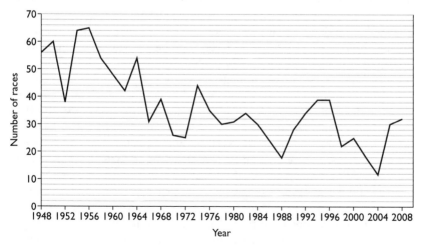

Figure 11.2 Total number of marginal U.S. House races, 1948–2008.

increase in the two most recent elections. Ultimately, the pattern in Figure 11.2 suggests that the majority of House incumbents are far less vulnerable today than they were 40 or 50 years ago.

In an attempt to better understand why elections have become less competitive over time, we shift our focus away from the question of why so many incumbents win each year to the equally interesting question of why some incumbents lose each election cycle. By doing this, we hope to offer new insights on specific factors contributing to declining levels of electoral competition in congressional races. Along the way, we also hope to offer differing explanations for incumbency defeats across the House and Senate given the greater volatility associated with Senate elections. We begin our discussion with several contextual factors that influence congressional elections. From there, we shift our attention to the actions of incumbents, the role of challengers, and the impact of money in determining candidate entry patterns and outcomes in House and Senate races.

Contextual Factors

Although ambition and personal considerations play an important role in determining the level of individual competition in congressional races, macro-level conditions may be equally important as well. Consider, for instance, national conditions as reflected by the overall state of the economy or levels of presidential approval. If the economy is perceived to be doing well or the incumbent president's approval levels are high, members of the out-party may have a much harder time justifying a decision to run for elected office. As such, incumbents may fare better in an upcoming election due to the lower probability of facing an experienced challenger. When national conditions are less favorable, however, incumbents have reason to be concerned about their electoral viability.[1] In these circumstances, more qualified candidates are likely to emerge and often have an easier time raising money, which places a greater number of sitting incumbents in increased electoral jeopardy.

In addition to national conditions, the nature of each individual congressional race can influence the outcome and level of competition. Open seat elections that lack an incumbent candidate are much more competitive than the typical incumbent-contested race (Gaddie and Bullock 2000; Jacobson 2009). Indeed, one could not discuss electoral competition without discussing open seat races. For the most part, races without an incumbent are rare in electoral politics—especially in the Senate. From 1980 to the present, the average number of open seats races in House elections was 43 (out of a possible 435). In 1984 and 1988 there were a mere 27 open seat races; however, in 1992 there were 91 open seat races. Since 2000, the number of open seats on average has declined even further to less than 30 per individual election. Without an incumbent in the race, experienced candidates are more likely to emerge since they feel that this may be their best chance to win an election (Banks and Kiewiet 1989; Jacobson 2009).

A third contextual factor that may influence aggregate patterns of candidate competition is the timing of a congressional election. Voter turnout fluctuates widely depending on whether or not it is a presidential election year. Midterm elections always lead to decreased voter turnout following the "surge" during the previous presidential election. Without the president at the top of the ballot, political interest among voters wanes. In addition, historically the president's party does far worse in midterm election years.[2] As a result, levels of electoral competition may be affected. Building on the earlier work of Angus Campbell (1960), James Campbell (1991) proposed a general theory of "surge and decline" that seeks to explain how many congressional seats the party of the president loses at the midterm election. According to the theory, the more seats the party of the president picks up during a presidential election, the more seats are at risk during a midterm election. Without the president's name on the ballot at the midterm, individual congressional candidates become more affected by local conditions, especially if the economy or national conditions have declined in the months preceding the election. Thus, the number of seats the president's party loses at the midterm (the decline) is a function of the number of seats gained in the previous presidential election (the surge).[3]

Two recent midterm elections—1998 and 2002—have challenged the conventional view associated with the surge-and-decline hypothesis. Rather than losing seats at each midterm, the president's party actually gained a few additional seats in each of these midterm elections. With the midterm losses for Republicans in 2006, it is unclear at the time of writing whether the traditional pattern of surge and decline for the president's party will continue in the 2010 midterm elections or how severe it might be for Democratic candidates. To a considerable extent, this will depend upon President Obama's ability to deliver on many of his campaign promises as reflected by his overall approval level, the state of the economy prior to the midterm elections, and the number of experienced Republican challengers willing to run against incumbent Democrats in 2010 (Jacobson 2009). With a congressional redistricting cycle looming on the horizon, the 2010 midterm elections could be the last hurdle the Democrats face to maintaining their majority status in the House for many years to come.

The Actions of Incumbents

For the past 40 years, students of congressional elections have documented a fairly stable pattern in the context of House and Senate elections: the relative ease with which incumbents seem to get re-elected. Beginning with the work of scholars who first recognized the underlying advantages of incumbency (see, e.g., Erikson 1971; Mayhew 1974b; Cover 1977; Ferejohn 1977; Fiorina

1977) and continuing with more recent and innovative attempts to estimate the extent of that advantage in congressional elections (see, e.g., Gelman and King 1990; Cox and Katz 1996, 1999, 2002; Erikson and Palfrey 1998; Ansolabehere, Snyder, and Stewart 2000; Brady, Cogan and Fiorina 2000), social scientists have widely examined both the causes and consequences of this recurring phenomenon. Although there is little doubt that incumbents have a substantial advantage over non-incumbents in congressional elections, there is considerably less agreement over the sources of the incumbency advantage and the causes of its growth over time. This is unfortunate, since elections go to the very heart of accountability and representation, and an insufficient understanding of how they are conducted as well as their direct and indirect effects limits our ability to generalize from them.

Why is the incumbency advantage so conceptually important to our understanding of electoral politics? The simple answer is that public-spiritedness and good intensions aside, once a person wins public office, her goal rapidly becomes staying in office. As classically stated by Mayhew (1974a), legislators value re-election above all other goals. Individuals may enter public office with altruistic intensions, but their proximate goal quickly becomes re-election. To accomplish their other goals they must be re-elected, and incumbency is their key advantage (Alford and Brady 1989). To some, the incumbency advantage is indicative of an electorate that is, by and large, content with the performance of its elected representatives. To many others, however, it raises potential concerns about the issue of democratic accountability, often resulting in increased demands for campaign finance reform or enactment of term limits for incumbents—issues that have received a widespread amount of attention since the early 1990s.

On the whole, concern about democratic accountability has sparked an interest among students of congressional elections to investigate the extent to which legislative behavior has discernible electoral consequences. While some scholars have focused on the electoral rewards associated with distributive benefits (see, e.g., Bickers and Stein 1994, 1996; Alvarez and Saving 1997; Sellers 1997), others have examined the potential advantages linked to casework (Alford and Hibbing 1981; Serra and Moon 1994) and incumbents' roll call voting records (Erikson 1971; Wright 1978; Jacobson 1993). Although far from conclusive, these studies have offered evidence that incumbents typically receive marginal benefits from these and other legislative activities. This, of course, has been a source of concern among journalists, pundits, and scholars alike who question whether potential advantages that accrue to incumbents make it impractical for quality challengers to mount an effective campaign. After all, how can we expect legislators to be responsive to their constituents if incumbents have little reason to believe that they will be defeated in the upcoming election?

To be sure, congressional incumbents spend a considerable amount of time engaging in activities that they anticipate will cultivate a sense of loyalty with their constituents and improve their chances of re-election. Indeed, Mayhew (1974a) finds that legislators split their time between advertising, credit claiming, and position taking in an effort to facilitate their re-election goal.[4] Fenno (1978) observes that incumbents cultivate a personal "home style" with their constituents in an attempt to foster a sense of trust and loyalty among prospective voters. Fiorina (1989) argues that Congress is responsible for the creation of a Washington establishment that allows individual legislators to frequently engage in pork barrel and casework activities, which brings them favor with their constituents. Incumbents also raise large sums of money with the expectation that it will enhance their prospects for re-election by discouraging the emergence of experienced, prospective challengers (Abramowitz 1989; Box-Steffensmeier 1996).

As the preceding studies suggest, there is little doubt that legislators believe that their actions and behavior impact upon their electoral fortunes. Given that voters directly elect legislators, most (if not all) recognize the importance and necessity of being responsive to their constituents. Since they also possess a finite amount of time and scarce resources, we should not expect them to act frivolously with regard to the allocation of these limited resources. Moreover, the extent to which we evaluate an incumbent as "marginal" or "safe" is largely contingent upon the activities that the legislator engages in while in office. Incumbents who appear "out of touch" with their constituencies will generally have a much harder time getting re-elected than those legislators who attempt to maintain a connection with their voters. As Mayhew (1974a: 37) explains, "what characterizes 'safe' representatives is not that they are beyond electoral reach, but that their efforts are very likely to bring them uninterrupted electoral success."

In light of the numerous advantages accruing to incumbents, why are some incumbents routinely defeated at the polls? Although there is little consensus in response to this question, there is some evidence to suggest that incumbents may not always be responsive enough to their constituents. As noted above, legislators strongly believe that their actions in office assist them in their re-election efforts. As such, if they fail to provide distributive benefits to their districts in the form of casework or pork barrel projects, there is the underlying perception that they are more likely to be defeated (Serra and Moon 1994; Sellers 1997). In addition, incumbents who focus more on goals such as policy or power within the chamber (see, e.g., Fenno 1973) may undermine their own chances of re-election if they forget what got them elected in the first place.

Another factor that may contribute to greater incumbency defeats is increased loyalty to one's political party. In any given Congress, numerous controversial and divisive issues come before the House and Senate chamber, often requiring individual legislators to express positions on legislation that may be unpopular with a large segment of their constituencies. If members of Congress represent moderate constituencies and are perceived as voting too often with their party on controversial legislation, then there is an increased chance that their voters will choose to vote for someone else in an upcoming election (Carson et al. 2010). One recent example of this is the health care reform bill that passed the House on March 22, 2010. Many "Blue Dog" Democrats who represented moderate districts were reluctant to vote "yes" on the legislation given the strong possibility of electoral repercussions in the fall. While it is unclear as of writing what the electoral effects will be on this highly visible vote, it is interesting to note that nearly all of the defections were by moderate members of the Democratic coalition.

One final point about incumbency defeats that should be made is that the actual number of losses might in fact be greater if incumbents did not behave strategically while in office. In any given election year, a few vulnerable incumbents decide not to seek re-election due to their precarious electoral circumstances. Although these strategic retirements are often couched in terms of legislators wanting to "spend more time with their families," in many respects these decisions are routinely made to avoid risking electoral defeat (Hall and Van Houweling 1995; Carson 2005). Indeed, the fact that incumbents do choose to retire strategically instead of risk the possibility of electoral defeat tends to inflate the extent to which incumbents actually are (or are perceived to be) re-elected (Cox and Katz 2002).

The Role of Challengers

In certain respects, focusing on the behavior of incumbents while in office can only tell us so much about candidate competition and electoral outcomes. Beyond legislators serving in the House and Senate, we also need to consider the role of their opponents, specifically in terms of who decides to challenge incumbents in a given election year. Although most of the attention in the incumbency advantage literature during the 1970s focused on the role of the incumbents, this began to change in the next decade. Starting with some early work by Jacobson (1980) and Jacobson and Kernell (1981) regarding strategic politicians, a shift in emphasis in congressional elections research began to occur. In this and much of the subsequent research on congressional elections, attention was given not just to incumbents and their legislative behavior, but to the role of challengers in explaining electoral outcomes. This development represented an important step in the congressional elections literature as scholars since then have regularly considered the effects of candidate experience when evaluating House and Senate elections.

Candidate Emergence

In shifting attention away from an exclusive emphasis on incumbents, Hinckley (1980) was among the first to observe that scholars of congressional elections were neglecting an important piece of the electoral equation. She argued that the incumbency advantage "may be less a matter of what incumbents do right than of what challengers do wrong—or not at all" (442). By only considering the actions of incumbents, scholars had neglected the other key player in congressional elections—the candidate running against an incumbent. Indeed, the great variation among candidates who decide to challenge incumbents could also drive varying levels of competition in congressional elections.

To systematically evaluate the impact of candidates, one must first ask, "Who runs for Congress?" Neither campaigning nor serving in Congress are simple tasks. Yet Kazee (1980) found that many candidates run for Congress solely because they enjoy campaigning for office. Subsequently, Kazee (1983) noticed that the presence of an incumbent candidate could serve as a deterrent for potential challengers. In follow-up studies of ambition and candidate emergence, a number of scholars have opted to employ a case study method examining who decides to emerge in a given congressional district (see, e.g., Fowler and McClure 1989; Kazee 1994). Ultimately, the study of candidate emergence can be especially challenging due to the inherent difficulty in identifying those potential candidates who opted *not* to run for elective office.

In an effort to overcome this potential limitation, Maisel and Stone (1997) first proposed an innovative approach to this question by studying the behavior of state legislators through their Candidate Emergence Project. Climbing up the political ladder of ambition, Maisel and Stone recognized that many career politicians move from state legislatures to the U.S. House. As a result, studying the emergence decisions of state legislators lends itself well to the study of the emergence of congressional candidates. Through their analysis of state legislators, Maisel and Stone find that potential candidates are most strongly influenced by their perceptions of success. Those state legislators who believe that they have a strong chance of winning a seat in the House of Representatives are the ones most likely to emerge as a candidate. More recently, Maestas et al. (2006) show how the costs and benefits of running for and holding elective office can influence candidate entry decisions among state legislators running for the House.

For a somewhat different perspective on candidate emergence, Fox and Lawless (2005) examine the lack of female candidates running for and serving in Congress. They evaluate this question by surveying individuals working in careers that are regarded as yielding the highest eligibility pool for political candidates (i.e., law, business, education, and political activism). Fox and Lawless find that women are significantly less likely to demonstrate the appropriate political ambition given the lack of significant role models. Women in their survey were less likely to be recruited to run for office and less likely to consider a candidacy for elective office. Ultimately, their work highlights the need to consider individual-level factors such as gender differences as well as the national political climate typically studied in analyses of candidate emergence (on this point, see also Lawless and Fox 2005).

Candidate Quality

Not all candidates who decide to challenge incumbents are created equal. Some bring more name recognition, campaign skill, and election experience than others. In their classic study of congressional elections, Jacobson and Kernell (1981) examine aggregate patterns of candidate emergence to identify whether or not challengers behave strategically. Through an analysis of congressional elections in the 1970s, they find that experienced candidates (those who have previously held an elected office) are more likely to run when national and partisan tides favor their candidacy. As a result, Jacobson and Kernell conclude that experienced challengers wait until the conditions are the most advantageous before deciding to emerge (on this point, see also Carson (2005) for comparisons across House and Senate elections).

Individual-level strategic decisions can combine to produce a major swing in the partisan composition of Congress even in the absence of a significant partisan shift in the electorate. As such, strategic decisions by congressional candidates, based on factors such as the perceived likelihood of victory, the apparent value of the seat to them, and the opportunity costs of running for office both reflect and enhance national partisan swings. Consequently, which candidates run, and when, is critical to the interpersonal and partisan dynamics that shape the legislative process in the U.S. Congress. National parties exhibit strategic behavior as well, providing campaign resources such as campaign appearances by party leaders to quality candidates running in competitive elections to increase their prospects for victory. Ultimately, a greater number of experienced candidates running for elective office can mean the difference between victory and defeat for incumbent legislators in vulnerable districts.

Jacobson (1989) provides additional support for his initial findings with Kernell using an expanded dataset that includes elections from 1946 to 1986. Although experienced challengers are most likely to emerge when there is an open seat (no incumbent seeking re-election), there is only a small percentage of open seats in any given election. In addition, if an incumbent appeared particularly vulnerable in their previous race or was involved in a political scandal, then a quality challenger is more likely to emerge. We can see this during the 2008 election when Nancy Boyda (D-KS) was targeted by the National Republican Congressional Committee as a vulnerable incumbent after winning her previous election by a narrow margin of 51 to 47 percent. As a result, two strong challengers stood in the Republican primary: State Treasurer Lynn Jenkins and former Congressman Jim Ryun. Jenkins emerged as the winner of the congressional primary and was able to narrowly defeat the incumbent.

Other scholars have developed alternative measures of candidate quality (see, e.g., Bond, Covington, and Fleisher 1985; Krasno and Green 1988), yet Jacobson's dichotomous measure has become widely used throughout the study of House elections. Certainly the somewhat blunt measure is not without potential flaws, as there are occasionally successful candidates who win elections with no previous elective experience (along with numerous quality candidates who are unable to unseat incumbent legislators). Yet the relative parsimony and ease of replication have made Jacobson's measure of previous elected experience a reliable measure in the study of House elections.

In their study of candidate competition, Banks and Kiewiet (1989) focus on a somewhat different question: given that most incumbents face some type of challenge each year, why do candidates without political experience elect to challenge incumbent members of Congress? Using primary elections data from 1980 to 1984, they find that the motivations of weaker, inexperienced candidates are similar to experienced challengers—both want to win. Weak candidates recognize that they are more likely to gain their party's nomination when an incumbent is present, than when there is an open seat. Although they will most likely lose in the general election, these candidates can increase their name recognition and electoral skill. If they wait until an incumbent retires, the primary field will most likely be filled with many experienced candidates, making it more difficult for them to receive their party's nomination.

While research on strategic politicians has offered valuable insight into House elections, relatively few scholars have considered the same phenomenon in the context of the Senate. For their part, Senate scholars who have studied candidate quality have been reluctant to adopt the dichotomous measure of previous elective experience. Lublin (1994) studies strategic politicians in the Senate from 1952 to 1990 and finds that members of the House of Representatives are the most successful Senate challengers. As a result, he proposes ranking previous elected experience of Senate candidates with members of the House of Representatives ranked above governors and other statewide officials. One would expect a governor to be a stronger Senate challenger having already represented the entire state, while members of the House are only familiar with a portion of the Senate constituency. Nevertheless, Lublin argues that voters most likely feel that service in the national government requires a different skill set than state-level elected office. In terms of his analysis, Lublin finds that candidates running for the Senate take into account similar factors as their House counterparts, such as economic, national, and partisan tides.

While most scholars agree that not all political candidates are created equal, they have to date been unable to identify what specific characteristics make an experienced candidate more likely to win. Is it their greater name recognition among the voters that gives them an electoral advantage? Are they simply better politicians, possessing certain skills making them more of an expert in the art of electioneering? Perhaps candidates who have previously won elected office better understand how to manage a campaign and utilize their resources such as time and money (on this point, see Steen 2006). Absent additional empirical work in this area, it would be difficult to accurately assess which of these competing explanations is most helpful in addressing these important questions. Moreover, the weights attached to each of these possible explanations have direct implications for assessing the health of representation and electoral accountability in the United States.

Money in Congressional Elections

In 2008, Ric Keller, a four-term Republican from Florida's 8th district, was outspent by his opponent to the tune of over $1.4 million dollars. Keller himself raised $1,168,536 for his unsuccessful re-election bid. However, challengers need not outspend their opponents by millions of dollars to unseat an incumbent member of Congress. Of the 19 incumbents who lost their seats in 2008, 11 outspent their opponents (Abramson, Aldrich, and Rohde 2010). Not surprising to most political observers, the average cost of campaigning for Congress has steadily risen each year. In 2006, for example, the average Senate campaign cost over eight million dollars while the average race for a House seat hovered at just under one million dollars (Jacobson 2009). Candidates for political office must have access to, or be able to raise, substantial sums of money just to be competitive in any congressional election.

With the passage of the Federal Election Campaign Act in the early 1970s, candidates for political office were required to disclose the amount of money raised and spent in their political campaigns. As such, it became easier to collect and analyze this information. Jacobson (1978, 1980) was among the first to systematically examine the nature of the relationship between campaign spending and election outcomes in congressional races. Indeed, Jacobson suggested that campaign spending may not have the same effects for incumbents and challengers. Based on his analyses of congressional elections from the 1970s, Jacobson (1978, 1980) found that the amount of money spent by challengers has a much more pronounced effect on election outcomes than does spending by incumbents. In a widely cited study, Jacobson (1978: 469) asserted that "the more incumbents spend, the worse they do." The reason for this somewhat counterintuitive claim, Jacobson (1978: 469) argues, is that incumbents "raise and spend money in direct proportion to the magnitude of the electoral threat posed by the challenger, but this reactive spending fails to offset the progress made by the challenger that inspires it in the first place." Challengers, in contrast, get more "bang for the buck" since they are starting with significantly lower levels of name recognition than incumbents.

Although surprising at first, Jacobson contends that this anomaly may best be understood in terms of the quality of the challenger and the perceived closeness of the race. Incumbents who run against a quality candidate in an election often have to raise and spend additional money in their campaign, but additional spending does not yield much in the way of further advantages since incumbents often start off with relatively high levels of name recognition. Moreover, high-quality or experienced candidates are usually adept at raising money themselves, which makes it more challenging for an incumbent to defeat them. Incumbents who perceive themselves to be in electoral danger can and do typically raise and spend more money than do incumbents who perceive themselves to be relatively safe in a particular election. Therefore, on average, incumbents who win by a large electoral margin spend relatively small amounts of money when compared to incumbents in close races. Thus, Jacobson concludes that increased spending can definitely help the challenger, but is almost always associated with lower vote shares for the incumbent.[5]

Beyond examining the effects of money in determining electoral outcomes, students of congressional politics have also examined the deterrent effects of incumbent fundraising. Most notably, some scholars believe that incumbents accumulate large sums of money in their war chests in an attempt to "scare off" potential challengers from running in a given election (Epstein and Zemsky 1995; Jacobson 1990a, 2009). Indeed, using a variety of different measures, several scholars have found that the amount of money raised by an incumbent does serve as a potential deterrent to candidate entry in congressional races (see, e.g., Goldenberg, Traugott, and Baumgartner 1986; Goidel and Gross 1994; Hersch and McDougall 1994; Box-Steffensmeier 1996; Carson 2003). Nevertheless, not everyone who studies congressional elections agrees with this conclusion about the deterrent effect of money. Several different students of legislative politics (see, e.g., Krasno and Green 1988; Epstein and Zemsky 1995; Milyo 1998; Ansolabehere and Snyder 2000; Goodliffe 2001, 2007) have found that the amount of money raised by an incumbent does *not* serve as an effective deterrent to entry of strong or experienced challengers in congressional races.[6]

Regardless of which side one falls with respect to these divergent findings, nearly everyone agrees that money is a critical component of electoral success. Moreover, and as noted earlier, there is little doubt that congressional elections, like presidential elections, have become much more expensive in recent decades. Growing disparities in spending patterns by incumbents and challengers raise obvious concerns about representation and democratic accountability in the context of House and Senate elections. Indeed, some view the lack of financial competitiveness in congressional races as a contributing factor in the decline of electoral competition during the post-World War II era (see, e.g., Jacobson and Kernell 1981; Abramowitz 1989, 1991). At the same time, how one views this important debate has important policy implications given recent discussions about campaign finance reform efforts in political races. In light of this, we hope to see additional work examine and resolve these important questions.

Why Incumbents Lose

So why, ultimately, do some incumbents lose their bids for re-election? Unfortunately for those incumbent members of the House and Senate planning their upcoming campaigns, there is no simple answer. Incumbents work diligently to cultivate a positive brand name for themselves at home in their district. Members of Congress who are unable to effectively advertise, credit-claim, or take positions may be the most electorally vulnerable (Mayhew 1974a). Yet another possibility is that incumbents lose or do worse than expected because they face highly qualified candidates with previous elected experience (Jacobson 1989). If incumbents are unable to ward off or deter a quality challenger from emerging, the race will likely be much more expensive. Unfortunately for incumbents, spending by challengers has been found to be more effective than incumbent spending as challengers are able to get more "bang for their buck" in congressional races (Jacobson 1980). Quality challengers able to raise large sums of money are likely to be the most competitive opposition an incumbent will face. Indeed, Jacobson (2009) finds that strong challengers with greater financial resources are 20 percent more likely to defeat incumbents than challengers lacking political experience.

In some cases national tides, outside of their control, may simply act against incumbents. This was clearly the case in 2006, when public approval of President Bush hovered at around 40 percent and Americans had grown weary of the ongoing wars in both Iraq and Afghanistan. Of the 22 incumbents who lost in 2006, all but one were Republicans (Jacobson 2007b). In many cases, party organizations target vulnerable incumbents who won their previous election by a small margin. The national parties then work to recruit qualified candidates and help raise large sums of money to unseat these incumbents. A final problem largely outside the control of incumbents is redistricting. Bauer and Hibbing (1989) argue that incumbents are most likely to lose only when they face a scandal or their district boundaries have been dramatically altered. Although redistricting is a concern that incumbents must deal with only every ten years, when it does occur, it may be a contributing factor to a small number of incumbent defeats.

Ultimately, while the vast majority of incumbents win re-election handily, they are not invincible as congressional candidates. Incumbents are not guaranteed certain victory in any given election. In the words of Mayhew (1974a: 37),

> When we say "Congressman Smith is unbeatable," we do not mean that there is nothing he could do that would lose him his seat. Rather we mean, "Congressman Smith is unbeatable as long as he continues to do the things he is doing."

If incumbents stray too far from the desires of their constituents or do not work diligently enough to provide the voters with distributive benefits or bureaucratic assistance, then an incumbent can expect stiff competition in the next election. However, the large majority of incumbents appear to be aware of how their actions can influence electoral outcomes and most work diligently to maintain their seat in Congress.

New Directions in Congressional Elections Research

As noted earlier, research on congressional elections has made remarkable progress since the early 1970s when scholars first observed that incumbents seemed to be winning re-election at much higher rates than in the past (Erikson 1971; Mayhew 1974b). Even with the decades of ensuing research, however, we believe several important areas have been overlooked in terms of further enhancing our understanding of congressional elections. To begin with, it is not an oversight on our part that most of the discussion in this chapter has focused almost exclusively on House elections; rather, this is reflective of the current state of the congressional elections literature. On the whole, we know a great deal about House elections but comparatively less about Senate elections as reflected in the asymmetry in the scholarship across the two chambers of Congress.

Many research questions, which have been systematically examined in the context of the House, have been virtually ignored in the upper chamber. In fact, and until very recently, much of the extant research on the U.S. Congress simply ignored the bicameral nature of the legislature and focused solely on the House. This is unfortunate, as a single Senate election has a far greater chance of being pivotal than a typical House election given the smaller size of the upper chamber. In addition, with the longer terms of office for U.S. Senators (six years compared to two for their counterparts in the House), the dynamics of the electoral connection may be significantly altered for legislators in the upper chamber. The increased length of time between elections may give senators greater leeway in the legislative process compared to legislators in the House, or it may make them less responsive except in the periods leading up to an election.

To systematically examine these types of issues in greater detail, we propose additional research be carried out on Senate elections. In particular, we would like to see new analyses that examine fundamentally important questions such as the incumbency advantage, the impact of challenger quality, and the effects of campaign fundraising in the context of Senate elections. This is certainly not to say that these questions have never been addressed (see, e.g., Abramowitz and Segal 1993; Krasno 1994). Distinct institutional differences between the two chambers may lead to significant variation in elections to both the House and Senate. For instance, a Senate election offers an incumbent the rare opportunity to watch someone else run a campaign for the same office with the same constituents. At some point during a senator's term, her other colleague from her home state will be forced to run for re-election. As such, senators may alter their campaign behavior based on the campaigns and elections of their counterparts. Unique facets of the Senate such as these merit more scholarly attention.

Another area ripe for additional research with respect to congressional elections is greater historical analyses of congressional elections. Most research on House elections artificially limits its sample to congressional elections from 1946 to the present, owing to the availability of these data. However, there is a wealth of congressional elections data prior to that time that is readily available for study. Turning to the study of historical election trends can offer additional leverage on questions relevant to the modern Congress that are more difficult to address in the modern era. For example, Carson, Engstrom, and Roberts (2007) find strong evidence that the incumbency advantage existed in House elections as far back as the late nineteenth century when many of the advantages naturally accruing to incumbents such as the perquisites of office simply did not exist. Studying congressional elections over longer time periods will allow for the development of more dynamic and generalizable theories of congressional elections.

A third area where additional research on House and Senate elections could be beneficial is greater emphasis on primary elections. Political scientists know very little about the actions of candidates in primaries and voters' decisions in congressional primaries. In many congressional districts dominated by one party, results from the general election make it appear as if there is little or no competition for the seat. However, there may be a great deal of competition at the primary level that is simply being overlooked, since relatively few scholars study these types of elections (for exceptions, see Banks and Kiewiet 1989; Galderisi, Ezra, and Lyons 2001). By ignoring this important stage of the electoral process, we may be missing a great deal of existing competition in congressional elections. Understanding when and under what conditions a candidate emerges in primary elections as well as what factors lead to a candidate's success in a field crowded with fellow partisans is essential.

One final area we would like to see scholars devote additional effort to in future research is trying to understand why certain candidates are more likely to run, and ultimately, to win. We know that candidates with previous elected experience perform better in elections to the House of Representatives than do their inexperienced counterparts, yet we cannot readily identify why this is the case. What is it about these quality challengers that makes them better candidates in these elections? Are they more successful fundraisers, having already built a base of support in previous electoral campaigns? Or is it simply that these individuals have greater familiarity with the voters, which obviously translates into increased voter recognition on Election Day?

Another possibility is that experienced challengers are better at running and managing a political campaign and, thus, are better suited to compete in congressional elections. Without additional research on House and Senate elections, however, we cannot adequately address these important questions, which are fundamental to our understanding of enhanced accountability, competition, and representation in our electoral system.

Conclusion

Competition is at the heart of electoral research. As noted from the outset of this chapter, the exceedingly high re-election rate of incumbent members of Congress (especially in the House of Representatives) suggests to many that the accountability and responsibility mechanism has been severed between constituents and their elected representatives. One should keep in mind, however, that simply because most elections are not competitive does not mean that electoral accountability does not exist. It may be that for the most part voters are content or happy with their current members of Congress. Furthermore, the advantages accruing to incumbents are not insurmountable for the most experienced and qualified candidates. When incumbents do stray from the interests of their constituents, or take their re-election for granted, they can be defeated. Scholars of both House and Senate elections should continue to seek new and innovative ways to understand competition and accountability in our electoral process.

Notes

1. Two recent examples of such elections are 1994 and 2006. The first was worse for Democratic candidates due to the unpopularity of President Clinton, while the latter was unfavorable for Republicans due to growing displeasure with President Bush and the ongoing Iraq War.
2. Since the Civil War, the president's party has lost seats in the House of Representatives in all but three midterm elections.
3. Several additional scholars offer various offshoots of the surge-and-decline theory also suggesting that the party of the president tends to lose seats during the midterm. See, for instance, Tufte (1975) and Kernell (1977) on negative voting and the economy, Fiorina (1981) in connection with retrospective voting, and Oppenheimer, Stimson, and Waterman (1986) on the exposure thesis.
4. For evidence supporting each of these contentions, see Cover and Brumberg (1982), Alford and Hibbing (1981), and Bovitz and Carson (2006) respectively.
5. This counterintuitive finding has come under intense criticism by congressional scholars who disagree over how to properly specify empirical models incorporating incumbent and challenger spending. For views contrary to those of Jacobson in the context of House elections, see Green and Krasno (1988), Ansolabehere and Gerber (1994), Levitt (1994), and Erikson and Palfrey (1998). For contrary evidence from Senate elections, see Gerber (1998).
6. Given the prevailing trends in other areas of congressional elections research, it should not come as a surprise that most of the research on the effects of money and elections has been examined using House elections.

Chapter 12

Presidential Elections

Campaigning within a Segmented Electorate

Scott D. McClurg and Philip Habel[1]

Presidential campaigns are arguably the most important political events in a citizen's life. According to the American National Election Study, a biennial random sample survey conducted among citizens aged 18 or older, interest in and attentiveness to presidential elections is considerable. On average, approximately a quarter of all Americans are "very interested" in presidential campaigns, with large majorities reporting that they monitor the campaign through print and broadcast media.[2] Moreover, among Americans eligible to vote, turnout in presidential elections from 1948 to 2008 averaged just under 60 percent.[3] Contests for control of the Executive Branch are among the few moments in time when Americans are collectively focused on government and politics.

As a consequence, political stakeholders—candidates, campaign managers, interest groups, pundits, to name a few—are acutely interested in communicating their priorities and positions to the public, creating opportunities for citizens to educate themselves on the health and direction of American society. Yet because stakeholders are self-interested actors they are not as committed to providing citizens with unbiased information that might facilitate "good" decisions as they are to advancing their agenda. It is this back-and-forth process among different actors that creates the unique patterns of information, emotion, and imagery and that constitutes the core of a presidential campaign and, ultimately, affects the outcome on Election Day.

An unavoidable product of this situation is the presence of stark differences in the amount and quality of information available to different groups of voters. Although presidential elections are ostensibly national debates about our collective concerns, in actuality they directly involve only a small part of the nation's states, media markets, communities, and voters. As political scientists have come to better understand how campaigns influence election outcomes and voting behavior, they have noted that the electorate is sliced into ever smaller pieces, that campaigns provide certain messages and information to some voters and not to others. This is what we call the segmented electorate. This segmentation holds important consequences for how individuals choose candidates, and ultimately, the kinds of outcomes we get from elections.

In this chapter, we offer this simple hypothesis about presidential campaigns in a media age: campaigns focus increasingly on narrower, more limited appeals to specific voters and eschew broader policy debates about the direction of government. The implication is that today's campaigns contribute to fragmentation in American government and fail to add coherence at the one moment in time when such a debate is possible. To demonstrate support for our point of view, we first describe significant transformations in presidential campaigns that are rooted in a combination of electoral reforms and technological innovation. We then identify how campaign strategies are developed in this environment, and we explain the implications this has for future presidential elections. From there we proceed to demonstrate how campaigns influence voters and provide some evidence that campaigns reach and mobilize a particular group that we call "peripheral partisans." The chapter concludes by addressing the question of how trends in information technology are leading us "back to the future," with campaigns focusing on ever narrower groups of voters rather than on more nationalized elections in which all voters are engaged.

The Operation of Presidential Campaigns

For us to explain and understand presidential campaigns—and ultimately their impact on the voters—we must understand the "rules of the game," particularly in terms of how they help us decide who wins and loses in presidential politics. While it is true that these rules have been more or less the same since our earliest efforts to select a president, the actors who must navigate them and the tools they have for achieving their goals have changed significantly over time. In this section, we discuss how the operation of presidential campaigns has evolved over time in order to explain why they segment the electorate and the challenges this holds for future campaigns. This sets the stage for our later discussion about the consequences that these strategies have for the voters who ultimately decide between candidates for president.

Background

To understand the modern campaign, we must look at the political history and institutional context under which presidential elections have taken place. The institution established by the Founders to select the president, the Electoral College, was devised as a means of insulating the choice of our chief executive from the whims and passions of the masses. The Electoral College represented a compromise among the states—awarding disproportionately more representation for states of lesser populations, while also maintaining numeric strength for states with greater populations—with the total number of electors equal to the number of Representatives and Senators for each state (Edwards 2004; Wayne 2011). Given this formula, and the fact that the

Constitution created a winner-take-all system, presidential candidates and party elites soon recognized the importance of creating a winning coalition comprising electors from certain states, states that were to become the target of their efforts. Even at the onset of U.S. democracy, and still true today, securing a plurality of voters nationally was only important inasmuch as it led to victory in the Electoral College (Davis 1997).

Party elites dominated early presidential elections. Congressional and state legislative caucuses controlled candidate nominations and exercised subsequent influence in the general election. Candidates themselves engaged in little active campaigning, leaving such matters to newspapers and party elites. Newspapers praised their preferred candidate and ridiculed the opposition, at times using accusations and slurs that would raise eyebrows today.[4] Although the election of 1828 witnessed the end of "King Caucus," party elites continued to exercise considerable influence over the nomination process through their control of both local party organizations and, ultimately, the convention delegates who chose the party nominees.

The dominance of party elites and the importance of local party organizations in campaigns outlasted a number of subsequent reforms, including efforts to reduce and later eliminate the poll tax; efforts to limit corruption, such as reforms to the civil service in the late 1800s; mandates on hiring bureaucrats based on merit rather than campaign service; and limits on the campaign activities of unions and corporations. Party organizations engaged in most of the actual campaign activity, based in part on their local organizational strength, while the candidates played a much less central role in the day-to-day affairs of the campaign. To offer some sense of how this era contrasts with today, consider the McKinley "front porch" campaign of 1896, where delegations of voters were invited to travel from across the country to Canton, Ohio for an opportunity to meet with McKinley, with an estimated 750,000 citizens availing themselves of the opportunity (Boller 2004).

Several additional reforms and technological advances eventually shifted power away from party elites in the twentieth century. The rise of the direct primary forced party elites to cede more control to the public during the nomination stage. The subsequent appearance of mass media—first in the form of radio, and later, television—permitted candidates to reach the electorate directly with their messages and mobilize voters. Given the government's creation of "media markets" dictating what geographic areas were to be covered (and excluded) by a given station's broadcast, campaigns could take advantage of unique media markets to target voters in high-stakes, battleground states. Indeed, television ushered in the advent of segmentation, where certain messages could be readily disseminated across the country, while other communications could be used to target audiences located in particular areas (Kendall 2000, Boller 2004). As early as the 1960s, candidates were cognizant of the ways in which television advertisements could be used strategically, and they shifted their efforts toward these techniques.

The transition in power away from parties culminated with the McGovern Fraser Commission's nomination reforms that were implemented in the aftermath of the 1968 election. Under these rules, the delegate vote at the convention was to be a close approximation of the results of the primary elections. The change brought about the beginnings of campaigns where candidates' fortunes were no longer governed by party elites (Polsby 1983). The reduced grip of parties on nominations offered opportunities for little-known candidates to gain momentum and rise to prominence, particularly with early primary/caucus wins in states such as New Hampshire and Iowa. It also widened the opening for other political stakeholders—including the media, interest groups, and other activists—to become more involved. Thus the campaign took on new importance, and candidates began to recognize the value of a well-coordinated and calculated effort to win.

The McGovern Fraser reforms had far-reaching effects, but the most important was the rise of candidate-centered elections. In contrast to party-based campaigns run by insiders, in this system, candidates cultivated their own message, image, and base—often in ways independent of the parties (Jamieson 1996; Campbell 2008b). Although candidates today still rely on the party for financial resources and expertise, particularly following the primaries, they enjoy greater liberty in dictating their fortunes than do the candidates of an earlier era. Today, messages, targets, and strategies are at the discretion of the campaign rather than the party.

The Strategic Environment of Modern Campaigns

With the rise of candidate-centered campaign organizations and the rise of direct voter contact through the media, a new style of electoral campaigning has evolved. The party insiders who once controlled primaries and wielded extensive field organizations have been replaced by the likes of political consultants, media strategists, data miners, and interest group liaisons who use money and technical expertise as their campaign weapons. The impact of their expertise and tools has shaped campaigns such that today we have highly segregated campaign environments, where certain people's votes are pursued by campaigns armed with important information, while other voters are taken for granted and ignored.

Campaign strategy ultimately revolves around decisions about how to distribute resources between states in order to build an Electoral College majority. The challenge facing candidates and their organizations is how to use their resources (time and money) to produce information environments (messages) that allow them to gain enough support (votes) in the right places in order to achieve that goal. In the contemporary campaign era, presidential campaign managers conceive of this decision in terms of efficiency and expediency. Efficiency captures the marginal cost associated with campaign activities, while expediency refers to the marginal gain in support given the cost of an activity. Daron Shaw's (2006) extensive research on campaign strategies based on internal campaign memos from the 2000 and 2004 elections illustrates what these concepts mean and what they imply.

Campaigns are concerned about efficiency because they do not want to waste scarce resources. A principal manifestation of this, according to Shaw (2006), is a focus on cost; all things being equal, a campaign would rather spend money in a market or state that is less expensive. As Shaw's data show, the cost of television advertising—and this is undoubtedly true for other forms of campaign, such as canvassing—varies substantially by both state and media market. For example, there are marked differences in the cost of 100 gross rating points in the 20 most efficient media markets.[5] As an example, even within the state of Missouri, the cost of 100 GRPs ranged from $2,000 in the Jefferson City-Columbia media market to $13,700 in St. Louis (Shaw 2006: 61). For a campaign short on the funds necessary to buy a blitz, the attractiveness of the Jefferson City market is clear.

But campaigns are not merely about efficiency, and decisions about how to spend resources are not based solely on cost. In order to win, decisions on where to spend must also be balanced by the potential gain in votes. The example we introduced from Missouri underscores this point. Although a campaign can purchase more ad time in Jefferson City-Columbia than in St. Louis due to the cost, the ad will reach fewer potential voters in Jefferson City—approximately 280,000 voters versus over 1,000,000 in St. Louis. In addition, depending upon which voters in Missouri support the campaign, and to what degree, it may be sensible to organize a smaller, more effective ad buy in St. Louis than a cheaper and more extensive (but less effective) campaign in Jefferson City-Columbia.

This is where expediency—the marginal gain in potential voters given the cost of campaign activities—factors into campaign strategy. As the popular Red state/Blue state metaphor suggests, there are significant differences in the politics of each state, and certain states are unlikely to be winnable for a given presidential campaign (Fiorina, Abrams, and Pope 2006; Gelman et al. 2008). This is illustrated in Table 12.1, which shows the last time each of the states switched from one major party candidate to another in successive elections. As may be seen in this table, voters in states like Wyoming and Utah have consistently favored the same party for around 40 years, while those in states such as Missouri and Colorado have been carried by candidates from different parties in recent elections.

How do these criteria—Electoral College votes, efficiency, and expediency—shape the different information environments to which voters are exposed? Shaw (1999b, 2006) and Huang and Shaw (2009) show that campaigns by the two major party candidates classify states into three categories that form the basis of their campaign strategy, and, by implication, campaign intensity varies by category. The first of these categories are what Shaw calls base states (such as Utah and Oklahoma), where the campaigns have very

Table 12.1 Last Election in which State Shifted Party Support from Previous Presidential Election

State	Year	State	Year	State	Year	State	Year	State	Year
Colorado	2008	Arizona	2000	Connecticut	1992	Massachusetts	1988	Minnesota	1976
Florida	2008	Arkansas	2000	Delaware	1992	New York	1988	Alaska	1968
Indiana	2008	Kentucky	2000	Illinois	1992	Oregon	1988	Idaho	1968
Iowa	2008	Louisiana	2000	Maine	1992	Rhode Island	1988	Kansas	1968
Nevada	2008	Missouri	2000	Maryland	1992	Washington	1988	Nebraska	1968
New Mexico	2008	Tennessee	2000	Michigan	1992	Wisconsin	1988	North Dakota	1968
North Carolina	2008	West Virginia	2000	New Jersey	1992	Alabama	1980	Oklahoma	1968
Ohio	2008	Georgia	1996	Pennsylvania	1996	Mississippi	1980	South Dakota	1968
Virginia	2008	Montana	1996	Vermont	1996	South Carolina	1980	Utah	1968
New Hampshire	2004	California	1992	Hawaii	1992	Texas	1980	Wyoming	1968

little incentive to compete, because one party is heavily favored to win. Not surprisingly, there is almost no campaigning in many of these states, particularly regarding campaign advertising and visits from the candidates. The second category includes marginal states where one party has a natural advantage because of the state's history, but where (typically) both campaigns expend resources in their efforts to build an Electoral College majority. The degree to which they put resources into these states is especially sensitive to the campaign's financial resources and the cost of media markets; if campaigns have sufficient funds and are doing well generally, they may compete harder in such states to broaden their base of support. Finally, there are the battleground states (such as Missouri and Colorado) where both campaigns input substantial time, effort, and money because they anticipate a close outcome. These states tend to be more costly because they are competitive, but their "winability" means that a campaign must spend considerable time and money winning over voters in those states. It is in these areas that the campaign is most intense and the voters are faced with a constant barrage of information.

In addition to differences driven by these strategic considerations, the level of electoral segmentation is also dependent on the national political context. Consider, as an illustration, the highly competitive 2000 presidential election juxtaposed with the far less competitive 2008 election. The 2000 election pitted former Senator and then current Vice-President Albert Gore against George W. Bush, the then popular governor of Texas and the son of former president George H.W. Bush. Despite a strong economy that should have benefited Gore, many voters suffered from "Clinton fatigue" due to the outgoing president's infidelities and scandals while in office. Thus it was difficult for Gore to claim credit for the previous administration's successes without being attached to its embarrassments. Bush's credentials, his image as a "compassionate conservative," and the national political context, facilitated his ability to fundraise, and therefore, compete. By contrast, the 2008 election was marked by an increasingly severe economic crisis and with discontent over eight years of the Bush administration, which significantly advantaged the Democratic candidate. The Democratic nominee, Barack Obama, raised substantial funds, while the Republican candidate, John McCain, accepted public funds for his campaign and the stringent fundraising limits that came with them. In the end, Obama was able to outspend McCain significantly.

As shown in Table 12.2, such disparate contexts produce different levels of electoral segmentation across the states and over time. In 2000, the campaign was competitive in a smaller range of states—as judged by the ad expenditure data—and especially intense in the battleground states, with both campaigns working fervently for the same votes. In contrast, the 2008 electoral terrain was dominated by the Democrat, Barack Obama, as witnessed in the spending data especially. Given the political context and his vast stores of funds, Obama was able to spend heavily in both battleground and marginal states, appar-

Table 12.2 Campaigning in the 2008 and 2000 Presidential Elections

	2008	*2000*
Republican spending[a]	$358	$185
Democratic spending	$760	$120
Number of battleground states[b]	10	15
States with Republican ad expenditures[c]	31	19
States with Democratic ad expenditures	36	15

Notes

a Spending data are for entire two-year reporting cycle. Obtained from www.fec.gov (Accessed May 17 2010).

b These are states, categorized as a battleground by at least one of the major party campaigns. Data obtained from Shaw (2006) and Huang and Shaw (2009).

c These are states shown as having an ad buy of one or more GRPs by Shaw (2006) and Huang and Shaw (2009).

ently with some success. By contrast, John McCain was left to focus on holding a base that was not overly enthusiastic about his candidacy.

The Future of Campaign Strategy

What then do the imperatives of efficiency and expediency imply about the future of presidential campaigns, particularly with regards to strategic and tactical decision-making? Ultimately, campaigns would like to spend their money on persuadable voters and, conversely, not spend on those who cannot be swayed. Accordingly, campaigns must both identify these persuadable voters and develop contacting strategies that allow them to focus singularly upon them.

Two trends have become apparent in recent campaigns as they try to distinguish between votes for which they will compete and those for which they will not: narrowcasting and micro-targeting. Concerning narrowcasting, in today's multi-channel, multi-audience world, campaigns can locate a great deal of information about the viewing habits of voters and the audiences for different television programs. As a consequence, campaign managers can decide what people are more likely to see advertisements and (for the campaigns with time and resources) potentially cast different versions of their message depending on the audience. Similarly, for micro-targeting, campaigns can shape their message and contacts to voters based on information they are able to compile about those individuals.

The distinction of today's campaign from earlier elections relates to the amount and variety of information collected on voters. Such information is typically based on a combination of both data mining (a process in which statisticians use material they access from data companies, such as magazine subscriptions), and opinion surveys, used to identify groups of voters with particular interests. Campaigns then compile these data to decide on what information voters receive, be it a certain campaign mailer or a knock on the door from a canvasser with a particular message. Although, ultimately, changes in privacy laws and the increasing reluctance of voters to participate in surveys may reduce the feasibility of certain tactics, the strategic imperatives of campaigns will accelerate the drive toward increased electoral segmentation. In an age where data on individual voters abound, the group of voters that are contacted will be, presumably, increasingly smaller and divided into ever narrower swathes.

Campaigns That Matter

The trend in the previous section toward narrower, more focused campaigns that do not engage in a "national conversation" has been documented by numerous studies (Shaw 1999a; Simon 2002; Johnston, Hagen, and Jamieson 2004; Holbrook and McClurg 2005; Shaw 2006; Wolak 2006; Hillygus and Shields 2008; McClurg and Holbrook 2009). Less clear from that discussion is whether voters exposed to the campaign behave differently than others. If true, such differences in behavior have consequences for both the outcome of a race and the behavior of presidents once they enter office. In this section, we first explain why it is that campaigns might have very limited consequences for voters, in order to demonstrate the limits and importance of segmentation. We then follow with an explanation for why this skepticism about important consequences for campaigns has abated in recent years. We show how the literature has evolved to a more sophisticated understanding of voting and elections where campaigns play an important role.

Do Campaigns Matter? Sources of Skepticism

Early political communication research advanced what became known as "minimal effects" understanding of campaigns (Berelson, Lazarsfeld, and McPhee 1954). According to this perspective, exposure to campaign advertisements did not change minds, but rather served to reinforce underlying predispositions, motivating partisans to act on their biases. A campaign did little more than activate latent preferences; it "crystallizes and reinforces more than it converts" (Berelson, Lazarsfeld, and McPhee 1954: 248).

With this as a foundation, scholars naturally focused on the causes and consequences of voters' political predispositions. One avenue of research examined socio-psychological factors that drove voting decisions. At the heart of this explanation, dubbed the "Michigan model" because of its origins among a group of scholars at the University of Michigan, was a focus on long-standing partisan affiliations that were, at times, superseded by temporary evaluations of parties, candidates, and issues (Campbell et al. 1960; Lewis-Beck et al. 2008). According to this model, partisan identities were strongly rooted in voters' social classes, religious affiliations, and group identities.

These factors then shaped how voters interpreted short-term factors. Through this lens campaigns were considered less important, largely because voters were seen as unwilling to move away from these core beliefs. Dissatisfied in part by what was perceived to be the Michigan model's downplaying of short-term factors in elections, a subsequent contribution developed a "retrospective voting" model. Seminal research in this vein noted that incumbent performance was a useful short cut in making electoral choices (Downs 1957) and could shape the preferences of those voters who were not strongly allied with a political party (Key 1966). In Fiorina's (1981) classic formulation, the author articulated how voters make decisions in the face of changing circumstances, particularly downturns in the economy. Yet despite a strong emphasis on issues and performance in this model, voters were still not considered to be heavily dependent on the campaign to inform their decision because "citizens need only calculate the changes in their own welfare. If jobs have been lost in a recession, something is wrong" (Fiorina 1981: 6). Here again, there was no reason to believe that campaigns played an important role in the decisions that voters made.

From a different vantage point, other research called into question the importance of both campaigns and the media by questioning their capacity to inform voters. In this vein of research the implication was that, even if voters were not driven by deeply rooted predilections and economic performance, there was not much to be learned about elections from the campaigns and media. As an example of this logic, consider that modern campaigns are dominated by negative advertisements. Conventional wisdom from campaign strategists and early empirical evidence suggests that negative ads will shape voter attitudes about the candidates, essentially generating ill-will toward the derided candidate. Indeed, some scholars suggest that such advertisements had deleterious consequences for democracy, fostering cynicism among the electorate and ultimately depressing turnout by as much as 5 percent (Ansolabehere et al. 1994; Ansolabehere and Iyengar 1995). However, as more work has been done on these issues, there has been meager support for such strong claims, particularly regarding the consequences for turnout or vote choice (see Lau et al. (1999) and Lau, Sigelman, and Rovner (2007) for reviews).

With respect to the mass media in elections, scholars and pundits alike have been wary of the power of the news media to offer voters the kind of information needed to make normatively good decisions. Such decisions, based on the rationality perspective of voting behavior (see Hinich and Munger (1997) for a review), suggests voters are "voting correctly" when they efficaciously translate their preferences to their vote choice (Lau and Redlawsk 2006). Faced with competing pressures to be financially viable—and in the case of the 24-hour news networks, to provide a constant stream of information—many have noted the dominance of news intended to appeal to audiences (and, therefore, advertisers)(Hamilton 2004). Many media critics have argued that such news compromises the quality of information which voters receive. In this market-driven model, the "news" is the information that captures the audience's attention—which can translate to entertainment-orientated soft news; information that is sensational, emphasizing conflict, scandal, or disaster; and information that covers familiar themes and personalities excessively (see Graber (2010) for a review). In the context of elections, Thomas Patterson (1993, 2002) finds that undue attention is granted to the game, the strategy decisions made among competing candidates; and, relatedly, to the horse race, changes in the polls among viable candidates leading up to Election Day. Such news coverage fails to elucidate the policy differences among the candidates, thereby obfuscating the information voters need to make a "correct" choice. The absence of quality news also creates an opportunity for candidates to cast their own message to voters, to frame issues and ideas according to their own perspective.

Finally, political scientists have shown that election outcomes are quite predictable, and well in advance of an election, which again calls into question the effect of campaigns.[6] Using a handful of variables such as the state of the economy and presidential approval ratings, researchers have been able to approximate the percentage vote for the presidential candidates weeks, and even months, before Election Day. Thus it may be argued that the campaign itself must be less consequential, with the outcome driven by other factors. In other words, the campaign is more of a consequence of the political and economic environment than a cause of the outcome.

How Do We Know Campaigns Matter?

Recent developments in political science scholarship, however, give pause to such skepticism about the limited ability of campaigns to influence voters. Much of this has been driven by innovations in survey research and data collection that provide a better picture of electoral dynamics. When we examine trends in voter preferences and "political markets" over the course of presidential campaigns, key events such as televised debates (Holbrook 1996), degrees of advertising (Shaw 1999a), and other campaign-related phenomena (Campbell 2000; Hillygus and Jackman 2003) are undeniably linked to changes in how the public evaluates and responds to the candidates. How is it that the public as a whole can show significant change over time when we know from earlier research that people come to elections with partisan biases and broad concerns about government performance? The key to answering this question lies in thinking about how evidence for these two points has been gathered and used.

Academic surveys have typically approached voters in the weeks preceding Election Day and asked them a variety of questions about their upcoming decision. Although such surveys capture the strength of voters' leanings at a given moment in time, they fail to uncover important changes in how voters assess the candidates' credibility, personality, and ideology over the course of a campaign. Importantly, changes in voters' evaluations are conceivable even if the partisan lens through which they evaluate information does not itself change. To see how, consider the following in the context of the 2008 election. Many Democratic voters who supported Hillary Clinton's bid for the nomination likely leaned toward Barack Obama over John McCain at the beginning of the campaign, but the length and bitterness of the nomination battle could have left these voters with reservations about Obama's candidacy. Had the Obama campaign not explicitly tried to strengthen those voters' initial predispositions through various issue appeals, the entire dynamic of the 2008 race could have changed.

More generally, this means that we have to be careful interpreting what even two snapshots of the electorate may mean about the consequences of a campaign. To illustrate, consider a case in which the percentage of voters favoring a particular candidate does not greatly change over time. Despite the temptation to do so, you cannot infer that the same voters preferred the same candidate at each point in time, and in campaigns, those changes may be even more consequential. To illustrate, conservative Democrats may initially lean toward a Democratic presidential candidate in an election but eventually defect toward a moderate Republican on the basis of ideology. If that defection is offset by an equal number of undecided voters moving toward the Democratic candidate, then the total support for the two candidates may not have necessarily changed significantly. Given that candidates are not seeking a plurality of votes but rather a majority of Electoral College votes, such changes in support for a candidate can be highly consequential depending upon what they signify about where and with whom a candidate is losing or gaining ground.

The 2000 presidential election serves as a suitable illustration of what we are arguing about campaign effects revealing themselves over the course of an election. The American National Election Study (ANES) interviewed a sample of registered voters at two time points in 2000, once shortly before Election Day and once again in the weeks following. In the pre-election survey, Gore was preferred by 49.7 percent of the respondents and Bush by 43.1 percent; in the post-election survey, these numbers were 51.0 percent and 45.3 percent, respectively. These percentages tentatively suggest that voters' preferences did not waver significantly.[7] Yet, in contrast, the data displayed in Figure 12.1— drawn from a survey that sought to interview nearly 100 respondents on a weekly basis over the last three months of the campaign—show significant change in how voters reacted to the ebb and flow of the campaign (Johnston, Hagen, and Jamieson 2004).

As we can see, there were important shifts in how potential voters viewed the candidates in 2000 that become clear when the data are collected at an interval (here, the week) that is much closer to the meaningful unit for campaigns (days), rather than at one or two moments in time. Although Gore started the campaign with a clear advantage, he eventually lost that lead

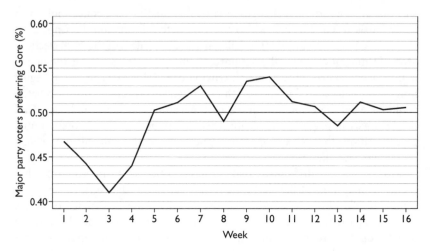

Figure 12.1 Percent preferring Gore over Bush, 2000 (source: 2000 National Annenberg Election Study).

around the time of the Republican Convention, only to spend the rest of the campaign playing catch-up. Were the campaigns "responsible" for this movement? Extensive analyses of the data that serve as the basis for this graphic and of other similar data suggest that the answer is a clear "yes." As the original analyses of these data show, Gore's comeback was driven by a message that focused on protecting Social Security (Johnston, Hagen, and Jamieson 2004). Given the closeness of that election, the implication is that had Gore's campaign focused on Social Security earlier, he might have won in November.

How Do Campaigns Influence Voters?

Such evidence of campaign effects helps assuage lingering doubts from earlier research about the importance of campaigns; however, the more central and perplexing question of how and why campaigns matter for voters remains. To address this, we need a model of voting that not only leaves room for decisions to be shaped by the campaign, but accounts for what we know from the earlier literature about the important roles of partisanship and retrospective evaluations. The mobilization model of campaign effects meets these criteria (Finkel 1993; Gelman and King 1993; Freedman, Franz and Goldstein 2004). This explanation of how voters change in response to information from campaigns is based on two assumptions consistent with prior evidence about voter decision-making. The first is that people with partisan predilections are more likely to pay attention to politics and are therefore more likely to respond to campaign information. The second assumption is that these same people—those who harbor partisan leanings—are also more likely to vote in the election, in part because they are more politically engaged, and in part because they are already more invested in politics. The implied contrast here is with those individuals who are apolitical or truly independent, meaning they are less attached to the naturally oppositional elements of politics. What is not assumed is that all voters with partisan views are equally committed or passionate about them, nor that they will inevitably cast a vote consistent with those views.

Campaign effects, then, are less about persuading independents and opponents and more about rekindling dormant loyalties and gathering support on Election Day. This mobilization perspective, to state it somewhat differently, suggests that campaigns tend to preach to a chorus of partisans who are more likely to say "Hallelujah" than they are to consider the merits of the sermon. Importantly, this fits with what we know about how campaigns make strategic decisions, focusing on persuadable voters and eschewing the strategy of engaging in a broad national debate.

Evidence from recent studies supports this perspective. Holbrook and McClurg (2005) find that as the amount of campaigning in a state increases, the composition of the voting day electorate becomes more partisan. In another study, they also found that the importance of ideology and partisanship for predicting votes in 1988 and 1992 increased for people who lived in battleground states (McClurg and Holbrook 2009). Other research uses continuous survey data (of the type displayed in Figure 12.1) to show that the so-called "fundamentals of voting"—factors, such as voter partisanship, interest, political evaluations that are presumably distinct from the campaign itself—become better predictors of election results as the campaign proceeds (Johnston, Hagen, and Jamieson 2004; Shaw 2006). The fundamental attributes that underlie voting behavior (such as partisanship) become activated and therefore more relevant over the course of the election, presumably because of information made available by the campaigns.

The Consequences of a Segmented Electorate

Campaigns "matter" in the sense that they mobilize the base voters of each party, a depiction that we believe fits well with the picture of the segmented electorate. In line with that expectation, the model suggests that the segregation of the electorate by campaigns does more to influence the beliefs of what we call "peripheral partisans." In contrast it offers less help to those voters whose beliefs are poorly anchored in the political system. Here we focus on using these understandings of campaign strategy and campaign effects to understand the consequences of segmentation for voting. We do this by focusing on the rise of more peripheral partisans who are likely to be persuaded by campaigns and the effect of living in areas saturated by campaign messages.

The Rise of the Peripheral Partisans

Although it is common for pundits and journalists to conceive of independent and undecided voters as blank slates, the truth is that most people harbor political prejudices that affect what information they acquire and that shape their behavior. In Figure 12.2, we provide two graphs that capture the percentage of strong partisans (Strong Identifiers), weak partisans (both Weak Identifiers and Leaners), and "true" independents and apolitical voters (Non-Identifiers) since the early 1950s. As shown on the left-hand side of Figure 12.2, the percentage of voters who have relatively weak partisan beliefs have

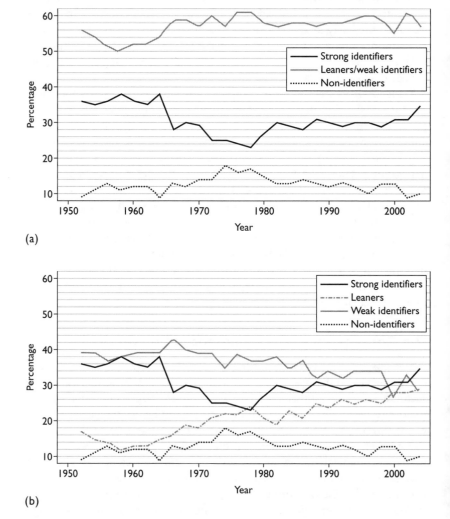

(a)

(b)

Figure 12.2 Trends in partisan identification, 1952–2004 (ANES data).

comprised over 50 percent of the electorate over the past 60 years.[8] This group is roughly twice the size of the most committed voters, the Strong Identifiers, and they outnumber Non-Identifiers by nearly six to one. In our view, it is the weak partisans who are the targets for campaigns because, while they have an affinity for one party or another, they also harbor more ambivalence toward the parties than do strong partisans. That is, they are more likely to be responsive to party messages (Petrocik 1996; Abbe et al. 2003) than Non-Identifiers and yet, importantly, they are less committed than strong partisans. In short, it is among these "peripheral partisans" where the campaign can get the most "bang for their buck."

Trends observed from the data in Figure 12.2 suggest that targeting weak partisans is becoming more important for the campaigns. Looking at the right-hand side of the figure, we observe a precipitous increase in the percentage of Leaners since the early 1960s. Importantly, the percentage of Non-Identifiers, the "true" independents, has generally decreased since the mid-1970s. Although much is made about the role of "independent" voters in dictating election outcomes, the growth in partisan leaners is of much greater consequence. Our conjecture is that the significant increase in "peripheral partisans" indicates that presidential candidates must attempt to bring these voters into the fold on Election Day.

If our interpretation holds, what some have suggested is merely partisans naturally returning to the fold as Election Day approaches is, rather, the result of a more complex set of factors driven by campaigns. Although a full test of this argument has yet to materialize, McClurg (2006) found that in the 2000 election, peripheral partisans were more responsive to the advertising strategies of the two parties than the other groups. In particular, he found that as the parties talked more about their traditional issues, peripheral partisans were more likely to favor the candidate of the party to which they had some allegiance.

Living in (or Near) a Battleground

If segmentation matters, then we should observe differential effects among those who are and are not targeted for campaign communications. Although this subject has only recently been broached by scholars, some research finds such differences. The first body of evidence stems from studies using so-called "field experiments" to study voter mobilization, which take place in a natural, real-world setting. Field experiments have distributed campaign messages to a randomly selected set of voters via phone, mail, or door-to-door canvassing. By randomly assigning the contacts to a sufficient number of voters, one can effectively rule out other potential causes of voter behavior and isolate the effect of the contact. In *Get Out the Vote!*, Alan Gerber and Donald Green (2004) use this cutting-edge technique to show that personal contacts, such as a neighborhood canvass, can increase voter turnout by as much as 7 percent.

Additional evidence comes from studies comparing the behavior of voters in battleground states to those who reside elsewhere. McClurg and Holbrook's (2009) analysis of the 1988 election shows that the controversial issue of race—clearly a center-piece of that campaign—played out differently in battleground states than in other areas. Likewise, they show that economic attitudes were more strongly related to battleground state voting in 1992 than in the other states. Other studies of both individuals (Wolak 2006) and groups of voters (Shaw 1999a, 2006; Johnston, Hagen, and Jamieson 2004) arrive at similar conclusions.

One reason, however, to give pause to our claim that campaign segmentation matters relates to a classic problem of inference known as selection bias. As noted, campaigns choose their targets carefully, which is another way of saying that voters in such locations have certain characteristics that set them apart from those in other areas. Thus if the people targeted by a campaign change their behavior, how can we know with confidence that this was because of the campaign instead of the characteristics that drew the campaign's attention in the first place? It is very difficult to distinguish between the effect of the campaign's message and the characteristics of the voters. Ideally, one would randomly contact some voters who are "good" targets, but not others, and study the behavior of the two groups.

One suitable approach to address selection bias, pioneered by Huber and Arceneaux (2007), has taken advantage of what one would call "accidental targets." Quite simply, these are voters who reside in media markets targeted by campaigns in competitive states, but who happen to live in a different state than the one focused on in the target. An example helps to illustrate the design of this research. Voters in the battleground state of Missouri have been heavily targeted in the past three presidential elections, while voters residing in neighboring Illinois and Kansas have not, given Illinois' and Kansas' status as base states (see Table 12.1). When the campaigns buy advertising time in Kansas City and St. Louis (not to mention in other media markets), a number of voters in Kansas and Illinois, respectively, are exposed to these ads because the cities' media markets cross state lines. These non-Missouri voters do not share the characteristics of the voters who were targeted with the ad, but they are exposed to the ad nonetheless. Thus one can study the effect of campaigns by examining such voters.

Using this method, Huber and Arceneaux (2007) consider three questions: Does advertising engage? Does advertising inform?, and Does advertising persuade? Regarding the first question, the authors find that, after taking into account other forms of campaign activity, advertising has little effect on turnout. Concerning the second, the authors find mixed evidence of learning, with citizens in these areas better able to gauge the presidential candidates' positions on only six issues. Finally, related to persuasion, the authors find evidence of campaign effects, with campaigns having their greatest influence among moderately aware voters. Voters with lower levels of awareness face fewer opportunities for persuasion, and those with higher levels of awareness and stronger prior beliefs are more resistant to the appeals in the advertisements. This latter finding is consistent with the mobilization model in that we have argued that campaigns have less influence among strong partisans (those with strong beliefs) and among Non-Identifiers (those with low awareness), and more influence among peripheral partisans who are more likely to have moderate levels of awareness. Although some of what Huber and Arceneaux find is not on its face consistent with the mobilization model (e.g., the lack of an effect of campaign message on turnout), their evidence is important for the argument we offer here for two reasons: (1) they provided the clearest evidence that it is campaign messages, as a part of the campaign, that have meaningful effects for voters; and (2) they raise the possibility that what we have called mobilization is not only a rekindling of blind loyalties, but a process of connecting those loyalties to policy positions.

Back to the Future

We have argued that campaign effects take place in the context of the mobilization model, and that increased segmentation is to be expected given the importance of targeting leaners; what we have yet to consider is what this means for future elections given the rise of new media, and what avenues of research students and scholars of political science might pursue. For this, we provide several examples of the use of new media for electoral segmentation in the past several elections. New media and the Internet represent the fourth information revolution, offering new opportunities for citizens, pundits and journalists, policy-makers, and other political stakeholders to readily transmit and share information (Bimber 2003). Unlike print or broadcast media, where campaigns had little control over whom, in a given media market, would be exposed to the content of advertisements, campaigns today can better isolate an audience, particularly in conjunction with the new data about voters that we described earlier. Moreover, the cost of communication through new media is far less than the cost of television ad buys. Using several examples below, we consider the prospects for increased segmentation in the new media era.

Looking at the 2004 campaign, two 527 groups highlight the use of new media to convey their respective messages: America Coming Together and Swift Boat Veterans for Truth. 527 groups, so-called because of their tax designation by the IRS, are organizations that must operate independently of the parties and candidates without explicitly endorsing a candidate. America Coming Together (ACT) and its sister organization, Media Fund, was orchestrated by former AFL-CIO director Steve Rosenthal and heavily financed by billionaire George Soros. The organizations were intended to forward the campaign of John Kerry, and moreover, to eventually become a permanent fixture in the advancement of liberal policies. With close to $200 million in seed money, these organizations targeted voters in battleground states with campaign ads and with door-to-door canvassers, focusing particular attention on a message criticizing the Republicans' handling of the war in Iraq. At the same time, they adopted an Internet strategy where voters could locate resources and information related to their efforts. Many pundits and journalists credited their push with mobilizing voters, although there is little academic research to confirm this conjecture.

Another 527 group taking advantage of new media in the 2004 election was the Swift Boat Veterans for Truth. Prior to the election, one of the purported strengths of Kerry as a candidate was his service record in Vietnam. Many believed that Kerry's criticisms of the war in Iraq would be perceived as credible, given his commendations for duty in Vietnam and his foreign policy experience in the Senate. The Swift Boat Veterans for Truth cut at the very core of Kerry's campaign, using ads that questioned the validity of Kerry's service, actions that were subsequently given the eponymous moniker of "swift boating." A series of veterans appeared in Internet and television ads targeted at certain markets in battleground states. These servicemen, who all noted "I served with John Kerry," admonished Kerry for acting distrustfully, for dishonorable behavior, and for betraying his country. Although the ads were initially run in only a handful of battleground states, they received considerable exposure due to the news media commenting on their controversial nature, with the 24-hour news networks devoting particular attention to them. Thus the organization received considerably more free air time than paid air time. In addition, for citizens who were intrigued, the Internet provided a means of locating and watching all of the ads on the Swift Boat Veterans' website. Kerry's response to the Swift Boat attacks came late, and by that time many pundits argued that the damage had been done.

As further evidence of segmentation, consider the get-out-the-vote (GOTV) campaigns of recent elections. In the 2002 midterm elections, Republicans mounted a "72-hour task force" effort, the branding referring to a concerted effort to contact voters in areas with contested elections in the 72 hours prior to the election. Armed with evidence suggesting that personal contacts could be an important means of mobilizing voters, Republican operatives directed by Karl Rove targeted areas in the states of New Jersey, Colorado, Florida, and Georgia, with mass mailings, phone calls, and door-to-door canvassing (Robinson 2004). These efforts were bolstered by visits from President Bush on behalf of the candidates. After some success in picking up congressional seats, Republicans reiterated this effort in the 2004 election, soliciting Evangelical voters, Latinos, and Catholics especially with targeted appeals.

The Obama campaign of 2008 allows for the opportunity to focus on the use of new media and electoral segmentation. The campaign can be considered on multiple fronts that tie into the goals of efficiency and expediency: the execution of the general message of "Hope" and "Change" from the initial announcement to the evening of the victory speech, and even continuing into the presidency; the ability to raise funds throughout the course of the election; the strategy of creating a winning coalition in the primary season by focusing both on important early elections and on communicating with voters in often-ignored primary states; and the subsequent targeting of voters in battleground states with visits and campaign ads during the general election. Several studies to date suggest that these and related strategies were effective in mobilizing leaners (Lupia 2010; Osborn, McClurg, and Knoll 2010).

The streamlined management of the Obama campaign was heralded by both pundits and scholars alike. First, the general themes of hope and change resonated with voters after eight years of Republican rule and the downward spiral of the economy late in the election season. While the McCain campaign struggled to find a unifying message, offering "Country First" and later highlighting "experience," the Obama campaign was able to cultivate its message of change by tying McCain directly to Bush, and to offer hope in the way of new policy solutions that appealed to specific groups of voters, such as tax cuts for the middle class (Thurber 2010). The campaign, perhaps cognizant of the poor timing of Kerry's reaction to the Swift Boat Veterans' ads, responded quickly to scandals and accusations using both information disseminated online and via transmissions to the press (Thurber 2010). The campaign encouraged interactions through social media particularly among young audiences, allowing voters to organize events, upload YouTube videos, and even doctor the official symbol of the campaign, the branded "O," to their liking. And Obama's campaign was the first to include advertisements in video games (Steinhorn 2010).

Second, Obama's fundraising operation was remarkably successful, particularly when seen in contrast to that of both Hillary Clinton and John McCain. Thanks to an innovative online presence attributed to such staff hires as one of the founders of Facebook, Obama was able to attract a large number of donors who gave incrementally and, importantly, repeatedly, particularly through the use of Internet messages and e-mail contacts (Steinhorn 2010). In contrast, while Clinton was successful in establishing what was initially a large war-chest, most donors provided the maximum contribution, and thus when the campaign found itself in need of funds following the Iowa and New Hampshire primaries, Clinton herself was forced to keep her campaign financially afloat. Obama continued to amass large amounts of money in the general election, outspending McCain by a significant amount (Corrado 2010; Nelson 2010; Thurber 2010).

Finally, concerning the general election, the campaign targeted leaners in battleground states in new and creative ways. Through online recruitment and social networking, the campaign was able to place more volunteers and staffers in battleground and even marginal states well before the McCain camp managed to establish a presence. Marginal states where Republicans were historically advantaged—places such as North Carolina, Virginia, Colorado,

Florida, Georgia, New Mexico—were targeted extensively by the Obama campaign. With the exception of Georgia, all were carried by Obama.

Our illustrations from the past several elections shed light on the mobilization model and point to increased electoral segmentation. What remains to be seen, however, is the extent to which new media enhance or detract from opportunities to micro-target and narrowcast in future elections. Consider the Swift Boat Veterans as an example of an initial intent to target voters in media markets in battleground states with their message, only to see the information go "viral" when picked up by the news media and accessed by thousands of Americans online. Indeed, campaigns must be increasingly aware that information can be widely disseminated. Whether this portends a return to more nationalized elections or whether we should expect greater segmentation remains to be seen. Both students and scholars should find this latter question of particular interest in future years.

Notes

1. We would like to thank Daron Shaw for generously sharing his data and Stephen Medvic for his helpful comments.
2. National Election Studies. 2010. "Political Involvement and Participation in Politics": The NES Guide to Public Opinion and Electoral Behavior. Available at www.electionstudies.org/nesguide/gdindex.htm#6 (accessed May 17, 2010).
3. McDonald, Michael. 2010. "Voter Turnout": United States Election Project. Available at http://elections.gmu.edu/ (Accessed May 17, 2010).
4. Consider Rachel Jackson, wife of Andrew Jackson, who was much maligned over her "adultery." According to her husband, such criticism contributed to her untimely death (Boller 2004). See Boller (2004) for a brief historical review of each presidential election.
5. Gross rating points represent an estimate of media penetration. Each 100 GRPs in a particular market suggest that an advertisement will be on average seen by every person in the market. For example, if an advertisement aired three times and reached 25, 30, and 35 percent of the audience, respectively, then the GRP would be 25 + 30 + 35, or 90. Shaw's state-based estimates are calculated by the weight of each media market's contribution to a particular state's electorate. See Shaw (2006: 76) for more details.
6. For a review, see a special edition of *PS: Political Science and Politics* edited by James E. Campbell, October 2008.
7. While these numbers show that Gore was preferred to Bush by nearly 5 percent among survey respondents, the actual election outcome was much closer, with Gore receiving slightly more than 1 percent to Bush. This serves as a reminder that national sample surveys are estimates of actual behavior, and that in some scenarios sampling errors can be meaningful. However, this is not problematic for the point we illustrate here.
8. These data were compiled from the American National Election Study.

Chapter 13

State and Local Elections
The Unique Character of Sub-National Contests

Timothy B. Krebs and Jonathan Winburn

In theory, electoral competition is the hallmark of a vibrant democracy. Without competitive elections there is little keeping elected officials from doing what they want as opposed to representing the needs of their constituents. Elections, in other words, hold elected officials' feet to the fire. In practice, however, incumbents get re-elected at alarmingly high rates at all levels, even in local contests where one might expect that voters could keep a closer eye on them and where one might expect challengers to have an easier time overcoming incumbents' electoral advantages.

While often linked together, studies of state and local politics are essentially distinct fields of study. The emphasis in the urban literature is on the role of institutions, population demographics, and descriptive representation. There is often a big city bias and a case study orientation to the research. Cities are significantly different than states, especially in terms of their institutional arrangements. Institutionally at least, states are more like mini-versions of the federal government with bicameral legislatures in 49 of the 50 states, governors, and independent judicial systems. By contrast, cities do not employ bicameral legislatures or independent judiciaries, and may or may not have a directly elected mayor. The effect of variation in these factors has been the focal point of state and local elections research.

We begin this chapter by discussing electoral competition in cities, before moving on to a discussion of electoral competition in states. The differences between elections at the city and state level are readily apparent, as are the methodological approaches employed by scholars in each area. From a scholarly standpoint there is one clear similarity, though: both areas of research offer scholars numerous opportunities to examine both old questions as well as new questions. In other words, there is much work to be done.

Local Campaigns and Elections

In this section we cover the nature of competition in city elections. Although the study of urban elections and campaigns remains in its infancy there are very promising signs of growth in this field. Consider that during the past 15 years there have been at least 11 works published that explicitly examine the role and influence of money in urban campaigns, and that prior to 1998 there were no systematic studies on this topic. Likewise, since 1990 there have been several studies of electoral competition in cities, with a focus on both incumbents and challengers, and employing a variety of methodological approaches. Here, there has been a serious effort at large-N, multivariate analyses.

Part of the reason for this lack of attention reflects data limitations. Unlike national and even state elections, there are no central repositories of urban election and campaign data. Although the Internet has made data collection much less arduous, especially on recent city elections, the ability to collect the same kinds of data on a large set of cities over time remains a substantial research challenge. Another reason has to do with the interests of urban politics scholars. Although there has been a concentrated research effort on the consequences of cities' institutional arrangements for descriptive representation, urban elections have largely remained at the periphery of the field. Thus, despite the fact that there are some 20,000 municipalities in the U.S., we know relatively little about elections in them, and what we do know comes largely from case studies.

City elections differ from state elections in many key respects. First are the rules that structure city elections and the nature of political representation. While all city councils are elected by the people, only 76 percent of cities directly elect their mayors, as indicated in Table 13.1. Approximately 77 percent of U.S. cities employ nonpartisan ballots in the selection of local officials (MacManus and Bullock 2003: 15). Some 17 percent of cities elect city councilors on the basis of single member districts, while 66 percent elect councilors at large or via multi-member districts. Seventeen percent of cities employ a combination of districts and multi-member districts, which are commonly referred to as mixed systems. Whereas state and national general elections typically occur at the same time, elections to local office are more often than not held in years in which state and national contests are not on the ballot. There are no bicameral councils, and the typical council has only

Table 13.1 Descriptive Data on Election Structures by Institution

City Councils		Mayors	
Average size	6	Directly elected	76%
District representation	17%	Directly elected (Mayor Council)	96%
At large representation	66%	Directly elected (Council Manager)	67%
Mixed representation	17%	1-year terms	14%
2-year terms	22%	2-year terms	35%
4-year terms	59%	3-year terms	6%
Staggered terms	85%	4-year terms	45%

Note
Data for cell entries are from MacManus and Bullock (2003) and Moulder (2008).

six members (Moulder 2008: 33). Term limits is a more recent institutional adaptation, but its reach is fairly limited, with only nine percent of cities using term limits (MacManus and Bullock 2003).

The second key difference with state and national elections is the nature of local populations, and, importantly, local electorates. Elections and campaigns in large U.S. cities—and increasingly in smaller suburban jurisdictions—are directly affected by the intense population diversity that exists in these places. This affects all aspects of the electoral process, from voter turnout, to candidate emergence, to election outcomes. This is especially true in elections for citywide office where multiethnic and multiracial candidate pools are commonplace, and where racial voting is a big part of the campaign storyline. Consequently, urban scholars have devoted considerable attention to the role of race and ethnicity in local elections.

Electoral Systems and Descriptive Representation

Urban politics scholars have spent a great deal of time examining the link between election systems—district or at large—and the representation of minorities and women on U.S. city councils. Importantly, research indicates that greater descriptive representation of minorities in elected positions leads to substantive policy gains (Browning, Marshall, and Tabb 2003). Because African Americans tend to be residentially concentrated in urban areas, district systems produce more adequate descriptive representation for this group than for Latinos, who are less residentially concentrated (Engstrom and McDonald 1981, 1982; Welch 1990; Zax 1990; Sass 2000; Trounstine and Valdini 2008). In terms of descriptive representation, districts matter less for groups that are either not concentrated or are so large that at-large systems are more beneficial to a group's electoral prospects, for example, women (Bullock and MacManus 1991; Trounstine and Valdini 2008). Nevertheless, because of changes in the law that have expanded black political opportunities, greater acceptability of black political involvement, and changes in the campaigns of black candidates, the negative effect of at-large systems for African Americans appears to have diminished over time (Sass and Mehay 1995; Hajnal 2007).

By turning to individual election outcomes at the mayoral level, two recent studies add to the important discussion of descriptive representation in cities. Hajnal and Trounstine's (2005) research on simulated election turnout and mayoral election outcomes in 10 large cities indicates that greater turnout by minority voters would have produced minority gains at the mayoral level. They also found that higher actual turnout is linked to significantly greater levels of city council representation of Latinos and Asian Americans, holding constant important institutional and social/demographic variables—representation system, minority population size—linked to descriptive representation on U.S. city councils.

Descriptive representation on city councils may also enhance the ability of minorities to win in mayoral elections. Marschall and Ruhil (2006) show that the election of an African American is a function in part of the degree to which blacks are represented on city councils. Although it is not clear why these relationships hold, one might speculate that minority presence on the council provides a kind of farm system for mayoral candidates as well as a base of official support in mayoral election campaigns. They also argue that African American mayors are more likely to be elected in unreformed systems (i.e., those that employ a council-manager form of government as opposed to the more politicized mayor-council form) because of the lack of strong parties or established organizations that may limit the advancement of "outsider" candidates. Studies of the effects of voter turnout on descriptive representation and possible connections among elected officials, political organizations, and the election of minority mayors offer new insights and new questions for scholars of urban elections and institutional effects.

Vote Choice in City Elections

Because urban electorates tend to be more racially and ethnically diverse than state and national electorates, a central issue is under what circumstances will voters of one race cross over to support candidates of another race. Some argue that cross-over voting is a function of context, and that voters who reside in diverse neighborhoods are more likely to support candidates of a different race (Carsey 1995). Others suggest that racial competition within voting precincts is likely to produce more racially polarized voting, and that cross-over voting is more likely when one group is dominant at the neighborhood or precinct level (Liu and Vanderleeuw 2007). In other words, racial polarized voting is more likely as groups compete at the local level, but diminishes when one group dominates. Racial factors may dominate urban elections only when race enters the campaign or issue environment (for example, in the event of a high-profile racial incident), and that under normal conditions party and ideology matter more in local voters' decisions (Kaufmann 2004; but see Abrajano, Nagler, and Alvarez 2005).

Others point to the role of performance in reducing the effect of race in voters' decisions. Stein, Post, and Ulbig's (2006) study of multiethnic Houston found that race mattered in minority candidates' first bid for office but that once in office, white and African American voters (but not Hispanics) evaluated incumbents on the basis of their performance. Hajnal (2007) examined 52 black challenger and black incumbent elections involving white opponents. He found that white candidate quality, and newspaper and party endorsements were more important considerations for white voters when black candidates were running as incumbents. Race alone, however, was a far more significant predictor of white support for black challengers. Because the shift in white support cannot be statistically attributable to indicators of job performance (crime rates, per capita income, and housing values), Hajnal argues that information generally, in particular experience under black leadership, explains whites' greater willingness to support black incumbents. One's race then (rather than qualifications or experience) would appear to be more important to white voters when black candidates make their first bid for office, and less when they run as incumbents.

Political candidates of course use campaigns to court voters and generate support. For minority candidates an important strategic consideration is whether or not to deracialize their appeals in an effort to attract white support. In a deracialized campaign racial issues are de-emphasized and issues with broader appeal are stressed (Hajnal 2007). The political downside of deracialized campaigning is that it may trigger a backlash among one's core supporters whose support on Election Day is only lukewarm (Austin-Wright and Middleton 2004). Considerable research has investigated the implications of deracialized campaigns.

Attracting cross-over votes is one strategic issue for minority candidates. A second is maintaining minority group unity in the face of internal threats. Internally, blacks may splinter on socioeconomic, religious, and issue lines, causing a failure to unify successfully behind black candidates (Jackson 1987). There may also be generational factors that divide older from younger minority voters (Jackson, Gerber and Cain 1994).

In Memphis, disagreements among blacks and a majority vote rule conspired to keep an African American from the mayoralty long after demographic conditions suggested it was possible. Only in 1991 with a direct appeal to black interests and a change in the rules allowing a plurality vote winner did Memphis elect its first black mayor (Vanderleeuw, Liu, and Marsh 2004). Machine-style politics in cities such as New York, Chicago, and Baltimore often splits minority group leaders aligned with white ethnic machine officials from more progressive minority leaders, creating a barrier to successful minority political action (Mollenkopf 2003; Orr 2003; Pinderhughes 2003). While the nature of black and Latino group cohesion is potentially problematic under the best of circumstances, recent immigration patterns that diversify these groups in terms of nationality further complicate the picture (Rogers 2006).

A much smaller but growing literature examines city council elections from the standpoint of individual candidates, and in this regard resembles work on state legislative and congressional elections (Hamm and Moncrief 2008; Jacobson 2009). Like legislative elections generally, local incumbents have an electoral advantage (DeSantis and Renner 1994: 40; Krebs 1998; Lieske 1989). Data from 1986 to 2001 indicate that approximately 86 percent of council incumbents who seek re-election win (Trounstine 2010).

Because of nonpartisan ballots local voters often rely on non-party cues in making their choices, the most important of which is incumbency status (Schaffner, Streb, and Wright 2001). Factors that enhance candidates' name recognition, familiarity, and legitimacy among voters are important variables. In addition to incumbency, newspaper endorsements have been shown to be important predictors of election outcomes (Stein and Fleischmann 1987), as have endorsements from nonpartisan slating organizations (Fraga 1988). Campaign spending also appears to be an important factor in city council elections (Gierzynski, Kleppner, and Lewis 1998). The main difficulty for council challengers is that incumbents, because they are more likely to win, are better able to raise money, secure endorsements, and scare off strong challengers (Krebs 1998), a vicious cycle seen in state and national legislative elections as well.

Oliver and Ha (2007) turned the focus away from large cities to suburban jurisdictions to understand if and how incumbents are advantaged. Their survey of voters suggested that the decision of suburban voters to vote for challengers is a function of candidate traits (such as whether they are personally likeable), issue agreement, shared partisan affiliation, and perceptions of local government performance. Context matters as well for whether a voter chooses to vote for an incumbent or challenger in a city council election. In smaller and more diverse suburbs, voters are significantly more likely to be interested in and aware of local political affairs and are therefore more likely to know something about challengers, a contextual effect that produces greater support for challengers. This research suggests that the incumbent advantage in city council elections may be limited to big cities, and that models of voting in legislative elections developed with data on state and national candidates may not apply to American suburbs.

Campaign Finance

Scant attention has been given to the topic of campaign finance in urban elections, despite the fact that Michael Bloomberg spent approximately $70 million of his own funds to win the mayoralty of New York City in 2001. A significant research complication is that there is no one place to go to gather fundraising and spending data on municipal candidates. Moreover, the laws are different across states and cities, complicating comparisons. The availability of information electronically has lessened the data collection problem considerably, but a number of issues regarding the quality of campaign finance reports remain. Existing work has focused entirely on a handful of big cities. In general, donors to local campaigns are strategic. Money tends to flow to the most important executive offices and to incumbents and candidates in open seat races (Fleischmann and Stein 1998).

Who donates to local campaigns? According to Fleischmann and Stein's (1998) study of contributions to local candidates in St. Louis and Atlanta, business and the legal community were the primary donors in these contests followed by donations from the development community (e.g., commercial/residential developers, property management, real estate, title firms, construction and contracting, planning, architecture, and engineering interests). Krebs (2005) found that corporate interests dominate campaign contributions in Los Angeles city elections, but not all corporate interests are equally active. Within the corporate community, professional and development interests are most active, followed by several different corporate interests (entertainment, financial, retail/services, miscellaneous business), and manufacturing and transportation/ public works concerns. Among non-corporate donors, homeowner, environmental, and social advocacy interests were key players. Both studies indicate that development interests are not as dominant in city politics as might be expected given the prominence of land use matters on local policy agendas.

Candidates' fundraising coalitions may depend upon the ideological and issue positions which candidates represent. For example, Chicago mayor Harold Washington's political coalition was based in neighborhood organizations and progressive activists. Consequently, he raised more money from political sources, public employee unions, and neighborhood interests and less from downtown corporate, real estate, and financial interests. By contrast, Richard M. Daley, a more centerist and pro-business mayor, raised more money from downtown corporate, real estate, and financial interests. As incumbents, however, both mayors' fundraising coalitions became more inclusive, as one would expect, given the power of incumbency (Krebs and Pelissero 2001). In open seat mayoral elections, competitive candidates draw funds from a remarkably similar coalition of donors, mainly from those in the business community, including real estate, legal, and financial sources, as well as smaller amounts from labor organizations (Adams 2007).

Although certain candidate attributes such as incumbency and political experience advantage some over others (Krebs 2001), the flow of contributions within local races is a dynamic process prone to change as candidates move up or down in the polls or are subject to positive and negative information about their campaigns. Fuchs, Adler, and Mitchell (2000) found that candidates in New York City mayoral elections benefitted from polls showing the race narrowing as Election Day neared. Using a measure of momentum based on positive and negative news coverage, Krebs and Holian (2005) found that candidates' weekly contributions largely tracked positive and negative news coverage in the 2001 Los Angeles mayoral elections. Both studies found that contributing behavior is a function of candidate ideology. Viable, but ideologically more extreme candidates benefitted from defensive contributing—the tendency of committed followers to rally to their favored candidate—in the face of negative information.

In concluding this section it is important to reiterate that American cities represent a tremendous research venue in which to test theories of campaigns and elections. Not only is the institutional structure of cities and suburbs highly variable, so too are their demographic profiles. Both of these features of city government have been at the center of urban electoral politics research. Both also serve to highlight aspects of local elections that differ from their state counterparts: nonpartisan ballots, greater use of multi-member districts, less frequent use of term limits, and more emphasis on the racial and ethnic dimensions of urban life and politics. As the country continues to diversify, it is very likely that scholars of state and national elections will turn to models of city elections to understand and interpret what is happening at higher levels as more minority candidates run for office. New directions in urban elections research are clearly seen in the areas of individual-level analyses of voters, candidates, and campaign contributors.

State Campaigns and Elections

State-level elections provide an interesting framework to study the workings of the American electoral system as 50 states elect essentially the same offices, but with substantial variation in the political, institutional, and electoral contexts. As Malcolm Jewell (1982) pointed out nearly 30 years ago, the states provide an opportunity to expand our theoretical understanding from the national level and our empirical findings within a comparative setting. The field of state politics has definitely moved on from the neglected world that Jewell discussed, since data collection is becoming less burdensome to test important questions of electoral politics. We examine new developments in state elections with an emphasis on electoral competition and research across the major institutions: legislative, executive, and judicial. Competition is a fundamental issue for understanding the workings of a representative democracy and serves as the starting point for much of the research into state electoral politics. With the exceptions of Brunell (2008) and Buchler (2005, 2007), most scholars, democratic theorists, and the conventional wisdom argue that electoral competition is the hallmark of a strong and vibrant democracy. As such, a sizable proportion of the state electoral research focuses on the factors that impede or facilitate competitive elections.

Legislative

With over 7000 seats, state legislative elections dominate the ballot and represent the largest and probably most well-developed part of state electoral research. However, this line of inquiry is by no means complete. The state legislatures provide a common electoral framework but with some interesting variation to study important theoretical questions.

Understanding the factors that promote or hinder electoral competition has always played a prominent role in legislative research. Overall, legislative races are not overly competitive, but with some important variations across the country in terms of incumbent re-election, contested seats, and competitive races (Niemi et al. 2006). In many ways, these trends look quite similar to congressional elections; however, some uniquely state-level factors greatly influence the variation between the states.

One unique factor, term limits, is "the most significant change to the legislative institution since the modernization movement of the 1960s and 1970s" (Moen, Palmer, and Powell 2005: 2) and has produced an enormous amount of research over the past decade and a half (Mooney 2009). Twenty-one states enacted term limits during the 1990s with full implementation usually not occurring until the 2000s. There are currently 15 states with active legislative term limits as six states had their term limits repealed by either the State Supreme Court or the legislature itself from 1972 to 2004. The impetus behind the term limit movement was to increase turnover and competition and bring fresh faces to the political table. However, emerging research suggests that the promises of the term limit movement have not always become reality.

We are now in a position to more fully understand the consequences of the term limits movement as they have been in place for almost a decade of elections in most of the 15 states. Since one of the primary claims of term limit reformers was to increase electoral competition and turnover, scholars have spent much time examining the theoretical bases and empirical realities of this claim. By definition, term limits have increased open seats, but the research is mixed on other increases in electoral competition, with more recent studies generally finding modest, if any, increases. Initially, several findings matched the reform movement rhetoric with an increase in competitive races along with a decrease in electoral spending (Daniel and Lott 1997), higher levels of contested seats (Carey, Niemi, and Powell 2000), and more opportunities for women and minorities to win office (Caress 1999; see Carroll and Jenkins (2001) for a counter-argument).

However, with time, many of these initial findings look less compelling. For example, Masket and Lewis (2007) show that open seat races are no more competitive with term limits in place and, after an initial suppression of campaign spending, spending returned to pre-term limits levels. In addition, term limits appear to make the redistricting process more partisan while benefitting the majority party (Schaffner, Wagner, and Winburn 2004). Overall, cross-sectional studies and those more focused within individual states keep coming to the same conclusion: term limits have not matched the reform goal of increasing electoral competition (see; Sarbaugh-Thompson et al. 2004; Cain, Hanley, and Kousser 2006), nor appear to have led to increased representational diversity (Schraufnagel and Halperin 2006).

As this research moves beyond testing the claims of the reformers, term limits is becoming an important staple as an independent variable in state legislative election research beyond questions of electoral competition. Similar to the professionalization research produced from the modernization movement, term limits provide interesting and important variations to test various theoretical propositions. Engstrom and Monroe (2006) use term limits to re-examine the incumbency advantage as term limits take strategic considerations out of incumbents' hands. Their findings lead to questions of both the conventional view and methodological measures of the incumbency advantage. Term limits also allow new ways to test theories of political ambition as both incumbents and challengers face a new landscape in which to plot their election goals. Meinke and Hasecke (2003) suggest term limits affect candidates' strategic considerations, especially Democrats, while Lazarus argues that "term limits have a much richer effect on state legislators' career choices" (2006: 377) while examining differing ambition models.

These are just two examples of how term limits can allow for new research into theories of elections and legislative institutions along with having the additional advantage of variation across the country in both use and design. This allows for stronger research designs to capture causal arguments and to better isolate specific effects on the electoral process (Mooney 2009).

Redistricting provides the foundation for the legislative elections that occur throughout the country, and it serves as one of the most political and contentious acts the states undergo every decade, and now potentially throughout a decade as well (Bullock 2010). While research into redistricting has a long and rich history, until recently, scholars have spent most of their time studying its effects in congressional elections. With the 2010 Census underway and another round of political fighting over redrawing electoral boundaries just around the corner, we look at the influence of redistricting control on electoral competition over the past decade. Specifically, with a major reform overhaul in California and calls for reform in other states, it is worth exploring the actual differences produced by the differing systems in place. For the reformers who stress the evils of redistricting, noncompetitive elections is often at the forefront of their concerns. The argument goes that the redistricting process erodes competition as partisans and/or incumbents strategically draw districts to prevent challengers from having a chance to succeed against already entrenched incumbents and/or partisans.

Across the country, states use both commissions and the traditional legislative process for conducting redistricting. Twenty states currently use some form of a commission in the process, with a neutral or bipartisan commission being the most popular format. The design of these commissions is to remove partisan politics, as much as possible, from the process. Other states use a partisan commission where one party has a clear majority of the positions on the commission. Five states use backup commissions that only become involved if the legislature fails to complete the process, and finally two states have commissions in an advisory capacity to the legislature. Iowa uses a unique format where the nonpartisan legislative staff members draw the maps and the legislature votes on them. The remaining states vest control completely in the hands of the legislature, with most governors having a veto over the outcomes with the exception of Maryland where the Governor controls the process.

When examining the influence of redistricting on electoral outcomes, it is important to know not who started the process, but rather who drew the districts used during an election. This specifically brings the courts into the fray;

in the 2000s the courts drew 13 plans throughout the decade. Within the legislatively drawn plans, it is important to make the distinction between those drawn under divided government, which theoretically should promote greater attempts at incumbent gerrymandering, and unified government that facilitates attempting a partisan gerrymander.

We generally expect that partisan plans should produce less competitive districts (more uncontested seats and fewer competitive races than neutral plans). The primary strategies of both partisan and incumbent gerrymandering lead to a base expectation of less competition as partisan gerrymanders attempt to insulate the controlling party and incumbent strategies are often seen as collusion between the parties to protect themselves against challengers.[1] Overall, we expect neutral commissions to produce more competitive outcomes than those implemented with distinct partisan strategies, since a goal of many of the neutral commissions is to promote competition. Finally, court-drawn plans should have fewer partisan biases and should lead to greater electoral competition.

To test these expectations we examine the rates of uncontested seats (those without two major party candidates) and competitive races (winner received less than 60 percent of the two-party vote) from the 2002, 2004, 2006, and 2008 elections.[2] As Figure 13.1 shows, the partisan redistricting methods did produce more uncontested seats than neutral methods. Across the four election cycles, chambers in states with partisan methods averaged 37 percent uncontested seats while those in neutral states averaged just 32 percent, and a difference of means tests is significant at the 0.05 level. In terms of competitive outcomes, Figure 13.2 shows a modest influence for redistricting control. Neutral commissions produced the highest rates of competitive races, with court-drawn plans having a similar effect. The three partisan methods

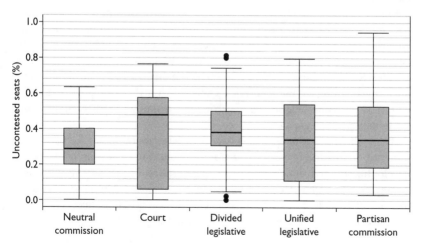

Figure 13.1 Rates of uncontested races by redistricting control, 2002–2008.

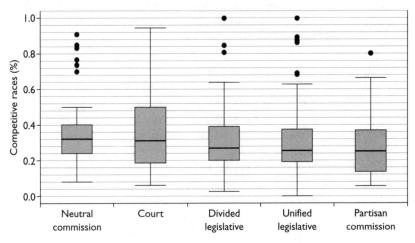

Figure 13.2 Rates of competitive races by redistricting control, 2002–2008.

produced almost identical numbers and had approximately 4 percent fewer competitive races than the nonpartisan methods. Across the decade, 35 percent of the races were competitive in neutral plans with the partisan states seeing 31 percent competitive races; however, this is a statistically insignificant difference.

Overall, Figures 13.1 and 13.2 highlight the relative lack of competition in legislative races over the past decade while also showing the variation between states as the whiskers extend quite far in these figures. In terms of redistricting, the results suggest that partisan redistricting may dissuade challengers from emerging, but does not necessarily produce less competitive races. These descriptive results also underscore the complexity of redistricting and its potential influences on electoral competition. While congressional redistricting receives much of the scholarly attention, state legislative redistricting is important from normative, theoretical, and empirical perspectives (Winburn 2008). From the normative view of who should actually draw the lines, to the theoretical concerns over the strategies used, to the empirical outcomes, legislative redistricting has many unanswered questions left to explore.

While the most developed area of state-level electoral research, there is still much to address on legislative elections. Beyond the topics discussed above, developing a better understanding of the workings of primary elections and linking policy behavior to electoral fortunes (see Hogan 2008) are other areas in need of further development. Fortunately, recent large-scale data collections are making these areas ripe for further development.[3]

Executive

"Scholars know little about gubernatorial elections" (Carsey 2000: 5). Although it is the most high-profile office in the states, researchers have not produced much consistent and systematic research on governors compared to legislative elections. Perhaps this is not surprising given the relative lack of attention to presidential studies, but the states at least provide some leverage on the small-N problem and also provide variation with an assortment of electoral rules and laws governing gubernatorial elections. In the past decade, research has begun to address some fundamental questions regarding the role of gubernatorial popularity and campaign spending often in relation to the incumbency advantage. King (2001) argues, not surprisingly, that gubernatorial popularity is an important determinant of an incumbent's re-election success, but that this popularity effect is also important in open seat races. Kang, Niemi, and Powell (2003) find an interactive relationship between incumbency and popularity as popular governors discourage competition and unpopular governors face stiffer competition. In addition, in an experimental setting, some initial tests show that participants' predictions based on candidate "appeal" or "charisma" are almost as effective as predictions based on incumbency (Benjamin and Shapiro 2009). While preliminary, the use of gubernatorial elections in an experimental setting shows promise for future research (see also Ballew and Todorov 2007).

While understanding the link between campaign spending and elections is often a central theme of election research, until recently, gubernatorial elections were not part of these studies. One major reason for this oversight has been the lack of data on gubernatorial races due to collection difficulties. As scholars begin to overcome these data hurdles, a new wave of gubernatorial research is slowly starting to emerge. This is a particularly important time for this line of research, as spending in gubernatorial campaigns has seen exponential growth over the past decade partly due to a jump in self-financed candidates willing to spend large sums of their own money (Beyle 2003).

Gubernatorial races provide a good context to study the role of money with significant variation on the use of campaign contribution limits and public financing as the states have traditionally placed greater limits on gubernatorial races than legislative races and many place stricter limits on individual contributions than does the Federal Election Commission (see Bardwell 2003a). Like other races, we know that "spending by candidates for state governor profoundly affects the outcomes of these contests" (Partin 2002: 228). Some initial research suggests that incumbent spending does little to increase a candidate's vote share while challenger spending plays a much more prominent role (Bardwell 2005). These studies provide a solid base to build future research that provide greater insight into the complex relationship between money and elections.

The influence of campaign finance laws is open to debate, as scholars are beginning to address these issues from differing theoretical and methodological perspectives. Initial studies show that contribution limits neither restrain spending nor hurt challengers, and they may actually reduce the incumbency advantage (Bardwell 2003b; Eom and Gross 2006). Others argue that contribution limits do not have a direct effect on competition (Gross, Goidel, and Shields 2002). One study suggests that these limits may have the intended effect of "democratizing" elections, in certain circumstances, by forcing candidates to rely upon smaller contributions from a larger number of contributors instead of simply being bankrolled by special interests (Eom and Gross 2007). However, public funds and spending limits do significantly help challengers and decrease spending by both incumbents and challengers who accept the funds (Bardwell 2003b). Spending limits have also been shown to have a negative effect on competition, but this is heavily contingent on the spending threshold (Gross, Goidel, and Shields 2002).

In many ways gubernatorial elections play a unique role in American electoral politics and scholars have only recently started to focus on these races in a systematic manner. As recent research suggests, gubernatorial elections are an excellent place to learn more about the role of campaign finance in electoral competition.

Judicial

The study of state judicial elections is an emerging and exciting area of research. Judicial elections are only found at the state level, as the federal judiciary follows the appointment/confirmation process. The states handle judicial selection in a variety of ways, and some states use different selection methods for trial and appellate courts. Overall, the most common methods are nonpartisan election and the hybrid merit plan. At the state Supreme Court level, 32 percent of the states use the merit or Missouri plan. This method allows for initial appointments, usually by the governor. The governor selects from a list compiled by a nonpartisan judicial commission. After a short term (between one and three years), the judge faces a retention election. These elections stand out as unique in the electoral system, as the voters decide whether they want to keep the current judge in office and do not choose among competing candidates. If a majority of voters decides to retain the judge, he or she then serves a longer term (ranges between six and 12 years) before facing another retention election. If the voters decide not to retain the judge, the process begins again. The second most popular selection method is nonpartisan elections (30 percent) with 14 percent of the states using partisan elections. Finally, 24 percent of the states use some version of an appointment process (Hall 2008). Overall, a majority of states give the voters some direct input on who becomes a part of the judiciary.

As such, much of the new research focuses on these judicial elections.

The ability of voters to effectively evaluate candidates and make informed decisions in these races is a fundamental question for assessing the utility of these types of elections. One common argument is that voters lack the information or ability to discern the appropriate qualifications of candidates for judicial elections and this undermines elections as a viable option for selecting members of the bench. However, some recent research suggests the opposite, as several studies argue that challengers make strategic decisions to enter when they might have a reasonable chance of winning, and voters, in turn, vote based on the quality of those challengers (Bonneau and Hall 2003; Hall and Bonneau 2006). Overall, these findings suggest that judicial elections follow similar patterns to those found in legislative races with competitive parties and quality challengers influencing the success of incumbent judges.

One fundamental concern regarding judicial elections and, specifically, the growing similarities between judicial campaigns and campaigns for other offices is the effect of these campaigns on judicial legitimacy. Perhaps owing largely to the federal model that the judiciary is supposed to be above politics, many view the courts' institutional role as different from the other legislative and executive branches of government. Moreover, the role of the judiciary is not to make public policy but rather to be a neutral arbiter in interpreting the law. Many see institutional legitimacy of the judicial branch as resting on the impartiality of judges who are free from political self-interest in making their rulings. However, as judicial elections become more competitive and candidates spend more on campaigns, we have seen an increase in the number of attack ads and policy-related campaign promises that some fear undermine these linchpins of institutional legitimacy (Gibson 2008). While comprehensive and clearly generalizable research does not exist in this area, some initial experimental work finds that campaign contributions and attack ads do in fact lead to a decrease in citizens' perceptions of legitimacy. However, these findings are not court specific, as a similar effect is also found in legislative elections (Gibson 2008).

Recent studies provide some important answers while opening the door to more questions in the area of judicial elections. Issues of accountability and the fundamental differences in what it means to campaign for a judicial office compared to traditional elected offices are two important areas. Overall, research on judicial elections is a burgeoning field with lots of questions to address both empirically and normatively regarding, among other issues, the relationship between campaign donations, electoral outcomes, and judicial decision-making.

The study of state elections provides important avenues for future research. These opportunities come in the form of the variation that having 50 independent states with a large degree of autonomy over their electoral rules and processes produces for testing and developing electoral theories. Further, scholars often use the states to bridge the gap between practical politics and academic endeavors, as the past decade has seen many attempts to provide fuller and more informed answers to major reform movements that have taken hold across the states (i.e., term limits, campaign finance, redistricting).

Conclusion

As this review demonstrates, there are many differences between elections to city and state offices, although it is common for scholars to link the two fields together under the heading of state and local politics. While this is fine for textbooks and for introducing students to the essential functions, elections, and types of state and local institutions, it has little utility in the real world of research on state and local elections. Indeed, those who study state elections are unlikely to do research on local elections, and vice versa, a fact that explains why this chapter is co-authored. Although scholars of state and local elections can learn from each other, what is clear is that both areas of study contain great potential for growth.

What do we know? In city elections we know that there is a link between the structure of city electoral institutions and the composition, both in terms of gender and race/ethnicity, of city councils. We know too that racial considerations play a significant role in voting in mayoral elections. Unclear are the conditions under which race may be less of a factor in voter choice. Some argue that racial voting is a function of neighborhood demographics, and that in the right context voters are more inclined to support candidates not of their race or ethnic background. Others argue that racial considerations matter only when an election has been racialized, and that in the absence of this, normal factors like party and ideology structure voting. Still others point to the role of performance in lessening the tendency of voters of one race to support candidates of the same race.

On the state side, similar to federal elections, the legislative research is the most developed, and within this literature we often see the application of a congressional theory tested at the state level. Across much of this research is the place of professionalization, as it tends to capture some of the most fundamental factors that drive electoral competition: resources, opportunity, and saliency. At the aggregate level, we know that state legislative elections are not very competitive, with incumbents having a major advantage, while in gubernatorial elections the incumbency advantage is slightly weaker and often the races are more competitive.

Beyond the study of city electoral institutions and the representation of minority groups and women on city councils, nearly all aspects of local elections deserve more scholarly attention. There are numerous areas of inquiry that have received next to no attention at the city level, but generous attention at the state level: election outcomes and the role of incumbency, candidate quality and spending; how opportunity influences patterns of candidate emergence; campaign finance; incumbent advantage in both city council and mayoral elections; and the effects of term limits on electoral competition. Moreover, this review was limited to elections to city office; thus it ignored elections to county offices, school boards, and special district governments, where all of these issues could be explored as well. Are there ideas that state elections scholars can borrow from urban elections scholars? Clearly as the country becomes more diverse, and as that diversity continues to spread into America's suburbs, there are going to be more multiracial and multiethnic contests for state legislatures and governors. For state scholars, the research agenda remains open and inviting as more large-scale data collections become available. Scholars will continue to examine the role of institutional reform (term limits, clean elections) on electoral outcomes while expanding questions of state legislative elections into less developed areas such as primaries. In addition, the sky is the limit on gubernatorial and judicial research as scholars are beginning to expand beyond legislative studies. It is in these areas that scholars would be wise to examine local research into how personal and contextual factors can play a significant role in determining who wins and who loses.

Notes

1. Of course, partisan gerrymandering strategy is more complicated and based on several factors, and could also lead to more competition in specific conditions.
2. States with odd year elections are included in the previous year's election totals. Maine and Montana did not redistrict until 2004; therefore, their 2002 results are not included. For states with multi-member districts, we consider the district competitive if the vote difference was less than 20 percent between the first loser and the last winner on the ballot.
3. The State Legislative Election Returns database and the Representation in America's Legislatures project are two examples of new data collections that should make it easier to conduct future research.

## Chapter 14

Election Reform

What Is Expected, and What Results?

Todd Donovan and Shaun Bowler

This chapter examines continuity and change in election rules. Rules governing the conduct of elections are fundamental to democratic institutions, and much can be learned from studying how, and when, electoral institutions change. Continuity may be the norm, but instances of change (or reform) allow us the possibility of examining how (or if) new rules might create different outcomes. We begin with a discussion of how, and when, electoral reform might occur. We then briefly consider the effects which three major changes in electoral rules may have had on voter behavior and attitudes—the adoption of legislative term limits, the introduction of direct democracy, and the adoption of proportional representation—in order to assess if these reforms have lived up to some of the expectations set by their proponents.

Structural Electoral Reform

American election rules may appear static in the short run, but over time they can change dramatically. We make a distinction here between structural reforms and administrative reforms. Structural reforms change rules about who may vote, the offices and issues that people vote on, rules about how campaigns are conducted, and rules about how votes are translated into seats. Advocates of proportional representation (PR), term limits, direct democracy, and lowering the voting age are proposing structural changes to elections. Administrative reforms change the conduct of elections without directly altering their structure. Examples include efforts to improve voting machinery, poll worker training, and voter registration records. This chapter focuses on structural reforms, since we expect that these are more likely to have major consequence on who governs—but each category of reforms may affect who wins and who loses elections.

Structural reforms occur in response to legislative statutes, constitutional amendment, court orders, and citizen initiatives. Calls to alter the structure of American elections are enduring. The right to vote has been one highly visible area where reform efforts have long sparked controversy (Keyssar 2000). The Progressive Era stands out as a distinct historical moment where American political and economic institutions were radically transformed with the diffusion of direct primaries, direct democracy, direct election of US Senators, and many other electoral reforms (Tolbert 2003).

After the Progressive Era, pressure for the sort of large-scale structural reforms waned. This is not to say that calls for structural reforms had disappeared. With varying levels of success, reform advocates continue to press for use of proportional (Hallett and Hoag 1940; Amy 1993) and semi-proportional (Guiner 1994) election systems in the US, legislative term limits (Will 1990), direct election of the president, expansion of the size of the US House (Bowen 2009), myriad campaign finance regulations, the expanded use of direct democracy, and many other proposals. The crisis of the 2000 presidential election also precipitated many changes to the administration of elections, without generating much momentum for altering the structure of presidential elections.[1] Administrative reforms included new standards for voting equipment, voter registration, provisional ballots, and early voting. The phrase "reform" is used perhaps too loosely by proponents of changes to electoral arrangements: advocates of particular changes may see the advancement of their causes as reform, while defenders of alternate arrangements may see changes in rules as retrogression. Whatever the meaning of the phrase "reform," advocates of change use the phrase "reform" when pressing for changes in electoral institutions.

Institutions, by definition, are bundles of enduring rules and practices that bring stability to a political system. Political institutions—legislatures, courts, electoral arrangements, and the like—may have difficulty functioning if the institutional rules that define them shift too frequently. Legislatures need the enduring norms and practices of their committee systems to operate. Courts require some commitment to precedent in order to function. Elections, furthermore, require some consistency of practice if the meaning of preferences aggregated in one election are to be compared to the meaning of those aggregated in another election. But different rules advantage (or disadvantage) different social groups. As we discuss below, many expect that by changing or reforming election rules, long-standing arrangements that give power to certain groups can be altered. Citizens' attitudes toward politics are expected to change in response to reform.

Reform and Incumbent Self-Interest

Since change in electoral rules is largely controlled by elected officials who hold office as a result of winning under status quo rules, we might expect "reforms" of electoral rules to be particularly difficult; especially if these rules threaten the interests of incumbents. Given the incentives incumbents have for protecting themselves by defending or changing institutional arrangements only when it suits their interests (Prezworski 1991; Boix 1999; Shepsele 2001; Benoit 2004), we might assume that most "reforms" or changes in electoral rules reflect the interests of incumbents—or at least the interests of an influential incumbent faction. Many major structural changes in electoral rules have been explained in terms of self-interested incumbents acting strategically—and at times pre-emptively—to change rules in anticipation of broader demographic trends that might work to their disadvantage. Ware (2002) offers this argument to explain the diffusion of the direct primary in the United States. Electoral arrangements produced by the practice of redistricting legislative districts in the United States are seen by many scholars as reflecting either the self-interest of a majority party that attempts to maximize its own seat share, or as a bipartisan cartel arrangement designed to protect as many incumbents as possible (e.g. Cain 1985; McDonald and Samples 2006).

There are many additional examples of major structural changes to election rules that might be explained in terms of incumbent (or majority) self-interest, including the change from plurality elections to ranked preference (majoritarian) vote methods in British Columbia in 1952 (Angus 1952; Jansen 2004) and Australia in 1924 (Hughes 1968; Farrell and McAllister 2005). In each instance, simple plurality rules meant that coalitions of conservatives and liberals risked splitting their electoral support across rival candidates and, by doing so, empowering a labor party. The adoption of limited voting in UK parliamentary elections in 1867 (McMillan 1997), as well as the adoption of cumulative voting in the Cape Colonies (Trapido 1964), Illinois (Dunn 1972) and Victorian England (Sutherland 1973) are similar examples where incumbents redesigned electoral rules in response to political circumstances that might have weakened incumbent influence were status quo rules to persist. Likewise, the Chifley Labor government moved to adopt proportional (single transferable vote, or STV) representation for Australian federal Senate contests in an attempt to limit the Liberals' future electoral prospects (Farrell and McAllister 2005). Repeal of STV PR in Cincinnati (Engstrom 1990) and New York City (Amy 1993) have also been explained in terms of protecting the electoral self-interest of a dominant political coalition threatened by how PR gave minority groups access to power.[2] The latter examples beg the question of how and why PR came to be adopted in the US in some places, but not in most others. Proportional representation was part of the Progressive Era reform toolkit in North America (Weaver 1986; Barber 1995), and was featured in the National Municipal League's model city charter (Amy 1993). Reform advocates had little success in using referendums to promote PR for the American states, but STV and other ranked choice voting systems were adopted for parts of Alberta and Manitoba in the 1920s, and in many cities between 1915 and 1936.

These examples illustrate the point that electoral rules are largely introduced, maintained, and reformed by the governments elected under those rules. Tsebelis (1990) describes electoral rules as redistributive institutions. Unlike other institutional arrangements that can produce net efficiency gains—such as rules that have drivers stop at red lights and drive on a particular side of the road—electoral institutions have zero-sum properties. Among those with access to power (such as established political parties) electoral rules define winners and losers. More broadly, they can define who has access to representation and who does not. Redistributive institutions either "preserve the interests of the dominant coalition, or they create a new majority composed of the previous losers and some of the previous winners" (Tsebelis 1990: 111).

The stakes involved with proposals to change electoral arrangements are thus particularly high. Indeed, we may safely assume that the majority of literature examining electoral rules and electoral arrangements portrays such rules as reflecting the strategic interests of incumbents, with incumbents attempting to protect their interests in response to ascendant social groups previously excluded from representation.[3] Explanations of the expansion of the franchise beyond a class of male property owners provide a classic example of this. As rudimentary party systems were taking root in new nation states in the nineteenth century, "one of the two competing factions of the dominant class" (Tsebelis 1990:113) was "often led to promote the enlargement of the electorate in order to be rewarded at the polls by the newly enfranchised" (Poggi 1978: 124; Roth 1962).

It is unlikely that each and every question of electoral reform fits perfectly into this description of redistributive institutions that have zero-sum properties, where any change leaves someone as a clear winner and someone else as a clear loser. But many reform proposals—both structural and administrative—have this quality. Indeed, it is difficult to think of questions about changes to electoral institutions where outcomes might be seen by interested parties as efficiency gains for everyone. Rules about judicial selection methods do fit somewhat awkwardly in the distributive versus efficiency institution dichotomy. American states moved through waves of reform of rules used to select state court judges. Through the first half of the nineteenth century, judges were appointed by politicians. Around 1900, most were selected in partisan elections. By the end of the twentieth century, most states were using nonpartisan elections or merit selection methods in order to maximize judicial independence (Hanssen 2004). An independent judiciary may be seen as a net efficiency gain for a democratic system, yet the redistributive aspects of switching from elections to merit appointments are clear. Judicial independence requires that legislators and executives yield much of their discretion over judicial selection. Electoral reforms that moved toward greater judicial independence (changing from competitive elections to merit appointment with retention) fared worse in states where one party held larger legislative majorities. This suggests that parties with a stronger hold on power were less likely to accept a reform that weakened the authority of the institution they controlled (Hanssen 2004: 431).

The politics of redistributive institutions is evident in other discussions of election reform. Discussions in the U.S. about seemingly mundane regulatory matters, such as where people can register to vote (online? by mail? in person at a government office that provides social services?) and rules about which forms of identification may be required at polling places generate enduring partisan divisions (Barreto, Nuño, and Sanchez 2009).

When Do Rules Change?

Any theory of electoral system change must thus place great emphasis on incumbent self-interest—and the competing interests of incumbents—as one reason why electoral rules remain static or change (Bowler, Donovan, and Karp 2006). Yet election rules do change in ways that are not always obviously in the interest of incumbents. What explains why, and when, electoral systems change?

There are prominent examples where electoral reforms have been adopted that appear to run counter to incumbent self-interest—or at least counter to the interests of the majority coalition in power at the time. Many of these involve reforms pushed by forces external to the government. Social movements, mandates from courts, and voter-approved initiatives are three such forces. Courts were instrumental in ordering the end to malapportionment of legislative districts that over-represented rural areas in the United States (*Baker* v. *Carr; Reynolds* v. *Sims*). The Voting Rights Act of 1965 (VRA) allowed groups to use the courts as a venue to challenge many state and local governments' districting practices that under-represented minority voters (Davidson and Grofman 1994). Despite substantial opposition from (white) incumbent office-holders, courts have used the VRA to order numerous local governments to abandon at-large local elections that, for decades, artificially over-represented the electoral influence of white voters (Engstrom and McDonald 1981; Bowler, Donovan, and Brockington 2003). Courts have also forced states to eliminate poll taxes, and rules that limit participation in primary elections to white voters. Even in these cases, the rule changes advantaged groups seeking access to the governing coalition.

The direct initiative is another venue that allows an end-run around incumbent self-interest that might block new rules from emerging from a legislature. The American experience provides several examples of initiatives being used to challenge status quo rules governing political parties (Bowler and Donovan 2006), to limit legislative tenure (Donovan and Snipp 1994), and take reapportionment authority from the legislature. These are rule changes that may be seen as running counter to the interests of elected representatives. Some American state constitutions allow voters to propose constitutional amendments independent of the legislature. Nearly every state that has adopted legislative term limits did so by citizen initiative, rather than by actions taken by legislative incumbents (Tolbert 1998).

The success of reforms promoted by direct voter initiative need not mean that theories of institutional change emphasizing incumbent self-interest are flawed. In the United States, proposals to place limits on the length of legislative terms, although widely popular with the public (Karp 1995; Bowler and Donovan 2007), have been successfully resisted by incumbent legislators in states that lack the constitutional initiative device. But reforms such as term limits, equality in apportionment, and expanded voting rights can advantage one of the key players in power prior to adoption of the reform. This is the nature of electoral rules as redistributive institutions. Incumbent self-interest may not be a unitary interest, as incumbency includes government and opposition.

It is not clear whether reforms associated with initiative efforts always run counter to incumbent interests. The citizen initiative process has been shown to have spread more rapid diffusion of campaign finance reforms that legislators might have resisted (Pippen, Bowler and Donovan 2002). Direct primary rules also appear to have diffused more rapidly in American states that had the initiative process (Lawrence, Bowler, and Donovan n.d.). These examples demonstrate that election reforms which incumbents might resist may eventually be adopted if groups outside of government have access to the initiative device. However, it is not clear if direct primaries run counter to incumbent interests (Ware 2002), and legislators often alter citizens' initiatives that voters approve. Elected representatives have been able to amend and weaken some voter-approved term limits (Smith 2003; Parry and Donovan 2009), campaign finance reforms (D. Smith 2001), and many other citizen initiatives (Gerber et al. 2001). Nor is it clear that the initiative uniformly speeds up the diffusion of reforms. As much as advocates for women's suffrage hoped that direct democracy would advance their cause early in the twentieth century (Banaszak 1996; Piott 2004), in many initiative states legislators were instrumental in promoting suffrage, even as voters rejected ballot measures promoting the reform (Ellis 2002: 240).

Election Reforms: More Than Incumbent Self-Interest

These examples of reforms adopted via the citizens' initiative process that appear to be anti-incumbent and anti-party present an interesting 'chicken-and-egg'-type question for the study of electoral reform: if direct democracy can be used to promote electoral reforms that run counter to the strategic interests of elected representatives, why would representatives ever allow the introduction of direct democracy? Studies of attitudes of candidates and legislators demonstrate that, although outsiders may find the idea of direct citizen legislation appealing, incumbent legislators (independent of their party) do not (Bowler, Donovan, and Karp 2002; Bowler et al. 2001). Candidates for Parliament in Australia have been shown to have an interest in direct democracy that wanes once they are in government (Williams and Chin 2000).

As much as these studies show incumbent resistance to direct democracy, it may also be argued that direct democracy serves the interests of incumbents in some situations. German political parties have experimented with greater direct participation as a way to increase the number of people who are engaged with parties (Scarrow 1999, 2001). American political parties regularly use initiatives to advance their policy goals and for strategic purposes in campaigns (Smith and Tolbert 2001). Despite all of this the direct initiative process as used in parts of the United States leaves incumbents with weaker control over the policy agenda, provides voters and organized groups with a mechanism to write their own laws and undo legislation which representatives approve, and, in some places, prevents representatives and the executive from amending laws that voters approve.

Given this, we might think of the adoption of direct democracy as the ultimate example of an electoral reform that runs counter to incumbent interests. These may be cases where incumbents were unable to avoid responding to popular demands for a major change in electoral arrangements. Why, then, did legislators in some states decide to adopt new rules that curtailed their power? The social movement pushing for major reforms at the dawn of the twentieth century likely had more strength in some states, and met more resistance in others. In the US, the more radical, populist versions of direct democracy were adopted between 1898 and 1918 in places where anti-incumbent and anti-monopoly forces—socialist parties, labor groups, miners organizations, and cooperative farming (Grange) groups were strongest (Goebel 2002; Lawrence, Bowler, and Donovan 2009). Where these forces were weakest, direct democracy was not adopted, or weaker versions were adopted—forms that were more difficult to use, and easier for legislators to amend (Bowler and Donovan 2006).

Thus, when faced with demands for direct democracy in the absence of a powerful social movement, incumbents may safely do nothing or, as in the late 1980s and 1990s when mild popular interest in direct democracy surfaced in Mississippi, New Zealand, and British Columbia, may safely adopt forms of direct democracy that are merely advisory or virtually impossible to use.

The key point is that incumbent self-interest alone provides an inadequate explanation of when, and if, electoral reforms occur. There are cases of major electoral reforms being adopted by incumbents that are difficult to place in terms of whether or not the reform furthered the interests of incumbents generally, or the interests of a new coalition of incumbents and groups previously out of power. Indeed, uncertainty about the effects of major reforms can make it difficult for incumbents to anticipate who will be advantaged by the change. Instances of early adoption of women's suffrage in Wyoming (1869), New Zealand (1893), South Australia (1894), Australia (1902), and several American states seem to be cases where incumbents bent to the will of broad-based social movements arguing for change in the name of basic fairness.[4] Expansion of suffrage in these cases occurred independent of external pressures on incumbents from courts or direct democracy. Early adoption of women's suffrage is another case where electoral institutions were newer, and incumbent interests may have thus been less entrenched and easier to deflect. This "newness" argument has also been made to explain the diffusion of reforms to judicial selection methods (Hanssen 2004) and direct democracy in the United States (Goebel 2002; Lawrence et al. 2009).

Adoption of the Voting Rights Act in the United States in the 1960s is another example of a major change that occurred in the face of a broad-based social movement. From the perspective of incumbent interests, it was likely seen at the time as something that could further the electoral interests of the majority Democratic Party. This assumes that Democrats could safely expect that newly registered African American voters in key states would remain loyal Democratic voters, and that this would produce a net gain to compensate for the loss of support from pro-segregationist voters who had previously voted Democratic.[5] More recently, Democrats and Republicans were divided internally about whether various aspects of the McCain Feingold (Bi-Partisan Campaign Reform Act of 2002) would advantage or disadvantage their respective parties.

Clearly, many incumbents likely evaluate election rules in terms of narrow partisan self-interest, but they also face substantial uncertainty about long-run effects of reforms (Andrews and Jackman 2005). They also apply broader principles such as procedural fairness when considering proposals for reforms. Surveys of legislators reveal that, in addition to their electoral self-interest, ideals about democratic processes also condition how they evaluate proposals for changing electoral rules (Bowler, Donovan, and Karp 2006). Unpopular election rules, particularly those seen to be grossly unfair, can become difficult for incumbents to defend and an ongoing defense of such rules might cost them political capital. The potential costs to incumbents of resisting proposed reforms that are widely popular (campaign finance regulations, disclosure requirements, enforcement of voting rights, some forms of direct democracy) might appear too steep for many incumbents to ignore. Moreover, some incumbents might champion popular reforms in order to build support among their constituents.

Even rule changes that may have been motivated by the short-term gain of one party, such as the adoption of STV for the Australian Senate, can be difficult to reduce to narrow partisan interest. Votes-to-seats distortions were so great under the pre-STV Senate electoral rules that even incumbents from parties advantaged by the bias would have been hard pressed to defend it. Menzies' Liberals who inherited the new STV system retained it, as did subsequent governments.[6] Radical changes to presidential nomination rules in the United States after 1968 may be attributed as much to the need of party officials to respond to a crisis in public confidence resulting from the disastrous Democratic convention in Chicago (Polsby 1983), as to party elites protecting their interests by modifying status quo rules. The same might be said about adoption of the Bi-partisan Campaign Reform Act of 2002—a bill that created substantial uncertainty for both Democrats and Republicans, but was motivated, in part, by the need to respond to public opinions about campaign finance abuse. Even when self-interested incumbents attempt to repeal reforms they do not like (as the British Columbia Legislative Assembly did shortly after adopting the Alternate Vote and as several U.S. state legislatures attempted after the initial adoption of direct democracy and term limits), if voters continue to signal support for the reforms the capacity that self-interested incumbents have to control rules may be limited. At some point, public support for reforms (or outrage over status quo conditions) can reach a point where incumbents must adapt by adopting or embracing reforms.

Election Reform: How Much Can It "Fix"?

We have much to learn, then, in studying the politics of election reform, since it sheds light on instances where political institutions change. The politics of election reform highlight many fundamental questions of practical politics and political science. What, exactly, are the links between particular institutional arrangements and the behavior and attitudes of citizens? Does the adoption of new rules have the potential to produce substantively important changes in how people and elected officials behave?

Reform advocates often link normative assumptions about the benefits of proposed reforms to empirical claims about how their proposal will change behavior. They often make explicit claims about how a change in election rules will affect the behavior of citizens, representatives, or both. Many of these claims are testable, at least indirectly. The larger normative arguments offered by reform advocates may be more difficult to address than the positive assumptions about how the reform actually affects behavior, but the empirical claims are testable.

As examples, champions of proportional representation claim that the winner-takes-all rules used in the United States depress participation in elections, because plurality systems discourage participation by political minorities who have no chance of electing like-minded representatives (Amy 1993). By presenting more choices, PR is also expected to encourage more people to form attachments to a political party. Advocates of greater two-party electoral competition in U.S. House races claim that the quality of democracy might improve if primary nomination or redistricting practices were reformed in a manner that made elections more competitive (Fiorina et al. 2002; McDonald and Samples 2006). Nonpartisan redistricting plans or open primaries might improve the quality of representation by altering the composition of the electorate and thus helping elect more "moderates" (Fiorina et al. 2002). Proponents of the use of direct democracy employ a similar logic. They claim that the process of making choices over ballot questions can encourage citizens to learn more about politics, and become more engaged with elections (Smith and Tolbert 2004). Much of the legal debate about campaign finance regulations in the United States hinges on assumptions that unregulated contributions and spending perpetuates the appearance of political corruption.[7] Implicit in all of these expectations is that a reform produces some normative gain by changing how people behave or how they are oriented to politics. These are not isolated examples. Advocates of Election Day Registration (EDR) assume there is a pool of people who might otherwise not vote if they have to register weeks in advance of an election—but that these people might be mobilized to participate if they could register on Election Day. Advocates for limits on legislative terms claimed that limits can make elections more competitive, improve the quality of candidates seeking office, reduce the power of narrow interest groups (Fund 1992), enhance the ability for women and minorities to win office, reduce levels of cynicism among the mass public, and increase participation (Will 1992).

Many reform advocates place priority on normative goals, such as procedural fairness, equal rights, and improvements in the quality of democracy. Advocates of proportional representation, term limits, and direct democracy made explicit claims about how these reforms should alter behavior. The politics of election reform thus merges important normative questions with positive questions about how changes in electoral institutions will somehow alter human behavior. Some of these causal claims are less explicit than others, but complex assumptions about relationships between institutions and behavior often lie beneath the normative claims of reform proponents. The empirical claims and questions, at least, are also testable.

Indeed, there are numerous studies assessing how differences in electoral arrangements correspond with variations in how people behave and how they are oriented to politics. In fact, for some of the assumptions that reform advocates advance, we have a pretty good understanding of how different rules that exist in various places are associated with different outcomes. As we discuss below, however, much less is known about whether or not *changes* in rules that exist in a particular place can *cause* a change in political behavior. Much of our understanding of the potential effects of election reforms is based on cross-sectional studies; little is achieved from studying the effects of particular rule changes over time. The issue of endogeneity thus inhibits our understanding of how much of a substantive effect we might expect when any election reform is adopted.

At the same time, we know relatively little about how effects of reforms (if there are any) might endure across time. Some sets of voters might become more interested in politics at the moment when their nation changes from plurality to PR rules, or when term limits or redistricting suddenly make an uncontested seat competitive. A referendum or initiative campaign might likewise stimulate more interest than usual and increase voter turnout. But by how much, and do we expect such events to have permanent effects on citizens, effects that transform them and leave them more interested in politics and more efficacious? How much, exactly, does the adoption of major reforms such as term limits and direct democracy actually offer as a vehicle for increasing political engagement and participation?

Effects of Term Limits

The adoption of term limits in American states in the 1990s provides another "before-and-after" opportunity to study the effects of a major election reform. Term limits are assumed to somehow improve democracy, indirectly, by making elections more competitive. In theory, term limits break incumbent advantages by forcing increased turnover of incumbents. The increase in the number of races with no incumbent should stimulate more campaign activity, boost voter interest, and also make representatives more responsive. Some term limits advocates also claimed that limits would reduce campaign spending, produce representatives who were less parochial, and eliminate "career politicians" (Fund 1992; Will 1992).

Term limits proved widely popular in the 1990s, and were adopted by voters in over a dozen states. Courts rejected some of these measures, but limits remained in place in many states, allowing us another rare opportunity to compare mass behavior in these states before and after the adoption of this reform.

Did term limits have the effects that proponents expected? Now that some time has passed since term limits have been in effect, it is possible to test for this. A number of studies show that the reform may have actually reduced electoral competition, or show that existing trends toward greater incumbent advantages simply continued after limits began terming out incumbents (Mooney 2007). Campaign spending was not reduced in California under term limits (Masket and Lewis 2007) and more incumbents ran unopposed, as potential challengers wait for the time when the seat will automatically become open (Sarbaugh-Thompson et al. 2004; Mooney 2007). Term limits have reduced professionalism in some chambers (Kousser 2005; but see also Weberg and Kurtz 2007) but, rather than putting an end to career politicians they may have shuffled ambitious politicians from lower offices into term-limited legislatures, and from the legislature to other offices (Carey et al. 1998; Powell 2000). There are no differences between limited and non-limited states in the type of people who seek office (Carey et al. 2006). There is evidence that term limited legislators are less informed, and thus less able to address state-wide issues (Powell et al. 2007).

Given this muted effect upon electoral competition, how much did the adoption of term limits affect voter participation? Term limit reformers expected a new level of competition provided by "leveling the playing field" in state legislative races. This assumes that a large proportion of incumbents were actually staying in office for longer than the limits, which typically restrict terms to three or four two-year terms in the lower house, and to two four-year terms in the upper house. Limits began to have major effects upon some state legislatures in the late 1990s. Between 1996 and 1998, a majority of upper house seats and 47 percent of lower house seats became open contests, since incumbents could not seek re-election. Limits also began to apply to legislatures in Colorado, Michigan, and Arkansas in 1998. That year, 58 percent of Michigan House seats, and 49 of 100 seats in the Arkansas lower house were open contests as a result of term limits. Limits hit hard in Missouri in 2002, when 73 of 163 seats were made open.

Figure 14.1 plots trends in general election voter turnout in these states. We might expect the spike in open seats resulting from term limits to have increased the mobilizing effects of campaigns. Open seat contests are known to attract quality candidates (Jacobson and Kernell 1983: 32), and involve far more total campaign spending than races that feature an incumbent (Jacobson and Kernell 1983: 41). Yet, although term limits force incumbents out, they do nothing to affect the partisan competition of the districts. Seats that are safe for one party due to the composition of voters in the district could remain safe for that party when an incumbent retires. This being the case, term limits could have limited effects, if any, on mobilizing voters via electoral competition.

There is little in Figure 14.1 to suggest that term limits affected voter turnout, at least at the state level. Despite most House seats being open contests in Michigan in 1998, and large proportions of legislators termed-out in Arkansas, California, and Colorado, turnout declined in each state that year. Turnout was up slightly in Missouri when limits opened many seats, but much if not all of the 6 percent increase in turnout over that state's previous midterm may be attributed to an incredibly close special election for a U.S.

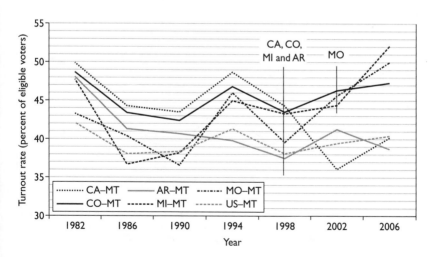

Figure 14.1 Trends in turnout, and effects of term limits (AR, CA, CO, MI, MO, US).

Senate seat,[8] and an unusually large number of initiatives and referendums on the ballot. Long after term limits have taken effect, we do see a rise in turnout in Michigan in 2006. Far fewer seats were open as a result of limits in Michigan (21 percent of lower house seats) in 2006 than in 1998 (when 58 percent of lower house seats were opened). Turnout in Michigan likely rose due to contested U.S. Senate and gubernatorial races, and a controversial state-wide anti-affirmative action ballot initiative.[9] Turnout was up slightly in Missouri in 2006 during that state's repeat of the highly competitive U.S. Senate race[10] and a nationally prominent ballot measure on stem cell research in 2006. With only 6 percent of lower house seats opened by term limits that year, the turnout effect would seem unrelated to term limits.

Figure 14.2 plots trends in voter turnout in Florida and Ohio. In both of these states, term limits began to have their largest impact in 2000. One half of the Ohio lower house, and 46 percent of the Florida lower house was termed-out in 2000. Turnout was up slightly in these states in 2000, but the turnout in Ohio and Florida that year largely matches national trends associated with the mobilizing effect of presidential elections. Again, any effect of term limits on voter engagement in these states is likely swamped by larger forces, particularly the closely fought presidential contests in Florida and Ohio.

We cannot conclude decisively that term limits failed to affect voter engagement with elections. Given that many state legislative districts are safe for one party only, it may be that term limits generated increased competition—and affected turnout—in isolated primaries in these states. However, state-wide turnout in primaries is much lower than turnout in general elections, so effects on participation for the broad electorate may still be limited.

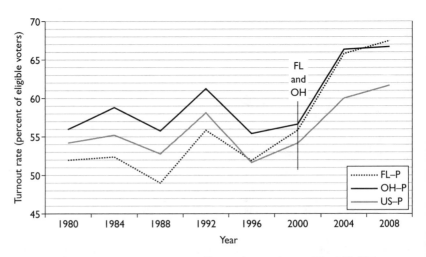

Figure 14.2 Trends in turnout, and effects of term limits (FL, OH, US).

Furthermore, an increase in competitive races might engage voters without mobilizing them if it encourages people to cast votes in legislative races they may have skipped had the contest been uncontested.

Effects of Direct Democracy

Early proponents of the adoption of direct democracy offered many arguments about how this reform would improve politics, and even change the behavior of citizens and their representatives. Smith and Tolbert (2004) note that early advocates stressed the "educative effects" of direct democracy on citizens. Apart from its effects on policy, Progressive Era "reformers viewed the process of citizen law-making as one of many ways to encourage citizens to become more actively engaged in the political process" (Smith and Tolbert 2004: 3). Populist and Progressive Era reformers looked to direct democracy not only for a tool to affect policy, but as a means to increase voter turnout by stimulating interest in public affairs (Munro 1912). Experience with initiative use was also seen as a means for getting citizens more engaged with politics (Reinsh 1912; Smith and Tolbert 2004). Many empirical studies have searched for links between initiative use, and various measures of civic engagement, including turnout, efficacy, and participation. The implicit causal argument from the Progressives is that initiative use stimulates interest, engagement, and efficacy, which, in turn, stimulates voter turnout.

Unlike the cases of PR and term limits, we have less ability to observe how things changed in places that adopted the initiative process. Most U.S. states that have freewheeling versions of direct democracy adopted the process prior to the advent of modern survey research. Rather, a large number of cross-sectional studies document potential differences between initiative and non-initiative states. Some identify a link between use of ballot initiatives and individual survey respondents' self-reported political efficacy in the U.S. (Bowler and Donovan 2002; Smith and Tolbert 2004); between initiative use and voter knowledge in the U.S. (Smith 2002); between referendums and efficacy in Canada (Mendelsohn and Cutler 2000), and between initiatives and life satisfaction in Switzerland (Frey and Stutzer 2000). Several cross-sectional studies document a link between initiative use, and higher voter turnout (see Tolbert et al. (2009) for a review).

Nearly all of these studies suffer from the same problems that bedevil cross-national research showing a correlation between PR and turnout. It is very difficult to assign causality to the use of direct democracy in a state, given that other features of that place co-vary with use of direct democracy (Marschall and Ruhil 2005). It is possible that states which adopted direct democracy shared some common social context that, a century later, continues to affect levels of efficacy and participation. Moreover, Dyck (2009a) notes that although efficacy is associated with turnout, changes in efficacy have a very weak relationship with trends in voter turnout (Rosenstone and

Hansen 1993: 214). Studies using panel data show that much of the relationship between efficacy and participation is endogenous, with the act of participating (Leighley 1991) or supporting winning candidates (Clarke and Acock 1989) driving efficacy. Given all of this, Dyck (2009a: 404) expects a weak relationship between initiative use and civic engagement. His reassessment (2009a) of several years of survey data from the U.S. shows that some of the reported links between direct democracy and external efficacy[11] in cross-sectional studies may be erroneous, but he confirms Bowler and Donovan's (2002) finding that initiative use was associated with higher internal efficacy in 1992.[12] Internal efficacy, however, has a very modest relationship with turnout. People scoring highest on a measure of internal efficacy are about 2.9 percent more likely to vote than people with low efficacy, whereas people scoring highest on external efficacy are about 10.6 percent more likely to vote (Rosenstone and Hansen 2003: 144–5). Many factors other than exposure to an occasional ballot measure (education, having an attachment to a political party, childhood socialization, media usage, etc.) all likely play a much greater role in determining an individual's level of political efficacy.

Thus, if direct democracy may only be loosely related to the weaker form of efficacy, how might direct democracy increase voter participation? How large is the substantive effect of direct democracy on turnout? The link between initiative use and turnout may have as much (or less) to do with direct democracy building civic engagement as with the mobilizing effects of expensive and sensationalist initiative campaigns—campaigns that often have anti-government themes that might actually stimulate distrust (Dyck 2009b). Nonetheless, there is a link between initiative use and participation—turnout is higher in initiative states generally (Smith and Tolbert 2004), and higher across initiative states where more initiatives are used (Tolbert et al. 2009). Depending on the study we consult and the years being examined, the substantive effects are rather modest. Smith and Tolbert report that a ballot initiative increased state-wide turnout by 0.5 percent in 1996, and by 1 percent in 1998 (2004: 51). A study of turnout from 1980 through 2002 estimated the effect at 0.7 percent for presidential years, and 1.7 percent for midterm elections (Smith and Tolbert 2005). Another study estimates that a ballot measure increased turnout by 2 percent in 1994, but that the presence of an initiative caused turnout to *decline* by 1 percent in 1996 (Tolbert et al. 2001: 641–2). This latter study further muddled the causality issue: initiative states were shown to have higher turnout in 1994, even if no initiatives were on the ballot that year. Another study examining turnout in 2002 and 2004 estimated the effect as a 1 percent increase in 2002, and a smaller effect for 2004 (Tolbert et al. 2009). A study pooling data from 1980 to 2006 showed the effects to be even smaller: 0.3 percent for presidential years, and 0.5 percent for midterm elections (Tolbert et al. 2008).

Put simply, reform advocates promoted direct democracy, at least in part, as a means to transform, educate, and engage citizens. Experience in the U.S.

suggests that direct democracy has a mixed record in terms of affecting engagement, and only a modest effect on voter participation.

Effects of Proportional Representation

Lacking accessible information on the use of PR in the U.S., we assess the effects of this reform in Australia and New Zealand. The anticipated behavioral effects of adopting PR could operate in a number of ways. More parties may lead to more campaign activity, which could stimulate voter interest over the long haul. Simply having new choices on a ballot representing new perspectives may empower people who were not engaged with long-established, major parties. This could make people who were previously not voting become more interested, and thus make them more likely to vote. There is ample cross-sectional empirical evidence that nations with PR rules have higher turnout (see Blais (2000) for review). Cross-national research also demonstrates that people report more attachments to parties and higher political efficacy in nations that use PR, and that supporters of smaller parties are more efficacious, and more likely to vote in PR nations than in places using plurality/majoritarian rules (Banducci and Karp 2008).[13] Even the most sophisticated statistical studies of the "effects" of PR have difficulty with questions about causality and endogeneity. Did nations with traditions of greater civic engagement or more participatory cultures or a wider range of social cleavages end up adopting PR, or does the adoption of PR have a predictable causal effect on engagement and participation, independent of the forces that led to its adoption?

We can answer this by examining what happens when a nation using plurality switches from plurality to PR. In Australia (STV in 1949) and New Zealand (mixed-member proportional, or MMP, in 1996), it is clear that adoption of new electoral formula affected the number of parties in Parliament (in both cases) and in government (at least in New Zealand).[14] Is there evidence to suggest that such reforms had the anticipated effects on citizen's attitudes and behavior? Unfortunately, other than the case of New Zealand in 1996, there are very few (if any) examples of this where panel survey data are available from before and after adoption of such a reform.

There is some evidence from New Zealand showing that the adoption of the new PR (MMP) electoral system corresponded with changes in behavior and attitudes about politics, but the results are a mixed bag when compared to the expectations of reform advocates. In the short term, there was a general shift of opinions among citizens in New Zealand toward greater efficacy and greater perceptions that government was responsive on some measures—particularly for political minorities (Banducci, Donovan, and Karp 1999). Turnout was up modestly in New Zealand's first PR election of 1996, but the two subsequent elections reached historic low points for turnout. In other words, PR in New Zealand did nothing to arrest a long-term decline in voter turnout—the same long-term decline in turnout that is occurring in many other democracies.

Despite what PR advocates suggest, attachments to parties eroded gradually in New Zealand over the two consecutive elections held after 1996, never coming close to the levels recorded prior to 1990 (Aimer and Vowles 2003). Aggregate measures of satisfaction with democracy were lower at the two elections conducted after 1996. There were also positive signs: more people trusted political parties after 1996 than before, fewer said that government was run by a few big interests, fewer said MPs were out of touch, and substantially fewer (17%) claimed they had no say in the two elections after PR was adopted (Vowles et al. 2006). Some of these effects are relatively modest,[15] and others are difficult to separate out from economic trends that correlate with trust and satisfaction.[16]

Australia's federal system provides a unique opportunity to study how changing electoral systems affected support for smaller parties. South Australia, West Australia, and Victoria have elected the upper chamber of their state legislatures (the Legislative Council) for many decades, with New South Wales moving from an appointed to an elected Council in 1978.[17] Different states adopted different electoral rules. New South Wales began electing its Legislative Council with PR, whereas elections in South Australia, West Australia, and Victoria were using majoritarian preference voting in the 1970s. Each of these latter states subsequently changed to proportional (STV) representation (South Australia in 1975, West Australia in 1989, and Victoria in 2006). This provides a natural experiment for assessing how differences in election systems across similar contexts, and changes in these electoral systems, might affect political behavior. If PR empowers some people by allowing them to cast a more efficacious vote, we should see support for smaller parties spike upon adoption of PR and remain at higher levels afterwards. PR is expected to give voters new opportunities to express meaningful preferences for smaller parties, perhaps voters who had previously resisted supporting their most preferred party out of fear of wasting their vote. PR advocates note that once empowered to express their real preferences, these voters will become more efficacious.

As expected, the distribution of seats in these chambers was altered by the change to PR. No minor party candidates were elected to the West Australian, South Australian, or Victorian legislative councils under majoritarian voting. A small number of Greens, Democrats, independents, and others have been elected in these states under PR, and votes-to-seats distortions are less pronounced.[18] However, the trends in support for minor parties in these states since the 1970s each look very similar. Independent of the election system, and independent of most changes in the state's election system, there has been a gradual increase in support for minor party candidates since the 1970s. Support for third party candidates was growing in Victoria prior to 2006 under majoritarian rules, just as it was in New South Wales under long-existing STV. Voters were increasingly casting ballots for third parties in West Australia under majoritarian rules, and the trend continued following the change to PR. Similar patterns are evident in New Zealand. Support for minor parties was no different in 2005 and 2008 under PR than it was in earlier years under plurality rules (see note 14). Given these very subtle differences (if any) in voter behavior associated with the presence and the adoption of proportional voting rules, it is difficult to expect that there were major changes in individual-level political efficacy associated with these electoral reforms. Admittedly, the substantive stakes are rather low in the Australian examples: changing from having an upper house of a state Parliament that had only two large parties to one that has two large parties and a small number of third party representatives.

The Inflated Promise of Electoral Reforms: Why Minimal Effects?

Given the wider discussion above, there are many reasons to anticipate only minimal effects of most electoral reforms on mass political engagement—even reforms that may be seen as major structural changes.

First, arguments promoting a link between electoral reforms and engagement may be like straw men. Proponents of some electoral arrangements may have incentives to make overblown, civic-minded claims about the effects of their proposals in order to mask instrumental motivations. Proposals to advance proportional representation sound more fair-minded when framed as a way to enhance civic engagement than when framed as a strategy to strengthen the hand of smaller parties trying to secure seats in Parliament. Proponents of direct democracy clearly had instrumental goals—not the least of which was challenging established parties' entrenched monopoly power (Goebel 2002). Term limits were largely promoted by well-funded conservative activists frustrated by Democratic majorities in the U.S. Congress and most state legislatures (Benjamin and Malbin 1992). Republicans were generally more supportive of term limits than Democrats in the 1990s (Donovan and Snipp 1994),[19] but an overtly strategic, partisan argument could have been less successful than one appealing to fairness and civic virtues. If instrumental motives are the primary force driving electoral reforms, and claims about civic engagement are at least partially rhetorical, than it may be no surprise that reforms show a limited capacity to build efficacy and participation.

Second, and related to this, the theory that electoral institutions affect levels of political engagement may simply be wrong or overstated. Politics is a very small piece of all the factors that affect how most people view their world, and the process of elections may be a small part of how they view politics. Larger forces include personal relationships, families, jobs, job searches, bills to pay, retirements to plan, chances for education, and myriad other concerns. Direct experiences with government as a student paying fees, as a taxpayer, as a person seeking services or dealing with bureaucrats may play a larger role than elections in shaping political efficacy or tweaks in electoral rules. Interpersonal trust is known to be built upon a host of broad life experiences, and, independent of experiences with electoral politics, is a strong predictor of trust in government (Donovan et al. 2007). Is a relatively small force, such as adding one more party to a legislative chamber, or improving the administration of elections, ever going to be large enough to rival the effects of these larger forces that shape efficacy, trust, and political engagement? These core attitudes are formed as a result of childhood socialization, education, income, life security, occupation, age, etc. Compared to all of these larger forces, how much can experiencing a competitive election, or a multiparty system in one chamber of a legislature, or voting on whether gays should be allowed to marry affect efficacy and trust for most people?

Third, even in the area of mass politics, electoral reforms that are aimed at increasing efficacy and participation may be running against much more politically and socially powerful tides. Although support for basic democratic processes remains stable, citizens in many of the world's advanced democracies—regardless of electoral arrangements—have weaker attachments to parties than in previous generations. Trust was eroding at similar rates in many nations as cynicism increased. Confidence in political institutions has eroded in a host of advanced democracies (Dalton 1999). For several decades, voter turnout has been in decline in many nations (Franklin 2002; Dalton 2004). Whatever it is that is driving these behavioral and attitudinal changes, the fact that they are so widespread, and occur across places with such a range of electoral arrangements, suggests that electoral institutions alone may not be the cause, or even the primary cause, behind changes in how contemporary citizens view their political world.

Fourth, incumbents still have strong control over what is adopted in the name of reform. Given that self-interested incumbents often have a hand in designing electoral reforms, the substantive scope of reforms may be quite limited. Direct democracy can scarcely be used in many places where it was adopted, and where it is used it may advance the cause of incumbent interests (Smith 1998; Ellis 2002). Proportional representation may change a party system only slightly, moving it from two parties, to two large parties and a handful of minors. Even the rules written to spite incumbents can be weak agents of change, and thus have weak potential to engage new voters. Term limits do not address what may be the root causes of incumbent advantages: safe partisan districts and incumbent advantages in fundraising. As such, they simply replace one set of relatively safe incumbents with another.

Where Do We Go From Here?

Despite our claim that election reforms might often have minimal effects, there is still a great deal to be learned about the politics of electoral reform.

This is an area of research that can inform us about how voters view institutions, and about how institutions affect voters. Many structural electoral reforms are proposals to change how elections are conducted. Some proposals reflect popular opinion, or a response to public perceptions that something "needs fixing." Other reform proposals might be generated with little public interest, but may nonetheless eventually require some level of popular approval. Yet we know relatively little about how—or if—citizens form meaningful preferences about institutions and proposals to change institutions. We know relatively little about how people reason about institutions and electoral reform proposals when presented with rival elite claims about the potential effects of rule changes. Furthermore, we know fairly little about why some reform proposals succeed—or at least diffuse widely—while other, seemingly popular, proposals languish.

Notes

1. The 1948 and 1968 election outcomes led Congress to consider (and come close to passing) structural, constitutional changes that would have altered or eliminated the Electoral College (EC). The 1968 election raised the prospect of no EC majority, and could have left a Democratic-controlled Congress to select the president after a Republican had narrowly won the popular vote. George Wallace came within 300,000 votes of leaving Nixon without an EC majority. This was not an issue in the 2000 election.
2. In Cincinnati, STV facilitated the election of black candidates. In New York, Communists were elected under STV.
3. Examples include: Rokkan 1970; Brady and Mo 1992; Lijphart 1992; Shugart 1992; Bawn 1993; Geddes 1996; Benoit 2004.
4. Norway (1913), Denmark and Iceland (1917) were also early in adopting women's suffrage. The origins of the suffrage movement are attributed to eighteenth-century France, but women's suffrage was not extended there until 1944 during Nazi occupation.
5. On signing the Civil Rights Act, Lyndon Johnson said to Bill Moyers, "I think we've just delivered the South to the Republican Party for the rest of my life, and yours" (as quoted in Gittinger and Fisher 2004).
6. This could be a case where an election reform appears more as an efficiency institution than as a redistributive institution, given the gross votes-to-seats distortions that both major parties suffered from prior to the reform.
7. In 2010, the United States Supreme Court saved social scientists from countless hours of fruitless research by resolving this empirical question definitively. In *Citizens United* v. *FEC*, "This court now concludes that independent expenditures, including those made by corporations, do not give rise to corruption or the appearance of corruption." With this issue resolved by the Court, social science may now move on to other matters.
8. The special election was to fill the seat of John Ashcroft. Ashcroft was defeated in 2000 by Mel Carnahan, a dead man. Carnahan's widow was appointed to serve until the special election of 2002, where she was defeated by Jim Talent, 49 percent to 48 percent.
9. Colorado also had two initiatives on gay marriage and a medical marijuana vote in 2006.

10. Claire McCaskil defeated Talent 49 percent to 47 percent.
11. External efficacy is measured with items that ask: "People like me don't have any say in what government does" and "Public officials don't care much what people like me think."
12. This is measured with items that ask: "I consider myself well qualified to participate in politics" and "Sometimes government and politics seem so complicated that a person like me can't really understand what's going on."
13. This begs the question of how to sample from the small pool of minor party supporters in nations with plurality systems.
14. Even in these cases, causation is not crystal-clear. Prior to the adoption of PR for Australia's Federal Senate seats in 1949, the average number of minor parties per state was increasing in both House and Senate races. This trend continued beyond 1949 for both chambers. Minor parties in Australia posted similar (upward) trends in support over time in the PR elected Senate and the majoritarian (AV) elected House. Prior to adoption of PR in New Zealand, third parties received 30 percent support in 1993. After the adoption in 1996 support for third parties went up to 38 percent, but dropped back to 31 percent in 1999. By 2005 and 2008 third parties received support under PR at levels similar to what was posted in 1978 and 1981 under plurality.
15. For example, 61 percent said MPs were out of touch in 1993; 52 percent said so in 1999.
16. A long-run decline from double-digit unemployment levels in New Zealand began around 1990 and continued through 2006. Likewise, economic growth was negative during a severe recession from 1991 to 1992, then began to recover in 1993.
17. Queensland Labor governments viewed the Legislative Council as a threat, and abolished it in 1921.
18. The states differ in how proportional their rules are. New South Wales has 21 seats per district; South Australia has 11, West Australia between five and seven, and Victoria five.
19. Republican elites' enthusiasm for term limits waned after the party took control of Congress in 1994.

Bibliography

AAPOR Opt-In Online Panel Task Force. 2010. "AAPOR Report on Online Panels," www.aapor.org/AAPOR_Releases_Report_on_Online_Survey_Panels/2263.htm.

Abbe, Owen, Jay Goodliffe, Paul Herrnson, and Kelly Patterson. 2003. "Agenda Setting in Congressional Elections: The Impact of Issues and Campaigns on Voting Behavior." *Political Research Quarterly* 56(4): 419–30.

Abrajano, Marisa A., Jonathan Nagler, and R. Michael Alvarez. 2005. "A Natural Experiment of Race-Based and Issue Voting: The 2001 City of Los Angeles Elections."*Political Research Quarterly* 58(2): 203–18.

Abramowitz, Alan I. 1989. "Campaign Spending in U.S. Senate Elections." *Legislative Studies Quarterly* 14 (November): 487–507.

Abramowitz, Alan I. 1991. "Incumbency, Campaign Spending, and the Decline of Competition in U.S. House Elections." *The Journal of Politics* 53(February): 345–6.

Abramowitz, Alan I. 2007. "Don't Blame Primary Voters for Polarization." The Forum: A Journal of Applied Research in Contemporary Politics, Issue 4, Article 4: www.bepress.com/forum/v5ol./iss4/art4/.

Abramowitz, Alan. 2010. "Ideological Realignment Among Voters," in *New Directions in American Political Parties*, ed. Jeffrey M. Stonecash. New York: Routledge.

Abramowitz, Alan and Jeffrey Segal. 1993. *Senate Elections*. Ann Arbor: University of Michigan Press.

Abramowitz, Alan I. and Kyle L. Saunders. 2006. "Exploring the Bases of Partisanship in the American Electorate: Social Identity vs. Ideology." *Political Research Quarterly* 59: 175–87.

Abramowitz, Alan I. and Kyle L. Saunders. 2008. "Is Polarization a Myth?" *Journal of Politics* 70: 542–55.

Abramson, Paul, John Aldrich, and David Rohde. 2010. *Change and Continuity in the 2008 Elections*. Washington, DC: CQ Press.

ActBlue. 2010. "About ActBlue." www.actblue.com/about (April 2, 2010).

Adams, Brian E. 2007. "Fundraising Coalitions in Open Seat Mayoral Elections." *Journal of Urban Affairs* 29(5): 481–99.

Aimer, Peter and Jack Vowles. 2003. "What Happened at the 2002 Election?" Revised paper presented at the New Zealand Political Studies Association Conference, University of Auckland, April.

Aistrup, Joseph. 1996. *The Southern Strategy Revisited*. Lexington: University of Kentucky Press.

Aldrich, John H. 1993. "Rational Choice and Turnout." *American Journal of Political Science* 37: 246–78.

Alexander, Herbert E. 1979. *Financing the 1976 Election.* Washington, DC: Congressional Quarterly Press.

Alford, John R. and David W. Brady. 1989. "Personal and Partisan Advantage in U.S. Congressional Elections, 1846–1986," in Lawrence C. Dodd and Bruce L. Oppenheimer, eds. *Congress Reconsidered,* 4th ed. Washington, DC: CQ Press.

Alford, John R. and John H. Hibbing. 1981. "Increased Incumbency Advantage in the House." *The Journal of Politics* 43(November): 104–261.

Allen, Cathy. 2000. "Get Out *Your* Vote." *Campaigns & Elections* (October/November): 202–5.

Alvarez, R. Michael. 1997. *Information and Elections.* Ann Arbor: University of Michigan Press.

Alvarez, R. Michael, Delia Bailey, and Jonathan N. Katz. 2007. "The Effect of Voter Identification Laws on Turnout." Unpublished manuscript. California Institute of Technology.

Alvarez, R. Michael and Thad E. Hall. 2005. "Rational and Pluralistic Approaches to HAVA Implementation: The Cases of Georgia and California." *Publius* 35 (4): 559–77.

Alvarez, R. Michael and Thad E. Hall. 2006. "Controlling Democracy: The Principal–Agent Problems in Election Administration." *Policy Studies Journal* 34 (4): 491–510.

Alvarez, R. Michael and Thad E. Hall. 2008. "Building Secure and Transparent Elections through Standard Operating Procedures." *Public Administration Review* 68 (5): 828–38.

Alvarez, R. Michael, Thad E. Hall, and Morgan Llewellyn. 2008. "Who Should Run Elections in the United States?" *Policy Studies Journal* 36 (3): 325–46.

Alvarez, R. Michael and Jonathan Nagler. 1998. "Economics, Entitlement, and Social Issues: Voter Choice in the 1996 Presidential Election." *American Journal of Political Science* 42: 55–96.

Alvarez, R. Michael and Jason L. Saving. 1997. "Deficits, Democrats, and Distributive Benefits: Congressional Elections and the Pork Barrel in the 1980s." *Political Research Quarterly* 50(December): 809–31.

Amy, Douglas. 1993. *Real Choices, New Voices.* New York: Columbia University Press.

Andres, Gary J. 1985. "Business Involvement in Campaign Finance: Factors Influencing the Decision to Form a Corporate PAC." *PS* 18 (2): 213–20.

Andrews, Josephine and Robert Jackman. 2005. "Strategic Fools: Electoral Rule Choice Under Extreme Uncertainty." *Electoral Studies.* 24(1): 65–84.

Angus, H.F. 1952. "Note of the British Columbia Election in June 1952." *Western Political Quarterly* 5(4): 585–91.

Ansolabehere, Stephen. 2007. Cooperative Congressional Election Study, 2006: Common Content. [Computer File] Release 2: November 14, 2007.

Ansolabehere, Stephen. 2009. Cooperative Congressional Election Study, 2008: Common content. [Computer File] Release 1: February 2, 2009.

Ansolabehere, Stephen, John M. de Figueiredo and James M. Snyder Jr. 2003. "Why is There so Little Money in U.S. Politics?" *Journal of Economic Perspectives* 17 (1): 105–30.

Ansolabehere, Stephen and Alan Gerber. 1994. "The Mismeasure of Campaign Spending: Evidence from the 1990 U.S. House Elections." *Journal of Politics* 56 (November): 1106–18.

Ansolabehere Stephen and Shanto Iyengar. 1995. *Going Negative: How Political Advertisements Shrink and Polarize the Electorate.* New York: Free Press.

Ansolabehere, Stephen D., Shanto Iyengar, and Adam Simon. 1999. "Replicating Experiments Using Aggregate and Survey Data: The Case of Negative Advertising and Turnout." *American Political Science Review* 93: 901–9.

Ansolabehere, Stephen, Shanto Iyengar, Adam Simon, and Nicholas Valentino. 1994. "Does Attack Advertising Demobilize the Electorate?" *American Political Science Review* 88: 829–38.

Ansolabehere, Stephen and Nathaniel Persily. 2007. "Vote Fraud in the Eye of the Beholder: The Role of Public Opinion in the Challenge to Voter Identification Requirements." *Harvard Law Review* 121: 173–4.

Ansolabehere, Stephen and Brian F. Schaffner. 2009. "Understanding the Political Distinctiveness of the Cell Phone Only Public: Results from the 2006 and 2008 CCES." Paper presented at the annual meeting of the American Association of Public Opinion Researchers, Ft. Lauderdale, FL.

Ansolabehere, Stephen and Brian F. Schaffner. 2010. "Residential Mobility, Family Structure, and the Cell-Only Population." *Public Opinion Quarterly* 74: 244–59.

Ansolabehere, Stephen and James M. Snyder. 2000. "Campaign War Chests in Congressional Elections." *Business and Politics* 2: 9–33.

Ansolabehere, Stephen, James M. Snyder, Jr., and Charles Stewart, III. 2000. "Old Voters, New Voters, and the Personal Vote: Using Redistricting to Measure the Incumbency Advantage." *American Journal of Political Science* 44 (January): 173–4.

Ansolabehere, Stephen, James M. Snyder, Jr., and Micky Tripathi. 2002. "Are PAC Contributions and Lobbying Linked? New Evidence from the 1995 Lobby Disclosure Act." *Business and Politics* 4 (2): 131–55.

Arceneaux, Kevin and David W. Nickerson. 2009. "Modeling Certainty with Clustered Data: A Comparison of Methods." *Political Analysis* 17: 177–90.

Arrington, Theodore S. and Gerald L. Ingalls. 1984. "Effects of Campaign Spending on Local Elections: The Charlotte Case." *American Politics Quarterly* 12: 117–27.

Atkeson, Lonna Rae, Lisa Ann Bryant, Thad E. Hall, Kyle Saunders, and Michael Alvarez. 2010. "A new barrier to participation: Heterogeneous application of voter identification policies." *Electoral Studies* 29 (1): 66–73.

Atkeson, Lonna Rae and Kyle L. Saunders. 2007. "The Effect of Election Administration on Voter Confidence: A Local Matter?" *PS: Political Science and Politics* 40 (4): 655–60.

Austin Wright, D. Sharon, and Richard T. Middleton, IV. 2004. "The Limitations of the Deracialization Concept in the 2001 Los Angeles Mayoral Election." *Political Research Quarterly* 57 (2): 283–93.

Bafumi, Joseph and Andrew Gelman. 2006. "Fitting Multilevel Models When Predictors and Group Effects Correlate." Paper presented at the annual meeting of the American Political Science Association, Philadelphia, PA.

Bailey, Michael. 2004. "The (Sometimes Surprising) Consequences of Societally Unrepresentative Contributors on Legislative Responsiveness." *Business and Politics* 6 (3): Article 2.

Ballew, Charles C. and Alexander Todorov. 2007. "Predicting Political Elections from Rapid and Unreflective Face Judgments." *Proceedings of the National Academy of Sciences of the United States of America* 104(46): 17948–53.

Banaszak, Lee Ann. 1996. *Why Movements Succeed or Fail: Opportunity, Culture and the Struggle for Woman Suffrage.* Princeton, NJ: Princeton University Press.

Banducci, Susan and Jeffrey Karp. 2008. "Political Efficacy and Participation in Twenty Seven Democracies: How Electoral Systems Shape Political Behavior." *British Journal of Political Science* 38 (2): 311–34.

Banducci, Susan, Todd Donovan and Jeffrey Karp. 1999. "Proportional Representation and Attitudes about Politics: Results from New Zealand." *Electoral Studies* 18(4): 533–55.

Banks, Jeffrey S. and D. Roderick Kiewiet. 1989. "Explaining Patterns of Candidate Competition in Congressional Elections." *American Journal of Political Science* 33 (November): 997–1015.

Barber, Kathleen. 1995. *Proportional Representation and Election Reform in Ohio.* Columbus: Ohio State University Press.

Bardwell, Kedron. 2003a. "Campaign Finance Laws and the Competition for Spending in Gubernatorial Elections." *Social Science Quarterly* 84(4): 811–25.

Bardwell, Kedron. 2003b. "Not All Money Is Equal: The Differential Effect of Spending by Incumbents and Challengers in Gubernatorial Primaries." *State Politics & Policy Quarterly* 3(3): 294–8.

Bardwell, Kedron. 2005. "Reevaluating Spending in Gubernatorial Races: Job Approval as a Baseline for Spending Effects." *Political Research Quarterly* 58(1): 97–105.

Barker, David C. 2002. *Rushed to Judgment.* New York: Columbia University Press.

Barreto, Matt A., Luis R. Fraga, Sylvia Manzano, Valerie Martinez-Ebers, and Gary M. Segura. 2008. "Should They Dance with the One Who Brung 'Em? Latinos and the 2008 Presidential Election." *PS: Political Science and Politics* 41: 753–60.

Barreto, Matt A., Stephen A. Nuño, and Gabriel R. Sanchez. 2007. "Voter ID Requirements and the Disenfranchisements of Latino, Black, and Asian Voters." Paper presented at the 2007 Annual Meeting of the American Political Science Association, Chicago, IL.

Barreto, Matt A., Stephen A. Nuño, and Gabriel R. Sanchez. 2009. "The Disproportionate Impact of Voter-ID Requirements on the Electorate—New Evidence from Indiana." *PS: Political Science and Politics* 42: 111–16.

Barreto, Matt A., Matthew J. Streb, Mara Marks, and Fernando Guerra. 2006. "Do Absentee Voters Differ from Polling Place Voters?" *Public Opinion Quarterly* 70 (2): 224–34.

Bartels, Larry M. 1996. Book review of Stephen Ansolabehere and Shanto Iyengar's *Going Negative: How Political Advertisements Shrink and Polarize the Electorate. Public Opinion Quarterly* 60: 456–61.

Bartels, Larry M. 2000. "Partisanship and Voting Behavior, 19521–996." *American Journal of Political Science* 44: 35–50.

Bauer, Monica and John R. Hibbing. 1989. "Which Incumbents Lose in House Elections: A Response to Jacobson's 'The Marginals Never Vanished'" *American Journal of Political Science,* 33 (February): 262–71.

Baumgartner, Frank R., Jeffrey M. Berry, Marie Hojnacki, Beth L. Leech, and David C. Kimball. 2009. *Lobbying and Policy Change: Who Wins, Who Loses, and Why.* Chicago: University of Chicago Press.

Baumgartner, Frank R. and Beth L. Leech. 1998. *Basic Interests: The Importance of Groups in Politics and in Political Science.* Princeton, NJ: Princeton University Press.

Bawn, Kathleen. 1993. "The Logic of Institutional Preferences: German Electoral Law as a Social Choice Outcome." *American Journal of Political Science* 37(4): 965–89.

Bedlington, Anne H. 1999. "The Realtors Political Action Committee: Covering All

Contingencies," in *After the Revolution: PACs, Lobbies and the Republican Congress*, R. Biersack, P.S. Herrnson, and C. Wilcox. New York: Allyn & Bacon.

Beniger, James R. 1986. *The Control Revolution: Technological and Economic Origins of the Information Society*. Cambridge, MA: Harvard University Press.

Benjamin, Daniel J. and Jesse M. Shapiro. 2009. "Thin-Slice Forecasts of Gubernatorial Elections." *Review of Economics & Statistics* 91(3): 523–56.

Benjamin, Gerald and Michael Malbin. 1992. *Limiting Legislative Terms*. Washington, DC: CQ Press.

Bennett, W. Lance. 2005. "The Twilight of Mass Media News." In *Freeing the Presses*, ed. Timothy E. Cook. Baton Rouge: Louisiana State University Press.

Benoit, Kenneth. 2004. "Models of Electoral System Change." *Electoral Studies* 23(3): 363–89.

Berelson, Bernard R., Paul F. Lazarsfeld, and William N. McPhee. 1954. *Voting: A Study of Opinion Formation in a Presidential Campaign*. Chicago: University of Chicago Press.

Berman, Ari. 2008. "The Dean Legacy." *The Nation*, February 28, www.thenation.com/article/dean-legacy, accessed June 30, 2010.

Beyle, Thad. 2003. "The Rising Costs of Gubernatorial Elections, 1977–2002." *Spectrum: Journal of State Government* 76(3): 282–9.

Bickers, Kenneth N. and Robert M. Stein. 1994. "Congressional Elections and the Pork Barrel." *Journal of Politics* 56(August): 377–99.

Bickers, Kenneth N. and Robert M. Stein. 1996. "The Electoral Dynamics of the Federal Pork Barrel." *American Journal of Political Science* 40(November): 1300–26.

Bickers, Kenneth N. and Robert M. Stein. 1997. *Perpetuating the Pork Barrel: Policy Subsystems and American Democracy*. New York: Cambridge University Press.

Biersack, Robert, Paul S. Herrnson and Clyde Wilcox. 1999. *After the Revolution: PACs, Lobbies, and the Republican Congress*. Boston: Allyn and Bacon.

Bimber, Bruce. 2003. *Information and American Democracy: Technology in the Evolution of Political Power*. New York: Cambridge University Press.

Bimber, Bruce and Richard Davis. 2003. *Campaigning Online: The Internet in U.S. Elections*. New York: Oxford University Press.

Bipartisan Campaign Reform Act, Public Law 107–55, 107th Cong., 2nd session (March 27, 2002).

Bishop, Bill. 2008. *The Big Sort: Why Clustering of Like-Minded Americans Is Tearing Us Apart*. New York: Houghton Mifflin.

Black, Earl and Merle Black. 1987. *Politics and Society in the South*. Cambridge, MA: Harvard University Press.

Black, Earl and Merle Black. 2002. *The Rise of Southern Republicans*. Cambridge, MA: Harvard University Press.

Blais, Andre. 2000. *To Vote or Not to Vote: The Merits and Limits of Rational Choice Theory*. Pittsburgh: University of Pittsburgh Press.

Blais, Andre. 2006. "What Affects Voter Turnout?" *Annual Review of Political Science* 9: 111–25.

Blumberg, Stephen J. and Julian V. Luke. 2009. "Wireless Substitution: Early Release of Estimates from the National Health Interview Survey, July–December 2008." Centers of Disease Control. Available at www.cdc.gov/nchs/data/nhis/earlyrelease/wireless200905.pdf.

Blumenthal, Mark M. 2005. "Toward an Open-Source Methodology: What We Can Learn from the Blogosphere." *Public Opinion Quarterly* 69(5): 655–69.

Blumenthal, Mark. 2009. "Is Polling As We Know It Doomed?" *National Journal* (August 10). Available at: www.nationaljournal.com/njonline/mp_20090810_1804.php.

Blumler, Jay G. and Denis McQuail. 1969. *Television and Politics*. Chicago, IL: University of Chicago Press.

Boatright, Robert G. 2007. "Situating the New 527 Organizations in Interest Group Theory." *The Forum* 5(2): Article 2.

Boatright, Robert G. and Michael J. Malbin. 2005. "Political Contribution Tax Credits and Citizen Participation." *American Politics Research* 33(6): 787–817.

Boix, Carles. 1999. "Setting the Rules of the Game: The Choice of Electoral Systems in Advanced Democracies." *American Political Science Review* 93(3): 609–24.

Boller, Paul F. 2004. *Presidential Campaigns: From George Washington to George W. Bush*. Oxford: Oxford University Press.

Bond, Jon R., Cary Covington, and Richard Fleisher. 1985. "Explaining Challenger Quality in Congressional Elections." *The Journal of Politics* 47(June): 510–29.

Bond, Jon R., Richard Fleisher, and Jeffrey M. Stonecash. 2009. "The Rise and Fall of Moderates in Congress." Delivered at the Conference on Bicameralism, Duke University March 26–29.

Bonneau, Chris W. and Melinda Gann Hall. 2003. "Predicting Challengers in State Supreme Court Elections: Context and the Politics of Institutional Design." *Political Research Quarterly* 56(3): 337–49.

Bosso, Christopher J. 2005. *Environment, Inc.: From Grassroots to Beltway*. Lawrence: University Press of Kansas.

Bovitz, Gregory L. and Jamie L. Carson. 2006. "Position-Taking and Electoral Accountability in the U.S. House of Representatives." *Political Research Quarterly* 59(June): 297–312.

Bowen, Daniel. 2009. "We Need More Politicians." Paper presented at the Electoral Reform Agenda Conference, Iowa City, IA, May.

Bowler, Shaun and Todd Donovan. 2002. "Democracy, Institutions and Attitudes about Citizen Influence on Government." *British Journal of Political Science* 32: 371–90.

Bowler, Shaun and Todd Donovan. 2006. "Direct Democracy and Political Parties in America." *Party Politics* 12(5): 649–69.

Bowler, Shaun and Todd Donovan. 2007. "Reasoning About Institutional Change: Winners, Losers and Support for Electoral Reform." *British Journal of Political Science* 37(July): 455–76.

Bowler, Shaun, Todd Donovan, and David Brockington. 2003. *Electoral Reform and Minority Representation: Local Experiments with Alternative Elections*. Columbus: Ohio State University Press.

Bowler, Shaun, Todd Donovan, and Jeffrey Karp. 2002. "When Might Institutions Change? Elite Support for Direct Democracy in Three Nations." *Political Research Quarterly* 55(4): 731–54.

Bowler, Shaun, Todd Donovan, and Jeffrey Karp. 2006. "Why Politicians Like Electoral Institutions: Self-Interest, Values, or Ideology?" *Journal of Politics* 68(2): 434–46.

Bowler, Shaun, T. Donovan, M. Neiman, and J. Peel. 2001. "Institutional Threat and

Partisan Outcomes: Legislative Candidates' Attitudes Toward Direct Democracy." *State Politics and Policy Quarterly* 1(4): 364–79.

Box-Steffensmeier, Janet M. 1996. "A Dynamic Analysis of the Role of War Chests in Campaign Strategy." *American Journal of Political Science* 40(May): 352–71.

Brader, Ted. 2005. "Striking a Responsive Chord: How Political Ads Motivate and Persuade Voters by Appealing to Emotions." *American Journal of Political Science* 49(2): 388–405.

Brader, Ted. 2006. *Campaigning for Hearts and Minds: How Emotional Appeals in Political Ads Work.* Chicago, IL: University of Chicago Press.

Brader, Ted and Bryce Corrigan. 2008. "Going Emotional: How Ads Sway Voters by Appealing to Discrete Emotions." Paper presented at the annual meeting of the Midwest Political Science Association, Chicago, IL.

Bradley, David W., John F. Cogan, and Douglas Rivers. 1997. "The 1996 House Elections: Reaffirming the Conservative Trend." *Hoover Essays in Public Policy* 75.

Brady, David, John Cogan, and Morris Fiorina. 2000. *Continuity and Change in House Elections.* Stanford, CA: Stanford University Press.

Brady, David and Jongryn Mo. 1992. "Electoral Systems and Institutional Choice." *Comparative Political Studies* 24(4): 405–29.

Brewer, Mark D. 2009. *Party Images in the American Electorate.* New York: Routledge.

Brewer, Mark D. and Jeffrey M. Stonecash. 2009. *The Dynamics of American Political Parties.* New York: Cambridge University Press.

Brians, Craig Leonard and Martin P. Wattenberg. 1996. "Campaign Issue Knowledge and Salience: Comparing Reception from TV Commercials, TV News, and Newspapers." *American Journal of Political Science* 40: 172–93.

Brooks, Deborah Jordan. 2006. "The Resilient Voter: Moving Toward Closure in the Debate over Negative Campaigning and Turnout." *The Journal of Politics* 68: 684–96.

Brooks, Deborah Jordan and John G. Geer. 2007. "Beyond Negativity: The Effects of Incivility on the Electorate." *American Journal of Political Science* 51(1): 11–16.

Brown, Clifford W., Jr., Lynda W. Powell, and Clyde Wilcox. 1995. *Serious Money: Fundraising and Contributing in Presidential Nomination Campaigns.* New York: Cambridge University Press.

Brown, Robert D., Robert A. Jackson, and Gerald C. Wright. 1999. "Registration, Turnout, and State Party Systems." *Political Research Quarterly* 52: 463–79.

Browning, Rufus P., Dale Rogers Marshall, and David H. Tabb, eds. 2003. *Racial Politics in American Cities*, 3rd edition. New York: Longman.

Brownstein, Ronald. 2007. *The Second Civil War: How Extreme Partisanship Has Paralyzed Washington and Polarized America.* New York: Penguin Press.

Brownstein, Ronald. 2008. "The First 21st Century Campaign." *National Journal,* April 19: 26–32.

Brunell, Thomas. 2008. *Redistricting and Representation: Why Competitive Elections are Bad for America.* New York: Routledge.

Buchler, Justin. 2005. "Competition, Representation and Redistricting: The Case against Competitive Congressional Districts." *Journal of Theoretical Politics* 17(4): 431–63.

Buchler, Justin. 2007. "The Social Sub-Optimality of Competitive Elections." *Public Choice* 133(34–): 439–56.

Buckley v. *Valeo*, 424 U.S. 1 (1976).

Bullock, Charles S., III. 2010. *Redistricting: The Most Political Activity in America.* Lanham, MD: Rowman & Littlefield.

Bullock, Charles S., III and M.V. Hood, III. 2002. "One Person, No Vote; One Vote, Two Votes: Voting Methods, Ballot Types, and Undervote Frequency in the 2000 Presidential Election." *Social Science Quarterly* 83(4): 981–93.

Bullock, III, Charles S. and Susan A. MacManus. 1991. "Municipal Electoral Structure and the Election of Councilwomen."*Journal of Politics* 53: 75–89.

Burden, Barry C., David T. Canon, Stéphane Lavertu, Kenneth R. Mayer, and Donald P. Moynihan. 2010. "Comparing Elected and Appointed Election Officials: The Impact of Selection Method on Policy Preferences and Turnout." Paper presented at the Midwest Political Science Association Annual Meeting. Chicago, IL.

Burden, Barry C. and David C. Kimball. 1998. "A New Approach to the Study of Ticket Splitting." *American Political Science Review* 92: 533–44.

Burnham, Walter Dean. 1982. *The Current Crisis in American Politics.* Oxford: Oxford University Press.

Cain, Bruce. 1985. Assessing the Partisan Effects of Redistricting. *American Political Science Review* 79(2): 320–33.

Cain, Bruce, John Hanley, and Thad Kousser. 2006. "Term Limits: A Recipe for More Competition?" in *The Marketplace of Democracy: Electoral Competition and American Politics*, eds. Michael P. McDonald and John Curtis Samples. Washington, DC: Brookings Institution Press.

Caldeira, Gregory A. and Samuel C. Patterson. 1982. "Contextual Influences on Participation in U.S. State Legislative Elections." *Legislative Studies Quarterly* 7: 359–81.

Caldeira, Gregory A., Samuel C. Patterson, and Gregory A. Markko. 1985. "Mobilization of Voters in Elections." *The Journal of Politics* 47: 490–59.

Calhoun-Brown, Allison. 1996. "African American Churches and Political Mobilization: The Psychological Impact of Organizational Resources." *The Journal of Politics* 58: 935–53.

Caltech/MIT Voting Technology Project. 2001. "Residual Votes Attributable to Technology: An Assessment of the Reliability of Existing Voting Equipment."

Campaign Finance Institute. 2008. "Reality Check: Obama Received About the Same Percentage from Small Donors in 2008 as Bush in 2004." Press Release, November 24. Available at www.cfinst.org/Press/PReleases/081-12-4/Realty_Check__Obama_Small_Donors.aspx, accessed June 13, 2010.

Campaign Finance Institute. 2010. "Executive Summary." Available at www.cfinst.org/president/pdf/CFI_ExecSumm.pdf (April 10, 2010).

Campbell, Angus. 1960. "Surge and Decline: A Study of Electoral Change." *Public Opinion Quarterly* 24: 397–418.

Campbell, Angus, Philip E. Converse, Warren E. Miller, and Donald E. Stokes. 1960. *The American Voter.* New York: Wiley.

Campbell, David E. and J. Quin Monson. 2007. "The Case of Bush's Re-Election: Did Gay Marriage Do It?" in *A Matter of Faith: Religion and the 2004 Presidential Election*, ed. D.E. Campbell. Washington, DC: Brookings.

Campbell, David, J., Quin Monson, and John C. Green. 2009. "Framing Faith: How Voters Responded to Candidates' Religions in the 2008 Presidential Campaign." Paper presented at the Annual Meeting of the American Political Science Association, Toronto, Ontario.

Campbell, James E. 1991. "The Presidential Surge and its Midterm Decline in Congressional Elections, 1868–1988." *Journal of Politics* 53(May): 477–87.

Campbell, James E. 2000. *The American Campaign: U.S. Presidential Campaigns and the National Vote*. College Station: Texas A&M Press.

Campbell, James E. 2008a. *The American Campaign: U.S. Presidential Campaigns and the National Vote*, 2nd edition. College Station: Texas A&M University Press.

Campbell, James E. 2008b. "Editor's Introduction: Forecasting the 2008 National Elections." *PS Political Science & Politics* 41: 679–82.

Campbell, Timothy C. 2006. *Wireless Writing in the Age of Marconi*. Minneapolis: University of Minnesota Press.

Caress, Stanley M. 1999. "The Influence of Term Limits on the Electoral Success of Women." *Women & Politics* 20: 45–63.

Carey, John, Richard Niemi, and Lynda Powell. 1998. "The Effects of Term Limits on State Legislatures." *Legislative Studies Quarterly* 23(2): 271–300.

Carey, John M., Richard G. Niemi, and Lynda W. Powell. 2000. *Term Limits in the State Legislatures*. Ann Arbor: University of Michigan Press.

Carey, John, Richard Niemi, Lynda Powell, and Gary Moncrief. 2006. "The Effects of Term Limits on State Legislatures: A New Survey." *Legislative Studies Quarterly* 31(1): 105–34.

Carney, Eliza Newlin. 2010. "Money Woes Could Stymie GOP Comeback: Party Donations from Lawmakers and Individuals are Down Sharply." *National Journal*, January 11. Available at www.nationaljournal.com/njonline/rg_20100108_8676.php (April 3, 2010).

Carroll, Susan J. and Krista Jenkins. 2001. "Do Term Limits Help Women Get Elected?" *Social Science Quarterly* 82(1): 197–201.

Carsey, Thomas M. 1995. "The Contextual Effects of Race on White Voter Behavior: The 1989 New York City Mayoral Election." *The Journal of Politics* 57(1): 221–28.

Carsey, Thomas M. 2000. *Campaign Dynamics: The Race for Governor*. Ann Arbor: University of Michigan Press.

Carson, Jamie L. 2003. "Strategic Interaction and Candidate Competition in U.S. House Elections: Empirical Applications of Probit and Strategic Probit Models." *Political Analysis* 11(Fall): 368–80.

Carson, Jamie L. 2005. "Strategy, Selection, and Candidate Competition in U.S. House and Senate Elections." *Journal of Politics* 67(February): 12–18.

Carson, Jamie, Erik Engstrom, and Jason Roberts. 2007. "Candidate Quality, the Personal Vote, and the Incumbency Advantage in Congress." *American Political Science Review* 101(May): 289–301.

Carson, Jamie, Greg Koger, Matthew Lebo, and Everett Young. 2010. "The Electoral Costs of Party Loyalty in Congress." *American Journal of Political Science* 54(3): 598–616.

Carter, James and Gerald Ford. 2002. *To Assure Pride and Confidence in the Electoral Process*. Washington, DC: Brookings Institution Press.

Catalist. 2006. "The Future of Progressive Organizing." Available at http://catalist.us/ (April 7, 2010).

Center for Media and Public Affairs. 2008. *Late-Nite Talk Shows Were Road to White House*. Research Report, Washington, DC: Center for Media and Public Affairs.

Center for Responsive Politics. 2009. "Leadership PACs." *Open Secrets*. Available at www.opensecrets.org/pacs/industry.php?txt=Q03&cycle=2008 (April 6, 2010).

Chaffee, Steven H. and Miriam J. Metzger. 2001. "The End of Mass Communication." *Mass Communication and Society* 4(4): 365–79.

Chaney, Carole, Michael Alvarez, and Johnathan Nagler. 1998. "Explaining the Gender Gap in US Presidential Elections: 1980–1992." *Political Research Quarterly* 2: 311–39.

Chang, Linchiat and Jon A. Krosnick. 2009. "National Surveys via RDD Telephone Interviewing versus the Internet: Comparing Sample Representativeness and Response Quality." *Public Opinion Quarterly* 73(4): 641–78.

Chang, Linchiat and Jon A. Krosnick. 2010. "Comparing Oral Interviewing With Self-Administered Computerized Questionnaires: An Experiment." *Public Opinion Quarterly* 74(1): 154–67.

Cigler, Allan J. 2006. "Interest Groups and Financing the 2004 Elections," in *Financing the 2004 Election*, eds. David B. Magleby, Anthony Corrado, and Kelly D. Patterson. Washington, DC: Brookings Institution Press.

Cigler, Allan J. Forthcoming. "Interest Groups and Financing the 2008 Elections," in *Financing the 2008 Elections*, eds. David B. Magleby and Anthony Corrado. Washington, DC: Brookings Institution Press.

Citizens United v. *Federal Election Commission*, 558 U.S. 50 (2010).

Claassen, Ryan L., David B. Magleby, J. Quin Monson, and Kelly D. Patterson. 2008. "'At Your Service': Voter Evaluations of Poll Worker Performance." *American Politics Research* 36(4): 612–34.

Clark, David G. 1962. "Radio in Presidential Campaigns: The Early Years (1924–1932)." *Journal of Broadcasting* 6(3): 229–338.

Clark, David G. 2004. *Politics Moves Online*. New York: Century Foundation Press.

Clarke, Harold and Alan Acock. 1989. "National Elections and Political Attitudes: The Case of Political Efficacy." *British Journal of Political Science* 19(4): 551–62.

CNN. 2004. "Sen. Corzine Enters New Jersey Governor's Race." December 2. Available at www.cnn.com/2004/ALLPOLITICS/12/01/corzine/index.html (accessed April 10, 2010).

Coleman, John J. and Paul F. Manna. 2000. "Congressional Campaign Spending and the Quality of Democracy." *The Journal of Politics* 62 (3): 757–89.

Colorado Republican Committee v. *FEC*, 518 U.S. 604 (1996).

Converse, Philip E. 1964. "The Nature of Belief Systems in Mass Publics," in *Ideology and Discontent*, ed. David E. Apter. London: Free Press of Glencoe.

Converse, Philip E. 2006. "Democratic Theory and Electoral Reality." *Critical Review* 18: 297–329.

Conway, M. Margaret. 2009. "The Scope of Participation in the 2008 Presidential Race: Voter Mobilization and Electoral Success," in *Winning the Presidency 2008*, ed. William J. Crotty. Boulder, CO: Paradigm Publishers.

Copeland, Gary W. 1983. "Activating Voters in Congressional Elections." *Political Behavior* 5: 391–401.

Corrado, Anthony. 1992. *Creative Campaigning: PACs and the Presidential Selection Process*. Boulder, CO: Westview Press.

Corrado, Anthony. 2005. "Party Finances," in *The New Campaign Finance Sourcebook*, eds. Anthony Corrado, Thomas E. Mann, Daniel R. Ortiz, and Trevor Potter. Washington, DC: Brookings Institution Press.

Corrado, Anthony. 2006. "The Regulatory Environment," in *Financing the 2004 Election*, eds. David B. Magleby, Anthony Corrado, and Kelly D. Patterson. Washington, DC: Brookings Institution Press.

Corrado, Anthony. 2010. "Fundraising Strategies in the 2008 Presidential Campaign." in *Campaigns and Elections American Style*, 3rd edition, eds. James A. Thurber and Candice J. Nelson. Boulder, CO: Westview Press.

Corrado, Anthony. Forthcoming. "The Regulatory Environment," in *Financing the 2008 Election*, ed. David B. Magleby. Washington, DC: Brookings Institution Press.

Corrado, Anthony, Thomas E. Mann, Daniel Ortiz, and Trevor Potter, eds. 2005. *The New Campaign Finance Sourcebook*. Washington, DC: Brookings Institution Press.

Cover, Albert D. 1977. "One Good Term Deserves Another: The Advantage of Incumbency in Congressional Elections." *American Journal of Political Science* 21(August): 523–41.

Cover, Albert D. and Bruce S. Brumberg. (1982). "Baby Books and Ballots: The Impact of Congressional Mail on Constituency Opinion." *American Political Science Review* 76(June): 347–59.

Cox, Gary W. and Jonathan N. Katz. 1996. "Why Did the Incumbency Advantage in U.S. House Elections Grow?" *American Journal of Political Science* 40(May): 478–97.

Cox, Gary W. and Jonathan N. Katz. 1999. "The Reapportionment Revolution and Bias in U.S. Congressional Elections." *American Journal of Political Science* 43(July): 812–41.

Cox, Gary W. and Jonathan N. Katz. 2002. *Elbridge Gerry's Salamander: The Electoral Consequences of the Reapportionment Revolution*. New York: Cambridge University Press.

Cox, Gary W. and Michael C. Munger. 1989. "Closeness, Expenditures, and Turnout in the 1982 U.S. House Elections." *American Political Science Review* 83: 217–31.

Creek, Heather M. and Kimberly A. Karnes. 2010. "Federalism and Election Law: Implementation Issues in Rural America." *Publius* 40(2): 275–95.

Curtin, R., S. Presser, and E. Singer. 2005. "Changes in Telephone Survey Nonresponse Over the Past Quarter Century." *Public Opinion Quarterly* 69: 87–98.

Dale, Allison and Aaron Strauss. 2009a. "Mobilizing the Mobiles: Text Messaging and Turnout," in *Politicking Online: The Transformation of Election Campaign Communications*, ed. Costas Panagopoulos. New Brunswick, NJ: Rutgers University Press.

Dale, Allison and Aaron Strauss. 2009b. "Don't Forget to Vote: Text Message Reminders as a Mobilization Tool." *American Journal of Political Science* 53: 787–804.

Dalton, Russell. 1999. "Political Support in Advanced Industrial Democracies," in *Critical Citizens*, ed. Pippa Norris. Oxford: Oxford University Press.

Dalton, Russell. 2004. *Democratic Challenges, Democratic Choices: The Erosion of Political Support in Industrial Democracies*. Oxford: Oxford University Press.

Daniel, Kermit and John R. Lott, Jr. 1997. "Term Limits and Electoral Competitiveness: Evidence from California's State Legislative Races." *Public Choice* 90(1–4): 165–84.

Dao, James (2004). "To Get Ohio Voters to the Polls, Volunteers Knock, Talk and Cajole." *The New York Times*, October 31, A17.

Davidson, Chandler and Bernard Grofman. 1994. *Quiet Revolution in the South*. Princeton, NJ: Princeton University Press.

Davis, James W. 1997. *U.S. Presidential Primaries and the Caucus-Convention System: A Sourcebook*. Westport, CT: Greenwood Press.

Davis, Richard. 1999. *The Web of Politics: The Internet's Impact on the American Political System*. New York: Oxford University Press.

Davis, Richard and Diana Owen. 1999. *New Media and American Politics*. New York: Oxford University Press.

Davis v. *Federal Election Commission*, 128 S. Ct. 2759 (2008).

Dawson, Michael C. 1994. *Behind the Mule: Race and Class in African American Politics*. Princeton, NJ: Princeton University Press.

Dawson, Michael C. 2001. *Black Visions: The Roots of Contemporary African-American Political Ideologies*. Chicago, IL: University of Chicago Press.

Denton, Robert E., ed. 2009. *The 2008 Presidential Campaign: A Communication Perspective*. Lanham, MA: Rowman & Littlefield.

De Rooij, Eline A., Donald P. Green, and Alan S. Gerber. 2009. "Field Experiments on Political Behavior and Collective Action." *Annual Review of Political Science* 12: 389–95.

DeSantis, Victor and Tari Renner. 1994. "Term Limits and Turnover Among Local Officials," in *Municipal Year Book, 1994*. Washington, DC: International City Management Association.

Dever, Jill, Ann Rafferty, and Richard Valliant. 2008. "Internet Surveys: Can Statistical Adjustments Eliminate Coverage Bias?" *Survey Research Methods* 2: 47–62.

Donovan, Todd, David Denemark, and Shaun Bowler. 2007. "Trust, Citizenship and Participation: Australia in Comparative Perspective," in *Australian Social Attitudes: The 2nd Report*, eds. D. Denemark et al. University of New South Wales Press.

Donovan, Todd and Joseph Snipp. 1994. "Support for Legislative Term Limitations in California: Group Representation, Partisanship and Campaign Information." *Journal of Politics* 56: 492–501.

Douglas, Susan J. 2004. *Listening In: Radio and the American Imagination*. Minneapolis: University of Minnesota Press.

Downs, Anthony. 1957. *An Economic Theory of Democracy*. New York: Harper & Row.

Druckman, James N., Martin J. Kifer, and Michael Parkin. 2009. "The Technological Development of Candidate Web Sites: How and Why Candidates Use Web Innovations," in *Politicking Online: The Transformation of Election Campaign Communications*, ed. Costas Panagopoulos. New Brunswick, NJ: Rutgers University Press.

Druckman, James N., Martin J. Kifer, and Michael Parkin. 2010. "Timeless Strategy Meets New Medium: Going Negative on Congressional Campaign Web Sites, 2002–2006," *Political Communication* 27: 881–903.

Duffy, Robert J., Kyle L. Saunders, and Joshua Dunn. Forthcoming. "Colorado 2008: Democrats Expand Their Base and Win Unaffiliated Voters," in *The Change Election: Money, Mobilization, and Persuasion in the 2008 Federal Elections*, ed. David B. Magleby. Philadelphia, PA: Temple University Press.

Dulio, David A. 2004. *For Better or Worse: How Political Consultants are Changing Elections in the United States*. Albany, NY: State University of New York Press.

Dunn, Charles. 1972. "Cumulative Voting: Problems in Illinois Legislative Elections." *Harvard Journal on Legislation* 9: 627–65.

Dwyre, Diana and Victoria A. Farrar-Myers. 2001. *Legislative Labyrinth*. Washington, DC: CQ Press.

Dyck, Joshua. 2009a "Direct Democracy and Political Efficacy Reconsidered." *Political Behavior* 31(3): 401–27.

Dyck, Joshua. 2009b. "Initiated Distrust: Direct Democracy and Trust in Government." *American Politics Research* 37(4): 539–68.

Edsall, Thomas Byrne and Mary D. Edsall. 1991. *Chain Reaction: The Impact of Race, Rights, and Taxes on American Politics*. New York: W.W. Norton.

Edsall, Thomas B. and James V. Grimaldi. 2004. "On Nov. 2, GOP Got More Bang For Its Billion, Analysis Shows." *Washington Post*, December 30. Available at www.washingtonpost.com/wp-dyn/articles/A350622-004Dec29.html (accessed June 24, 2010).

Edwards, George C. III. 2004. *Why the Electoral College is Bad for America*. New Haven, CT: Yale University Press.

Eismeier, Theodore J. and Philip H. Pollock. 1986. "Strategy and Choice in Congressional Elections: The Role of Political Action Committees." *American Journal of Political Science* 30(1): 197–213.

Eldersveld, Samuel J. 1956. "Experimental Propaganda Techniques and Voting Behavior." *American Political Science Review* 50: 154–65.

electiononline.org. 2007. "Helping Americans Vote: Poll Workers ". Washington, DC: Pew Center on the States.

Ellis, Richard. 2002. *Democratic Delusions*. Lawrence, KS: University Press of Kansas.

Elmendorf, Christopher S. 2006. "Election Commissions and Electoral Reform: An Overview." *Election Law Journal* 5(4): 425–6.

Engstrom, Richard. 1990. "Cincinnati's 1988 Proportional Representation Initiative." *Electoral Studies* 9(3): 217–25.

Engstrom, Erik J. and Nathan W. Monroe. 2006. "Testing the Bias of Incumbency Advantage: Strategic Candidates and Term Limits in the California Legislature." *State Politics and Policy Quarterly* 6(1): 12–20.

Engstrom, Richard and Michael McDonald. 1981. "The Election of Blacks to City Councils: Clarifying the Impact of Electoral Arrangements on the Seats/Population Relationship." *American Political Science Review* 75: 344–54.

Engstrom, Richard and Michael McDonald. 1982. "The Underrepresentation of Blacks on City Councils: Comparing the Structural and Socioeconomic Explanations for South/Non-South Differences." *Journal of Politics* 44: 1088–99.

Eom, Kihong and Donald A. Gross. 2006. "Contribution Limits and Disparity in Contributions between Gubernatorial Candidates." *Political Research Quarterly* 59(1): 99–110.

Eom, Kihong and Donald A. Gross. 2007. "Democratization Effects of Campaign Contribution Limits in Gubernatorial Elections." *Party Politics* 13(6): 695–720.

Epstein, David and Peter Zemsky. 1995. "Money Talks: Deterring Quality Challengers in Congressional Elections." *American Political Science Review* 89(June): 295–308.

Erikson, Robert S. 1971. "The Advantage of Incumbency in Congressional Elections." *Polity* 3(Spring): 395–445.

Erikson, Robert S. and Thomas R. Palfrey. 1998. "Campaign Spending and Incumbency: An Alternative Simultaneous Equations Approach." *Journal of Politics* 60(May): 355–73.

Evans, Diana. 1988. "Oil PACs and Aggressive Contribution Strategies." *The Journal of Politics* 50 (4): 1047–56.

Ewald, Alec C. 2009. *The Way We Vote: The Local Dimension of American Suffrage*. Nashville, TN: Vanderbilt University Press.

Farfoush, Rahaf. 2009. *Yes We Did: An Inside Look at How Social Media Built the Obama Brand*. Berkeley, CA: New Riders.

Farrell, David and Ian McAllister. 2005. "1902 and the Origins of Preferential Electoral Systems in Australia." *The Australian Journal of Politics and History* 52(2): 155–67.

Farrell, David M. and Paul Webb. 2000. "Political Parties as Campaign Organizations," in *Parties without Partisans: Political Change in Advanced Industrial Democracies*, eds. Russell J. Dalton and Martin P. Wattenberg. New York: Oxford University Press.

Faucheux, Ron. 1999. "Hitting the Bull's Eye." *Campaigns & Elections* (July): 20–5.

Federal Election Commission. 2007. "FEC Announces Updated Contribution Limits." Press Release, January 23. Available at www.fec.gov/press/press2007/20070123limits. html (accessed April 10, 2010).

Federal Election Commission. 2008. "Candidate Summary Reports, 2007–2008 Cycle, Mitt Romney." Available at http://query.nictusa.com/cgi-bin/cancomsrs/?_08+ P80003353 (accessed June 1, 2010).

Federal Election Commission. 2009a. "Congressional Candidates Raised $1.42 Billion in 2007–2008." Press Release, December 29. www.fec.gov/press/press2009/2009Dec 29Cong/2009Dec29Cong.shtml (accessed April 3, 2010).

Federal Election Commission. 2009b. "Growth in PAC Financial Activity Slows." Press Release, April 24. Available at www.fec.gov/press/press2009/20090415PAC/2009042 4PAC.shtml (accessedApril 3, 2010).

Federal Election Commission. 2009c. "Party Financial Activity Summarized for the 2008 Election Cycle." Press release, May 28. Available at www.fec.gov/press/press20 09/05282009Party/20090528Party.shtml (accessed April 3, 2010).

Federal Election Commission v. *Christian Coalition*, 52 F. Supp. 2d 45 (D.D.C.) (1999).

Federal Election Commission v. *Wisconsin Right to Life, Inc* 551 US 449 (2007).

Fenno, Richard F. 1973. *Congressmen in Committees*. Boston, MA: Little, Brown.

Fenno, Richard F. 1978. *Home Style: House Members in their Districts*. New York: HarperCollins.

Ferejohn, John A. 1977. "On the Decline of Competition in Congressional Elections." *American Political Science Review* 71(March): 166–76.

Ferry, Christian. 2009. "Deputy Campaign Director, John McCain for President." *The Change Election* Press Event, Washington, DC, June 23.

Finkel, Steven. 1993. "Reexamining the 'Minimal Effects' Model in Recent Presidential Elections." *Journal of Politics* 55: 1–21.

Finkel, Steven E. and John G. Geer. 1998. "Spot Check: Casting Doubt on the Demobilizing Effect of Attack Advertising." *American Journal of Political Science* 42: 573–95.

Fiorina, Morris P. 1977. "The Case of the Vanishing Marginals: The Bureaucracy Did It." *American Political Science Review* 71(March): 177–81.

Fiorina, Morris P. 1981. *Retrospective Voting in American National Elections*. New Haven, CT: Yale University Press.

Fiorina, Morris P. 1989. *Congress: Keystone of the Washington Establishment*. New Haven, CT: Yale University Press.

Fiorina, Morris P., Samuel J. Abrams, and Jeremy C. Pope. 2002. *Culture Wars? The Myth of a Polarized America*. New York: Pearson Longman.

Fiorina, Morris P., Samuel J. Abrams, and Jeremy C. Pope. 2006. *Culture War? The Myth of a Polarized America*, 2nd edition. New York: Pearson Longman.

Fischer, Eric A. and Kevin J. Coleman. 2008. "Election Reform and Local Election Officials: Results of Two National Surveys." Washington, DC: Congressional Research Service.

Fleischmann, Arnold and Lana Stein. 1998. "Campaign Contributions in Local Elections." *Political Research Quarterly* 51(3): 673–89.

Foner, Eric. 1998. *The Story of American Freedom.* New York: W.W. Norton.

Foot, Kirsten A. and Steven M. Schneider. 2006. *Web Campaigning.* Cambridge, MA: MIT Press.

Fowler, Erika F. and Travis N. Ridout. 2009. "Local Television and Newspaper Coverage of Political Advertising." *Political Communication* 26(2): 119–36.

Fowler, James H. and Oleg Smirnov. 2007. *Mandates, Parties, and Voters.* Philadelphia, PA: Temple University Press.

Fowler, Linda L. and Robert D. McClure. 1989. *Political Ambition: Who Decides to Run for Congress.* New Haven, CT: Yale University Press.

Fox, Richard L. and Jennifer L. Lawless. 2005. "To Run or Not to Run for Office: Explaining Nascent Political Ambition." *American Journal of Political Science* 49: 642–59.

Fraga, Luis Ricardo. 1988. "Domination Through Democratic Means: Nonpartisan Slating Groups in City Electoral Politics." *Urban Affairs Quarterly* 23: 528–55.

Francia, Peter L. 2006. *The Future of Organized Labor in American Politics.* New York: Columbia University Press.

Francia, Peter L., John C. Green, Paul S. Herrnson, Lynda W. Powell, and Clyde Wilcox. 2003. *The Financiers of Congressional Elections: Investors, Ideologues, and Intimates.* New York: Columbia University Press.

Frank, Thomas. 2004. *What's the Matter with Kansas? How Conservatives Won the Heart of America.* New York: Metropolitan Books.

Franklin, Mark. 2002. "The Voter Turnout Puzzles." Paper presented at the Fulbright Brainstorm Conference on Voter Turnout, Lisbon, February.

Franklin, Mark N. 2004. *Voter Turnout and the Dynamics of Electoral Competition in Established Democracies since 1945.* New York: Cambridge University Press.

Franz, Michael M. 2008. *Choices and Changes: Interest Groups in the Electoral Process.* Philadelphia, PA: Temple University Press.

Franz, Michael M., Paul B. Freedman, Kenneth M. Goldstein, and Travis N. Ridout. 2008a. *Campaign Advertising and American Democracy.* Philadelphia, PA: Temple University Press.

Franz, Michael M., Paul Freedman, Ken Goldstein, and Travis N. Ridout. 2008b. "Understanding the Effect of Political Advertising on Voter Turnout: A Response to Krasno and Green." *The Journal of Politics* 70: 262–8.

Freedman, Paul, Michael M. Franz, and Kenneth Goldstein. 2004. "Campaign Advertising and Democratic Citizenship." *American Journal of Political Science* 48(4): 723–41.

Freedman, Paul and Ken Goldstein. 1999. "Measuring Media Exposure and the Effects of Negative Campaign Ads." *American Journal of Political Science* 43(4): 1189–208.

Freedman, Paul and L. Dale Lawton. 2001. "Beyond Negativity: Advertising Effects in the 2000 Virginia Senate Race." Paper presented at the 2001 annual meeting of the Midwest Political Science Association. Chicago, April 19–22.

Frey, Bruno and Alois Stutzer. 2000. "Happiness, Economy and Satisfaction." *The Economic Journal* 110: 918–38.

Fridkin, Kim Leslie and Kenney, Patrick J. 2004. "Do Negative Messages Work? The Impact of Negativity on Citizens' Evaluations of Candidates." *American Politics Research* 32: 570–605.

Frijda, Nico H. 1986. *The Emotions*. Cambridge: Cambridge University Press.

Fuchs, Ester R., Adler, E. Scott, and Lincoln A. Mitchell. 2000. "Win, Place, Show: Public Opinion Polls and Campaign Contributions in a New York City Election." *Urban Affairs Review* 35: 479–501.

Fund, John. 1992. "Term Limitation: An Idea Whose Time Has Come," in *Limiting Legislative Terms*, eds. G. Benjamin and M. Malbin. Washington, DC: CQ Press.

Gaddie, Ronald Keith and Charles S. Bullock, III. 2000. *Elections to Open Seats in the U.S. House: Where the Action Is*. New York: Rowman & Littlefield.

Galderisi, Peter, Marni Ezra, and Michael Lyons. 2001. *Congressional Primaries and the Politics of Representation*. New York: Rowman & Littlefield.

Garramone, Gina M., Charles K. Atkin, Bruce E. Pinkleton, and Richard T. Cole. 1990. "Effects of Negative Political Advertising on the Political Process." *Journal of Broadcasting & Electronic Media* 34: 299–311.

Geddes, Barbara. 1996. "Initiation of New Democratic Institutions in Eastern Europe and Latin America," in *Institutional Design in New Democracies*, eds. A. Lijphart and C. Waisman. Boulder, CO: Westview Press.

Geer, John G. 2006. *In Defense of Negativity: Attack Ads in Presidential Campaigns*. Chicago, IL: The University of Chicago Press.

Geer, John G. and James H. Geer. 2003. "Remembering Attack Ads: An Experimental Investigation of Radio." *Political Behavior* 25(1): 69–95.

Gelman, Andrew and Gary King. 1990. "Estimating Incumbency Advantage Without Bias." *American Journal of Political Science* 34(November): 1142–64.

Gelman, Andrew and Gary King. 1993. "Why Are American Presidential Election Campaign Polls So Variable When Votes are So Predictable?" *British Journal of Political Science* 23: 409–51.

Gelman, Andrew, David Park, Boris Shor, Joseph Bafumi, and Jeronimo Cortina. 2008. *Red State, Blue State, Rich State, Poor State: Why Americans Vote The Way They Do*. Princeton, NJ: Princeton University Press.

Gerber, Alan. 1998. "Estimating the Effect of Campaign Spending on Senate Election Outcomes Using Instrumental Variables." *American Political Science Review* 92(June): 401–11.

Gerber, Alan, James G. Gimpel, Donald P. Green, and Daron R. Shaw. Forthcoming (2011). "How Large and Long-Lasting Are the Persuasive Effects of Televised Campaign Ads? Results from a Randomized Field Experiment." *American Political Science Review*.

Gerber, Alan S. and Donald P. Green. 2000a. "The Effect of a Nonpartisan Get-Out-the-Vote Drive: An Experimental Study of Leafletting." *The Journal of Politics* 62: 846–57.

Gerber, Alan S. and Donald P. Green. 2000b. "The Effects of Personal Canvassing, Telephone Calls, and Direct Mail on Voter Turnout: A Field Experiment." *American Political Science Review* 94: 653–43.

Gerber, Alan S. and Donald P. Green. 2004. *Get Out the Vote! How to Increase Voter Turnout*. Washington, DC: Brookings Institution Press.

Gerber, Alan S., Donald P. Green, and Christopher W. Larimer. 2008. "Social Pressure and Voter Turnout: Evidence from a Large-Scale Field Experiment." *American Political Science Review* 102: 334–8.

Gerber, Elisabeth, Arthur Lupia, Mathew McCubbins, and D.R. Kiewiet. 2001. *Stealing the Initiative*. Upper Saddle River, NJ: Prentice Hall.

Gershtenson, Joseph. 2003. "Mobilization Strategies of the Democrats and Republicans, 1956–2000." *Political Research Quarterly* 56: 293–308.

Gibson, James L. 2008. "Challenges to the Impartiality of State Supreme Courts: Legitimacy Theory and 'New-Style' Judicial Campaigns." *American Political Science Review* 102(1): 597–605.

Gibson, Rachel and Stephen Ward. 2009. "Parties in the Digital Age—A Review Article." *Representation* 45: 871–900.

Gierzynski, Anthony, Paul Kleppner, and James Lewis. 1998. "Money or the Machine: Money and Votes in Chicago Aldermanic Elections." *American Politics Research* 26: 160–73.

Gilliam, Franklin D. 1985. "Influences on Voter Turnout for U.S. House Elections in Non-Presidential Years." *Legislative Studies Quarterly* 10: 339–51.

Gimpel, James G., Frances E. Lee, and Shanna Pearson-Merkowitz. 2008. "The Check is in the Mail: Interdistrict Funding Flows in Congressional Elections." *American Journal of Political Science* 52(2): 373–94.

Gittinger, Ted and Allen Fisher. 2004. "LBJ Champions the Civil Rights Act of 1964." *Prologue Magazine* 36 (Summer).

Glaeser, Edward L. and Bryce A. Ward. 2006. "Myths and Realities of American Political Geography." *Journal of Economic Perspectives*, 20(2): 119–44.

Goebel, Thomas. 2002. *A Government by the People: Direct Democracy in America.* Chapel Hill, NC: University of North Carolina Press.

Goidel, Robert K. and Donald A. Gross. 1994. "A Systems Approach to Campaign Finance in U.S. House Elections." *American Politics Quarterly* 22: 125–53.

Goidel, Robert K., Donald August Gross, and Todd G. Shields. 1999. *Money Matters: Consequences of Campaign Finance Reform in U.S. House Elections.* Lanham, MD: Rowman & Littlefield.

Goldenberg, Edie N., Michael W. Traugott, and Frank R. Baumgartner. 1986. "Preemptive and Reactive Spending in U.S. House Races." *Political Behavior* 8: 32–40.

Goldstein, Kenneth, Michael Franz, and Travis Ridout. 2002. "Political Advertising in 2000." Combined File [dataset]. Final release. Madison, WI: The Department of Political Science at the University of Wisconsin-Madison and the Brennan Center for Justice at New York University.

Goldstein, Ken, and Paul Freedman. 2002a. "Campaign Advertising and Voter Turnout: New Evidence for a Stimulation Effect." *Journal of Politics* 64: 721–40.

Goldstein, Ken, and Paul Freedman. 2002b. "Lessons Learned: Campaign Advertising in the 2000 Election." *Political Communication* 19(1): 52–8.

Goldstein, Kenneth M. and Matthew Holleque. 2010. "Getting Up Off the Canvass: Rethinking the Study of Mobilization," in *The Oxford Handbook of American Elections and Political Behavior*, ed. Jan E. Leighley. Oxford: Oxford University Press.

Goldstein, Kenneth and Travis N. Ridout. 2004. "Measuring the Effects of Televised Political Advertising in the United States." *Annual Review of Political Science* 7: 205–26.

Goldstein, Kenneth and Patricia L. Strach, eds. 2004. *The Medium and the Message.* Upper Saddle River, NJ: Prentice Hall.

Gonzalez, Nathan L. 2009. "Direct Mail Not Dead Yet." *The Rothenberg Political Report*, February 20. Available at http://rothenbergpoliticalreport.blogspot. com/2009/02/direct-mail-not-dead-yet_20.html (accessed March 30, 2010).

Goodliffe, Jay. 2001. "The Effect of War Chests on Challenger Entry in U.S. House Elections." *American Journal of Political Science* 45(October): 830–44.

Goodliffe, Jay. 2007. "Campaign War Chests and Challenger Quality in Senate Elections." *Legislative Studies Quarterly* 32(February): 135–56.

Gorman, Steve. 2008. "Obama Buys First Video Game Campaign Ads," Reuters.com, October 15. Available at www.reuters.com/article/idUSTRE49EAGF20081015 (accessed June 16, 2010).

Gosnell, Harold F. 1926. "An Experiment in the Stimulation of Voting." *American Political Science Review* 20: 869–74.

Gosnell, Harold F. 1927. *Getting Out the Vote: An Experiment in the Stimulation of Voting*. Chicago, IL: University of Chicago Press.

Gosnell, Harold F. 1948. "Mobilizing the Electorate." *Annals of the American Academy of Political and Social Science* 259: 981–3.

Graber, Doris. 2010. *Mass Media and American Politics*, 8th edition. New York: Congressional Quarterly Press.

Graf, Joseph, Grant Reeher, Michael J. Malbin, and Costas Panagopoulos. 2006. "Small Donors and Online Giving: A Study of Donors to the 2004 Presidential Campaign." *Campaign Finance Institute* and *Institute for Politics, Democracy, and the Internet*. March. Available at www.cfinst.org/pdf/federal/president/IPDI_SmallDonors.pdf (accessed April 12, 2010).

Gray, Virginia and David Lowery. 1996. "A Niche Theory of Interest Representation." *The Journal of Politics* 58(1): 91–111.

Green, Donald Philip and Jonathan S. Krasno. 1988. "Salvation for the Spendthrift Incumbent: Reestimating the Effects of Campaign Spending in House Elections. *American Journal of Political Science* 32(November): 884–907.

Green, Donald P. and Alan S. Gerber. 2002. "Reclaiming the Experimental Tradition in Political Science," in *Political Science: State of the Discipline*, eds. Ira Katznelson and Helen V. Milner. New York: W.W. Norton.

Green, Donald P. and Alan S. Gerber. 2008. *Get Out the Vote: How to Increase Voter Turnout*, 2nd edition. Washington, DC: Brookings Institution Press.

Green, John C. and Nathan S. Bigelow. 2002. "The 2000 Presidential Nominations: The Costs of Innovation," in *Financing the 2000 Election*, ed. David B. Magleby. Washington, DC: Brookings Institution Press.

Green, Joshua. 2007. "The Rove Presidency." *Atlantic Monthly* (September).

Grenzke, Janet M. 1989. "PACs and the Congressional Supermarket: The Currency is Complex." *American Journal of Political Science* 33(1): 1–24.

Gronke, Paul and Daniel Kratz Toffey. 2008. "The Psychological and Institutional Determinants of Early Voting." *Journal of Social Issues* 64(3): 503–24.

Gross, Donald A., Robert K. Goidel, and Todd G. Shields. 2002. "State Campaign Finance Regulations and Electoral Competition." *American Politics Research* 30(2): 143–65.

Gross, Donald A. and Penny M. Miller. 2000. "Kentucky Senate and Sixth District Races." In *Outside Money: Soft Money and Issue Advocacy in the 1998 Congressional Elections*, ed. David B. Magleby. Maryland: Rowman & Littlefield.

Gueorguieva, Vassia. 2008. "Voters, MySpace, and YouTube: The Impact of Alternative Communication Channels on the 2006 Election Cycle." *Social Science Computer Review* 26: 288–900.

Guerra, Fernando. 1992. "California: Conditions Not Met," in *From Rhetoric to*

Reality: Latino Politics in the 1988 Election, eds. Rodolfo de la Garza and Louis DeSipio. Boulder, CO: Westview Press.

Guiner, Lani 1994. *The Tyranny of the Majority*. New York: Free Press.

Gulati, Garish J. 2009. "No Laughing Matter: The Role of New Media in the 2008 Election," in *The Year of Obama*, ed. Larry J. Sabato. New York: Longman.

Gulati, Girish J. "Jeff" and Christine B. Williams. 2009. "Closing Gaps, Moving Hurdles: Candidate Web Site Communication in the 2006 Campaigns for Congress," in *Politicking Online: The Transformation of Election Campaign Communications*, ed. Costas Panagopoulos. New Brunswick, NJ: Rutgers University Press.

Gurin, Patricia, Shirley Hatchett, and James S. Jackson. 1989. *Hope and Independence: Blacks' Response to Electoral and Party Politics*. New York: Russell Sage Foundation.

Hajnal, Zoltan L. 2007. *Changing White Attitudes toward Black Political Leadership*. Cambridge: Cambridge University Press.

Hajnal, Zoltan and Jessica Trounstine. 2005. "Where Turnout Matters: The Consequences of Uneven Turnout in City Politics."*The Journal of Politics* 67(2): 515–35.

Hall, Melinda Gann. 2008. "State Courts: Politics and the Judicial Process," in *Politics in the American States: A Comparative Analysis*, 9th edition, eds.Virginia Gray and Russell L. Hanson. Washington, DC: CQ Press.

Hall, Melinda Gann and Chris W. Bonneau. 2006. "Does Quality Matter? Challengers in State Supreme Court Elections." *American Journal of Political Science* 50(1): 20–33.

Hall, Richard L. and Robert P. Van Houweling. 1995. "Avarice and Ambition in Congress: Representatives' Decisions to Run or Retire from the U.S. House." *American Political Science Review* 89(March): 121–36.

Hall, Thad E., J. Quin Monson, and Kelly D. Patterson. 2007. "Poll Workers and the Vitality of Democracy: An Early Assessment." *PS: Political Science and Politics* 40(4): 647–54.

Hall, Thad E., J. Quin Monson, and Kelly D. Patterson. 2009. "The Human Dimension of Elections: How Poll Workers Shape Public Confidence in Elections." *Political Research Quarterly* 62(3): 507–22.

Hall, Thad E. and Charles Stewart, III. 2010. "Voter Attitudes toward Poll Workers in the 2008 Election," in *Caltech-MIT Voting Technology Project*. Cambridge, MA: Harvard University Press.

Hallett, George and C. Hoag. 1940. *Proportional Representation: The Key to Democracy*. New York: National Municipal League.

Hamilton, James T. 2004. *All the News That's Fit to Sell: How the Market Transforms Information into News*. Princeton, NJ: Princeton University Press.

Hamm, Keith and Gary Moncrief. 2008. "Legislative Politics in the States" in *Politics in the American States: A Comparative Analysis*, 9th edition, eds.Virginia Gray and Russell L. Hanson. Washington, DC: CQ Press.

Hanmer, Michael J., Won-Ho Park, Michael W. Traugott, Richard G. Niemi, Paul S. Herrnson, Benjamin B. Bederson, and Frederick C. Conrad. 2010. "Losing Fewer Votes: The Impact of Changing Voting Systems on Residual Votes." *Political Research Quarterly* 63(1): 129–42.

Hanssen, F. Andrew. 2004. "Learning about Judicial Independence: Institutional Change in the State Courts." *Journal of Legal Studies* 33(2): 431–73.

Harfoush, Rahaf. 2009. *Yes We Did: An Inside Look at How Social Media Built the Obama Brand*. Berkeley, CA: New Riders.

Harris Interactive. 2008. "More Than Half of Americans Never Read Political Blogs." March 10, Available at *harrisinteractive.com.*, www.harrisinteractive.com/harris_poll/index.asp?PID=879 (accessed August 14, 2009).

Hart, Roderick P. 1999. *Seducing America.* Thousand Oaks, CA: Sage.

Hasen, Richard L. 2005. "Beyond the Margin of Litigation: Reforming U.S. Election Administration to Avoid Electoral Meltdown." *Washington and Lee Law Review* 62: 937–99.

Hayes, Danny and Seth McKee. 2008. "Toward a One Party South?" *American Politics Research* 36(1): 33–42.

Heberlig, Eric S., Peter L. Francia, and Steven H. Greene. Forthcoming. "The Conditional Party Teams of the 2008 North Carolina Federal Elections," in *The Change Election: Money, Mobilization, and Persuasion in the 2008 Federal Elections*, ed. David B. Magleby. Philadelphia, PA: Temple University Press.

Hendricks, John Allen and Robert E. Denton, Jr. eds. 2010. *Communicator-in-Chief: How Barack Obama Used New Media Technology to Win the White House.* Lanham, MD: Lexington Books.

Herrnson, Paul S. 1992. "Campaign Professionalism and Fundraising in Congressional Elections." *The Journal of Politics* 54: 859–70.

Herrnson, Paul S. 2009. "The Roles of Party Organizations, Party-Connected Committees, and Party Allies in Elections." *The Journal of Politics* 71: 1207–224.

Herrnson, Paul S., Atiya Kai Stokes-Brown, and Matthew Hindman. 2007. "Campaign Politics and the Digital Divide: Constituency Characteristics, Strategic Considerations, and Candidate Internet Use in State Legislative Elections." *Political Research Quarterly* 60: 31–42.

Herrnson, Paul S., Richard G. Niemi, Michael J Hamner, Benjamin B. Bederson, Frederick C. Conrad, and Michael W. Traugott. 2008. *Voting Technology: The Not-So-Simple Act of Casting a Ballot.* Washington, DC: Brookings Institution Press.

Hersch, Philip L. and Gerald S. McDougall. 1994. "Campaign War Chests as a Barrier to Entry in Congressional Races." *Economic Inquiry* 32(September): 630–41.

Hershey, Marjorie Randon. 1974. *The Making of Campaign Strategy.* Lexington, MA: D.C. Heath.

Hetherington, Marc J. and Jonathan D. Weiler. 2009. *Authoritarianism and Polarization in American Politics.* Cambridge: Cambridge University Press.

Highton, Benjamin. 2004. "Residential Mobility, Community Mobility, and Electoral Participation." *Political Behavior* 22(2): 109–20.

Hill, Kim Quaile and Jan E. Leighley. 1993. "Party Ideology, Organization, and Competitiveness as Mobilizing Forces in Gubernatorial Elections." *American Journal of Political Science* 37: 1158–78.

Hill, Kim Quaile and Jan E. Leighley. 1996. "Political Parties and Class Mobilization in Contemporary United States Electorates." *American Journal of Political Science* 40: 787–804.

Hill, Seth J., James Lo, Lynn Vavreck, and John Zaller. 2007. "The Opt-In Internet Panel: Survey Mode, Sample Methodology, and the Implications for Political Research." Unpublished manuscript.

Hillygus, D. Sunshine. 2005. "Campaign Effects and the Dynamics of Turnout Intention in Election 2000. *The Journal of Politics* 67: 50–68.

Hillygus, D. Sunshine and Simon Jackman. 2003. "Voter Decision-Making in Election

2000: Campaign Effects, Partisan Activation, and the Clinton Legacy." *American Journal of Political Science* 47: 583–96.

Hillygus, Sunshine and Todd Shields. 2005. "Moral Issues and Voter Decision Making in the 2004 Presidential Election." *P.S. Political Science and Politics* 38(2): 201–19.

Hillygus, D. Sunshine and Todd G. Shields. 2008. *The Persuadable Voter: Wedge Issues in Presidential Campaigns*. Princeton, NJ: Princeton University Press.

Hinckley, Barbara. 1980. "House Re-Elections and Senate Defeats: The Role of the Challenger." *British Journal of Political Science* 10(October): 441–60.

Hindman, Matthew. 2009. *The Myth of Digital Democracy*. Princeton, NJ: Princeton University Press.

Hinich, Melvin J. and Michael C. Munger. 1997. *Analytical Politics*. Cambridge: Cambridge University Press.

Hirano, Shigeo and Jr. Snyder. 2009. "Using Multimember District Elections to Estimate the Sources of the Incumbency Advantage." *American Journal of Political Science* 53(2): 292–306.

Hogan, Robert E. 2008. "Policy Responsiveness and Incumbent Reelection in State Legislatures." *American Journal of Political Science* 52(4): 858–73.

Hojnacki, Marie and David C. Kimball. 2001. "PAC Contributions and Lobbying Contacts in Congressional Committees." *Political Research Quarterly* 54(1): 161–80.

Holbrook, Thomas. 1996. *Do Campaigns Matter?* Newbury Park, CA: Sage.

Holbrook, Thomas and Scott D. McClurg. 2005. "Mobilization of Core Supporters: Campaigns, Turnout, and Electoral Composition in United States Presidential Elections." *American Journal of Political Science* 49(4): 689–703.

Howard, Philip N. 2006. *New Media Campaigns and the Managed Citizen*. New York: Cambridge University Press.

Huang, Taofang and Daron R. Shaw. 2009. "Beyond the Battlegrounds: Electoral Strategies in the 2008 Presidential Elections." *Journal of Political Marketing* 8(4): 272–91.

Huber, Gregory A. and Kevin Arceneaux. 2007. "Identifying the Persuasive Effects of Presidential Advertising." *American Journal of Political Science* 51(4): 957–77.

Huber, Gregory A. and John Lapinski. 2006. "The 'Race Card' Revisited: Assessing Racial Priming in Policy Contests." *American Journal of Political Science* 48(2): 375–401.

Huber, Gregory A. and John Lapinski. 2008. "Testing the Implicit-Explicit Model of Racialized Political Communication." *Perspectives on Politics* 6(1): 125–34.

Huckfeldt, Robert and John Sprague. 1992. "Political Parties and Electoral Mobilization: Political Structure, Social Structure, and the Party Canvass." *American Political Science Review* 86: 405–23.

Huddy, Leonie and Anna Gunnthorsdottir. 2000. "The Persuasive Effects of Emotive Visual Imagery: Superficial Manipulation or the Product of Passionate Reason?" *Political Psychology* 21(4): 745–78.

Hughes, C.A. 1968. *A Handbook of Australian Government and Politics, 1890-1964*. Canberra: Australian National University Press.

Hutney, Bev. 2008. Quoted in Liz Halloran, "Obama's Money Magic? Get Them to Give Again?" *National Public Radio*, December 5. Available at www.npr.org/templates/story/story.php?storyId=97878010 (accessed March 30, 2010).

Imbens, Guido W. and Jeffrey M. Wooldridge. 2009. "Recent Developments in the Econometrics of Program Evaluation." *Journal of Economic Literature* 47(1): 58–86.

Iyengar, Shanto and Adam Simon. 2000. "New Perspectives and Evidence on Political Communication and Campaign Effects." *Annual Review of Psychology* 51: 149–69.

Jackman, Robert W. 1987. "Political Institutions and Voter Turnout in the Industrial Democracies." *American Political Science Review* 81: 405–23.

Jackman, Simon. 2009. "Data Wars (Can You Trust Internet Samples?)." Available at http://jackman.stanford.edu/blog/?p=1186 (accessed April 22).

Jackson, Brooks. 1988. *Honest Graft: Big Money and the American Political Process.* New York: Knopf: Distributed by Random House.

Jackson, Byran O. 1987. "The Effect of Racial Group Consciousness on Political Mobilization in American Cities." *Western Political Quarterly* 40: 631–46.

Jackson, Byran O., Elisabeth R. Gerber, and Bruce E. Cain. 1994. "Coalitional Prospects in a Multi-Racial Society: African American Attitudes toward Other Minority Groups." *Political Research Quarterly* 47: 277–94.

Jackson, Robert A. 1993. "Voter Mobilization in the 1986 Midterm Election." *The Journal of Politics* 55: 1081–99.

Jackson, Robert A. 1996a. "A Reassessment of Voter Mobilization." *Political Research Quarterly* 49: 331–49.

Jackson, Robert A. 1996b. "The Mobilization of Congressional Electorates." *Legislative Studies Quarterly* 21: 425–45.

Jackson, Robert A. 1997. "The Mobilization of U.S. State Electorates in the 1988 and 1990 Elections." *The Journal of Politics* 59: 520–37.

Jackson, Robert A. 2002. "Gubernatorial and Senatorial Campaign Mobilization of Voters." *Political Research Quarterly* 55: 825–44.

Jackson, Robert A. and Jason C. Sides. 2006. "Revisiting the Influence of Campaign Tone on Turnout in Senate Elections." *Political Analysis* 14: 206–18.

Jackson, Robert A. and Thomas M. Carsey. 2007. "U.S. Senate Campaigns, Negative Advertising, and Voter Mobilization in the 1998 Midterm Election." *Electoral Studies* 26: 180–95.

Jacobson, Gary C. 1978. "The Effects of Campaign Spending in Congressional Elections." *American Political Science Review* 72(June): 469–91.

Jacobson, Gary C. 1980. *Money in Congressional Elections.* New Haven, CT: Yale University Press.

Jacobson, Gary C. 1989. "Strategic Politicians and the Dynamics of U.S. House Elections, 1946–1986." *American Political Science Review* 83(September): 773–93.

Jacobson, Gary C. 1990a. "The Effects of Campaign Spending in House Elections: New Evidence for Old Arguments." *American Journal of Political Science* 34(May): 334–62.

Jacobson, Gary C. 1990b. *The Electoral Origins of Divided Government.* Boulder, CO: Westview Press.

Jacobson, Gary C. 1993. "Deficit-Cutting Politics and Congressional Elections." *Political Science Quarterly* 108(Autumn): 375–402.

Jacobson, Gary C. 1997. "The 105th Congress: Unprecedented and Unsurprising," in *The Elections of 1996*, ed. Michael Nelson. Washington, DC: Congressional Quarterly.

Jacobson, Gary C. 1999. "The Effect of the AFL-CIO's 'Voter Education' Campaigns on the 1996 House Elections." *The Journal of Politics* 61(1): 185–94.

Jacobson, Gary C. 2007a. *A Divider, Not a Uniter: George W. Bush and the American People.* New York: Pearson Longman.

Jacobson, Gary C. 2007b. "Referendum: The 2006 Midterm Congressional Elections." *Political Science Quarterly* 122(Spring): 1–24.

Jacobson, Gary C. 2009. *The Politics of Congressional Elections*, 7th edition. New York: Pearson Longman.

Jacobson, Gary C. and Samuel Kernell. 1981. *Strategy and Choice in Congressional Elections*. New Haven, CT: Yale University Press.

Jacobson, Gary C. and Samuel Kernell. 1983. *Strategy and Choice in Congressional Elections*, 2nd edition. New Haven, CT: Yale University Press.

Jamieson, Kathleen Hall. 1988. *Eloquence in the Electronic Age*. New York: Oxford University Press.

Jamieson, Kathleen Hall. 1992. *Dirty Politics*. New York: Oxford University Press.

Jamieson, Kathleen Hall. 1996. *Packaging the Presidency: A History and Criticism of Presidential Campaign Advertising*. Oxford: Oxford University Press.

Jamieson, Kathleen Hall and Joseph N. Cappella. 2008. *Echo Chamber*. New York: Oxford University Press.

Jamieson, Kathleen Hall, Paul Waldman, and Susan Sherr. 2000. "Eliminate the Negative? Categories of Analysis for Political Advertisements," in *Crowded Airwaves*, eds. James Thurber, Candice Nelson, and David Dulio. Washington, DC: Brookings Institution Press.

Jansen, Harold. 2004. "The Political Consequences of the Alternative Vote: Lessons from Western Canada." *Canadian Journal of Political Science* 37(3): 647–69.

Jenkins, Henry. 2006. *Convergence Culture*. New York: New York University Press.

Jewell, Malcolm E. 1982. "The Neglected World of State Politics." *Journal of Politics* 44(3): 638–57.

Johnson, Dennis W. 2007. *No Place for Amateurs: How Political Consultants Are Reshaping American Democracy*, 2nd edition. New York: Routledge.

Johnson, Thomas J. and Barbara K. Kaye. 2003. "A Boost or Bust for Democracy? How the Web Influenced Political Attitudes and Behaviors in the 1996 and 2000 Presidential Elections." *Harvard International Journal of Press/Politics* 8: 9–34.

Johnston, Richard, Michael Hagen, and Kathleen Hall Jamieson. 2004. *The 2000 Presidential Election and the Foundations of Party Politics*. New York: Cambridge University Press.

Judd, Nick. 2010. "Maybe, This Year, All Politics is Social," techpresident.com, June 14. Available at http://techpresident.com/blog-entry/maybe-year-all-politics-social (accessed June 23, 2010).

Justice, Glen. 2004. "Kerry Kept Money Coming With the Internet as His ATM." *New York Times*, November 6. www.nytimes.com/2004/11/06/politics/campaign/06internet.html (accessed April 10, 2010).

Kahn, Kim Fridkin and Patrick J. Kenney. 2004. *No Holds Barred: Negativity in U.S. Senate Campaigns*. Upper Saddle River, NJ: Pearson Prentice Hall.

Kahn, Kim Fridkin and Patrick J. Kenney. 1999. "Do Negative Campaigns Mobilize or Suppress Turnout? Clarifying the Relationship between Negativity and Participation." *American Political Science Review* 93: 877–89.

Kaid, Lynda Lee and Anne Johnston. 2001. *Videostyle in Presidential Campaigns: Style and Content of Televised Political Advertising*. Westport, CT: Praeger.

Kamarck, Elaine Ciulla. 1999. "Campaigning on the Internet in the Elections of 1998," in *Democracy.com? Governance in a Networked World*, eds. Elaine Ciulla and Joseph S. Nie Kamark. Hollis, NH: Hollis Publishing.

Kang, Insun, Richard G. Niemi, and Lynda W. Powell. 2003. "Strategic Candidate

Decision Making and Competition in Gubernatorial Nonincumbent-Party Primaries." *State Politics & Policy Quarterly* 3(4): 353–66.

Karlan, Pam and Daniel Ortiz. 2002. "Congressional Authority to Regulate Elections," in *To Assure Pride and Confidence in the Electoral Process*, eds. J. Carter and G. Ford. Washington, DC: Brookings Institution Press.

Karol, David. 2009. *Party Position Change in American Politics: Coalition Management*. New York: Cambridge University Press.

Karp, Jeffrey. 1995. "Explaining Public Support for Legislative Term Limits." *Public Opinion Quarterly* 59: 373–91.

Karpf, David. 2009. "Blogosphere Research: A Mixed-Methods Approach to Rapidly Changing Systems." *IEEEI Intelligence Systems* 24 (5): 67–70.

Katz, Elihu. 1996. "And Deliver Us from Segmentation." *Annals of the American Academy of Political and Social Science* 546: 22–33.

Kaufmann, Karen. 2004. *The Urban Voter: Group Conflict and Mayoral Voting Behavior in American Cities*. Ann Arbor: University of Michigan Press.

Kayden, Xandra. 1978. *Campaign Organization*. Lexington, MA: D.C. Heath.

Kazee, Thomas A. 1980. "The Decision to Run for the U.S. Congress: Challenger Attitudes in the 1970s." *Legislative Studies Quarterly* 5: 791–800.

Kazee, Thomas A. 1983. "The Deterrent Effect of Incumbency on Recruiting Challengers in U.S. House Elections." *Legislative Studies Quarterly* 8: 469–80.

Kazee, Thomas A. 1994. *Who Runs for Congress? Ambition, Context, and Candidate Emergence*. Washington, DC: CQ Press.

Keeter, Scott. 2006. "The Impact of Cell Phone Noncoverage Bias on Polling in the 2004 Presidential Election." *Public Opinion Quarterly* 70(1): 88–98.

Keeter, Scott, Michael Dimock, and Leah Christian. 2008. Calling Cell Phones in '08 Pre-Election Polls." Available at http://people-press.org/reports/pdf/cell-phone-commentary.pdf.

Keith, Bruce E., David B. Magleby, Candice J. Nelson, Elizabeth Orr, Mark C. Westlye, and Raymond Wolfinger. 1992. *The Myth of the Independent Voter*. Berkeley: University of California Press.

Kelley, Stanley, Jr. 1956. *Professional Public Relations and Political Power*. Baltimore, MD: The Johns Hopkins University Press.

Kendall, Kathleen. 2000. *Communication in the Presidential Primaries: Candidates and the Media, 1912–2000*. New York: Praeger Publishers.

Kern, Montague. 1989. *30-Second Politics: Political Advertising in the Eighties*. New York: Praeger.

Kernell, Samuel. 1977. "Presidential Popularity and Negative Voting: An Alternative Explanation of the Midterm Congressional Decline of the President's Party." *American Political Science Review* 71(March): 44–66.

Key, V.O., Jr. 1949. *Southern Politics in State and Nation*. New York: Knopf.

Key, V.O., Jr. 1958. *Politics, Parties, and Pressure Groups*. New York: Thomas Y. Crowell.

Key, V.O., Jr. 1966. *The Responsible Electorate*. Cambridge, MA: Harvard University Press.

Keyssar, Alexander. 2000. *The Right to Vote: The Contested History of Democracy in the United States*. New York: Basic Books.

Kim, Hakkyun, Akshay R. Rao, and Angela Y. Lee. 2009. "It's Time to Vote: The Effect of Matching Message Orientation and Temporal Frame on Political Persuasion." *Journal of Consumer Research* 35(6): 877–89.

Kimball, David C. and Brady Baybeck. 2010. "Is There a Partisan Way to Administer Elections?," in *Midwest Political Science Association Annual Meeting*, Chicago, IL.

Kimball, David C., Brady Baybeck, Jennifer Collins-Foley, Connie Schmidt, and Chere Maxwell. 2010. "Survey of Poll Worker Training Practices by Local Election Officials." Pew Charitable Trusts.

Kimball, David C., Brady Baybeck, Cassie Gross, and Laura Wiedlocher. 2009. "Poll Workers and Election Administration: The View from Local Election Officials," in Midwest Political Science Association Annual Meeting, Chicago, IL.

Kimball, David C., and Martha Kropf. 2006. "The Street-Level Bureaucrats of Elections: Selection Methods for Local Election Officials." *Review of Policy Research* 23(6): 1257–68.

Kimball, David C., Martha Kropf, and Lindsay Battles. 2006. "Helping America Vote? Election Administration, Partisanship, and Provisional Voting in the 2004 Election." *Election Law Journal: Rules, Politics, and Policy* 5(4): 447–61.

Kinder, Donald R. 1994. "Reason and Emotion in American Political Life," in *Beliefs, Reasoning, and Decision Making*, eds. Roger Schank and Ellen Langer. Hillsdale, NJ: Lawrence Erlbaum.

King, James D. 2001. "Incumbent Popularity and Vote Choice in Gubernatorial Elections." *The Journal of Politics* 63(2): 585–97.

Koch, Jeffrey W. 2008. "Campaign Advertisements' Impact on Voter Certainty and Knowledge of House Candidates' Ideological Positions." *Political Research Quarterly* 61(4): 609–21.

Koger, Gregory, Seth Masket, and Hans Noel. 2009. "Partisan Webs: Information Exchange and Party Networks." *British Journal of Political Science* 39 (3): 633–53.

Koster, Josh. 2009. "Long-Tail Nanotargeting: Al Franken's Online Ad Buys Earned an Unbelievable Return on Investment," *Politics* 30 (February): 222–6.

Kousser, Morgan J. 1974. *The Shaping of Southern Politics: Suffrage Restrictions and the Establishment of the One-Party South*. New Haven, CT: Yale University Press.

Kousser, Thad. 2005. *Term Limits and the Dismantling of State Legislative Professionalism*. New York: Cambridge University Press.

Kramer, Gerald H. 1970. "The Effects of Precinct-Level Canvassing on Voter Behavior." *Public Opinion Quarterly* 34: 560–72.

Krasno, Jonathan S. 1994. *Challengers, Competition, and Reelection: Comparing Senate and House Elections*. New Haven, CT. Yale University Press.

Krasno, Jonathan S. and Donald Philip Green. 1988. "Preempting Quality Challengers in House Elections." *Journal of Politics* 50(November): 920–36.

Krasno, Jonathan S. and Donald P. Green. 2008a. "Do Televised Presidential Ads Increase Voter Turnout? Evidence from a Natural Experiment." *The Journal of Politics* 70: 245–61.

Krasno, Jonathan S. and Donald P. Green. 2008b. "Response to Franz, Freedman, Goldstein, and Ridout." *The Journal of Politics* 70: 269–71.

Krebs, Timothy B. 1998. "The Determinants of Candidates' Vote Share and the Advantages of Incumbency in City Council Elections." *American Journal of Political Science* 42: 921–35.

Krebs, Timothy B. 2001. "Political Experience and Fundraising in City Council Elections." *Social Science Quarterly* 82: 537–51.

Krebs, Timothy B. 2005. "Urban Interests and Campaign Contributions: Evidence from Los Angeles."*Journal of Urban Affairs* 27: 1651–75.

Krebs, Timothy B. and David B. Holian. 2005. "Competitive Positioning, Deracialization, and Attack Speech: A Study of Negative Campaigning in the 2001 Los Angeles Mayoral Election." *American Politics Research* 35: 123–49.

Krebs, Timothy B. and John P. Pelissero. 2001. "Fund-Raising Coalitions in Mayoral Campaigns."*Urban Affairs Review* 37: 67–84.

Krigman, Eliza. 2008. "Races to Watch VIII: Top Self-Funders." Open Secrets Capital Eye Blog, October 6. Available at https://www.opensecrets.org/news/2008/10/races-to-watch-viii-top-selffu.html (accessed April 10, 2010).

Krosnick, Jon A. 1999. "Survey Research." *Annual Review of Psychology* 50: 537–67.

Krupnikov, Yanna. 2010. "Who Votes? How and When Negative Campaign Advertisements Demobilize Voters." Indiana University Manuscript.

Lamb, Karl A. and Paul A. Smith. 1968. *Campaign Decision-Making: The Presidential Election of 1964.* Belmont, CA: Wadsworth Publishing Company.

Langer, Gary. 2009. "Study Finds Trouble for Opt-in Internet Surveys." *ABC News,* September 1. Available at http://blogs.abcnews.com/thenumbers/2009/09/study-finds-trouble-for-internet-surveys.html.

La Raja, Raymond J. 2008. *Small Change: Money, Political Parties, and Campaign Finance Reform.* Ann Arbor, MI: University of Michigan Press.

Lariscy, Ruth Ann Weaver and Spencer F. Tinkham. 1999. "The Sleeper Effect and Negative Political Advertising." *Journal of Advertising* 28(4): 13–30.

Lasswell, Harold. 1930. *Psychopathology and Politics.* Chicago, IL: University of Chicago Press.

Lau, Richard R. 1982. "Negativity in Political Perception." *Political Behavior* 4(4): 353–78.

Lau, Richard R. and Gerald M. Pomper. 2001. "Effects on Negative Campaigning on Turnout in U.S. Senate Elections, 1988–1998." *The Journal of Politics* 63: 804–19.

Lau, Richard R. and Gerald M. Pomper. 2004. *Negative Campaigning: An Analysis of U.S. Senate Elections.* Lanham, MD: Rowman & Littlefield.

Lau, Richard R. and David P. Redlawsk. 2006. *How Voters Decide: Information Processing During Campaigns.* Cambridge: Cambridge University Press.

Lau, Richard R., Lee Sigelman, Caroline Heldman, and Paul Babbitt. 1999. "The Effects of Negative Political Advertisements: A Meta-Analytic Assessment." *American Political Science Review* 93: 851–75.

Lau, Richard R., Lee Sigelman, and Ivy Brown Rovner. 2007. "The Effects of Negative Political Campaigns: A Meta-Analytic Reassessment." *Journal of Politics* 69: 1176–209.

Lavrakas, Paul J., Charles D. Shuttles, Charlotte Steeh, and Howard Feinberg. 2007. "The State of Surveying Cell Phone Numbers in the United States." *Public Opinion Quarterly* 71 (5): 840–54.

Lawless, Jennifer L. and Richard L. Fox. 2005. *It Takes a Candidate: Why Women Don't Run for Office.* New York: Cambridge University Press.

Lawrence, Eric, Shaun Bowler, and Todd Donovan. n.d. "The Adoption of the Direct Primary in the United States." Working paper.

Lawrence, Eric D., Todd Donovan, and Shaun Bowler. 2009. "Adopting Direct Democracy: Tests of Competing Explanations of Institutional Change." *American Politics Research* 37(6): 1024–47.

Lawrence, Eric, John Sides, and Henry Farrell. 2010. "Self-Segregation or Deliberation? Blog Readership, Participation, and Polarization in American Politics." *Perspectives on Politics* 8(1): 141–57.

Lawson-Borders, Gracie and Rita Kirk. 2005. "Blogs in Campaign Communication." *American Behavioral Scientist* 49(4): 548–59.

Layman, Geoffrey. 2001. *The Great Divide: Religious and Cultural Conflict in American Party Politics.* New York: Columbia University Press.

Lazarus, Jeffrey. 2006. "Term Limits: Multiple Effects on State Legislators' Career Decisions." *State Politics and Policy Quarterly* 6: 357–83.

Lazarus, Richard S. 1991. *Emotion and Adaptation.* New York: Oxford University Press.

Leighley, Jan. 1991. "Participation as a Stimulus of Political Conceptualization." *Journal of Politics* 53(1): 198–211.

Leighley, Jan E. and Jonathan Nagler. 1992. "Individual and Systemic Influences on Turnout: Who Votes? 1984." *The Journal of Politics* 54: 718–40.

Levendusky, Matthew. 2009. *The Partisan Sort: How Liberals Became Democrats and Conservative Became Republicans.* Chicago, IL: University of Chicago Press.

Levin, Murray B. 1962. *The Compleat Politician: Political Strategy in Massachusetts.* New York: Bobbs-Merrill.

Levitt, Stephen D. 1994. "Using Repeat Challengers to Estimate the Effect of Campaign Spending on Election Outcomes in the U.S. House." *Journal of Political Economy* 102(August): 777–98.

Levy, Michael S., and Sven Windahl. 1984. "Audience Activity and Gratifications: A Conceptual Clarification and Exploration." *Communication Research* 11: 517–18.

Lewis-Beck, Michael S., William G. Jacoby, Helmut Norpoth, and Herbert F. Weisberg. 2008. *The American Voter Revisited.* Ann Arbor: University of Michigan Press.

Lewis-Beck, Michael S., Charles Tien, and Richard Nadeau. 2010. "Obama's Missed Landslide: A Racial Cost?" *PS: Political Science & Politics* 43: 69–76.

Liasson, Mara. 2008. "Romney, McCain Trade Blows at GOP Debate." *National Public Radio,* January 30. Available at www.npr.org/templates/story/story.php?storyId=18566967 (accessed April 15, 2010).

Liebschutz, Sarah F. and Daniel J. Palazzolo. 2005. "HAVA and the States." *Publius* 35 (4): 497–514.

Lien, Pei-te, M. Margaret Conway, and Janelle Wong. 2004. *The Politics of Asian Americans: Diversity and Community.* New York: Routledge.

Lieske, Joel. 1989. "The Political Dynamics of Urban Voting Behavior."*American Journal of Political Science* 33(1): 1507–14.

Lijphart, Arend. 1992. *Parliamentary Versus Presidential Government.* Oxford: Oxford University Press.

Lindauer, Charles. 1999. "Tactical Cartography." *Campaigns & Elections* (April): 48–51.

Link, Michael W. and Ali H. Mokdad. 2005. "Alternative Models for Health Surveillance Surveys: An Experiment with Web, Mail, and Telephone." *Epidemiology* 16(5): 701–4.

Liscio, Rebecca, Jeffrey M. Stonecash, and Mark D. Brewer. 2011. "Unintended Consequences: Republican Strategy and Winning and Losing Voters," in *The State of the Parties,* 5th edition, ed. John C. Green. New York: Rowman & Littlefield.

Liu, Boadong and James Vanderleeuw. 2007. *Race Rules: Electoral Politics in New Orleans, 1965–2006.* Lanham, MD: Lexington Books.

Loviglio, Jason. 2005. *Radio's Intimate Public: Network Broadcasting and Mass-Mediated Democracy.* Minneapolis: University of Minnesota Press.

Lublin, David I. 1994. "Quality, Not Quantity: Strategic Politicians in U.S. Senate Elections, 1952–1990." *The Journal of Politics* 56(February): 228–41.

Lupia, Arthur. 2010. "Did Bush Voters Cause Obama's Victory?" *PS: Political Science & Politics* 43: 239–41.

Lupia, Arthur and Tasha S. Philpot. 2005. "Views from Inside the Net: How Websites Affect Young Adults' Political Interest." *Journal of Politics* 67(4): 1122–42.

Mackay, Jenn Burleson. 2010. "Gadgets, Gismos, and the Web 2.0 Election," in *Communicator-in-Chief*, eds. John Allen Hendricks and Robert E. Denton, Jr. Lanham, MD: Lexington Books.

MacManus, Susan A. and Charles S. Bullock III. 2003. "The Form, Structure, and Composition of America's Municipalities in the New Millennium," in *The Municipal Year Book 2003*. Washington, DC: International City/County Management Association.

Maestas, Cherie D., Sarah A. Fulton, L. Sandy Maisel, and Walter J. Stone. 2006. "When to Risk It? Institutions, Ambition, and the Decision to Run for the U.S. House." *American Political Science Review* 100(May): 195–208.

Magleby, David B. 2000a. *Dictum Without Data: The Myth of Issue Advocacy and Party Building*. Provo, UT: Center for the Study of Elections and Democracy.

Magleby, David B. 2000b. "Interest-Group Election Ads," in *Outside Money: Soft Money and Issue Advocacy in the 1998 Congressional Elections*, ed. David B. Magleby. Lanham, MD: Rowman & Littlefield.

Magleby, David B., ed. 2000c. *Outside Money: Soft Money and Issue Advocacy in the 1998 Congressional Elections*. Lanham, MD: Rowman & Littlefield.

Magleby, David B., ed. 2002. *Financing the 2000 Election*. Washington, DC: Brookings Institution Press.

Magleby, David B. 2004. "The Importance of Outside Money in the 2002 Congressional Elections," in *The Last Hurrah? Soft Money and Issue Advocacy in the 2002 Congressional Elections*, eds. David B. Magleby and J. Quin Monson. Washington, DC: Brookings Institution Press.

Magleby, David B. 2010. "Political Parties and Consultants," in *The Oxford Handbook of American Political Parties and Interest* Groups, eds. L. Sandy Maisel and Jeffrey M. Berry. New York: Oxford University Press.

Magleby, David B. Forthcoming(a). "A Change Election," in *The Change Election: Money, Mobilization, and Persuasion in the 2008 Federal Elections*. Philadelphia, PA: Temple University Press.

Magleby, David B., ed. Forthcoming(b). *The Change Election: Money, Mobilization, and Persuasion in the 2008 Federal Elections*. Philadelphia, PA: Temple University Press.

Magleby, David B. Forthcoming(c). "Elections as Team Sports," in *The Change Election: Money, Mobilization, and Persuasion in the 2008 Federal Elections*, ed. David B. Magleby. Philadelphia, PA: Temple University Press.

Magleby, David B. Forthcoming(d). "Political Parties and the Financing of the 2008 Elections," in *Financing the 2008 Election*, ed. David B. Magleby. Washington, DC: Brookings Institution Press.

Magleby, David B. and J. Quin Monson. 2004. *The Last Hurrah? Soft Money and Issue Advocacy in the 2002 Congressional Elections*. Washington, DC: Brookings Institution Press.

Magleby, David B., J. Quin Monson, and Kelly D. Patterson. 2007. "Introduction," in *Dancing Without Partners*, eds. David B. Magleby, J. Quin Monson, and Kelly D. Patterson. Lanham, MD: Rowman & Littlefield.

Magleby, David B., J. Quin Monson, and Kelly D. Patterson. 2008. "Evaluating the Quality of the Voting Experience: A Cross Panel Pilot Study of the November 7 2006 Election in Franklin County OH, Summit County, OH, and the State of Utah." Provo, UT: Center for the Study of Elections and Democracy, Brigham Young University.

Magleby, David B. and Candice J. Nelson. 1990. *The Money Chase: Congressional Campaign Finance Reform*. Washington, DC: Brookings Institution Press.

Magleby, David B. and Kelly D. Patterson, eds. 2007. *War Games: Issues and Resources in the Battle for Control of Congress*. Provo, UT: Center for the Study of Elections and Democracy.

Magleby, David B. and Nicole Carlisle Squires. 2004. "Party Money in the 2002 Congressional Elections," in *The Last Hurrah: Soft Money and Issue Advocacy in the 2002 Congressional Elections*, eds. David B. Magleby and J. Quin Monson. Washington, DC: Brookings Institution Press.

Magleby, David B. and Jonathan W. Tanner. 2004. "Interest-Group Electioneering in the 2002 Congressional Elections," in *The Last Hurrah? Soft Money and Issue Advocacy in the 2002 Congressional Elections*, eds. David B. Magleby and J. Quin Monson. Washington, DC: Brookings.

Maisel, L. Sandy and Walter J. Stone. 1997. "Determinants of Candidate Emergence in U.S. House Elections: An Exploratory Study." *Legislative Studies Quarterly* 22(February): 79–96.

Malbin, Michael J., Clyde Wilcox, Mark J. Rozell, and Richard Skinner. 2002. "New Interest Group Strategies: A Preview of Post McCain-Feingold Politics?" *Election Law Journal* 1(4): 541–55.

Malchow, Hal. 1998. "Predicting Voter Turnout: A New Targeting Approach." *Campaigns & Elections* (July): 444–6.

Malchow, Hal. 2000. "Predicting Voter Turnout: Applying New Tools." *Campaigns & Elections* (April): 69–71.

Mann, Thomas E. Forthcoming. "Lessons for Reformers," in *Financing the 2008 Election*, ed. David B. Magleby. Washington, DC: Brookings Institution Press.

Marcus, George E., W. Russell Neuman, and Michael MacKuen. 2000. *Affective Intelligence and Political Judgment*. Chicago, IL: University of Chicago Press.

Margetts, Helen. 2006. "Cyber Parties," in *Handbook of Party Politics*, eds. Richard S. Katz and William Crotty. Thousand Oaks, CA: Sage.

Margolis, Michael, David Resnick, and Jonathan Levy. 2003. "Major Parties Dominate, Minor Parties Struggle: US Elections and the Internet," in *Political Parties and the Internet: Net Gain?*, eds. Rachel Gibson, Paul Nixon, and Stephen Ward. New York: Routledge.

Marinucci, Carla. 2007. "Who is the Person Behind the Clinton Attack Ad?" SFGate.com, March 19. Available at http://articles.sfgate.com/20070–31–9/bay-area/17237231_1_ad-clinton-s-campaign-early-presidential-campaign (accessed June 22, 2010).

Marschall, Melissa J. and Anirudh V.S. Ruhil. 2005. "Fiscal Effects of the Voter Initiative Reconsidered: Addressing Endogeneity." *State Politics and Policy Quarterly* 5(4): 327–55.

Marschall, Melissa and Anirudh Ruhil. 2006. "The Pomp of Power: Black Mayoralties in Urban America." *Social Science Quarterly* 87: 828–50.

Marshall, Thomas R. 1999. "Why PAC, Why Bundle? Patterns of Interest Group Donations." *American Review of Politics* 20 (Fall): 245–60.

Martin, Paul S. 2004. "Inside the Black Box of Negative Campaign Effects: Three Reasons Why Negative Campaigns Mobilize." *Political Psychology* 25(4): 545–62.

Masket, Seth E., Michael T. Heaney, Joanne M. Miller, and Dara Z. Strolovitch. 2009. "Networking the Parties: A Comparative Study of Democratic and Republican National Convention Delegates in 2008." Paper presented at The State of the Parties: 2008 and Beyond, 15–16 October. Ray C. Bliss Institute, University of Akron.

Masket, Seth E., and Jeffrey B. Lewis. 2007. "A Return to Normalcy? Revisiting the Effects of Term Limits on Competitiveness and Spending in California Assembly Elections." *State Politics and Policy Quarterly* 7(1): 203–8.

Masters, Marick F. and Gerald D. Keim. 1985. "Determinants of PAC Participation Among Large Corporations." *The Journal of Politics* 47(4): 1158–73.

Mayhew, David R. 1974a. *Congress: The Electoral Connection*. New Haven, CT: Yale University Press.

Mayhew, David R. 1974b. "Congressional Elections: The Case of the Vanishing Marginals." *Polity* 6: 295–317.

McCarty, Nolan, Keith Poole, and Howard Rosenthal. 2006. *Polarized America: The Dance of Ideology and Unequal Riches*. Cambridge, MA: Massachusetts Institute of Technology Press.

McClurg, Scott D. 2006. "Campaign Intensity, Partisan Cues, and the Activation of Voters in the 2000 Elections." Paper Presented at the 2006 Annual Meeting of the American Political Science Association.

McClurg, Scott D. and Thomas Holbrook. 2009. "Living in a Battleground: Presidential Campaigns and Predictors of Vote Choice." *Political Research Quarterly* 62(3): 495–506.

McConnell v. *Federal Election Commission*, 540 US 93 (2003).

McDonald, Michael and John Samples. 2006. *The Marketplace of Democracy: Electoral Competition and American Politics*. Washington, DC: Brookings Institution Press.

McMillan, Alistair. 1997. "The Limited Vote in Britain: A Failed Attempt at PR." *Representation* 33(3): 85–90.

McQuail, Denis. 2000. *McQuail's Mass Communication Theory*, 4th Edition. London: Sage.

McQuail, Denis, Jay G. Blumler, and J.R. Brown. 1972. "The Television Audience: A Revised Perspective," in *The Sociology of Mass Communications*, ed. Denis McQuail. Baltimore, MD: Penguin Press.

McQuail, Denis and Sven Windahl. 1981. *Communication Models for the Study of Mass Communication*. New York: Longman.

Medvic, Stephen K. 2001. *Political Consultants in U.S. Congressional Elections*. Columbus, OH: Ohio State University Press.

Medvic, Stephen K. 2005. "Campaign Organization and Political Consultants," in *Guide to Political Campaigns in America*, ed. Paul S. Herrnson. Washington, DC: CQ Press.

Medvic, Stephen K. 2006. "Understanding Campaign Strategy: 'Deliberate Priming' and the Role of Professional Political Consultants." *Journal of Political Marketing* 5 (1/2): 11–32.

Medvic, Stephen K. 2009. "Political Management and the Technological Revolution," in *Routledge Handbook of Political Management*, ed. Dennis W. Johnson. New York: Routledge.

Medvic, Stephen K. and Silvo Lenart. 1997. "The Influence of Political Consultants in the 1992 Congressional Elections." *Legislative Studies Quarterly* 22: 61–77.

Meinke, Scott R. and Edward B. Hasecke. 2003. "Term Limits, Professionalization, and Partisan Control in U.S. State Legislatures." *The Journal of Politics* 65(3): 898–908.

Meirick, Patrick. 2002. "Cognitive Responses to Negative and Comparative Political Advertising." *Journal of Advertising* 31(1): 494–9.

Meirick, Patrick. 2005. "Political Knowledge and Sponsorship in Backlash from Party- and Candidate-Sponsored Attacks." *Communication Reports* 18(1/2): 75–84.

Mellow, Nicole. 2008. *The State of Disunion: Regional Sources of Modern American Partisanship*. Baltimore, MD: Johns Hopkins University Press.

Mendelberg, Tali. 1997. "Executing Hortons: Racial Crime in the 1988 Presidential Campaign." *Public Opinion Quarterly* 61: 134–57.

Mendelberg, Tali. 2001. *The Race Card: Campaign Strategy, Implicit Messages, and the Norm of Equality*. Princeton, NJ: Princeton University Press.

Mendelberg, Tali. 2008. "Racial Priming Revived." *Perspectives on Politics* 6(1): 109–23.

Mendelsohn, Matthew and Fred Cutler. 2000. "The Effects of Referenda on Democratic Citizens." *British Journal of Political Science* 30: 669–98.

Mendelsohn, Matthew and Richard Nadeau. 1996. "The Magnification and Minimization of Social Cleavages by the Broadcast and Narrowcast News Media." *International Journal of Public Opinion Research* 8(4): 374–89.

Merriam, Charles E. and Harold F. Gosnell. 1924. *Non-Voting: Causes and Methods of Control*. Chicago, IL: University of Chicago Press.

Milkis, Sidney M. 2003. "Parties versus Interest Groups," in *Inside the Campaign Finance Battle: Court Testimony on the New Reforms*, eds. Anthony Corrado, Thomas E. Mann, and Trevor Potter. Washington, DC: Brookings Institution Press.

Milkis, Sidney M. 2006. "Lyndon Johnson, the Great Society, and the Modern Presidency," in *The Great Society and the High Tide of Liberalism*, eds. Sidney M. Milkis and Jerome M. Mileur. Amherst, MA: University of Massachusetts Press.

Miller, Arthur H., Martin P. Wattenberg, and Oksana Malanchuk. 1986. "Schematic Assessments of Presidential Candidates." *American Political Science Review* 80: 521–40.

Miller, Mark. 2008. "The End of Mass Media: Aging and the US Newspaper Industry," in *The Silver Market Phenomenon*, eds. Florian Kohlbacher and Cornelius Herstatt. Berlin: Springer Berlin Heidelberg.

Miller, Sean. 2010. "2010 Midterms Will Be the Most Expensive in History With More than $1 Billion in Play." *The Hill Newspaper*, July 9.

Milyo, Jeffrey. 1998. *The Electoral Effects of Campaign Spending in House Elections*. Los Angeles, CA: Citizens' Research Foundation.

Milyo, Jeffrey. 2002. "Bribes and Fruit Baskets: What does the Link Between PAC Contributions and Lobbying Mean." *Business and Politics* 4 (2): 157–60.

Moen, Matthew C., Kenneth T. Palmer, and Richard J. Powell. 2005. *Changing Members: The Maine Legislature in the Era of Term Limits*. Lanham, MD: Lexington Books.

Mollenkopf, John. 2003. "New York: Still the Great Anomaly," in *Racial Politics in American Cities*, 3rd edition, eds. Rufus P. Browning, Dale Rogers Marshall, and David H. Tabb. New York: Longman.

Monson, J. Quin and J. Baxter Oliphant. 2007. "Microtargeting and the Instrumental

Mobilization of Religious Conservatives," in *A Matter of Faith: Religion in the 2004 Presidential Election*, ed. David E. Campbell. Washington, DC: Brookings Institution Press.

Monson, J. Quin, Kelly D. Patterson, and Jeremy C. Pope. 2009. "The Campaign Context for Partisan Stability." Paper presented at the 2009 State of the Parties Conference, Akron, OH.

Montjoy, Robert S. and Jeffrey L. Brudney. 1991. "Volunteers in the Delivery of Public Services: Hidden Costs ... and Benefits." *The American Review of Public Administration* 21(4): 327–44.

Montjoy, Robert S. and Douglas M. Chapin. 2005. "The U.S. Election Assistance Commission: What Role in the Administration of Elections?" *Publius* 35(4): 617–34.

Mooney, Christopher. 2007. "The Effects of Term Limits in Professionalized State Legislatures," in *Legislating without Experience*, eds. R. Farmer, C. Mooney, R. Powell, and J. Green. Lanham, MD: Lexington Books.

Mooney, Christopher Z. 2009. "Term Limits as a Boon to Legislative Scholarship: A Review." *State Politics and Policy Quarterly* 9(2): 204–28.

Moulder, Evelina R. 2008. "Municipal Form of Government: Trends in Structure, Responsibility and Composition," in *The Municipal Year Book 2008*. Washington, DC: International City/County Management Association.

Moynihan, Donald P. and Carol L. Silva. 2008. "The Administrators of Democracy: A Research Note on Local Election Officials." *Public Administration Review* 68(5): 816–27.

Munro, William. 1912. *The Initiative, Referendum and Recall*. New York: Appleton.

Munro, William B. 1928. "APSA Presidential Address: Physics and Politics: An Old Analogy Revised." *American Political Science Review* 22: 1–11.

Mutz, Diana C. and Paul S. Martin. 2001. "Facilitating Communication across Lines of Political Difference: The Role of Mass Media." *American Political Science Review* 95(1): 97–114.

Nadeau, Richard and Michael Lewis-Beck. 2001. "National Economic Voting in U.S. Presidential Elections." *Journal of Politics* 63: 159–81.

Nagourney, Adam. 2008. "The '08 Campaign: Sea Change for Politics as We Know It." *New York Times*, November 4, A1.

Nelson, Candice J. 2010. "Strategies and Tactics of Fundraising in 2008," in *Campaigns and Elections American Style*, 3rd Edition, eds. James A. Thurber and Candice J. Nelson. Boulder, CO: Westview Press.

Nickerson, David W. 2007. "Quality is Job One: Professional and Volunteer Voter Mobilization Calls." *American Journal of Political Science* 51: 269–82.

Nickerson, David W. 2008. "Is Voting Contagious? Evidence from Two Field Experiments." *American Political Science Review* 102: 49–57.

Nickerson, David W. 2009. "The Impact of E-Mail Campaigns on Voter Mobilization: Evidence from a Field Experiment," in *Politicking Online: The Transformation of Election Campaign Communications*, ed. Costas Panagopoulos. New Brunswick, NJ: Rutgers University Press.

Nie, Norman, Sidney Verba, and John Petrocik. 1976. *The Changing American Voter*. Cambridge, MA: Harvard University Press.

Niemi, Richard G., Lynda W. Powell, William D. Berry, Thomas M. Carsey, and James M Snyder, Jr. 2006. "Competition in State Legislative Elections, 1992–2002," in *The Marketplace of Democracy: Electoral Competition And American Politics*, eds.

Michael P. McDonald and John Curtis Samples. Washington, DC: Brookings Institution Press.

Niemi, Richard G. and Herbert F. Weisberg, eds. 2001. *Controversies in Voting Behavior*, 4th edition. Washington, DC: CQ Press.

Nimmo, Dan. 1970. *The Political Persuaders: The Techniques of Modern Election Campaigns*. Englewood Cliffs, NJ: Prentice-Hall.

Nisbet, Adam. 2010. "Online Social Interactive Media: Opportunities for Democratic Deliberation and Political Participation." Paper presented at New American Spaces, 2010 Chesapeake American Studies Association Annual Conference. Georgetown University, Washington, DC.

Nou, Jennifer. 2009. "Privatizing Democracy: Promoting Election Integrity through Procurement Contracts." *Yale Law Journal* 118: 744–93.

Oliver, J. Eric and Shang E. Ha. 2007. "Vote Choice in Suburban Elections."*American Political Science Review* 101(3): 393–408.

Olson, Laura R. and John C. Green. 2006. "The Religion Gap." *PS: Political Science & Politics* 39: 455–9.

Open Secrets. 2009. "Presidential Candidate John McCain (R)." Available at www.opensecrets.org/pres08/summary.php?cycle=2008&cid=N00006424 (accessed April 5, 2010).

Oppenheimer, Bruce I., James A. Stimson, and Richard W. Waterman. 1986. "Interpreting U.S. Congressional Elections: The Exposure Thesis." *Legislative Studies Quarterly* 11(May): 227–47.

O'Reilly, Tim. 2005. "What is Web 2.0: Design Patterns and Business Models for the Next Generation of Software," oreilly.com, September 30, 2005. Available at http://oreilly.com/web2/archive/what-is-web-20.html (accessed June 10, 2010).

Orr, Marion. 2003. "The Struggle for Black Empowerment in Baltimore," in *Racial Politics in American Cities*. 3rd edition, eds. Rufus P. Browning, Dale Rogers Marshall, and David H. Tabb. New York: Longman.

Osborn, Tracy, Scott D. McClurg, and Benjamin Knoll. 2010. "Voter Mobilization and the Obama Victory." *American Politics Research* 38: 211–32.

Overacker, Louise and Victor J. West. 1932. *Money in Elections*. New York: The Macmillan Company.

Owen, Diana. 1991. *Media Messages in American Presidential Elections*. Westport, CT: Greenwood Press.

Owen, Diana. 1997. "Talk Radio and Evaluations of President Clinton." *Communication Research* 14: 333–53.

Owen, Diana. 2008. "Election media and youth political engagement." *sowi.net*. October. sowi.net/owen (accessed November 25, 2008).

Owen, Diana. 2009. "The Campaign and the Media," in *The American Elections of 2008*, eds. Janet M. Box-Steffensmeier and Steven E. Schier. New York: Rowman & Littlefield.

Owen, Diana and Richard Davis. 2008. "United States: Internet and Elections," in *Making a Difference: A Comparative View of the Role of the Internet in Election Politics*, eds. Stephen Ward, Diana Owen, Richard Davis, and David Taras. Lanham, MD: Lexington Books.

Pace, Joseph Michael. 1994. "Public Funding of Presidential Campaigns and Elections: Is There a Viable Future?" *Presidential Studies Quarterly* 24(1): 139–52.

Panagopoulos, Costas. 2009. "Technology and the Modern Political Campaign: The

Digital Pulse of the 2008 Campaigns," in *Politicking Online: The Transformation of Election Campaign Communications*, ed. Costas Panagopoulos. New Brunswick, NJ: Rutgers University Press.

Panagopoulos, Costas and Daniel Bergan. 2009. "Clicking for Cash: Campaigns, Donors, and the Emergence of Online Fund-Raising," in *Politicking Online: The Transformation of Election Campaign Communications*, ed. Costas Panagopoulos. New Brunswick, NJ: Rutgers University Press.

Park, Hun Myoung, and James L. Perry. 2008. "Do Campaign Web Sites Really Matter in Electoral Civic Engagement? Empirical Evidence From the 2004 Post-Election Internet Tracking Survey." *Social Science Computer Review* 26 (2): 1902–12.

Park, Hun Myoung and James L. Perry. 2009. "Do Campaign Web Sites Really Matter in Electoral Civic Engagement? Empirical Evidence from the 2004 and 2006 Post-Election Internet Tracking Survey," in *Politicking Online: The Transformation of Election Campaign Communications*, ed. Costas Panagopoulos. New Brunswick, NJ: Rutgers University Press.

Parry, Janine and Todd Donovan. 2009. "Leave the Rascals in: Explaining Support for Extending Term Limits." *State Politics and Policy Quarterly* 8(3): 293–308.

Partin, Randall W. 2002. "Assessing the Impact of Campaign Spending in Governors' Races." *Political Research Quarterly* 55(1): 213–23.

Patterson, James T. 1967. *Congressional Conservatism and the New Deal: The Growth of the Conservative Coalition in Congress, 1933–1939*. Lexington: University of Kentucky Press.

Patterson, Kelly D. 2006. "Spending in the 2004 Election," in *Financing the 2004 Election*, ed. David B. Magleby, Anthony Corrado, and Kelly D. Patterson. Washington, DC: Brookings Institution Press.

Patterson, Samuel C. and Gregory A. Caldeira. 1983. "Getting Out the Vote: Participation in Gubernatorial Elections." *American Political Science Review* 77: 675–89.

Patterson, Thomas E. 1980. *The Mass Media Election*. New York: Praeger.

Patterson, Thomas. 1993. *Out of Order*. New York: Alfred A. Knopf.

Patterson, Thomas. 2002. *The Vanishing Voter: Public Involvement in an Age of Uncertainty*. New York: Knopf.

Petrocik, John R. 1996. "Issue Ownership in Presidential Elections, with a 1980 Case Study." *American Journal of Political Science* 40(3): 825–50.

Petty, Richard E. and John T. Cacioppo. 1986. "The Elaboration Likelihood Model of Persuasion," in *Advances in Experimental Social Psychology*, ed. Leonard Berkowitz. New York: Academic Press.

Pew Research Center for the People and the Press 2008a. "Internet's Broader Role in Campaign 2008." *people-press*.org, January 11. Available at http://people-press.org/report/384/internets-broader-role-in-campaign-2008 (accessed November 20, 2008).

Pew Research Center for the People and the Press. 2008b. "High Marks for Campaign; High Bar for Obama." *pewresearch*.org, November 13. Available at http://people-press.org/report/?pageid=1429 (accessed November 20, 2008).

Pew Research Center for the People and the Press. 2009a. "Dissecting the 2008 Electorate: Most Diverse in U.S. History." Available at http://pewresearch.org/pubs/1209/racial-ethnic-voters-presidential-election (accessed July 15, 2010).

Pew Research Center for the People and the Press. 2009b. "Obama's Approval Ratings Slide: By the Numbers". Available at http://pewresearch.org/pubs/1333/obama-approval-falls-across-most-major-demographics (accessed July 13, 2010).

Pew Research Center for the People and the Press. 2010. "Blacks Upbeat about Black Progress, Prospects." Available at http://people-press.org/report/576/ (accessed July 13, 2010).

Pinderhughes, Dianne M. 2003 "Chicago Politics: Political Incorporation and Restoration," in *Racial Politics in American Cities*, 3rd edition, eds. Rufus P. Browning, Dale Rogers Marshall, and David H. Tabb. New York: Longman.

Piott, Steven. 2004. *Giving Voters a Voice: Origins of the Initiative and Referendum in America*. Columbia, MO: University of Missouri Press.

Pippen, John, Shaun Bowler, and Todd Donovan. 2002. "Election Reform and Direct Democracy: The Case of Campaign Finance Regulations in the American States." *American Politics Research* 30(6): 559–82.

Pitts, Michael J. 2008. "Empirically Assessing the Impact of Photo Identification at the Polls through an Examination of Provisional Balloting." *Journal of Law and Politics* 24: 475–528.

Plambeck, Joseph. 2010. "Newspaper Circulation Falls Nearly 9%." *New York Times*, April 26: B2.

Plouffe, David. 2009. *The Audacity to Win: The Inside Story and Lessons of Barack Obama's Historic Victory*. New York: Viking.

Poggi, Gianfranco. 1978. *The Development of the Modern State*. Stanford, CA: Stanford University Press.

Polsby, Nelson W. 1983. *Consequences of Party Reform*. New York: Oxford University Press.

Polsby, Nelson W. 2005. *How Congress Evolves: Social Bases of Institutional Change*. New York: Oxford University Press.

Polsby, Nelson W. and Aaron Wildavasky. 2008. *Presidential Elections*, 12th edition. New York: Rowan & Littlefield.

Pomper, Gerald M. 1979. "The Impact of *The American Voter* on Political Science." *Political Science Quarterly* 93: 617–28.

Postelnicu, Monica, Justin D. Martin, and Kristen D. Landreville. 2006. "The Role of Campaign Web Sites in Promoting Candidates and Attracting Campaign Resources," in *The Internet Election: Perspectives on the Web in Campaign 2004*, eds. Andrew Paul Williams and John C. Tedesco. Lanham, MD: Rowman & Littlefield.

Potter, Trevor. 2005. "The Current State of Campaign Finance Law," in *The New Campaign Finance Sourcebook*, eds. Anthony Corrado, Thomas E. Mann, Daniel Ortiz, and Trevor Potter. Washington, DC: Brookings Institution Press.

Powell, G. Bingham, Jr. 1986. "American Voter Turnout in Comparative Perspective." *American Political Science Review* 80: 17–43.

Powell, Lynda, Richard Niemi, and Michael Smith. 2007. "Constituent Attention and Interest Representation," in *Institutional Change in American Politics: The Case of Term Limits*, eds. K. Kurtz, B. Cain and R Niemi. Ann Arbor: University of Michigan Press.

Powell, Richard J. 2000. "The Impact of Term Limits on Candidacy Decisions of State Legislators in US House Elections." *Legislative Studies Quarterly* 25: 645–61.

Prewworski, Adam. 1991. *Democracy and the Market*. New York: Cambridge University Press.

Prior, Markus. 2007. *Post-Broadcast Democracy*. Princeton, NJ: Princeton University Press.

Pritzker, Penny. 2009. Quoted in Richard Wolffe, *Renegade: The Making of a President*. New York: Crown Publishers.

Putnam, Robert D. 2000. *Bowling Alone: The Collapse and Revival of American Community*. New York: Simon & Schuster.

Rackaway, Chapman. 2009. "Trickle-Down Technology? The Use of Computing and Network Technology in State Legislative Campaigns," in *Politicking Online: The Transformation of Election Campaign Communications*, ed. Costas Panagopoulos. New Brunswick, NJ: Rutgers University Press.

Rae, Nicol. 1989. *The Decline and Fall of Liberal Republicans from 1952 to the Present*. New York: Oxford University Press.

Ramakrishnan, S. Karthick, Janelle Wong, Taeku Lee, and Jane Junn. 2009. "Race-Based Considerations and the Obama Vote: Evidence from the 2008 National Asian American Survey." *DuBois Review: Social Science Research on Race* 6: 219–38.

Reinsh, Paul 1912. "The Initiative and Referendum." *Proceedings of the Academy of Political Science* 3: 155–61.

Reiter, Howard L. and Jeffrey M. Stonecash. 2011. *Counter-Realignment: Political Change in the Northeast*. New York: Cambridge University Press.

Ricci, David M. 1984. *The Tragedy of Political Science: Politics, Scholarship, and Democracy*. New Haven, CT: Yale University Press.

Ridout Travis N. and Erika Franklin Fowler. 2009. "Explaining Perceptions of Campaign Tone." Paper presented at the annual meeting of the American Political Science Association, September 26, Toronto.

Ridout, Travis N. and Glen R. Smith. 2008. "Free Advertising: How the Media Amplify Campaign Messages." *Political Research Quarterly* 61(4): 598–608.

Rigamer, Greg. 1998. "Targeting and Predicting Voter Turnout." *Campaigns & Elections* (October/November): 424–5.

Rivers, Douglas and Delia Bailey. 2009. "Inference from Matched Samples in the 2008 U.S. National Elections." Paper presented at the Joint Statistical Meetings, August 19, Washington, DC.

Rivers, Doug. 2009. "Second Thoughts about Internet Surveys." Pollster.com, September 6. Available at www.pollster.com/blogs/doug_rivers.php.

Rivers, Douglas. n.d. "Sample Matching: Representative Sampling from Internet Panels." Available at www.polimetrix.com/documents/YGPolimetrixSampleMatching.pdf.

Robbins, Suzanne M. and Maksim Tsvetovat. 2008. "Guns, Babies, and Labor: Campaign Finance Networks in 2000," in *Political Networks Paper Archive*. Southern Illinois University Carbondale.

Roberts, Gene. 2008. "The Race Beat." *The Richardson Lecture, American Studies Program, Georgetown University*. Washington, DC.

Robinson, Will. 2004. "The Ground War: The Importance of Organizing the Field," in *Campaigns and Elections American Style*, 2nd edition, eds. James A. Thurber and Candice J. Nelson. Boulder, CO: Westview Press.

Rogers, Reuel R. 2006. *Afro-Caribbean Immigrants and the Politics of Incorporation: Ethnicity, Exception, or Exit*. New York: Cambridge University Press.

Rohde, David. 1991. *Parties and Leaders in the Postreform House*. Chicago, IL: University of Chicago Press.

Rokkan, Stein. 1970. *Citizens, Elections, Parties*. Oslo: Universitetforlaget.

Römmele, Andrea. 2003. "Political Parties, Party Communication and New Information and Communication Technologies," *Party Politics* 9: 72–80.

Rose, Richard. 1967. *Influencing Voters: A Study of Campaign Rationality*. New York: St. Martin's Press.

Rosenstone, Steven J. and John Mark Hansen. 2003. *Mobilization, Participation, and Democracy in America*. New York: Longman.

Rospars, Joe. 2009. "Obama for America New Media Director." Telephone interview by David Magleby, January 28.

Roth, Guenther. 1962. *The Social Democrats in Imperial Germany*. Totowa, NJ: Beminster Press.

Rozell, Mark J., Clyde Wilcox, and David Madland. 2006. *Interest Groups in American Campaigns: The New Face of Electioneering*, 2nd edition. Washington, DC: CQ Press.

Ruggeiro, Thomas E. 2000. "Uses and Gratifications Theory in the 21st Century." *Mass Communication and Society* 3(1): 33–7.

Sabato, Larry J. 1981. *The Rise of Political Consultants: New Ways of Winning Elections*. New York: Basic Books.

Saltman, Roy G. 2006. "The Great Awakening after Florida, Through July 2005," in *The History and Politics of Voting Technology*. New York: Palgrave Macmillan.

Sanchez, Gabriel R. 2006. "The Political Role of Group Consciousness in Latino Public Opinion." *Political Research Quarterly* 59: 435–46.

Sarbaugh-Thompson, Marjorie, Lyke Thompson, Charles D. Elder, John Strate, and Richard C. Elling. 2004. *The Political and Institutional Effects of Term Limits*. New York: Palgrave Macmillan.

Sass, Tim R. 2000. "The Determinants of Hispanic Representation in Municipal Government." *Southern Economic Journal* 66: 609–30.

Sass, Tim R. and Stephen L. Mehay. 1995. "The Voting Rights Act, District Elections, and the Success of Black Candidates in Municipal Elections." *Journal of Law and Economics* 38: 367–92.

Saunders, Kyle L. and Alan I. Abramowitz. 2004. "Ideological Realignment and Active Partisans in the American Electorate." *American Politics Research* 32: 285–309.

Scarrow, Susan. 1999. "Parties and the Expansion of Direct Democracy." *Party Politics* 5(3): 341–62.

Scarrow, Susan. 2001. "Direct Democracy and Institutional Change: A Comparative Investigation." *Comparative Political Studies* 34(6): 651–65.

Schaffner, Brian F. 2010. "Partisan Bias and Perceptions of Campaign Strategies." Paper presented at the Annual Meeting of the Midwest Political Science Association, April 22–25, Chicago, IL.

Schaffner, Brian F., Matthew Streb, and Gerald Wright. 2001. "Teams Without Uniforms: The Nonpartisan Ballot in State and Local Elections." *Political Research Quarterly* 54: 73–80.

Schaffner, Brian F., Michael W. Wagner, and Jonathan Winburn. 2004. "Incumbents Out, Party In? Term Limits and Partisan Redistricting in State Legislatures." *State Politics and Policy Quarterly* 4(4): 396–414.

Scheufele, Dietram A. and Matthew C. Nisbet. 2002. "Being a Citizen Online: New Opportunities and Dead Ends." *Harvard International Journal of Press/Politics* 7: 55–75.

Schraufnagel, Scot and Karen Halperin. 2006. "Term Limits, Electoral Competition, and Demographic Change: The Case of Florida." *State Politics and Policy Quarterly* 4: 448–62.

Schudson, Michael. 1998. *The Good Citizen*. New York: The Free Press.

Schwartz, Mildred A. 1990. *The Party Network: The Robust Organization of Illinois Republicans*. Madison: University of Wisconsin Press.

Scola, Nancy. 2009. "Why You Build Ahead of Time: Wilson's Outburst Turns ActBlue Tap On for Miller [Updated]." techpresident.com, September 11. Available at http://techpresident.com/blog-entry/why-you-build-ahead-time-wilsons-outburst-turns-actblue-tap-miller (accessed June 22, 2010).

Scotto, Thomas J., Harold D. Clarke, Allan Kornberg, Jason Reifler, David Sanders, Marianne C. Stewart, and Paul Whiteley. Forthcoming. "The Dynamic Political Economy of Support for Barack Obama During the 2008 Presidential Election Campaign." *Electoral Studies*.

Secor, Justin. 2010. "Multimedia Project: Citizen Journalism on Wikipedia and Flickr." *justinsecor.com*. May 10. Available at http://justinsecor.com/mediapolitics/health-care.php (accessed May 15, 2010).

Seeyle, Katharine Q. 2007. "Democrats Supply Video, You Make the Ad." The Caucus, nytimes.com, November 27. Available at http://thecaucus.blogs.nytimes.com/2007/11/27/democrats-supply-the-video-you-make-the-ads/ (accessed June 16, 2010).

Sellers, Patrick J. 1997. "Fiscal Consistency and Federal District Spending in Congressional Elections." *American Journal of Political Science* 41(July): 1024–41.

Serra, George and David Moon. 1994. "Casework, Issue Positions, and Voting in Congressional Elections: A District Analysis." *Journal of Politics* 56(February): 200–13.

Shadish, William R., Thomas D. Cook, and Donald T. Campbell. 2002. *Experimental and Quasi-Experimental Designs for Generalized Causal Inference*. Boston, MA: Houghton-Mifflin.

Shafer, Byron E. 2003. *The Two Majorities and the Puzzle of Modern American Politics*. Lawrence: the University of Kansas Press.

Shah, Dhavan V., Jaeho Cho, Seungahn Nah, Melissa R. Gotlieb, Hyunseo Hwang, Nam-Jin Lee, Rosanne M. Scholl, and Douglas M. McLeod. 2007. "Campaign Ads, Online Messaging, and Participation: Extending the Communication Mediation Model." *Journal of Communication* 57(4): 676–703.

Shao, Guosong. 2008. "Understanding the Appeal of User-Generated Media: A Uses and Gratifications Perspective." *Internet Research* 19(1): 72–5.

Shaw, Daron R. 1999a. "The Effect of TV Ads and Candidate Appearances on Statewide Presidential Votes, 1988–1996." *American Political Science Review* 93: 345–61.

Shaw, Daron R. 1999b. "The Methods Behind the Madness: Presidential Electoral College Strategies, 1988–1996." *Journal of Politics* 61(4): 893–913.

Shaw, Daron R. 2006. *The Race to 270: The Electoral College and the Campaign Strategies of 2000 and 2004*. Chicago, IL: University of Chicago Press.

Shaw, Daron, Rodolfo O.de la Garza, and Jongho Lee. 2000. "Examining Latino Turnout in 1996: A Three-State, Validated Survey Approach." *American Journal of Political Science* 44: 338–46.

Shea, Daniel M. 1996. *Campaign Craft: The Strategies, Tactics, and Art of Political Campaign Management*. Westport, CT: Praeger.

Shea, Daniel M. 1998. "Get-Out-the-Vote: 5-Step Process." *Campaigns & Elections* (October/November): 48.

Shen, Fuyuan. 2004. "Chronic Accessibility and Individual Cognitions: Examining the

Effects of Message Frames in Political Advertisements." *Journal of Communication* 54(1): 123–37.

Shepsle, Kenneth. 2001. "A Comment on Institutional Change." *Journal of Theoretical Politics* 13: 321–5.

Shirky, Clay. 2008. *Here Comes Everybody: The Power of Organizing Without Organizing.* New York: Penguin Books.

Shugart, Matthew. 1992. "Electoral Reform in Systems of Proportional Representation." *European Journal of Political Research* 21: 207–24.

Sides, John and Andrew Karch. 2008. "Messages that Mobilize? Issue Publics and the Content of Campaign Advertising." *The Journal of Politics* 70: 466–76.

Sigelman, Lee and Mark Kugler. 2003. "Why Is Research on the Effects of Negative Campaigning So Inconclusive? Understanding Citizens' Perceptions of Negativity." *The Journal of Politics* 65: 142–160.

Silberman, Michael. 2008. "The Meetup Story," in *Mousepads, Shoe Leather, and Hope: Lessons from the Howard Dean Campaign for the Future of Internet Politics,* eds. Zephyr Teachout and Thomas Streeter. Boulder, CO: Paradigm Publishers.

Simon, Adam. 2002. *The Winning Message: Candidate Behavior, Campaign Discourse, and Democracy.* New York: Cambridge University Press.

Simpson, Glenn R. 2007. "Lender Lobbying Blitz Abetted Mortgage Mess; Ameriquest Pressed for Changes in Laws; a Battle in New Jersey." *The Wall Street Journal,* December 31.

Sinclair, Barbara. 2006. *Party Wars: Polarization and the Politics of National Policy Making.* Norman: University of Oklahoma Press.

Sinclair, Brendan. 2008. "Obama's In-Game Ad Bill: $44.5K," GameSpot.com, October 29. Available at www.gamespot.com/news/6200232.html?sid=6200232 (accessed June 16, 2010).

Skinner, Richard. 2005. "Do 527s Add Up to a Party? Thinking about the 'Shadows' of Politics." *The Forum* 3(3).

Slatecard. 2008. "Slatecard is a Utility to Support and Enhance Republican Activism," January 18. Available at http://slatecard.com/ (accessed April 5, 2010).

Smith, Ben. 2008. "Palin Raises $8 Million—For Obama." *Politico,* September 4. Available at www.politico.com/blogs/bensmith/0908/Palin_raising_for_Obama_.html (accessed June 1, 2010).

Smith, Daniel. 2001. "Homeward Bound? Micro-Level Legislative Responsiveness to Ballot Initiatives." *State Politics and Policy Quarterly* 1(1): 506–11.

Smith, Daniel. 2003. "Overturning Term Limits: The Legislature's Own Private Idaho?" *PS: Political Science and Politics* 35: 215–20.

Smith, Daniel and Caroline Tolbert. 2001. "The Initiative to Party: Partisanship and Ballot Initiatives in California." *Party Politics* 7(6): 739–57.

Smith, Daniel and Caroline Tolbert. 2004. *Educated by Initiative: The Effects of Direct Democracy on Citizens and Political Organizations in the American States.* Ann Arbor: University of Michigan Press.

Smith, Daniel and Caroline Tolbert. 2005. "The Educative Effects of Ballot Initiatives on Voter Turnout." *American Politics Research* 33(2): 283–309.

Smith, Daniel A. and Caroline Tolbert. 2010. "Direct Democracy, Public Opinion, and Candidate Choice." *Public Opinion Quarterly* 74(1): 85–108.

Smith, Mark A. 2001. "The Contingent Effects of Ballot Initiatives and Candidate Races on Turnout." *American Journal of Political Science* 45: 700–6.

Smith, Mark A. 2002. "Ballot Initiatives and the Democratic Citizen." *Journal of Politics* 64: 892–903.

Sonenshein, Raphael. 1993. *Politics in Black and White: Race and Power in Los Angeles.* Princeton, NJ: Princeton University Press.

Sorauf, Frank J. 1988. *Money in American Elections.* Glenview, IL: Scott Foresman/ Little Brown College Division.

Squire, Peverill, Raymond E. Wolfinger, and David P. Glass. 1987. "Residential Mobility and Voter Turnout." *American Political Science Review* 81(1): 45–65.

Steen, Jennifer A. 2006. *Self-Financed Candidates in Congressional Elections.* Ann Arbor: University of Michigan.

Stein, Lana and Arnold Fleischmann. 1987. "Newspaper and Business Endorsements in Municipal Elections: A Test of Conventional Wisdom."*Journal of Urban Affairs* 9: 325–36.

Stein, Robert M., Stacey Ulbig, and Stephanie Post. 2005. "Voting for Minority Candidates in Multi-Racial/Ethnic Communities." *Urban Affairs Review* 41: 157–81.

Stein, Robert M. and Greg Vonnahme. 2008. "Engaging the Unengaged Voter: Vote Centers and Voter Turnout." *The Journal of Politics* 70(2): 487–97.

Stein, Robert M., Greg Vonnahme, Michael Bryne, and Daniel Wallach. 2008. "Voting Technology, Election Administration, and Voter Performance." *Election Law Journal* 7(2): 123–35.

Steinberg, Jacques. 2008. "The Buzz on the Bus: Pinched, Press Steps Off." *nytimes. com,* March 26. Available at www.nytimes.com/2008/03/26/us/politics/26bus. html?hp (accessed November 1, 2008).

Steinhorn, Leonard. 2010. "The Selling of the President in a Converged Media Age," in *Campaigns and Elections American Style,* 3rd edition, eds. James A. Thurber and Candice J. Nelson. Boulder, CO: Westview Press.

Stelter, Brian. "Enticing Text Messagers in a Get-Out-the-Vote Push." *New York Times,* August 18, A12.

Stevens, Daniel. 2008. "Measuring Exposure to Political Advertising in Surveys." *Political Behavior* 30(1): 47–72.

Stevens, Daniel. 2009. "Elements of Negativity: Volume and Proportion in Exposure to Negative Advertising." *Political Behavior* 31(3): 429–54.

Stoker, Laura and Jake Bowers. 2002. "Designing Multi-Level Studies: Sampling Voters and Electoral Contexts," in *The Future of Election Studies,* eds. Mark Franklin and Chris Wlezien. New York: Elsevier.

Stone, Walter J., L. Sandy Maisel, and Cherie D. Maestas. 2004. "Quality Counts: Extending the Strategic Politician Model of Incumbent Deterrence." *American Journal of Political Science* 48(3): 479–95.

Stonecash, Jeffrey M. 2006. *Political Parties Matter: Realignment and the Return of Partisan Voting.* Boulder, CO: Lynne-Rienner.

Storey, David D. 2002. "The Amendment of Section 527: Eliminating Stealth PACs and Providing a Model for Future Campaign Finance Reform." *Indiana Law Journal* 77 (167): 167–87.

Stratmann, Thomas. 2005. "Some Talk: Money in Politics. A (Partial) Review of the Literature." *Public Choice* 124(1/2): 1351–6.

Stromer-Galley, Jennifer. 2000. "On-Line Interaction and Why Candidates Avoid It." *Journal of Communication* 50: 111–32.

Stroud, Natalie Jomini. 2007. "Media Use and Political Predispositions: Revisiting the Concept of Selective Exposure." *Political Behavior* 30(December): 341–66.

Stuart, Guy. 2004. "Databases, Felons, and Voting: Bias and Partisanship of the Florida Felons List in the 2000 Elections." *Political Science Quarterly* 119(3): 453–75.

Sutherland, Gillian. 1973. *Policy Making in Elementary Education, 1870-1895*. New York: Oxford University Press.

Tate, Gayle T. 1994. "How Antebellum Black Communities Became Mobilized: The Role of Church, Benevolent Society and Press," in *The Challenge to Racial Stratification*, ed. Matthew Holden. New Brunswick, NJ: Transaction Publishers.

Tate, Katherine. 1993. *Black Faces, Black Interests: The Representation of African Americans in Congress*. Cambridge, MA: Harvard University Press.

Teachout, Zephyr and Thomas Streeter. 2008. *Mousepads, Shoe Leather, and Hope: Lessons from the Howard Dean Campaign for the Future of Internet Politics*. Boulder, CO: Paradigm.

Tedesco, John C. 2002. "Televised Political Advertising Effects: Evaluating Responses during the 2000 Robb-Allen Senatorial Election." *Journal of Advertising* 31(1): 37–48.

Tewksbury, David. 2005. "The Seeds of Audience Fragmentation: Specialization in the Use of Online Media." *Journal of Broadcasting and Electronic Media* 49(3): 332–48.

Thomas, Evan. 2008. "Center Stage." *Newsweek*, November 6. Available at www.newsweek.com/id/167905 (accessed April 15, 2010).

Thompson, Dennis F. 1993. "Mediated Corruption: The Case of the Keating Five." *The American Political Science Review* 87(2): 369–81.

Thurber, James A. 2010. "Dynamics and Transformation of American Campaigns," in *Campaigns and Elections American Style*, 3rd edition, eds. James A. Thurber and Candice J. Nelson. Boulder, CO: Westview Press.

Tokaji, Daniel P. 2005. "Early Returns on Election Reform: Discretion, Disenfranchisement, and the Help America Vote Act." *George Washington Law Review* 73(5/6): 1206–53.

Tolbert, Caroline. 1998. "Changing the Rules for State Legislatures: Direct Democracy and Governance Policy," in *Citizens as Legislators*, eds. Shaun Bowler, Todd Donovan, and Caroline Tolbert. Columbus, OH: Ohio State University Press.

Tolbert, Caroline. 2003. "Direct Democracy and Institutional Realignment in the American States." *Political Science Quarterly* 118(3): 467–89.

Tolbert, Caroline, Daniel Bowen, and Todd Donovan. 2009. "Initiative Campaigns: Direct Democracy and Voter Mobilization." *American Politics Research* 37(1): 155–92.

Tolbert, Caroline, Todd Donovan, Bridgett King, and Shaun Bowler. 2008. "Election Day Registration, Competition, and Voter Turnout," in *Democracy in the States: Experiments in Election Reform*, eds. Bruce E. Cain, Todd Donovan, and Caroline J. Tolbert. Washington, DC: Brookings Institution Press.

Tolbert, Caroline, John Grummel, and Daniel Smith. 2001. "The Effect of Ballot Initiatives on Voter Turnout in the American States." *American Politics Research* 29(6): 625–48.

Tolbert, Caroline J. and Ramona S. McNeal. 2003. "Unraveling the Effects of the Internet on Political Participation." *Political Research Quarterly* 56(2): 175–85.

Tomz, Michael and Robert P. Van Houweling. 2003. "How Does Voting Equipment Affect the Racial Gap in Voided Ballots?" *American Journal of Political Science* 47: 46–60.

Trapido, Stanley. 1964. "Origins of the Cape Franchise Qualification 1853." *Journal of African History* 20: 37–53.

Trippi, Joe. 2004. *The Revolution Will Not Be Televised: Democracy, the Internet, and the Overthrow of Everything.* New York: HarperCollins.

Trippi, Joe. 2008. "Howard Dean Campaign Manager and Participant in John Edwards Campaign." Interview by David Magleby, December 18.

Trounstine, Jessica. 2010. "Incumbency and Responsiveness in Local Elections." Working Paper.

Trounstine, Jessica and Melody E. Valdini. 2008. "The Context Matters: The Effects of Single-Member versus At-Large Districts on City Council Diversity." *American Journal of Political Science* 52: 554–69.

Tsebelis, George. 1990. *Veto Players.* Princeton, NJ: Princeton University Press.

Tufte, Edward R. 1975. "Determinants of the Outcomes of Midterm Congressional Elections." *American Political Science Review* 69(September): 812–26.

Unruh, Jesse M. 1962. Quoted in "Politics: Hale Fellows at Yale." *Time Magazine,* December 14. Available at www.time.com/time/magazine/article/0,9171,872928,00.html (accessed March 22, 2010).

Vaccari, Cristian. 2008. "From the Air to the Ground: the Internet in the 2004 US Presidential Campaign." *New Media & Society* 10(4): 647–65.

Valentino, Nicholas A., Vincent L. Hutchings, and Ismail K. White. 2002. "Cues That Matter: How Political Ads Prime Racial Attitudes." *American Political Science Review* 96: 75–90.

Valentino, Nicholas A., Vincent L. Hutchings, and Dmitri Williams. 2004. "The Impact of Political Advertising on Knowledge, Internet Information Seeking, and Candidate Preference." *Journal of Communication* 54(2): 337–54.

Valentino, Nicholas, Ted Brader, Eric W. Groenendyk, Krysha Gregorowicz, and Vincent Hutchings. Forthcoming (2011). "Election Night's All Right for Fighting: The Role of Anger versus Anxiety in Political Participation." *Journal of Politics.*

Vanacore, Andrew. 2010. "US Newspaper Circulation Falls 8.7 Percent." *washingtonpost.com,* April 26. Available at www.washingtonpost.com/wp-dyn/content/article/2010/04/26/AR2010042601659.html (accessed April 26, 2010).

Vanderleeuw, James, Liu, Baodong, and Gregory March. 2004. "Applying Black Threat Theory, Urban Regime Theory and Deracialization: The Memphis Mayoral Elections of 1991, 1995 and 1999."*Journal of Urban Affairs* 26(4): 505–19.

Vargas, Jose Antonio. 2008. "Obama Raised Half a Billion Online." 44: The Obama Presidency, washingtonpost.com, November 20. Available at http://voices.washingtonpost.com/44/2008/11/20/obama_raised_half_a_billion_on html (accessed June 13, 2010).

Verba, Sidney and Norman H. Nie. 1972. *Participation in America: Political Democracy and Social Equality.* New York: Harper & Row.

Verba, Sidney, Kay Lehman Schlozman, and Henry E. Brady. 1995. *Voice and Equality: Civic Voluntarism in American Politics.* Cambridge, MA: Harvard University Press.

Vowles, Jack, Susan Banducci, and Jeffrey Karp. 2006. "Forecasting and Evaluating the Consequences of Electoral Change in New Zealand." *Acta Politica* 41: 267–84.

Ward, Stephen, Rachel Gibson, and Paul Nixon. 2003. "Parties and the Internet: An Overview," in *Political Parties and the Internet: Net Gain?,* eds. Rachel Gibson, Paul Nixon, and Stephen Ward. New York: Routledge.

Ware, Alan. 2002. *The American Direct Primary*. Cambridge: Cambridge University Press.

Ware, Alan. 2006. *The Democratic Party Heads North, 1877–1962*. New York: Cambridge University Press.

Wattenberg, Martin P. 1991. *The Rise of Candidate-Centered Politics: Presidential Elections of the 1980s*. Cambridge, MA: Harvard University Press.

Wattenberg, Martin P. and Craig Leonard Brians. 1999. "Negative Campaign Advertising: Demobilizer or Mobilizer?" *American Political Science Review* 93: 891–9.

Wayne, Stephen J. 2011. *Is This Any Way to Run a Democratic Election?*, 4th edition. Washington, DC: Congressional Quarterly Press.

Weaver, David and Dan Drew. 2001. "Voter Learning and Interest in the 2000 Presidential Election: Did the Media Matter?" *Journalism and Mass Communication Quarterly* 78(Winter): 787–99.

Weaver, Leon. 1986. "The Rise, Decline and Resurrection of Proportional Representation in Local Governments in the United States," in *Electoral Laws and Their Political Consequences*, eds. B. Grofman and A. Lijphart. New York: Algora Publishing.

Weaver, Vesla M. 2009. "The Electoral Consequences of Skin Color: The "Hidden" Side of Race in Politics." Unpublished manuscript.

Weberg, Brian and Karl Kurtz. 2007. "Legislative Staff," in *Institutional Change in American Politics: The Case of Term Limits*, eds. K. Kurtz, B. Cain, and R. Niemi. Ann Arbor: University of Michigan Press.

Weissman, Steve. 2009. *Soft Money Political Spending by 501 (C) Nonprofits Tripled in 2008 Election*. Washington, DC: Campaign Finance Institute.

Weissman, Stephen R. and Ruth Hassan. 2006. "BCRA and 527 Groups," in *The Election After Reform: Money, Politics, and the Bipartisan Campaign Reform Act*, ed. Michael J. Malbin. Lanham, MD: Rowman & Littlefield.

Weissman, Stephen and Kara D. Ryan. 2006. *Non-Profit Interest Groups' Election Activities and Federal Campaign Finance Policy: A Working Paper*. Washington, DC: Campaign Finance Institute.

Welch, Susan. 1990. "The Impact of At-Large Elections on the Representation of Blacks and Hispanics." *Journal of Politics* 52: 1050–76.

Wielhouwer, Peter W. and Brad Lockerbie. 1994. "Party Contacting and Political Participation, 1952–90." *American Journal of Political Science* 38: 211–29.

Wilcox, Clyde. 1989. "Organizational Variables and Contribution Behavior of Large Pacs: A Longitudinal Analysis." *Political Behavior* 11(2): 157–73.

Wilcox, Clyde and Marc Genest. 1991. "Member PACs as Strategic Actors." *Polity* 23(3): 461–70.

Wilcox, Clyde and Rentaro Iida. 2010. "Interest Groups and American Elections," in *The Oxford Handbook of American Political Parties and Interest Groups*, eds. L. Sandy Maisel and Jeffrey M. Berry. New York: Oxford University Press.

Wilcox, Clyde and Carin Larson. 2006. *Onward Christian Soldiers? The Religious Right in American Politics*, 3rd edition. Boulder, CO: Westview Press.

Wilcox, Clyde and Carin Robinson. 2010. *Onward Christian Soldiers: The Christian Right in American Politics*. 4th edition. Boulder, CO: Westview Press.

Will, George. 1990. *Restoration: Congress, Term Limits and the Recovery of Deliberative Democracy*. New York: Free Press.

Williams, Andrew Paul and John C. Tedesco, eds. 2006. *The Internet Election*. Lanham, MD: Rowman & Littlefield.

Williams, Christine B. and Girish J. "Jeff" Gulati. 2009. "The Political Impact of Facebook: Evidence from the 2006 Elections and the 2008 Nomination Contest," in *Politicking Online: The Transformation of Election Campaign Communications*, ed. Costas Panagopoulos. New Brunswick, NJ: Rutgers University Press.

Williams, George and Geraldine Chin. 2000. "The Failure of Citizens' Initiated Referenda Proposals in Australia: New Directions for Popular Participation?" *Australian Journal of Political Science* 35: 27–48.

Wilson, William J. 1978. *The Declining Significance of Race: Blacks and Changing American Institutions*. Chicago, IL: University of Chicago Press.

Winburn, Jonathan. 2008. *The Realities of Redistricting: Following the Rules and Limiting Gerrymandering in State Legislative Redistricting*. Lanham, MD: Lexington Books.

Wolak, Jennifer. 2006. "The Consequences of Presidential Battleground Strategies for Citizen Engagement." *Political Research Quarterly* 59(3): 353–61.

Wolfinger, Raymond E. 1965. "The Development and Persistence of Ethnic Voting." *American Political Science Review* 59: 896–908.

Wolfinger, Raymond E. and Steven J. Rosenstone. 1980. *Who Votes?* New Haven, CT: Yale University Press.

Wooldridge, Jeffrey M. 2007. "Control Functions and Related Methods." *What's New in Econometrics?* NBER.

Wright, Gerald C., Jr. 1978. "Candidates' Policy Positions and Voting in U.S. Congressional Elections." *Legislative Studies Quarterly* 3(August): 445–64.

Wright, John R. 1985. "PACs, Contributions, and Roll Calls: An Organizational Perspective." *The American Political Science Review* 79(2): 400–14.

Xenos, Michael and Kirsten A. Foot. 2005. "Politics as Usual, or Politics Unusual: Position-Taking and Dialogue on Campaign Web Sites in the 2002 U.S. Elections." *Journal of Communication* 55: 165–89.

Yeager, David S., Jon A. Krosnick, LinChiat Chang, Harold S. Javitz, Matthew S. Levendusky, Alberto Simpser, and Rui Wang. 2009. "Comparing the Accuracy of RDD Telephone Surveys and Internet Surveys Conducted with Probability and Non-Probability Samples." Unpublished manuscript.

Yegiyan, Narine S. and Maria Elizabeth Grabe. 2007. "An Experimental Investigation of Source Confusion in Televised Messages: News versus Advertisements." *Human Communication Research* 33(3): 379–95.

Yoon, Kak, Bruce E. Pinkleton, and Wonjun Ko. 2005. "Effects of Negative Political Advertising on Voting Intention: An Exploration of the Roles of Involvement and Source Credibility in the Development of Voter Cynicism." *Journal of Marketing Communications* 11(2): 95–112.

Zax, Jeffrey S. 1990. "Election Methods and Black and Hispanic City Council Membership. *Social Science Quarterly* 71: 338–55.

Index

absentee voting 6, 11
ActBlue 29, 71–2
administrative reforms 238, 239
Affective Intelligence Theory 82
African Americans: as candidates 177–8,
179, 180; interaction with technology
13; local-level representation 223–5;
voting behavior 175, 176–8
age: and media use 159; and political
participation 42–3
America Votes 34, 36
American Association for Public
Opinion Researchers (AAPOR) 56–7
American Crossroads 131, 133, 143
American Federation of Labor-Congress
of Industrial Organizations (AFL-
CIO) 20, 129, 134, 136, 140
American Medical Association (ASA) 33,
142
American National Election Study
(ANES) 39, 41, 51–3, 56, 101, 124, 200,
211
American Seniors Association 132
American Voter (Campbell et al.) 164,
165
Americans Coming Together (ACT) 134,
140, 142, 143, 217–18
Ameriquest 132
Arab Americans, voting behavior 180–1
Arizona, term limit effects 249–50
Arlington Group 142
Asian Americans: local-level
representation 223; voting behavior
176–80
Association of Trial Lawyers of America
(ATLA) 29, 139
Australia, proportional representation
253–5

auxiliary websites 66

battleground states 206–7, 213, 215–17,
218, 219
Bipartisan Campaign Reform Act
(BRCA) 20–2, 28, 31, 33–4, 136, 245,
246
Blue Swarm 72
Boxer, Barbara 66–7
broadcast communication model 146–7,
152
Buckley v. *Valeo* (1976) 19–20, 33
Bush, George W.: approval ratings 51–2;
campaign finance 23, 35, 68; campaign
management 73; image 121–2; interest
group support 132–3, 143

California, term limit effects 249–50
Caltech/MIT Voting Technology Project
13
campaign advertising: airings data 85–6;
costs 204; interest groups 139–40;
measuring "dosage" 84–7, 90–4;
methodological baseline 87–93;
narrowcasting/micro-targeting 207;
quality/quantity 84–7, 90–4; recent
developments in study of 80–4;
regulations on 136–7; suggestions for
future study 84–93; use of ICT 70
campaign, contact surveys of 52–3
campaign bureaucracy, history of 60–1
campaign communication, evolution of
146–50
Campaign Finance Institute 68
campaign finance: capacity to inform
209–10; Congressional elections
194–5; distribution between states
203–6; executive elections 233–4;

eBooks – at www.eBookstore.tandf.co.uk

A library at your fingertips!

eBooks are electronic versions of printed books. You can store them on your PC/laptop or browse them online.

They have advantages for anyone needing rapid access to a wide variety of published, copyright information.

eBooks can help your research by enabling you to bookmark chapters, annotate text and use instant searches to find specific words or phrases. Several eBook files would fit on even a small laptop or PDA.

NEW: Save money by eSubscribing: cheap, online access to any eBook for as long as you need it.

Annual subscription packages

We now offer special low-cost bulk subscriptions to packages of eBooks in certain subject areas. These are available to libraries or to individuals.

For more information please contact webmaster.ebooks@tandf.co.uk

We're continually developing the eBook concept, so keep up to date by visiting the website.

www.eBookstore.tandf.co.uk